To Dad.

Love Jimmy Glenice and family 1994.

Love Jimmy Glenice and family 1994.

WHEN DRAGONS FLEW

WHEN DRAGONS FLEW

An illustrated history of
The 1st Battalion The Border Regiment 1939-45

Stuart Eastwood   Charles Gray   Alan Green

Published by the Regimental Museum
in association with
SILVER LINK PUBLISHING LTD

To all ranks who served in the Battalion during the
Second World War and in memory of those who lost their lives
in the service of their country.

The Airborne Prayer

May the Defence of the Most High be around us and within us,
in our going out and our coming in,
in our rising up and in our going down,
all our days and all our nights until the Dawn
when the Sun of Righteousness
shall arise with Healing in his Wings
for the Peoples of the World
through Jesus Christ our Lord, Amen.

© Stuart Eastwood, Charles Gray and Alan Green
1994

First published in September 1994

British Library Cataloguing in Publication Data

A catalogue record for this book is available from the
British Library.

ISBN 1 85794 048 2

Illustrations credited 'BRM' are from the collection of
The Border Regiment Museum; those credited 'IWM'
are reproduced by courtesy of the Imperial War
Museum; and those credited 'MAF' by courtesy of the
Museum of Army Flying, Middle Wallop.

Silver Link Publishing Ltd
Unit 5
Home Farm Close
Church Street
Wadenhoe
Peterborough PE8 5TE
Tel/fax (0832) 720440

The Regimental Museum of The Border Regiment
and The Kings Own Royal Border Regiment
Queen Mary's Tower
The Castle
Carlisle
Cumbria CA3 8UR
Tel (0228) 32774

Printed and bound in Great Britain

Title page A Handley Page Halifax with a Horsa gilder in tow
becomes airborne at Tarrant Rushton airfield in Dorset in mid-
1944. *Taylor Library*

Contents

Lt Col Tommy Haddon, Commanding Officer 1st Battalion The Border Regiment July 1943 to September 1944.

Tommy Haddon was commissioned into the Regiment in 1933 and served with the 2nd Battalion in India, before joining the 1st Battalion in Aldershot in 1939. He served as a Company Commander and was Adjutant during the retreat to Dunkirk. In 1941 he went to the Staff College and was later appointed as Assistant Secretary of the Joint Intelligence Sub-Committee at the War Cabinet Offices. He rejoined the Battalion as 2i/c in late 1942, and after the Sicily Operation, during which his glider crashed and he swam ashore, he succeeded Lt Col G. V. Britten MBE as Commanding Officer in July 1943. Despite his glider making forced landings twice en route to Arnhem, he finally made his way to the Rhine and crossed the river with the Dorsets opposite the Westerbouwing Heights, where he was taken PoW.

He returned to the War Cabinet Offices in 1945 and served as 2i/c of the 1st Battalion in the Middle East and Africa, before moving to Hong Kong as GSO1 (awarded OBE) and to Whitehall. In December 1955 he was appointed to command the 1st Battalion again in Gottingen and Berlin. Under his leadership the Battalion was one of the best units in the Army. Promoted Brigadier in 1958, he held important posts in Hong Kong and Singapore prior to retirement from active duty in 1968; he received the CBE and had been appointed as an ADC to HM the Queen.

He had a tremendous interest in his Regiment and was appointed President of the Border Regiment Association in 1966 and Vice-President Border Affairs in the new King's Own Royal Border Regimental Association in 1975. A greatly respected man, he died during the Easter weekend of 1993 at the age of 80. *BRM/Mrs C. Haddon*

Introduction

Alan Green's book about the 1st Battalion The Border Regiment at Arnhem was published by the Regimental Museum in 1991 and was the result of his considerable research into the battle. Combining as it did official accounts with personal reminiscences, the book gave well-deserved prominence to a Battalion that fought at Arnhem, often overlooked in many other accounts, and served successfully as a fitting tribute to the men who can best tell their own unique story. Since publication, additional information has become available, and with the 50th Anniversary of the Battle of Arnhem occurring in 1994, the authors decided to produce this book, which incorporates the material used in the 1991 publication.

The authors hope that the book will appeal to a broad cross-section of the general public, whatever their reason for interest, but it is primarily intended for those with a Regimental connection and particularly those of The Border Regiment. The book also provides a far broader view of the 1st Battalion's role and actions during the Second World War. Though the period is essentially dominated by the Battalion's Airborne role, it is important, if something of their manner is to be understood, to follow the path that led its officers and men from embarkation in September 1939 as part of the BEF to garrison duties in Germany in October 1945, by way of Dunkirk, Sicily and Arnhem. Indeed, in the authors' opinion, so powerful is the unpretentious message conveyed by the surviving veterans that little has been done other than to place these recollec-

tions within a chronology. Although in some cases the very nature and confusion of battle makes sequential recording difficult in the extreme, the essence of recollections has been preserved.

The book does not pretend to be a work of social history or a study of strategy and tactics. The authors have acted more as editors or collators to tell the story of this Battalion's involvement in operations in Belgium, France, North Africa, Sicily, Italy, Holland and Norway. In doing so there is little or no analysis, with or without the benefit of hindsight, or passing judgement on failure or success. The book chronicles the spirit of fellowship and triumph over adversity that was so clearly demonstrated throughout the Second World War and was manifest in the Battalion at each stage of its deployment.

In this respect 1 Border was probably no different from any other battalion or unit, but their lot required them to take on a new and wholly experimental role in late 1941 and apply those largely untried skills to an entirely novel method of prosecuting the fight against the enemy. Therefore the book is a commentary about combat and training at a very personal level, and in that respect the surviving veterans are their own authority. In addition, when in writing an account of a particular action or event, the individual recollections reflect what each man saw or experienced, which was often very different from his neighbour's experience, who may have only been 20 yards away in another slit-trench.

The authors make no apologies for publishing

The Border Regiment cap badge used above the chapter titles in this book
incorporates a Wreath awarded to the 34th (Cumberland) Regiment for their
rearguard action at the Battle of Fontenoy in 1745, and the Dragon superscribed with
CHINA was awarded to the 55th (Westmorland) Regiment for service in China
1841-42. These two Regiments were amalgamated and in 1881 became the
1st and 2nd Battalions respectively of The Border Regiment.

photographs that will have been seen before in other works. However, their inclusion has not been an attempt to seduce the reader with familiar or popular photographic references, but a real effort to provide more detail about the image, where perhaps other works have not been so able.

This book would not have been produced without the selfless co-operation of many former members of the 1st Battalion and their families, who have given so freely of their time and, sometimes painful, recol-

lection. This assistance was given in 1988-89 to help Alan Green, and was again so prevalent in 1993-94. Many others, both as individuals and those representing institutions, have also assisted the authors, and the acknowledgements at the end of the book are testament to that weight of authority and altruism.

**The Castle
Carlisle
September 1994**

REMEMBRANCE Since the end of the War, veterans of the Battalion have made numerous visits to Oosterbeek, particularly on the dates of the Annual Pilgrimage in September; that in 1994 was very special, as many planned to be there for the 50th Anniversary Commemoration of the Battle, and some of them would be returning for the first time since 1944.

On 8 October 1993, 14 veterans of 1 Border went to Oosterbeek to act as bearers and escorts at the funeral service for Pte Ernest Ager and Pte Douglas Lowery, both of C Company, who were killed in action on 22 and 24 September 1994 respectively. Their remains had been found earlier in the year near Van Lennepweg in Oosterbeek, where they had fallen in action. The funeral was also attended by representatives of the King's Own Royal Border Regiment, the British Military Attache in The Hague, the Dutch Army, the Commonwealth War Graves Commission, the Netherlands Grave Service, the Mayor of Oosterbeek, staff of the Airborne Museum Hartenstein, and local people.

The photograph shows Jim Longson carrying the 1 Border Veterans Standard, David Stubbs carrying the Carlisle Branch Standard of the King's Own Royal Border Regimental Association, the local British Legion Standard Bearer, and the Rev Geoffrey Allen, preceding Tom Northgraves, Len Scully, Jack Heaton, Ken Briggs, Ron Graydon and Jack Hardwick with Pte Ager's coffin, and Jim McDowell, Wilf Oldham, Ernie Westerman, Bill Homer, Eric Blackwell and Johnnie Peters with Pte Lowery's coffin. At the rear are RSM Bob Flynn and Cpl Conrad Craven (bugler) of the 1st Battalion The King's Own Royal Border Regiment. *BRM*

Chapter 1

Off to War: BEF and Dunkirk

The 1st Battalion left Palestine in April 1939 after an extremely active three-year tour, during which they reached high peaks of success and efficiency under the command of Lt Col W. O. Lay DSO. Their send-off reflected the respect from Divisional and Brigade Staffs and also from Arab and Jew. Lt Col Lay was presented with a scimitar by Chief Faris Irshaid with the words, 'You gave us some hard knocks at the beginning, but we asked for it and we have no complaints. We are glad to know we part as friends. This sword is not a symbol of war, but a gift in friendship'.

In early April the Battalion embarked on the *Dominion Monarch* at Haifa, and received the following tribute from Brigadier A. R. Godwin-Austen, Commander of 14th Infantry Brigade, in a letter to the Colonel of the Regiment:

'April 23rd 1939

Dear General

I write just as a very sad day for me and for the whole Brigade is coming, the day on which we lose your 1st Battalion.

I don't suppose any Battalion has earned the same admiration from everyone in Palestine as they have done. In fighting they have invariably been outstanding, whether in action on a big scale, as in the early days of the Rebellion when big gangs were encountered, or in the smaller actions and raids by platoons or small parties under junior leaders.

You will have heard and read of a good many of their triumphs, but it is their sustained energy and drive and high quality all through that have brought their sum total of achievements up to something with which those of no other Battalion can compare. They are good all

through, no matter by what standard one may judge them. Lay has thrown his heart and soul into the business of restoring order here and, quite apart from the operational side of this business, has controlled his area in a way that no one else has approached. His roads are better than anyone else's and his troops the envy of the rest in the country in their soldierly bearing and workmanlike smartness.

I can hardly express what I owe to him personally and to your Regiment as a whole for setting an example which others have sought to imitate, and so raising the level of the whole brigade.

To myself their example too has been so valuable because, coming fresh to the job three months ago, there were many occasions on which one wondered whether or not something could be done. Your Regiment showed me there was little that could not be done and done well.'

After disembarkation in England the Battalion proceeded to Aldershot and occupied the newly built Mandora Barracks. Some little while later Colonel Lay was posted to command the Lucknow Brigade and was succeeded by Lt Col W. H. F. 'Dolly' Chambers MC. In Aldershot the Battalion formed part of 4th Infantry Brigade, along with 2nd Battalion Royal Scots and 1st Battalion Royal Norfolks. In turn the Brigade was assigned to the 2nd Infantry Division as part of 1 Corps commanded by General Sir John Dill.

This period was characterised for the Battalion, as for the whole country, by rumours of war and mounting tension in Europe. Then, on 1 September 1939, the Battalion received orders for mobilisation and moved a few miles from Aldershot to a tented encampment at Ewshott Camp. Bandsman Doug Payne remembers well the new equipment for mobilisation that was issued while at Ewshott, and new 37 Pattern web equipment replaced the older 08 Pattern. Gas masks, gas capes, cream and eye-shields, groundsheets and blankets were distributed, and the side-cap replaced the old peaked forage-cap. The old pattern Service Dress was still worn and the Battalion did not change over to Battle Dress until they were in France.

Bandsman Alex Turner, who had joined the 1st Battalion in 1934, recalls that as they returned from Sunday Church Parade on 3 September he heard Prime Minister Neville Chamberlain announce on the radio that England was at war with Germany. On Monday the 4th Reservists arrived from the Regimental Depot at Carlisle, followed by another draft of 55 other ranks (ORs) on the 7th to bring the

Battalion up to war strength; ten officers also joined between 3 and 5 September. Mobilisation was completed on the 10th.

On 13 September Major F. R. Morgan and two ORs left for the Advance party, followed on the 16th by Lts Cowburn and Stewart MC, 2Lt Fitzgerald, the Carrier Platoon, all the Transport (MT) and baggage. On 20 September the Battalion left for Southampton, embarked on the *Royal Sovereign* and landed at Cherbourg the following morning. That evening they left Cherbourg by train, the wagons designated, as might be expected for soldiers, 'Hommes 40 Chevaux 8'. On arrival at Noyen En Sarthe they were billeted until the 28th, when they moved to a divisional concentration area near Bapaume on the old Somme battlefield.

The rest of the Battalion had arrived by the 26th and between 28 and 30 September they moved via Arnouville Les Mantes to Biache St Vaast, where they were joined by the Chaplain, Rev C. F. Holt; 2Lt Kay and 21 ORs from the Anti-Tank (A/T) Platoon left to join the Brigade. On 3 October the MT and Bren Carriers moved by road and the remainder of the Battalion by train to Mouchin on the Franco-Belgian frontier, where they occupied Blockhouse Defences before moving to Orchies, 13 miles south-south-east of Lille, on 6 October, where they went into Divisional Reserve. For the next few weeks the Battalion spent most of the time digging trenches and preparing defences; this continued into November. On 23 October the Battalion suffered its first fatality when 3594129 Pte R. Humphreys was killed in a motor accident. WO2 (CSM) A. Brackpool took over the Duties of RSM from A/WO1 (RSM) W. Matthews on Arroyo Day, 28 October 1939.

Four photographs taken at Orchies, France, on 13 October 1939. In the first (*above left*), a despatch rider takes a message from Major F. R. Morgan at Battalion HQ in the town. *IWM 0129*

Left Bren Carriers of the 1st Battalion exercising near Orchies. The 'cross-keys' sign of the 2nd Infantry Division can be clearly seen on the front mud-guard of the nearest vehicle. *IWM 0131*

Bandsman Doug Payne, who was at the time serving with D Company recalls: 'Eventually we reached Orchies, which was to be our home for a few months. Here it was Monday to Friday march out to the "Diggings", where we dug trenches, drainage ditches, communication trenches, weapon pits and erected barbed wire defences. On Saturday mornings it was marching nearer the border where we laboured for the Royal Engineers who were building pill-boxes. Sunday morning was Church Parade, and the service was held in the local cinema, whose walls and ceiling were covered with murals of naked and semi-naked women. . . It was during this time that we were issued with the new Boyes .5-inch anti-tank rifle. It was great fun firing at disposable petrol cans filled with earth, knocking them into the air and trying to hit them again whilst still airborne. . .' (3597704 Pte D. A. Payne)

Joe Hardy, then the Battalion Signal Sergeant, recalls: 'We quickly found out that the part of La Belle France that we had arrived in was not the Riviera, nor was the accommodation in any way comparable to the Ritz. Our first billet was in the town of Orchies, a hay loft near the junction of the main street and the railway crossing, and the best thing about that was the fact that it was next door to an *estaminet* [bar/cafe].

'As the winter set in it became so cold that it was really hard to bear, and as we were generally

Above right Bren carriers of the Battalion move through the town. *IWM 0134*

Right A Bren LMG team of the Battalion with the gun on an improvised AA mounting in a Morris CS8 15 cwt truck outside 2nd Division HQ. As was typical during the phoney war, the men are still wearing Service Dress with collar badges and shoulder titles. *IWM 0152*

employed on digging trenches, the rain, mud and cold shook the morale more than a little. We would return to the billet wet to the skin, take our wet clothes off, put on a pair of long underpants, puttees and an over-coat, and sneak away to the *estaminet*. The Army could not see its way to allowing a common soldier the luxury of two sets of clothing, but they did allow two sets of underclothing. It might have been differ-ent had they (the Army) realised that this would cause quite a lot of British soldiery to end up in the back room of a French cafe, trouserless every time they got themselves wet through during the day. The two sisters who owned the place, Maggie and Lucy, just accepted out trouserless state as being very natural. . .' (3597312 Sgt J. S. D. Hardy)

Bandsman Alex Turner again recalls that '. . .the Band adopted their wartime role as stretcher-bearers and medical orderlies, organised by the MO Capt

Men of the Battalion shopping, and the Corps of Drums playing, in Orchies market-place in October 1939. *IWM 0154 & 0150*

Geoffrey Black, being allocated four to each company.' Alex joined B Company, commanded by Capt Tommy Haddon. 'For eight months we trained, dug trenches on the Belgian border and slept on straw pal- liasses in hay lofts. Social life was nil apart from "cafe au lait", or "cafe avec rhum"; the odd lorry went to Lille for a change or shopping. Although the regi- mental drums were taken to war, our Band instru-

Above Issuing the cigarette ration at Orchies on 13 October 1939. Note the security poster to the right of the door. *IWM 0469*

Right Examples of two security posters issued to the BEF in 1939-40. *BRM*

ments were left behind, but with the long "Phoney War" the instruments were sent out and we formed a concert party to entertain the troops and villagers.' (3597414 Pte A. Turner)

November continued much in the same vein as October, with little or no training apart from one exercise at the end of the month. On 4 December the Battalion was deployed on various duties in the Orchies area, and on the 5th HM King George VI inspected the Battalion.

The 4th Battalion The Border Regiment, which had been sent to France to carry out duties on the Lines of Communication, took over the billets in Orchies as the weather started to become very cold. Before Christmas 1 Border exchanged one officer and four NCOs with 5 Border, which was still in the UK with 42nd Division. Capt W. Y. K. Blair-Oliphant left on 9 December with the NCOs to be instructors;

Capt A. S. Miller joined with a Colour Sergeant and three Sergeants from 5 Border to replace them on 8 December.

As there was no contact with the enemy on the Belgian frontier, one British Brigade at a time was sent to the Saar to gain experience and occupy the various lines (or in French 'lignes') of defence along the Maginot Line. 4th Infantry Brigade received their orders to move on 22 December, and with the impending move Christmas was celebrated a week early with turkey, pudding and all the trimmings served to the soldiers by the officers, as was the custom.

The move took place on Christmas Eve, with the MT drivers, Pioneer Platoon and Light Mortar Platoon entraining at Douai and the remainder of the Battalion at Rosolt. D Company 1st Battalion Royal Welch Fusiliers proceeded with 1 Border, as D Company had been left at Orchies attached to HQ 6th Infantry Brigade. This was done to ensure that all battalions received some experience of trench and open warfare in contact with the enemy. The train

Men of the Battalion reply to the toast of their officer at the Battalion Christmas dinner, held early on 18 December 1939 prior to the Battalion's move to the Maginot Line. *IWM 02182*

journey lasted through the night and the Battalion finally arrived at Quartier De Vallieres on the northern outskirts of Metz at 15.00 hrs on Christmas Day 1939. The Battalion marched to Bousse and Rurange on 30 December. The M1 Platoon was kept busy during the night starting up all vehicles every 15 minutes to prevent them from freezing.

The following day the Battalion moved to a hutted camp in woods at Kedanje and took over responsibility from the French for the 'Ligne D'Arret' in the rear of the Maginot Line. 1 Border then moved to the 'Ligne de Contact' with HQ Company at Waldweisstroff and A, B, C and D Companies at Halsroff. Some enemy shell and MG fire was reported on the Battalion left front during the evening of 5 January 1940. Joe Hardy again recalled that '. . .we were moved down to Metz and through the Maginot Line, where we were actually in contact with those dreadful people of the Third Reich. The most memorable experience about the trip was that I never realised that it could get so terribly cold. We found it a completely new experience to have a battery of French 75mm guns come up at full gallop to a place just behind us, shoot off perhaps 20 or 30 rounds, then get the hell out of there before the enemy could return their fire. The enemy shells always fell on the place that they had been, but where we still were! It struck me at the time that, if these gunners were our friends, the blokes in field-grey at the bottom end of the paddock might not be such bad enemies; I had a lot to learn.'

There was little contact with the enemy, although on 7 January a patrol of 2 Royal Norfolks was fired upon heavily and one of the officers, a 2Lt Everett, was found to be missing. The severe cold and icy conditions continued, and on 10 January the Battalion was inspected by General Gamelin and General Ironside, Chief of the Imperial General Staff (CIGS). They were then relieved in the front line by 1 Royal Scots and proceeded to the 'Ligne De Recueil' in the area of St Francois Lacroix. Battalion HQ, HQ and A Companies were in the forward locations; B Company remained under command of 1 Royal Scots at Hastroff; C Company were at Rodlich; and D Company (RWF) were at St Anne's Farm.

Tommy Haddon, who was commanding B Company at the time, recalled: 'I think we spent a week in each of the three lines. The front line was the worst, trenches in deep snow where we had to keep a careful watch, not only for the enemy, but also for frostbite; my moustache used to freeze and was most uncomfortable. Brigade HQ organised the reconnaissance patrols. By this time I was commanding a Company. I had bought in Metz a dozen or so white nightdresses for patrols to wear at night. Our Padre, who spoke good German, volunteered to go out with a patrol and brought back a lot of useful information, which was sent up to higher HQ. In return all he got was a rocket for going into enemy territory as a non-combatant!

'In fact we had no real excitement. German gunners shelled an unoccupied bit of our line and our gunners replied at the same time every day. By mistake our gunners fired out of hours, as it were, and the Germans were furious, and replied viciously, although they inflicted little damage. . .' The Battalion returned to Metz on 13 January, leaving three days later for Orchies, where D Coy 1 RWF rejoined their Battalion and D Coy 1 Border rejoined from attachment to 1 RWF at Mouchin.

The Battalion moved out of the billets in Orchies on 17 January, and 2 Wiltshires occupied them. After guarding Bouigny airfield and Orchies station, 1 Border moved to Rumegies to relieve 2 Royal Norfolks and occupied forward positions on the Belgian frontier. The severe cold weather continued, but training schemes at Company level began in addition to the mundane work of building pill-boxes and digging ditches; various parties left for Dannes Ranges near Boulogne for field firing. On 15 February B Company area was visited by more VIPs, who included the Minister of War, Lord Gort VC, the GOC BEF, Lord Milne, and others. The Press photographed C Company searching a village on 21 February, and both Company and Battalion exercises were carried out, despite the bad weather. It was B Company's turn again for the VIPs on 25 February when Field Marshals Birdwood, Montgomery-Massingberd and Jacob visited a Company blockhouse.

Further training schemes were carried out at Company, Battalion and Brigade levels during March. Sport and other activities were mixed in with the training, and included a trip by Company Commanders and WOs under the Commanding Officer to Beaumont-Hamel on the Somme battlefield to visit the areas held by 1 Border in 1916. The Battalion participated in a Brigade scheme on the River Authie on 15-16 March and returned to Rumegies on 19 March after a 70-mile drive without lights. On 8 April the Battalion began continuous wiring operations along its front, and on 14 April was placed on 6 hours notice to move. Word came on 19 April to resume normal training, but several other units remained on 6 hours notice.

1 Border received notice to join 42nd Division on 25 April, and the 2-pounder anti-tank guns fired on Flines ranges on the 26th. The Battalion was played out of the station at Rumegies by the Pipes of 1 Royal Scots and arrived at Comines at noon on 4 May. Tommy Haddon, who had taken over as Adjutant

Left A section of the Battalion crossing a stream during an exercise on 22 February 1940. *IWM F2682*

Right Searching a haystack on the same exercise. *IWM F2683*

Left A camouflaged section post being erected near Rumegies by men of the Battalion, 22 February 1940. *IWM F2754*

Above right A Section of the Battalion moving up to a blockhouse near Rumegies on 29 February 1940. *IWM F2862*

Right The Section inside the block-house. *IWM F2865*

from Major P. Ryding at the beginning of February, recalled that even in the most urgent of situations, bureaucracy still occasionally reared its ugly head: 'I remember being wakened in the middle of the night shortly before the invasion of Belgium by a despatch rider with an urgent demand for the number of prayer-books held by our Battalion; this from the HQ of the Brigade.'

The Battalion replaced 1/8th Lancashire Fusiliers (TA) in 125th Infantry Brigade of 42nd (East Lancashire) Division TA, which had arrived in France during April and formed part of III Corps commanded by Lt Gen Sir Ronald F. Adam. The other two Battalions in the Brigade were 1/5th and 1/6th Lancashire Fusiliers (TA). Over the next few days cadres were sent to 1/5th and 1/6th LFs and arrangements were made for a party to go to Dannes ranges. The German invasion of Belgium changed all that.

Tommy Haddon also recalled that at some stage, probably at the beginning of May, due to a disagreement with his TA Brigadier, Lt Col Chambers MC was relieved of his command of the Battalion and was succeeded by Major Hennessey DSO MC.

Between 10 May 1940, the date of the German invasion of Holland and Belgium, and 16 May the Battalion were guarding vital bridges on the Franco-Belgian frontier at Comines, Warneton and Deulemont, regulating the mass of refugee traffic out of Belgium. B Company were sent to guard Bondue aerodrome, north of Lille. Since Belgium had maintained strict neutrality, there had been no discussions with the

Belgian General Staff for a co-ordinated plan in the event of invasion. The French High Command assumed that the Belgian defences on their eastern frontier and on the Albert Canal would hold out for a few days; this view was further reinforced by Belgian preparations of anti-tank obstacles between Wavre and Namur. The first line of defence was to be the Albert Canal and the Meuse, and behind this lines on the rivers Dyle, Senne, Dendre and the Escaut.

The BEF, located in and around Lille, advanced 60 miles to the River Dyle as planned and took up positions between Wavre and Louvain, with the French 1st Army on its right between Namur and Wavre, the Belgian Army on its left, and the French 7th Army on its extreme left between Louvain and Antwerp. British cavalry units with armoured cars moved forward beyond the River

Below Cleaning a Bren and a Boyes anti-tank rifle at Rumegies in February 1940. *IWM F2871*

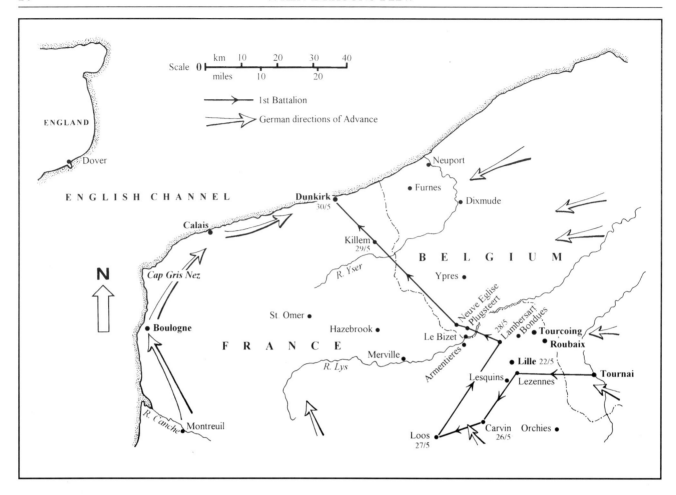

The route of the Battalion in France and during the retreat to Dunkirk in May 1940.

Dyle to observe the approaches from the east and make contact with the enemy. Two Corps occupied the British Front: 1st Corps on the right on a two-division front, with 1st Division on its left, 2nd Division on its right in contact with the French, and 48th Division in reserve; and II Corps on the left, with 3rd Division forward, the Belgians on their left and 4th Division in reserve. The 5th and 50th Divisions were in general reserve and would move forward when required, while III Corps, including 42nd and 44th Divisions, were deployed in depth on the River Escaut.

By 15 May a defence of the River Dyle was proving impractical, and the French High Command ordered a phased withdrawal over three days to the Senne, the Dendre, and finally to the River Escaut, which began on the evening of the 16th. On the morning of 17 May the situation in the south had become serious, as German armour and mobile forces were reported to have broken through the French lines, crossed the River Oise and to be heading for the sea, which would cut off the Allies; this threatened the right

flank of the BEF, the Rear GHQ, communications over the Somme and the base areas. 1 Border received orders to move on the morning of the 17th, and at 15.00 hrs began a 25-mile march to Don on the Canal La Bassee, where they arrived at dawn on 18 May. That afternoon the Battalion again moved by troop carriers and MT to Chereng, arriving at around midnight.

To protect the British right flank, an ad hoc task-force was formed under Major-General F. N. Mason Macfarlane, known as 'Macforce'. 127th Brigade (4 East Lancs, 5 Manchesters, 1 HLI) of 42nd Division with 1st Army Tank Brigade and 223 Battery of 56th Anti-tank Regiment (King's Own) RA TA were ordered to cover the right rear of the BEF and deny the enemy the crossings over the River Scarpe from Rache to St Amand. 126th Brigade (5 King's Own, 1 East Lancs, 5 Border) moved to a position on the Escaut near Tournai, supported by 222 Battery. 125th Brigade with 221 Battery were detached as a special force north of Tournai, forming a tank trap on the Tournai-Lille line to destroy an enemy armoured force that had broken through towards Arras, and which it was thought would try to rejoin its main body.

The front line was withdrawn from the Dendre to

the Escaut in daylight on 19 May. 125th Brigade rejoined 42nd Division on the same day and took over 126th Brigade's position on the Escaut at Froyennes, north of Tournai. With the other two battalions of the Brigade in support, 1 Border held a front 3,500 yards long with a line of forward defences on the west bank of the River Escaut. These positions were overlooked by high ground to the east, and communications between Battalion HQ and the companies were impeded by two ditches in the rear without any crossing points.

The Battalion War Diary for 19 May recorded: 'The right and centre of the front consisted of a narrow strip of land behind the FDLs (Forward Defensive Locations), the two anti-tank ditches with houses on the right and wooded country in the middle as far back as the railway line to a depth of 1,000 yards. The left of the position consisted of marshy open country from the FDL, almost to the railway line to a depth of 2,000 yards. The position necessitated putting three companies up and one in reserve on the left centre. C Company was on the right, B in the middle, A on the left and D in reserve. Battalion HQ, owing to the length of the front, was 3,000 yards back from the FDLs. . .

'The enemy was seen to occupy the east bank of the Escaut with strong mortar positions along the whole front; a particularly strong detachment was established behind a factory opposite C Company. Sniper posts in abandoned houses overlooking our FDLs and in most cases enemy occupying the top stories of houses on the opposite bank could see the bottom of our trenches. A gap of 1,000 yards was discovered on our left and the Carrier Platoon was despatched to help 100 Sappers who had stepped in to the breach. . .'

The Battalion were attacked on 20 and 21 May. On the 20th the forward positions were mortared heavily and the enemy were reported between these positions, B Company and C Company HQ; C Company HQ was fired on. British artillery brought down fire on the enemy mortar position behind the factory opposite C Company and counter-preparation fire along the whole front. Communications within the Battalion were already difficult due to the length of the front and the distance between Battalion HQ and the Companies; field telephone lines broken by shelling made communications even more difficult. A Platoon of A Company were sent to drive the ground behind the forward positions towards Bren Carriers posted on the line of the railway, and several enemy casualties were reported.

The following day was no better. It began quietly, but at about 06.00 hrs enemy artillery shelled the whole length of the forward positions. B and C

Companies reported that a large number of the enemy had appeared behind their front and in front of C Company HQ. Heavy enemy mortar fire was directed on C Company's front, and it was reported their forward positions had been wiped out and Company HQ was being attacked. B Company also reported their forward positions overrun and their Company HQ being fired at with MG fire. A Platoon of D Company were sent to hold the line of the railway, and another platoon to the high ground overlooking the railway. The Carrier Platoon, commanded by 2Lt D. K. Fitzgerald, were despatched to reinforce C Company. However, the Carrier Platoon's attack was unsuccessful, and Fitzgerald was among a number of the Battalion's fatal casualties.

By 11.00 hrs there were no telephone links with the Companies, and messages from C and B Companies, brought by runner, reported the area forward of the railway line overrun by the enemy and the forward posts surrounded. Battalion HQ was prepared for its own defence, but as no field of fire or view could be obtained, it moved out on to the hill to the south-east at 11.00 hrs and prepared to advance to try and secure the line of the railway.

The 1/6th LFs had meanwhile been preparing for a counter-attack and came through at about 14.00 hrs. Battalion HQ troops advanced with the counter-attack, which made the line of the railway without opposition; Battalion HQ was then re-occupied. Meanwhile, A and D Companies had remained in position, and it was ascertained later that elements of B and C Companies had remained in their forward posts. By 19.00 hrs an artillery barrage was put down in front of the railway and the 1/6th LFs advanced under the barrage to the west bank of the river and re-occupied the original front; they suffered over 100 casualties as they made a tremendous charge against heavy fire and restored the situation. 1 Border were then withdrawn to Brigade Reserve at 22.00 hrs, leaving a company attached to 1/6th LFs as a reserve company.

The Bandsmen were kept very busy as stretcher-bearers. Bandsman Alex Turner recalls that during this period he and his colleagues took ammunition and rations up to the Company forward positions and brought the wounded back with them to the Regimental Aid Post to be treated by the MO. This was hazardous due to the exposed positions of the Company and the difficulties posed by obstacles such as the anti-tank ditches. At one stage they tipped a woodman's caravan into the ditch to enable them to bring the stretchers across. The casualties at Froyennes were buried in the village churchyard; Alex returned regularly to the village after the war to play Last Post and Reveille at the annual service.

Four members of the Battalion were later recommended for the Military Medal (MM) for their actions during this period (see Appendix 3): L/Sgt Cyril Butler for carrying wounded to safety under fire (received an MiD); L/Cpl Alfred Fairweather for helping to evacuate wounded under fire over a 5-hour period (received an MiD); L/Cpl Albert Woods, also for tending wounded and bringing in casualties under fire (received an MiD); and Pte John McCluskie of the Signals Platoon for repairing signal cables under fire (received the MM). Another of the Battalion's stretcher-bearers, Bandsman Donald Clark, was also recommended for the MM for going out under fire to tend wounded and help to bring in casualties on the 22nd. Platoon Sergeant Major Sidney Usher was awarded the DCM for leadership and maintaining his rear-guard position under heavy fire.

On 22 May an enemy crossing of the Escaut developed into an attack on the whole front, forcing 42nd Division to withdraw west to prepared positions on the Franco-Belgian frontier; further casualties were suffered. 1 Border moved into reserve at Marquaisne, and at dusk the whole Brigade withdrew, the Battalion occupying a defensive position at Lezennes, south-east of Lille, with A and B Companies forward filling a gap near Ascqu, between the left of 42nd Division and the right of 1st Division to the north. These positions were held for three days on a 2,000-yard front, with a French Battalion on the left and 1 East Lancs on the right. Three companies were in forward positions and A Company in reserve (later attached to 1 East Lancs).

At 11.00 hrs on 26 May 1 Border were ordered to move south-west to take part in a counter-attack following an enemy breakthrough near Carvin. However, when the main body arrived at Barques the situation had been restored. HQ with C and D Companies billeted there; A and B Companies billeted at Ronchin. Orders were received that night to withdraw to the River Deule and occupy a position on a 4,000-yard front in the Loos area west of Lille.

On 27 May the Battalion's position on the Deule Canal was strung out. There was no sign of the enemy and at 17.00 hrs a patrol led by 2Lt Machell and a recce party were sent out; Machell had not reported back at 24.00 hrs. New positions were occupied the following day on either side of the Citadel, north-west of Lille, until noon, when the Battalion received orders to withdraw by thinning out gradually and RV at Ploegsteert. Several enemy patrols were seen and engaged, but no serious fighting took place. While French forces streamed across the river, news of the Belgian surrender was received at noon. With the left flank of the BEF exposed, the bridges over the Deule were blown and the withdrawal to the Dunkirk perimeter ordered.

Bandsman Alex Turner recalled that 'we were told to make for Dunkirk. We got the walking wounded away and made our serious casualties comfortable, marking the letter "M" on their foreheads so that the Germans would know that they had been given morphia.'

Major Hennessey later wrote in a letter to Brigadier G. Hyde Harrison DSO, the Colonel of the Regiment, that 'on the 28th we were left at Lille. The rest of the Brigade had gone, and the most forward British troops were some 15 to 20 miles further back. German tanks were already well past us on the flanks when we came out of the line at 3 o'clock in the afternoon. We were able to get hold of some lorries of a Bridging Section on the morning of the 28th, because they were full of explosives and the Bosche was shelling them and consequently their owners were only too glad to hand them over and leave us to unload the explosives. I have no doubt that but for these lorries the Battalion would have quite easily been mopped up by the Bosche.' The Bridging Section were instructed officially to hand over all their lorries and anti-tank mines to 1 Border, and not to burn any of the vehicles but to destroy all the bridging equipment.

I Border duly left by road to the RV covered by the Carrier Platoon, which left at 15.00 hrs accompanied by the CO and Adjutant. At Ploegsteert they were ordered to rendezvous at Neuve Eglise, where B echelon transport and two parties from A and B Companies, detached for traffic duties, rejoined. Captain C. S. Mackay in command was informed to proceed to Killem, the RV for 42nd Division. With no member of Brigade or Divisional Staff to be found at any of the RVs, the Battalion moved by the given route to Killem.

Despite total confusion on the roads, 1 Border reached Killem in convoy at 21.30 hrs, but Battalion HQ and other men from various companies had become separated. Joe Hardy, who had been riding up and down the convoy on his motorcycle trying to keep the vehicles in touch, found that the column soon became strung out. However, on the 28th 5 Border picked up about 80 other ranks of the Battalion at Le Bizet, a few miles south of Ploegsteert. As no further orders were received at Killem, 1 Border moved by companies to the Dunkirk perimeter and spent the whole of the 29th on the beaches.

Bandsman Doug Payne wrote that during the retreat '. . .one evening we pulled up in a village and I was sent to pull a Military Police van out of a ditch. Sergeant Wallace the Platoon Sergeant came with me. When we returned the Battalion had vanished and Sergeant Wallace and I spent a long time trying to find them. After a few days of hair-raising escapades, we were told by a Brigadier no less to head for Dunkirk. After much haggling with MPs, etc, I managed to drive my truck right to the sand dunes behind the beaches at Dunkirk.'

Bandsman Alex Turner was told 'to make for the black smoke on the skyline, which we later found to be the blazing oil tanks at the docks at Dunkirk. A young stretcher-bearer and I set off after commandeering a Bren-gun and tins of Maconochies, fish and stewed steak. At one stage we befriended a frightened horse and rode it until our rumps were sore. An MP at one of the crossroads into town met us, gave us a carton of 200 Players cigarettes each and directed us to the beach. Here everything was in chaos, and although the bulk of the BEF had been evacuated, burning vehicles took up a large area.

'I began using my first-aid kit on the casualties around me, interrupted continuously by the Stuka dive-bombers. We dug some pits in the lea of the dunes for the wounded and sent the walking wounded off to the queues for the boats. I replenished our stock of dressings, splints, etc, from the damaged ambulances. After a couple of days an officer insisted that we join his squad at the wooden jetty and that we were now Royal Engineers under his command. Day lifts had ceased and we waited until nightfall when we clambered over the damaged jetty down on to a fishing-boat below. Water and bread was all the fishermen could offer, but we fell asleep on the deck before eating. We awoke to the bustle and noise of Ramsgate pier; we were given sandwiches, chocolate and fruit, then directed to the trains at the station. . .'

Bandsman Doug Payne again: 'I helped with the evacuation of casualties from a convoy of ambulances that had been shot up. On the way we picked up L/Cpl Butler from our Signal Platoon, who stayed with us. We left Dunkirk on a Lowestoft drifter *The Golden Gift* heading for Dover. Before night set in we ran aground on the Goodwin Sands. Next morning we were taken off in small groups by a small naval launch and taken to the *Sandown*, which took us in to Ramsgate on 4 June.'

Joe Hardy remembers that his '. . .only option left was to join one of the queues and take my turn at getting away in one of the small boats. It all seemed very hopeless. After many hours standing chest deep in the water I reached the head of the queue, only to find that there was a very young and extremely gallant officer organising the loading of the boats. He could not remember how long he had been there, but it was very obvious that if he stayed there any longer he would go under. I told him that he was unfit to do the job any longer and insisted that he be the first man into the next boat and that I would take his place organising at the head of the queue. . .

'I have never been very sure just how long I did that job, but during the time I was doing it three or four Bandsmen of the Regiment reached the head of the queue and stayed with me to help lift others into the boats. As a group we finally talked ourselves into catching a boat and handing over to the next Sergeant to come along. He took over as though it were the most natural thing in life, shook hands with us and wished us luck.'

Sgt Hardy and his group then boarded a Dutch tramp steamer, which had grounded as the tide went out. They later rowed across to one of the naval ships and were eventually taken aboard a destroyer, which landed them at Margate.

Captain Robert Stockwell, the Battalion Signals Officer, was in command of one group of about 300 all ranks. He signalled a destroyer, possibly HMS *Eskimo*, which embarked the whole party from Dunkirk harbour at 02.00 hrs on the 30th and disembarked them at Margate. Two other groups under Captains Mackay and Millar arrived at 06.00 hrs. Captain Stockwell was recommended for and received an MiD for his leadership (see Appendix 3). Battalion HQ arrived at the beaches on 30 May and took control of a position north of Dunkirk. Major Hennessey DSO MC and Captain Haddon managed to collect between 70 and 100 ORs, who had become separated from their companies, many recognised by their helmets, which had been painted in distinguishing colours (green and black camouflage pattern). Later that day HQ 4th Brigade arrived and took over control of the area from 1 Border, who were then embarked on a flat-bottomed Thames barge and taken to Margate.

During this period, 17-30 May, the Battalion lost some 250 all ranks, killed, wounded and PoW. The Battalion also lost virtually all its Band and Drums property amongst all its other equipment and transport left in France.

During the retreat to Dunkirk Capt John 'Jackie' Cowburn was recommended for the MC (received an MiD) after being captured, disarming his captors and escaping with his ration party in an attempt to force his way through enemy lines to the Battalion; he was subsequently re-captured and held in Oflag VIIB. Lt Arthur Miller was recommended for an MiD for carrying out a lone reconnaissance under fire on the 28th (see Appendix 3).

Other officers of the Battalion taken prisoner included Lt T. L. Barlow-Massicks, who had been wounded (Oflag VIIB), 2Lt P. McDonald (Oflag VIIB), and Lt J. E. Whitmore (Oflag VIIB). Amongst the men taken prisoner was L/Cpl Joseph Hall of Blackpool; he subsequently escaped from PoW camp with a Capt Richard Broad and was awarded the

DCM for his exploits; Broad received the MC and later presented Hall with a silver identification tag engraved 'A souvenir of the dangers and hardships that we endured together, and as a small token to the courage with which you bore them'. Hall received his DCM from HM King George VI at an investiture at Buckingham Palace in April 1942. Sadly, after transferring to the Royal Irish Fusiliers, with whom he served in North Africa, Hall was killed during the fighting around Catania, Sicily, on 6 August 1943.

L/Cpl Joseph Hall DCM from Blackpool with his daughter outside Buckingham Palace in April 1942, when he was presented with his DCM by HM King George VI. He was killed on Sicily while serving with the Royal Irish Fusiliers and is buried in Catania War Cemetery. Note the BORDER shoulder title and Airborne badges taken into wear in 1942. *BRM*

Chapter 2

From Mules to Gliders

On arrival in England the units of 42nd Division were collected and reformed in the Durham area, and from 5 June onwards the Battalion was gradually reformed at Crook, a small mining town south-west of Durham; A/Lt Col Hennessey DSO MC was confirmed as the Commanding Officer. The rebuilding process took some time and was particularly difficult due to the acute shortages of all types of weapons, vehicles, supplies and equipment, which was exemplified by the QM collecting a stock of obsolete '08 Pattern equipment on 9 June. Large drafts of men arrived on 22 and 25 June: six officers and 232 ORs from the Infantry Training Centre (ITC) at Carlisle, and 45 ORs from No 6 Infantry Base Depot (IBD) at Halifax. As many of the ORs had only between six and nine weeks training, and a separate 'IBD' Company was established to improve their training; this Company was maintained until the end of October. Further drafts of men and equipment continued to arrive and by October the Battalion was fully up to strength.

On 1 July the Battalion moved 25 miles to Prudhoe in Northumberland, where they remained until 4 September. Their role, as the reserve Battalion of 42nd Division, was to act as a mobile column, for which 25 buses were allocated as transport. They were also responsible for guarding five bridges over the River Tyne and for the local defence of Prudhoe. Bandsman Doug Payne recalled that his Platoon was turned into a 'tank-hunting platoon'. Due to the shortage of military vehicles, they were given three commandeered civilian vans, his being a 12 cwt red Domestos Company vehicle with 'DOMESTOS' in large gold lettering on the side. Another was a Fordson laundry van and the third a small Commer from a local electrical contractor. The Platoon was also equipped with bicycles, and their main offensive

weapons were Molotov cocktails carried in beer crates in the vans.

On 5 September, 1 Border moved by road to Ainderby Steeple, where at 22.00 hrs on the 7th the code-word CROMWELL for invasion was received; the Battalion got as far as Northallerton when the alert was called off. The following day notice was given for a move to the Oxford area, and on the 9th the Battalion left in two trains from Northallerton for Burghclere in Hampshire. Billets were found in Kingsclere for HQ, C and D Companies, with A and B in Burghclere. This was followed by a move to Leiston in Suffolk at the beginning of November to take over the coastal defences, Battalion HQ being based at Stone House in Leiston.

The names of several other officers, NCOs and ORs were submitted for awards in the New Years Honours List by the Battalion, sadly without success (see Appendix 3). At the end of November the Battalion was notified that it would be joining 31st Independent Infantry Brigade, and on 1 December they left 42nd Division and moved by road and rail to Welwyn Garden City in Hertfordshire. The 1st Battalion Royal Ulster Rifles, 2nd Battalion Oxfordshire and Buckinghamshire Light Infantry and 2nd Battalion South Staffordshire Regiment, who had recently returned from India, formed the rest of the Brigade. The Brigade had its own support units: 31st Independent Reconnaissance Company, 9th Field Company RE, 181 Field Ambulance RAMC, 31 Independent Infantry Brigade Ordnance Workshop and Field Park, an RASC Company and an RASC Motor Coach Company, Brigade HQ, Brigade Signals and an anti-tank battery formed by 223 Battery of 56th Anti-Tank Regiment (King's Own) RA TA, which had left its parent regiment and the 42nd Division in July; one troop of guns was attached in

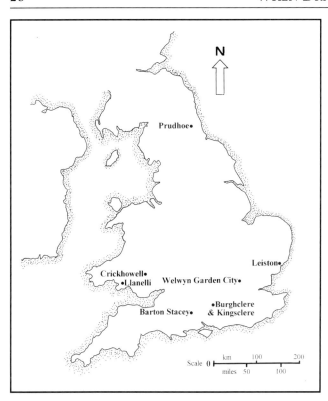

support of each of the Brigade's Battalions. The Brigade formed part of IV Corps, its role being to co-operate with 2nd Armoured Division.

Between 16 and 18 February 1941 the Brigade moved from Welwyn to Glanusk Park near Crickhowell in South Wales and began training in the Black Mountains. On 2 April they began experiments with pack-transport, the object being to evaluate if and how an Infantry Brigade with Field Ambulance, RE Company and Brigade HQ could be carried on pack transport. For the Battalion it was decided that some 350 animals would be required, and trials in mule loading began on 12 May. The number of mules was revised down to 200, then to 140 in June, and the final trials were completed at the

Left Locations of the 1st Battalion in England and Wales from June 1940 to May 1943.

Below The WOs and Sergeants of the 1st Battalion at Kingsclere in Hampshire, September 1940. Seated on the first row: — , CSM Pope, CSM Duffy, CSM Bradshaw, RSM Potts, 2i/c Major Murphy, the CO Lt Col Hennessey DSO MC, Adjutant Capt T. Haddon, Bandmaster Wallace, CSM Gardner, — , — . *BRM*

Above The Band at Kingsclere in September 1940.
Back row: Bob Cox, Joe Kitchen, Tom Jackson, Jock Fairweather, Jack Crooks, Smith 14, Hank Johnson, Olly Gainor, Sandy Sanderson, Doug Payne, — , — , — , Tarzan Smith 37, Lackery Wood.

Third row: — , Herbert Heaseman, L/Cpl Tom 'Pop' Ferguson, Jock Hyndman, Bill Fenwick, Alex Turner, Stan Munday, — , — , George Curtis, George Wombwell, G. Powell, Cap Thorne, — , Bill Bailey.

Second row: L/Cpl Titchener, — , Nobby Clarke, W. Windross, Melvyn Dunkerley, Joss Elliot, D. Davey, L/Cpl J. 'Nobby' Casey, Harry Burge, Bandmaster Wallace, — , Barney Steel, Tich Froud, — , — , G. Hay, Sgt Eric Buffel, CSM Bull Harrison, L/Cpl G. Blumsden.
Front Row: Capt Haddon, Lt Col Hennessey DSO MC, Major Murphy, Major Mackay. *BRM/Doug Payne*

Right Officers of the Battalion at Kingsclere in September 1940.
Back row: 2/Lt Baker, 2/Lt Pertwee, 2/Lt McIlvenna.
Middle row: Lt Smith (RASC), Lt R. J. Turner, 2/Lt M. W. Grubb, Capt W. J. Churcher, 2/Lt Dorman, Capt R. Stewart MC, Capt A. S. Miller, 2/Lt Kay, 2/Lt Pearl (RASC).
Front row: Lt J. W. (QM) Smith, Capt F. Fineron, Capt A. G. S. Smith, Capt C. M. R. Spedding, Major Murphy, Lt Col Hennessey DSO MC, Capt T. Haddon, Major C. S. Mackay, Capt R. Stockwell, 2/Lt Machell, Padre J. Rowell. *BRM*

This page A Mortar Platoon with pack mules during 31st Independent Infantry Brigade exercises in the Black Mountains, South Wales, 26 June 1941. With the mules is an Indian RASC Handler, seen in the third photograph. *IWM H11141/50/55*

beginning of July. Attached to the Battalion were a Platoon from the Indian RASC, who acted as the Mule Handlers.

Jimmy McDowell (3601450), who had joined the Battalion from 6 Border in the summer of 1940, recalls that each mule had an Indian Handler or Muleteer; Mohammed Lal and Mohammed Yassin were two of the names. Jimmy served in the Mortar Platoon for virtually the whole of his service in the Battalion and recalls that each box of six mortar bombs (packed in threes) had to be fastened simultaneously and carefully on to the mule pack-saddle, to avoid both the whole lot falling on the ground and giving the animal the slightest excuse to bolt! Each section of two mortars (there were three sections in the Mortar Platoon) used approxi-

Above The Mortar Platoon crossing a river. *IWM H11144*

Right Training with assault boats. *BRM/Tony Stafford/IWM H11157*

Below right A Sentry standing guard. *IWM H11159*

mately ten mules, one carrying the mortar tube, tripod and base-plate with four to carry the boxes of ammunition. The bipod and base-plate were slung on each side of the pack-saddle with the tube fastened on the top.

On 13 August the Battalion moved to the Llanelli area with companies based in several locations. The day before has a significant entry in the War Diary - 'Twelve Battalion pigs sold for £99 2s 3d.' The Battalion had been able to run a farm, under the direction of Capt Montgomery, on Lord Glanusk's estate.

In September 1941 it was announced that the Brigade was to become the 1st Air-Landing Brigade of the newly formed 1st Airborne Division, and on 10 October it was re-designated; at the end of that month Brigadier G. F. Hopkinson OBE MC was selected to command it. Having just

Above Llanelli, August 1941. The Band on the March led by Bandmaster Chic Young. From the right the members are Plum Wardle, Jack Crooks, Jock Fairweather, Smith 67, Boy Parsons, Bunker Bailey, Butch Smith, Ned Notley, Jackson, Walter Earl, Alex Turner, Doug Phillips, Stan Munday, Pop Ferguson and Jock Hyndman. *Alex Turner*

Left 2/Lt Tony Stafford leads his platoon through the town. The Lance-Corporal in the centre of the first rank carries a .3-inch P14 rifle, one of the many imported from the USA to meet the shortage of rifles post-Dunkirk. *BRM/Tony Stafford*

completed training in a light, self-contained role, the group now had to evolve the organisation, equipment and training of a formation to be carried by gliders or aircraft. The first main task was to sort out personnel. Individuals were given the option of transferring to other units, but most elected to take on the new role.

Joe Hardy, then the Signal Platoon Sergeant, recalled that 'all Airborne soldiers were supposedly Volunteers - it was judged to be a risky business. The way in which they had us volunteer was to announce

that in future the Battalion was to be designated an Airborne Unit, and that those men who did not want to take part in Airborne Operations should report to the Orderly Room and apply to be transferred to other units. We had one man in the Battalion who had sufficient guts to say that he did not want to fly; he was transferred out, and the rest of us were deemed to have volunteered.' The War Diary records that some 30 ORs left the Battalion on 30 December 1941 as 'unfit' for the new role.

2/Lt Tony Stafford and Lt Williamson, the MTO, at Llanelli. Note the BORDER title in black on a khaki patch sewn on to the Battle Dress, rather than being worn as a slip-on over the epaulette. Below this title can be seen the badge of 31st Independent Infantry Brigade. *BRM/Tony Stafford*

All the units in 31 Brigade remained with the new one apart from the Reconnaissance Company, which became 1st Airborne Reconnaissance Squadron in April 1942, and the RASC Company, which was also re-designated as Divisional troops in August 1942. As each Battalion in the Brigade established its own Heavy Weapons or Support Company, the Brigade anti-tank battery was re-designated as 1st Air-Landing Anti-Tank Battery in June 1942 and went as the anti-tank support of the 1st Parachute Brigade. Later 2nd Air-Landing Anti-Tank Battery was formed for the 4th Parachute Brigade. The Airborne Division consisted of two Parachute Brigades, one Air-landing Brigade, Royal Signals, RAMC and RE units. Lt Col R. H. Bower KOYLI (later to command 1st Air-Landing Brigade) replaced Lt Col Hennessey DSO MC as CO of 1 Border on 15 October 1941.

Training carried on very much as normal at Llanelli with Battalion and Company schemes. The earliest reference to any glider training is in November, when Lt Col Bower and Major Mackay, the 2i/c, went to RAF Ringway, near Manchester (now Manchester Airport), where the Glider Training Unit had been established in

June 1941. Both men were injured in a glider accident; the CO spent five days in Davyhulme Hospital with concussion. Sadly, worse was to follow in December.

At the end of the month the Battalion prepared for another move, which took place between 2 and 4 December 1941. The 1st Airborne Division moved to the Salisbury Plain area and 1 Border arrived at B Camp, Barton Stacey, near Winchester in Hampshire. Barton Stacey was a purpose-built hutted wartime camp and the Battalion were together for the first time in three months.

Joe Hardy recalls the first experience of glider activity, a flight in a Hotspur glider from RAF Ringway on 19 December 1941 intended to test for air-sickness: '. . .when they asked for volunteers for what was to be the first live glider load, as it was to take place in the Manchester area, where a lot of the Regiment came from, there was no shortage of volunteers at all. They asked for, I think, 18 men - they could have got 80! The glider crashed and the passengers were all killed.'

These were Sergeant Harrison and Privates Felton, Hornby, Keogh, Marshall and Pilkington (see Appendix 1); the pilot, who was also injured, was Lt Col J. F. Rock, the first CO of the Glider Pilot Regiment.

'In the British Army, all equipment that is issued must be fully accounted for, gathered together and be struck off strength when it is unfit for further usage.

The 1st Battalion Rugby XV at B Camp, Barton Stacey, early in 1942.
Back row, left to right: Lt Ingram Cleasby, Pte E. Wood, Pte V. Smith, Lt Charles Wilson, Lt G. A. Porter, Lt Arthur Springbett, Lt Geoffrey Costeloe, Lt Bob Coulston.
Front row: Pte L. Tremble, S/Sgt W. Evans APTC, Pte J. Hands, Capt Godfrey Black, Cpl Campbell, Lt Ernie Gaff, Pte Horrocks. *BRM/Tony Stafford*

The equipment that had belonged to the men was obviously unfit for further usage, so some efficient soul collected it all from the crash site and stacked it in front of the main dining-room; it probably never entered the man's head that all the "Never Yet Flown" men in the Battalion would have to pass the twisted blood-stained heap six times a day on their way to and from the dining-room. I feel that many soldiers at that time, myself included, decided that the only good thing about gliding was getting out of the damned things after they had landed.'

Nevertheless this particular tragedy did not prevent two officers and 123 ORs volunteering almost immediately to become glider pilots! Needless to say, Lt Col Bower denied the requests. The Battalion now started to be allocated vacancies on all kinds of courses, beginning in January 1942 with 20 officers and 50 ORs attending a Mortar/MMG course at the Small Arms School, Hythe; at the same time another group went on a Bisley course there. The conversion to an

Airborne role meant that the Battalion required a larger establishment, as well as needing men to make up existing shortfalls in manpower. Notices were posted throughout the UK asking for volunteers for the Airborne forces, and on 14-15 January Captain A. Miller visited Edinburgh to interview 110 young soldiers from various 70th (Young Soldiers) Battalions, who had volunteered for Airborne duties.

Having converted to their new role, 'T' (Training) Company was formed to improve training of the existing personnel in the Battalion, with great emphasis placed on both physical fitness and military skills beyond those of a normal infantry battalion, to develop morale, endurance and ability. These skills were essential, as on operations the Battalion could be expected to secure an objective behind enemy lines, hold on to it and confront the enemy, relying on what equipment and weapons they took with them and air re-supply until relieved.

Rev Ingram Cleasby, then a Lieutenant in the Battalion, recalls: 'I think "T" Company was the brainchild of Lt Col Bower. On taking command and on arrival at Barton Stacey he appointed me Weapon Training Officer (WTO), responsible directly to himself. As far as I know there had been no previous WTO, so I was given a very free hand to co-operate with Company Commanders in providing facilities for individual and Platoon training; looking for suitable training areas; devising assault courses (wading through a muddy local river up to their thighs, crawling through a culvert under roads and scrambling up the chalk sides of a railway cutting - it probably wasn't very popular) as well as a great deal of weapon practice with live ammunition, which was easily available as the Airborne Division had priority.'

Like other companies in the Battalion, T Company wore a slip-on company shoulder designation in black on both epaulettes. As far as can be ascertained the Company Colours were introduced by Lt Col Bower after the Battalion had joined the Airborne Division, to foster company esprit de corps within the unit. These designations were retained by the 1st Battalion until amalgamation in 1959 (see Appendix 8).

Rev Ingram Cleasby recalls that 'as the training was developed, it was decided to improve the calibre of men in the Battalion by inviting volunteers for the Airborne Forces from all branches of the Army. As a result we received periodic intakes of excellent young men, but from very varied backgrounds. Lt Col Bower saw the need for them to receive a short period of basic training to ensure that they could join one of the infantry companies on an equal footing with the existing members.' The volunteers were therefore initially posted to T Company; in 1943 it was redesignated as "R" (Reserve) Company.

Capt Dickie Stewart MC commanded T Company with Lt Cleasby as his 2i/c; Stewart looked after the administration of the Company and Cleasby ran the training programme. 'I think there were three platoons with picked Sergeants and Platoon officers. . .but they were also new members of the Battalion, who had volunteered. . . The course was probably not longer than two months, and consisted chiefly of section training, use of ground, a great deal of weapon training and movement by night. My recollection is that they were mostly very keen, and I think quite enjoyed their time with the Company, or perhaps it was just my own enthusiastic wishful thinking!'

Lt Col Bower selected 50 volunteers from the 70th (Young Soldiers) Battalion of The Border Regiment on 28-30 March 1942. In April 75 men joined the Battalion as reinforcements, comprising 48 from 70th Border, two

from 41 ITC, one from 8 Royal Scots, three from the East Yorks, 14 from the Northumberland Fusiliers, and six from the KOSB. Bill George and George Boardman, who had both joined the Loyal Regiment in May 1940, transferred first to 10 Manchesters and then to the 70th Battalion Border Regiment before volunteering for the Airborne Forces in 1942. They both attended a pre-selection course at Fulwood Barracks, Preston, and ended up in the queue for glider troops as opposed to parachutists. They both joined B Company at Barton Stacey under Major Armstrong. Sammy Black, a regular soldier with the King's Liverpool Regiment pre-war, volunteered for Airborne service while stationed with 9 King's at Dover in 1942. On completion of training he joined 16 Platoon of C Company, with whom he served for the remainder of the war. Bill Thompson joined the Battalion in February 1943 from 6 Border.

Wilf Oldham and a colleague, Private Hill, volunteered for the Airborne Forces while serving with the 30th Battalion The King's Regiment at Swanage in 1942. He recalls: '. . .we went down to Dorchester to be interviewed and having been accepted then proceeded to Barton Stacey to join the Battalion. At first we were posted to T Company under Lt Cleasby. All new recruits to the Battalion spent about five weeks training in T Company before joining their respective Company in the Battalion. After our training we were posted to B Company.' (3391058 Private W. E. Oldham, 12 Platoon B Company).

In similar circumstances Drummer Alexander 'Sandy' Masterton and Piper Malcolm Cockerill of the 70th Battalion Argyll & Sutherland Highlanders, stationed at Fort George near Inverness, saw a notice

Private Alexander 'Sandy' Masterton (left), Private Joe Cunnington and Private William 'Jock' Gillies, photographed in Germany in 1946.
BRM/Sandy Masterton

in 1942 asking for volunteers for Airborne duties; they applied and also joined T Company in August.

Sandy, who had originally enlisted in the 8th (Territorial) Bn A&SH in March 1938, recalls that Lt Cleasby was better known by his nickname 'Tracker' and his oft-quoted phrase 'We'll catch the Bosche with his trousers down'. 'Along with other volunteers,' he recalls, 'I was in Training Company and I think that we were told we had a month to prove ourselves fit for Airborne duties. Those that failed were RTU'd [returned to unit]. In charge of training were Lt Cleasby and Sergeant Clark, who was later to win the DCM at Arnhem. Training was hard, over fields, through muddy stinking drains and the dreaded run and walks. For this you wore full kit, steel helmet and carried your rifle. Then you were marched on to the road. When "Tracker" blew his whistle you ran a distance of two telegraph poles, walked two telegraph poles then ran for two poles; this was kept up for miles until you thought you were going to die. Our instructors were also in full kit, so they must have been very fit. Those that fell out were medically examined and usually given another chance before being RTU'd.' (2981724 Pte A. E. Masterton, H Company 1 Border)

According to Rev Cleasby, 'Tracker' was bestowed upon him by Major John Gibbon after he had taught members of the Intelligence Section how to light a fire and cook a meal for themselves while they were training at Glanusk Park in 1941.

Cyril Crickett and a fellow comrade, Joe Southwood, serving in the 1st Battalion The Manchester Regiment, saw the notices for volunteers for Airborne Forces and volunteered, joining the Battalion in the spring of 1942 after a medical examination at Catterick.

He recalls arriving at Barton Stacey, which was '. . . a hutted camp. It was very comfortable with well-equipped kitchens and the food was very good. Also we had the luxury of hot showers. On arrival we were told that there would be six weeks of training and that during this period you could ask to be RTU'd, or be RTU'd if it was considered that you couldn't make the grade. Moreover, at the end of the six weeks you were told whether or not you had been accepted and that even following acceptance you could still be RTU'd at any time for misconduct. Indeed, RTU'd for misconduct was the punishment most feared. Regardless of rank every man reverted to Private on acceptance. The first couple of weeks were very basic training, then it became steadily more demanding; the last week or two everything was at the double between Reveille and Last Post. As far as I remember during this period we were not allowed out of camp. . .'

'Apart from T Company, intensive battalion training was carried out at Barton Stacey, including personnel sent on various courses and companies sent to the ranges at Bulford. One particular exercise we did on a number of occasions was called the Otter Run, which involved crossing and re-crossing the River Test about seven times, after which you had to climb a haystack. We practised river crossing by rope, going hand over hand and often falling in. Another method was to strip naked apart from your helmet, wrap all your clothes and equipment in your gas-cape and float this with your rifle on top in front of you. To see a platoon of men wearing nothing but tin helmets is a sight not to be forgotten.' (3531268 Pte C. Crickett, 13 Platoon B Company)

The Battalion was organised into four Rifle Companies, each with an HQ and four Platoons, an HQ Company and an H (Heavy) Company consisting of one Platoon of eight 3-inch mortars, two Platoons each of four 6-pounder anti-tank guns, one Platoon of Vickers MMGs and one Platoon of 6 AA guns (Hispano 20mm cannons). The Company evolved during 1942 and early 1943 under the guidance of Captain Dickie Stewart and Lt Cleasby, but it was not until after the Sicily operations that the true 'S' (Support) Company was formed.

The first air experience exercises began on 19 February and thereafter groups from the Battalion

Members of 13 Platoon B Company, all of whom joined the Battalion as volunteers in 1942. From the left they are John Walker, Jim Longson, Cyril Crickett and Horace Adey, photographed before the Battalion embarked for North Africa. *Jim Longson/BRM*

Officers and NCOs, principally from the units of 1st Air Landing Brigade, who attended a 20mm Hispano AA course at Manorbier, Cornwall, from 24 June to 1 July 1942. Fourth from the left on the front row is Captain Dickie Stewart MC, and second from the right is Lt Tony Stafford. Fourth from the left on the second row is Lt Colin Douglas. *Tony Stafford/BRM*

went to various airfields including Andover, Chilbolton, Kidlington and Old Sarum. The Glider Pilot Regiment had also moved to the Salisbury Plain area, with its training depot established at Tilshead near Amesbury. Formed in December 1941, it had initially been commanded by and under the guidance of Colonel John F. Rock RE. The Regiment was organised in Sections, Platoons and Companies similar to most infantry regiments, its personnel being trained to both fly gliders and fight as infantrymen on the ground. Later the nomenclature of organisation changed to reflect a close kinship with the RAF - Wing and Squadron replaced Battalion and Company. At Netheravon was 38 Wing, which had been formed in January 1942 by the RAF Army Co-operation Command with the specific role of airlifting the 1st Airborne Division. 296 Glider Exercise Squadron, which had been formed at Ringway in January, was also based here flying Hawker Hector

and Harts as glider tugs until the arrival of Whitleys in June 1942.

From 19 to 21 March the Battalion acted as enemy to 5th Corps on Exercise 'Yorker'. The War Diary records: 'Operation quite successful. Bn remained in position until completely encircled by 38th and 47th Div troops and had a considerable nuisance value for a day and a half. A great number of guns, equipment, and prisoners were captured - including one Brigadier complete with Staff!'

From 13 to 17 April 1942 the 1st Airborne Division held a Divisional Tactical Week. Pat Stott, who joined the Battalion from OCTU in March 1942, recalls that during the Air to Ground demonstration at Imber Ranges, near Warminster, on 13 April 1942 one of the fighter aircraft misjudged the target area and a number of officers and ORs were killed and wounded. These included 2Lt James C. Poole, who was killed, and 2Lt Dodds, who was wounded; both officers had joined 1 Border with Pat from the same OCTU course.

On 16 and 17 April B Company were selected to take part in 'Demonstration Magnum', the first combined glider and parachute operation held at Netheravon. The demonstration was carried out with

12 Whitleys for the paratroops and nine Hector biplanes towing Hotspur gliders, and was before an invited audience that included Churchill and General George Marshall, the Chief of the US General Staff. Lt Bob Reese took part in the exercise and rode 2nd pilot in his Hotspur glider. It came in too low on its landing approach, hit a tree and crashed, killing the pilot in front and Private O'Malia sitting behind the Corporal; Bob Reese suffered a broken ankle and the other passengers were injured. The exercise was repeated the following day without mishap. Both Reese and Dodds were 'Y' listed and posted to 18 ITC

at Carlisle; Bob Reese was able to rejoin the Battalion on 12 August.

Glider flying experience in Hotspur gliders then

Below Watched by Prime Minister Winston Churchill in the foreground, a section de-planes from a Hotspur glider during 'Demonstration Magnum' at Netheravon on 16-17 April 1942. B Company provided the glider loads, one of which crashed on the 16th, injuring the occupants, one of whom, Pte O'Malia died of his injuries. *The Lawrence Wright Collection, MAF*

Bottom Men from B Company deploy from their Hotspur gliders during the Demonstration. *Lawrence Wright Collection, MAF*

A pair of Airspeed Hotspur gliders in flight in 1942.
BRM/IWM CH6030

began in earnest, 336 men being flown on 18-19 April, 189 on the 25th and 189 on the 26th, all from Kidlington in Oxfordshire. A Company went to Kidlington for two weeks to take part in extensive trials with RAF and Glider Pilot Regiment personnel, which included numerous glider flights. C Company replaced them on 30 April, followed by 120 men from HQ Company on 3-4 May and D Company on 12 May. On 29 April six RAF Sergeant Pilots joined the Battalion for 14 days for an insight into the infantry training of an Airborne Battalion.

The British Airspeed Hotspur was the first transport glider produced by the Allies during the Second World War; it was used for training only, towed by Hawker Hart, Hector, Demon or Fury tugs. Of all-wood construction, each glider carried two pilots, who boarded by way of the hinged plexi-glass canopy, and six troops, who entered by doors on each side.

Joe Hardy recalls that the seating arrangement in the Hotspur was 'normally first and second pilot in tandem, with six men, three on each side of the fuselage, with legs intertwined, each man looking directly at the opposite side of the fuselage and seeing nothing else. It was rather like being locked in a cupboard under the stairs. I was fortunate on my first flight - I was the senior soldier, so I sat behind the pilot in the second pilot's seat. He was an Australian and seemed to know all about these frightful machines.

'We were pulled into the air by some sort of very ancient biplane, towed 30 or 40 miles around Oxford, and when within about 15 miles of our base at Kidlington, we cast off and started the glide back home. Beautiful, it was a lovely day, no turbulence at all - it was like sitting in an armchair and the noise of the wind on the outer casing was the only thing that gave us any notion of moving. Sat where I was, it was a wonderful experience - for the lads in the fuselage it was anything but. When we were within perhaps 8 miles of the landing strip, the pilot, without any warning at all, stood the machine on its nose and came straight down for what seemed an eternity. It took my guts at least three eternities to catch up with my stomach, when he finally pulled out of the dive. I

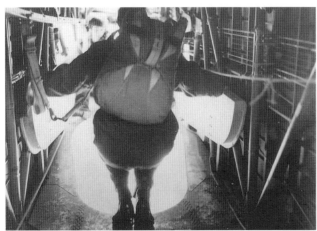

demanded of him "What the hell happened there?", and he gave me the simple answer that had he not done something like that we should never have known we had been flying. Had he had sufficient brains to tell us what he was going to do, we might have quite enjoyed the experience - as it was, he merely gave us all another perfectly good reason for not liking this flying business. The Hotspur glider had me quite unimpressed!'

Private Wilf Pridmore, who had joined the Battalion from 6 Border, echoed similar sentiments. He endured a flight in similar circumstances, possibly in this same glider as Joe Hardy, but was one of the more unfortunate passengers in the fuselage; like Joe he had a distinct feeling of being prepared to meet his maker. At least the extra pay of 1 shilling was earned after the required three training flights were completed.

On 27 April the first trials began with two types of folding bicycle, and members of the Battalion were asked to provide suggestions for an Airborne Division motto. The emblem of Bellerphon and Pegasus was designed by a Major Edward Seago and authorised to be worn with the title AIRBORNE on the upper arm of the Battle Dress blouse; the maroon berets were issued soon after.

HM King George VI and Queen Elizabeth visited the Airborne Division on 21 May at Bulford and watched a demonstration of parachute and glider landing. The Air Landing Brigade provided a composite company commanded by Major John Gibbon, OC of A Company, which included a Platoon from B Company.

The training became even more intensive at all levels, and on 2 June A Company carried out a night scheme with gliders, perhaps the first. Exercise 'Icarus', held from 1 to 3 July, saw the Battalion involved in an inter-Battalion exercise with 1 RUR in the Romsey-Burley-Bournemouth area.

Wilf Pridmore recalls that a group from the Battalion attended the Parachute Training School at Ringway, where they were trained by RAF Sergeant Instructors. Seven jumps qualified them for the parachute badge, often referred to as the 'light-bulb', worn on the lower right sleeve of the Battle Dress blouse. A large number of men from the Battalion opted to take the parachute courses, both to relieve the monotony of training, but also because it increased their pay! Three officers were the first from the Battalion to qualify in early April.

'After training,' Wilf remembers, 'we were taken up

Top 'Wait for it, Pridmore! We haven't taken off yet!' A contemporary cartoon.

Centre and bottom Preparing to jump through the hatch of a Whitley bomber, and 'Man gone'. BRM/Tony Stafford

in a balloon and dropped on a static line. Next we went in Whitley bombers and dropped through an aperture in the floor, again by static line fixed to the side of the plane. We trained in sticks of ten men, five on each side of the aperture in the aircraft. We did one drop on to the lake at Tatton Park; this was to practise the quick release in case we were dropped into rivers, lakes, etc, on actual operations.' (3600733 Pte Wilfred Pridmore, H Company 1 Border)

Jumping out of the hole sometimes had its problems: lean back and the chute hit the rear ledge, lean too far forward and you stood a good chance of cracking your head. Wilf actually did his course at Ringway between 25 June and 22 July 1942; in his AB 64 the details were entered: 'Parachute Course qualified'.

Pat Stott completed his parachute course between 26 June and 10 July. The preliminary training was done at Hardwick Hall in Derbyshire, using a fixed frame with a harness simulating jumping off and landing; this taught the men how to fall and roll. Then he proceeded to Ringway, where similar apparatus was installed in one of the hangars and the simulation was repeated. Four jumps were then made, two from a balloon from about 800 feet with three others, then two from Whitleys over Tatton Park. The added benefit of the course for Pat was that it allowed him to lodge nearby at home.

Sgt Fred Grimshaw completed his parachute course at Hardwick Hall and he was amongst several who volunteered for the Parachute Regiment when notices appeared at Barton Stacey. Mindful of his own Battalion, the CO refused the request, but allowed Fred to go on a second parachute course with three other senior NCOs at Chesterfield. Jimmy McDowell also went on the course at Hardwick, he reckons during October 1942, but did not complete it owing to a bout of pleurisy that landed him in Chesterfield Hospital.

By the time Sandy Masterton had completed T Company and received his coveted red beret, he was posted to H Company. The Battalion had to wait for their anti-tank guns, but then received the new 6-pounder. The first and subsequent training 'shoots' were held on the Royal Artillery ranges at Larkhill. Sandy's gun was named 'Scimitar Hill'; it was commanded by Sgt Johnny Molloy with Pte Danny Farrel as the No 1, Sandy as No 2, Gordon Ennion as No 3 and Gordon Haskins the jeep driver; all the eight guns in the two A/T Platoons were jeep-hauled. All the 6-pounders were named after Regimental Battle Honours: 'Arroyo', 'Marne', 'Ypres', 'Somme', 'Arras', 'Cambrai', 'Gallipoli', 'Scimitar Hill', 'Suvla Bay' and 'Hellespont'. If a gun was lost or replaced, the name was carried on, as for example 'Gallipoli II'.

At the end of August the Battalion proceeded to Ilfracombe for three weeks intensive training with RA and RE units from the Division attached. Cyril Crickett recalls: 'Whilst we were there, we did a simulated attack on a radar location post - Bruneval - and were taken off by sea. Moreover, we did a number of exercises where we were taken out by truck, abandoned and told to get back to Ilfracombe. We had one spell making rafts for motor-bikes and floating them out to sea. . .we used the canvas cover and frame from the trucks to make a boat capable of carrying ten or more men. We also did an exercise in which we swam across a reservoir and climbed the concrete dam with the aid of lengths of willow fencing. This method was also used to cross patches of bog, ponds, etc.

A 6-pounder anti-tank gun with its loading channels and chocks as it would be secured inside a Horsa glider. The Anti-Tank Platoons in the Air Landing Brigade received the 6-pounder as soon as they were available and the gun was adapted for easier loading into the Horsa - the gunshield armour was reduced, the axle was narrowed and the trail legs altered so that they could be folded for loading. Photographed at Netheravon in November 1942. *IWM H25689*

Above Pte Fred Jackson, 14 Platoon B Company. Fred joined the Battalion at the age of 15 in 1942, having lied about his age; he was the youngest man to serve in the Battalion and was taken prisoner at Arnhem. *BRM/Fred Jackson*

Above Early training in a Horsa in 1942. The men are from the Oxford and Bucks LI, as identified by the flashes on the side of their helmets; some men still wear the normal steel helmet and others the Airborne pattern. This early mark of Horsa had the large door on the port side, while later models also had a removable tail section that enabled jeeps and guns to be unloaded quickly. *BRM*

Below A group of possibly 13 Platoon of B Company led by Lt J. McCartney marching past a line of Horsas, ready for air-experience trials. The men are wearing no equipment except for the safety harness. This photograph was probably taken in the autumn of 1942 or spring of 1943, prior to leaving for North Africa. *BRM/Mr V. G. Murray*

A Corporal from A Company 1 Border takes cover, while the rest of his section prepares to leave their Hotspur glider on an exercise near Netheravon in October 1942. The coloured BORDER shoulder title is clearly visible, as well as the green Company Colour tab on his epaulette. *IWM TR170*

A Corporal from A Company 1 Border briefs the Glider Pilot on exercise near Netheravon in October 1942. *IWM TR171*

A closer view of the previous group. IWM TR171A

Badges worn by the 1st Battalion the Border Regiment 1939-1959 and its successor the King's Own Royal Border Regiment from 1959 to date.

Top centre W/M ORs' cap and collar badges, brass ORs' shoulder title and Officers' bronzed OSD cap badge; *top right* slip-on shoulder title 1940-41; *top left* woven shoulder title worn on the Battle Dress 1942-51; *centre left* woven and printed examples of the Airborne Division patch and title; glider qualification badge; *centre right* parachute course qualification badges; *centre* plastic cap badge 1943-46 and printed shoulder title 1943-59; *lower centre* Y printed badge of the 5th Infantry Division 1945; printed and woven 'glider' shoulder titles worn on the Battle Dress 1951-59; cloth shoulder title worn by the 1st Battalion King's Own Royal Border Regiment on Battle Dress 1959-64; *lower left* Officers' No 1 Dress glider badge 1952 to date; *bottom centre* Officers' and WOs' Service Dress glider badge c1952 to date; ORs' glider badge and Full Dress/Mess Dress glider badge. For full details see Appendix 8.

Above A Platoon of soldiers deploy after landing in their Horsa glider on exercise near Netheravon in December 1942. In the foreground a soldier carries a Mk 2 Sten SMG. The Airborne forces often received priority on new equipment and were some of the first to use the new Sten. Clearly visible on the lower right sleeve of his Battle Dress blouse is the glider qualification badge, a blue Horsa on a khaki background. *IWM H26175*

Below A Glider soldier from the same Platoon with a 2-inch mortar, also at Netheravon in December 1942. The coloured strip on the epaulette of his Battle Dress blouse indicates that he is from 1 Border. *IWM H26176*

Right An Airborne Division soldier in full fighting order, December 1942; the absence of parachute wings suggests that he may be from the 1st Air-Landing Brigade. He wears the standard 1937 pattern equipment, fighting order, and carries a 2-inch mortar as well as his No 4 rifle. The later 1943-pattern gas-mask is worn fastened on to the waist belt and the 08 pattern entrenching tool, re-introduced and adapted for wear with the 37 pattern equipment, is worn. The helve is the earlier pattern; the

later pattern had a metal fitting on the end similar to the muzzle of the No 4 rifle. The spike bayonet could be fitted to the helve for use as a mine-prodder. Also carried is a toggle rope and a cotton bandolier of extra .303-inch ammunition. *IWM H26184*

Top Officers and Sergeants of the Battalion at B Camp, Barton Stacey, on Arroyo Day, 28 October 1942.

On the front row in the centre is Brigadier George Hyde Harrison DSO, the Colonel of The Regiment; to his right are Lt Col Roger Bower, the Commanding Officer, later OC 6th and then 1st Air-Landing Brigades, and Lt Tony Stafford the Adjutant; to his left are Major George Britten MBE, the 2i/c, and RSM George Gardner (killed on Sicily on 10 July 1943). *BRM*

Above Officers of the Battalion photographed at Barton Stacey in the spring of 1943 prior to leaving for North Africa.

Front row from left to right: Lt Bob Coulston, Lt Tony Howe, Lt Joe Tate, Lt Doug Skilton, Major Stuart Cousens, Major

Tom Armstong, Capt Tony Stafford, Major Freddie Fineron, Major Tommy Haddon, Lt Pat Stott, Lt George Coulthard, Lt Joe Hardy, Lt Gordon Welch, Lt Ted Newport, Capt Godfrey Black, Lt Ingram Cleasby.

Middle row: — , Lt Alan Green, Lt Bob Reese, Capt T. Montgomery, Lt Arthur Springbett, Lt Hamish Law, Capt Howard Wilkie, Lt Colin Douglas, Lt Ronald Hope-Jones, Lt Col George Britten MBE, Capt Bob Stockwell, Lt Joe Poad, Capt Jock Neill, Lt Charles Wilson, Padre John Rowell, — , Lt Bill Hodgson.

Back row: — , — , Major John Gibbon, Lt John Mears, Lt Grant Louden, Capt Dickie Stewart MC, Capt Charles Scruby, Capt Ernie Gaff, Capt Dennis Morrissey, Lt John Horsley, Lt Bill Budgeon, Lt Mike Holman, — , — . *Pat Stott*

'Towards the end of our stay we went to Woolacombe for our baptism of fire. . .we had to walk in line abreast along the shore whilst MG and rifle fire was aimed from the front, above and behind us. On reaching two lines in the sand about 8 feet apart we had to lie down between the lines. There was a further session of firing with bullets flying over you and some hitting the sand close to your head. We then rose to our feet, continued to advance with more firing, and on reaching the end told that was it. Just as we all relaxed an explosion 20-30 yards away show-

ered us with sand! However, we found time to help out on the local farms and were rewarded with lovely home-made bread, cheese and scrumpy.' (Pte Cyril Crickett, 13 Platoon B Company) The Battalion then returned to Barton Stacey, but to a new site, C Camp.

The glider used in the largest numbers on operations was the Airspeed Horsa glider, which was first successfully test-flown in September 1941. It was larger than the US Waco, having a wingspan of 88 feet, a length of 68 feet and a capacity of 28 troops plus the two pilots. As the Horsa gliders and their Whitley

The Intelligence section at Barton Stacey on Arroyo Day, 28 October 1942.
Back row left to right: L/Cpl C. R. Thirlwell, Pte D. F. Blythe (PoW Arnhem), L/Cpl D. Doran, Pte Hughes.
Front row: Pte Leonard Mein, Pte Anderson, Lt John Horsley, Sgt Wolstencroft, Pte Carter.

Thirlwell and Mein served with the Intelligence Section throughout the war; the latter was renowned for his prowess as an artist and used to draw cartoons on air letters for members of the Battalion in North Africa. John Horsley handed over to Lt Ronald-Hope Jones as IO before North Africa. After the Battalion had returned to the UK, he joined 21st Independent Parachute Company, and was killed at Arnhem on 27 September 1944. *BRM/Ian Thirlwell*

bomber tugs became available, training and flights took place. The first reference to the use of Horsas by the Battalion is in October 1942, when H Company were sent to Brize Norton for flying experience. The Battalion celebrated Arroyo Day on 28 October, and this was followed by Glider Exercise 'Osprey' on 16 November, when C Company, Battalion HQ and some of H Company, with 21st Independent Parachute Company, flew in 15 Horsas. Further flights were made from Kidlington, Croughton and Kingston Bagpuize. A further exercise, 'Cormorant', was held on 29 December at Membury using 10 Horsas.

On 3 December Major G. V. Britten MBE, Northamptonshire Regiment, who had joined the Battalion as 2i/c in July, succeeded Lt Col R. H. Bower as Commanding Officer, when the latter was posted to the War Office. Colonel Roger Bower, who had done so much to influence, encourage and develop the Battalion in its new role, maintained close links with 1 Border until after the end of the war.

On 19 January 1943 C Company went to Brize Norton for flying experience on Horsas. On the 27th Major Tommy Haddon returned to the Battalion as 2i/c. Over the next few months, prior to the Battalion's departure for North Africa, a number of small drafts joined the Battalion to bring it up to full war establishment. These included officers and men from 2 Loyals, 6 Border, 5 King's, 7 DWR, 10 Royal Sussex and 9 King's. As with previous groups of vol-

unteers, many of these arrived on probation and had to make the grade before being accepted. Training continued apace with the first courses for the new PIAT (Projector Infantry Anti-tank) were held from 22 to 25 March, while the A/T platoons begin serious range work in late March at Foulness. A full field firing exercise was held at Swanage on 12 April, when sadly Pte Barker was accidentally shot and killed.

On 2 April HM King George VI inspected the 1st Airborne Division at Bulford, and five days later mobilisation orders for active service were received. The 1st Parachute Brigade of the Division had gone to North Africa in October 1942 and had seen extremely heavy fighting with the 1st Army in Algeria and Tunisia. The remainder of the Division now left to join them. At this point the 1st Air Landing Brigade was divided: 1 Border and 2 South Staffords went to North Africa, while 2 Oxfordshire & Bucks LI and 1 Royal Ulster Rifles remained in the UK to form 6th Air-Landing Brigade of the new 6th Airborne Division.

The Battalion Transport left by road for Southampton on 8 May under the command of Major Freddie Fineron, OC C Company. The accompanied baggage was loaded at Andover station on the 13th under Major du Boulay, OC H Company, Home details were posted to the 2 Oxfordshire & Bucks LI, and on the 16th the Battalion left Andover in three parties.

Chapter 3

A Soldier's Guide to North Africa and Sicily

The departure of the Battalion from England to North Africa was superbly recorded by Major Tony Stafford, then the Adjutant of 1 Border, in an article published in the Border Regiment Magazine. He wrote: 'On 16 May 1943, after living and training for 17 months under ideal conditions at Barton Stacey, the first part of 1 Border's move overseas began. For many weeks preparations had been in full swing. All baggage, transport and equipment had been despatched in stages and there remained only the Bodies to be manoeuvred by bounds to the destination. There was to be no ceremonial send-off, for as part of the 1st Airborne Division the departure was secret. An exit by the back door shorn of all the glamour; berets, divisional signs and wearing FS caps without badges to fox the enemy.

'The Battalion departed on three special trains leaving Andover Junction for Liverpool at 19.30, 03.30 and 07.30 hrs, the officer in charge of each being Major H. S. Cousens, Major T. Haddon, and Lt Col Britten. Thirty Home details remained behind due to low medical categories under command of an officer loaned by 2 Ox & Bucks LI. By 08.00 hrs the Battalion had left and all that remained was their reputation.

'By early evening everyone was on board the troopship MV *Staffordshire* at Liverpool, the gangways were lifted and the ship moved into the Mersey. Throughout the following day the ship lay at anchor while all on board sorted themselves out and became accustomed to the ship's routine.

'About 09.30 on 19 May the Battalion set sail with three other troopships for the Clyde to pick up the remainder of the convoy with its strong destroyer escort and an aircraft carrier. To the delight of all the troops on board, the training facilities were practically nil and consequently for the most part of the day they were free to do as they pleased without being bothered by parades. The officers, however, suffered numerous lectures and discussions on various tactical problems, but even these were restricted due to the lack of deck space for such gatherings. For five days the convoy sailed on and gradually the sea became bluer, the weather more settled, sunbathing started and KD became more fashionable.'

Lt Ronald Hope-Jones, the Intelligence Officer, wrote in his diary on 22 May: '. . .tried most valiantly to lecture to R Coy (late T Coy) in the fetid atmosphere of F3 Mess Deck. . . The conditions in which the men have to live are really ghastly, herded together like sheep. In fact "Baa" has become a Battalion cry. The scene at night is astonishing. All the floor and table-space occupied by interlacing mattresses and above them a moving mass of swaying hammocks. The officers' quarters were fine, the first class lounge with plenty of easy chairs, sofas and writing desks. . . Tobacco is 1s 9d or 2s a quarter pound, a fifth of the price at home, and this more than compensates for the fact that the ship is dry. . . The cuisine in the dining saloon is extraordinarily good - breakfasts have many, many courses, often with fish and meat, and always the most delicious rolls and marmalade. . .'

Tony Stafford continues: 'The Battalion was now due west of Gibraltar. One afternoon, while enjoying the sun on the pool-deck, they were suddenly surprised to see a column of water leap up close to the escorting aircraft carrier. Immediately the AA guns in the vicinity started to loose off at seemingly nothing. This outburst was short-lived, for there were no more water spouts and no enemy raiders descended into the sea. Apart from the destroyers scurrying up and down the convoy listening and watching for submarines, the convoy continued unmolested. Late on the

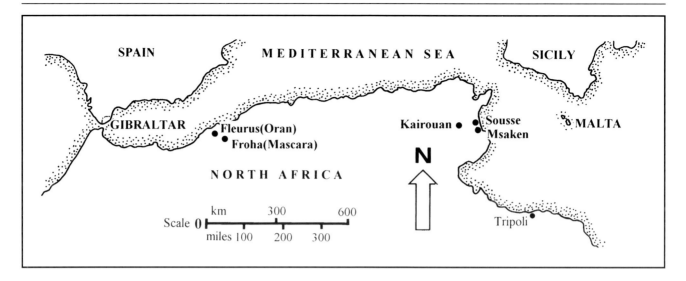

Locations of the 1st Battalion in North Africa, May-September 1943.

evening of 24 May the lights of Tangier could be seen on the starboard bow. The rock of Gibraltar was seen at about the same time the following day.

'The Battalion arrived at Oran in Algeria at 22.30 hrs on 26 May and made a systematic exodus from the ship by the glare of arc lights on the quay, then boarded trucks driven by American negroes, most of whom were smoking enormous cigars. The destination was a staging camp 15 miles east of Oran. Packed like sardines and hurtling through the deserted streets at a breakneck speed served as a shattering contrast to the calm and serenity of the sea convoy. The Battalion arrived at the camp in the early hours of 27 May and the Companies were immediately given areas in which to bed down. The remaining few hours were given to sleep, but this was hardly conducive in the cold cheerless night, punctuated by howling dogs in the nearby village and the buzzing of mosquitoes much closer at hand.

'The camp was located on a wide expanse of sparse, uncultivated land bordered by the main Oran road and the village of Fleurus and dominated by a small hill surmounted by a round broken tower. Acres of grapevines stretched in every other direction. After breakfast at about 06.30, Companies moved to new bivouac areas on the slope of the hill. Company HQs and cook-houses were sited and attempts were made to improvise some form of cover against the sun, as there were no tents or accommodation stores. Below the Battalion in a more permanent residential part of the staging area was a contingent of the US Navy. 1 Border seemed to have been sited in their latrine area, for a long line of wooden benches seldom unoccupied and fully exposed graced the top end of our camp.

'The stay at Fleurus was short, as the Battalion

moved to the 1st Airborne Divisional concentration area around Mascara 85 miles south-east of Oran on 8 June 1943. Up to the 8th the Battalion underwent its first climatic inoculation; scorching sun, dust-storms, flies, mosquitoes and all the other natural torments that go to make life unpleasant. The MO, Capt Godfrey Black RAMC, soon became the busiest man in the Battalion, for everyone in turn went to him suffering from a "gippy tummy". The cause of this complaint was the most popular topic of conversation amongst all ranks. Some blamed the mecaprine tablets (anti-malaria), which had to be taken four times a week, while others insisted that the water, flies, dust or American tinned products were responsible.

'Vehicle requirement could only be met by judicious scrounging from neighbouring US units, as all the Battalion transport and equipment was still in transit on another convoy. A bottle of Scotch got the use of a jeep and driver for the day. Arthur Royall, then OC of 12 Platoon, wrote that "a bottle of Scotch certainly worked wonders at Mascara. Jock Armstrong made friends with an American Scot in charge of supplies and one bottle ensured Chicken (tinned) for the whole of B Company on Sunday."

'Mornings and evenings were spent on individual training since Battalion training was impractical. Every afternoon was observed as a rest period, flies willing. The local village was a conglomeration of evil-smelling side streets and drinking saloons, the inhabitants mostly Arabs clad in filthy rags and lacking the halo of romanticism placed on their heads by popular fantasy. Their abodes were squalors of filth clustered together in their own particular quarter of the village. A small and decrepit railway station existed, at which an occasional train halted on its way along a single track to Oran. The troops soon discovered the potency of the local wine and learned of its after-effects from bitter experience.

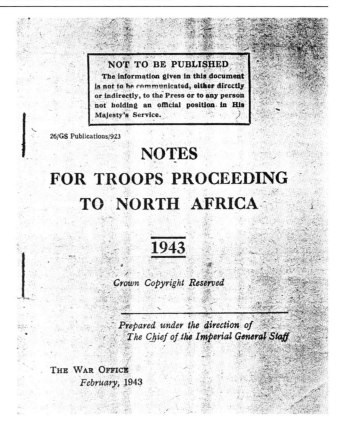

'An elaborate system of shower baths had been built by the Americans, but unfortunately the local water supply was not what it might have been and the water frequently ran out before everyone had bathed. To supplement this, parties were taken bathing in the Mediterranean and, if transport was available, to Khrystall, a small place on the coast 15 miles from Fleurus. These outings were very popular and there was great competition amongst the Companies as to whose turn it was to use the transport. The Orderly Room took a firm hand to ensure that all went in their turn.

'Being on US rations, the food and drink differed somewhat from what we had been used to. Instead of being able to drink tea with all meals, coffee, cocoa and lemonade were the stock beverages. Biscuits instead of bread and the lack of potatoes were not to the liking of the troops, who complained that they never felt satisfied. Tinned fruit and fruit juices were very appetising, but lacked body and only after constant overtures to higher authorities were the rations eventually supplemented by a special issue of tea and bread.

'Orders were suddenly received to move, and an advance party, consisting of the QM 'Uncle' Barnes, Capt Howard Wilkie and a Platoon of A Company, were sent off on 2 June to prepare for the arrival of the Battalion at its new location, Froha, 7 miles south of Mascara. The main body moved by road on 8 June;

heavy equipment was sent by light railway. The column consisted of 24 vehicles provided by the RASC and, as the road surfaces were very poor, the speed had to be kept fairly slow. Crossing the Tell Atlas Mountains by way of the road to Timbuktu sounds fantastical, but at one stage on the journey a signpost clearly indicated that the Battalion was within 2,000 km of that City of the French Sudan, on the southern edge of the Sahara Desert.

'The road was one long series of nightmare twists and turns and hazardous hairpin bends. Other traffic was few and far between, but the heavy US Army lorries driven in the opposite direction by the negroes swept round corners regardless of both danger and other road users. The incline became steeper, the drops more sheer, until the summit was eventually reached and the town of Mascara, famous for its wine, could be seen amidst a sea of vineyards. The small nondescript village of Froha lay about 7 miles beyond the town. After negotiating a series of tracks across country, the Battalion arrived at a small French farmhouse, part of which had been requisitioned for use by the HQ 1st Air-Landing Brigade. 1 Border's camp was situated on what a few weeks previously had been a vast wheatfield, lying in a wide valley running from north to south and bounded on the east and west by long ranges of bare hills.

'The tents, which had all been pitched, were rapidly filled and the troops' kits unpacked. The 1st Air-

Landing Brigade HQ were the immediate neighbours and 2 South Staffords were about a mile further down the valley. The site was a definite improvement on Fleurus, although the wheat stubble soon became trodden into a fine red dust that rose in dense clouds at the slightest provocation from vehicles or the wind.' (Lt N. A. H. Stafford, Adjutant 1st Battalion, 1943)

In the area several airstrips had been constructed at Froha, Matmore, Thiersville and Relizane for the training of gliders and their tugs.

It had been decided to begin the invasion of Italy with the seizure of Sicily, and planning for the operation had begun in late 1942. Following a meeting of the Combined Chiefs at Casablanca, it was decided to launch the operation to invade Sicily in July 1943 and detailed planning began in February. At the beginning of May, Eisenhower's planners chose 10 July as D-Day for Operation HUSKY. This would give favourable moonlight early in the night of 9 July for an airborne drop and complete darkness after midnight to favour the amphibious invasion force and its naval task-force.

The main invasion force would comprise General George S. Patton's US 7th Army and General

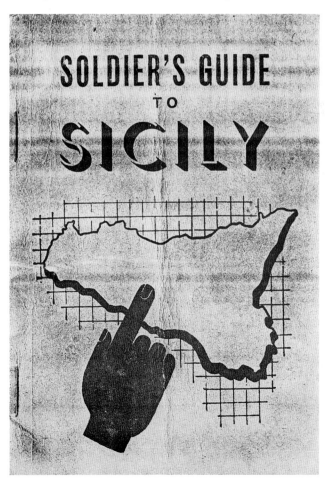

Montgomery's 8th Army. Patton's troops were to land on the south coast and work across the island towards Palermo, then swing east to link up with the British at Messina. Montgomery's troops were to make the main landing on the east coast below Syracuse, then move quickly north up to via Syracuse and the Catania Plain to Messina to prevent Axis forces escaping across the Straits to Italy.

The final planning stage in May brought the British 1st Airborne and the US 82nd Airborne Divisions into the operation. They were to be parachuted in on the night of 9-10 July to capture key roads and bridges leading inland from the invasion areas on the south and east coasts. The planning for the British Airborne element of the operations was the responsibility of Lieutenant-General F. A. M. Browning DSO, GOC Airborne Forces. However, the original plan did not involve the glider elements of 1st Airborne Division. Indeed, the only planned role for gliders was to ferry supplies to airfields in Sicily after the invasion troops had moved well inland. Therefore the planners waited until mid-March before requesting the shipment from the USA of 500 crated CG-4A Waco gliders (Hadrians to the British), to be sent by sea to Algeria. There were no British gliders in North Africa at all.

Shortly before the 1st Air-Landing Brigade arrived in Algeria, Montgomery reviewed the airborne operation plans. He had discussions with Major-General G. F. Hopkinson OBE MC, GOC 1st Airborne Division and the former Commander of 1st Air-Landing Brigade, who put the case for glider troop involvement. The objective of the British paratroops was the seizure on the night of 9 July of the Ponte Grande bridge, a vital crossing south-west of Syracuse. The second objective to be taken a few days after the initial invasion was the capture of the Primasole bridge north of Catania, over which the British troops would advance towards Messina. Worried about landing the paratroopers accurately at night on the drop zones, Montgomery decided that Ponte Grande should be seized by glider-borne troops instead.

This decision considerably upset the planners, but Montgomery insisted on it. The immediate problem resulting from the decision was the total lack of gliders available in North Africa for such an operation. Time was crucial, as the CG-4A Wacos ordered in mid-March from the USA only began to arrive in North African ports in early May. Moreover, as each glider required five separate crates, which had to be carefully unloaded at the dockside and carefully reassembled before they were ready for test flights, it would take some time before these were available in sufficient numbers.

Attached to the 1st Airborne Division was the 1st

Battalion of the Glider Pilot Regiment (GPR) commanded by Colonel George Chatterton. Shortly after arriving from England at the end of April 1943, Chatterton was summoned to Allied Forces HQ at Algiers by Major-General Hopkinson, who briefed on the operation to capture the Ponte Grande bridge. Chatterton described the meeting in his history of the Glider Pilot Regiment *The Wings of Pegasus*. He realised that the planned operation was only three months away and that there were no tug aircraft, gliders or airstrips available. His worries increased after being shown the aerial photographs of the proposed landing area and told that they would be using American gliders. Aware that his men were all recent graduates of glider school with a maximum of eight hours flying time and no experience of a tactical landing with troops, Chatterton added that they lacked flying practise, very few had flown at night and their experience was solely with the British Horsa glider. Despite his misgivings, Chatterton was told by Hopkinson that he had half an hour to consider the operation, or he would be relieved of his command; faced with dismissal before a combat operation, Chatterton reluctantly agreed.

Men from 1 Border with their Waco/Hadrian glider on one of the airstrips around their base at Froha, Algeria, in June 1943. The photograph was probably taken prior to Exercise 'Eve' on 20 June, or a few days later when a large proportion of the Battalion were airlifted to the 1st Airborne Division's operational base at Sousse in Tunisia. The men are entering by one of the doors to the cargo compartment. A C-47 Dakota tug stands on the edge of the runway. *IWM NA3842*

Some of the first of the crated Wacos to arrive were assembled at La Senia airfield near Oran by six officers and 62 ORs of the GPR from 8 May onwards. They were assisted by two USAF fitters, and they assembled 52 in ten days, which were flown to airstrips at Thiersville and Froha. A number of gliders were assembled by other USAF personnel, including some Glider Pilots. A detachment of 110 US Glider Pilots had arrived in February 1943 and were based in Egypt, tasked with assembling gliders on their arrival at Casablanca and flying them to forward bases in Algeria. The pilots had moved to Algeria in March 1943; however, they had to wait until May before their cargoes arrived, due to the late amendment of the original operational plan, which had not required gliders for the initial landings on Sicily.

At the end of May 240 Wacos had arrived at various ports in Africa, but assembly was slow. The assembly was therefore given priority over everything, so by 13 June 346 gliders had been assembled, test-flown and delivered to British and American airfields in Algeria and Tunisia, less than a month before D-Day! Even then there were maintenance and structural problems with the aircraft. Many of the US Glider Pilots were sent as flight instructors to the British 1st Airborne Division base in Algeria, although they had less actual flying experience than their British counterparts. The Americans were warmly welcomed by the Glider Pilot Regiment and began training on 20 Wacos delivered earlier. They provided first-hand knowledge of the flight characteristics and the basics of loading the CG-A4. The first training flights then began with the

Wacos towed by C-47s of the USAF 51st Troop Carrier Wing, which had been assigned to transport the 1st Airborne Division. Initially British Glider Pilots acted as Co-pilots to their USAF counterparts, but on all succeeding flights the roles were reversed. At the beginning of June 296 Squadron RAF of 38 Wing with their Albemarle tugs arrived at Froha from England.

The likelihood of an operation in the near future soon became obvious. Lt Col Britten and Lt Ronald Hope-Jones, the IO, began to work together in the Intelligence Office, a marquee located on the edge of the camp, to which only they and Major Haddon, the 2i/c, had access. Ronald Hope-Jones recalls: 'I was initiated into the projected operation on 9 June, and started on a trace showing routes, topographical details and located enemy posts for the approach march. I was disturbed to discover two pill-boxes sited exactly at the point where I expected to land. I not only worked very hard in the Planning Room, I had to sleep in it.' In his diary he recorded that 'I have vast quantities of air photos, which never seem to cover the particular area I want to examine, and spend much time trying to make traces with sand-clogged Indian ink. . .' The temperature rose to 104°

in the shade and the red dust blown up by the wind settled on everyone and everything.

Tony Stafford wrote that 'training soon got into its stride, and the Companies were constantly out on day and night exercises, all of which were designed to test the men's endurance in the most trying of circumstances. Live practise ammunition was fairly plentiful and mock battles in the hills were almost a daily feature, much to the consternation of the local Arabs. Even Battalion HQ participated in this orgy of training, and shortly after breakfast each morning such celebrities as the CO, 2i/c, IO, RSM George Gardner, Orderly Room Staff and, on occasion, the Adjutant, would be seen clad in PT kit under the APTCI clambering up mountains with a new-found energy.'

Two Airborne exercises known as 'Adam' and 'Eve' were carried out successfully with troops of 1st Air-Landing Brigade. 'Adam' was held on 14 June, less than a month before D-Day, and the Battalion watched as 2 South Staffords were lifted in 56 Waco gliders piloted by British Glider Pilots and towed by C-47s. Flying in four-plane formations at 2-minute intervals, they were towed over a 70-mile course and released to glide down to Froha airfield.

A Waco coming into land in North Africa, possibly at the end of Exercise 'Adam' or 'Eve', 14 or 20 June 1943. The CG-4A was built by a number of US companies in large quantities from a prototype developed by the Waco Aircraft Corporation of Ohio. Known to the British as the Hadrian, it had a wingspan of 83.6 feet and an overall length of 48 feet. The cockpit and fuselage consisted of a simple all-welded tubular metal framework, which was fabric-covered with a floor made of honeycombed plywood providing great strength with minimal weight. The wings and tailplane were constructed of wood covered in canvas. Weighing 3,440 lbs empty, it could carry an operational weight of 4,060 lbs. The principal feature was that the whole nose section, basically the pilot's compartment, was hinged at the top and swung upwards to open, giving a 60 x 70-inch opening facilitating loading of a variety of equipment. However, it could only take 16 men, or a few men with a jeep. For the Anti-tank Platoons this presented a serious problem, as a combined load of a jeep with a 6-pounder anti-tank gun could be loaded together into the Horsa, but required two Wacos to carry the same load. *BRM/Tony Stafford/IWM NA3852*

On the evening of the 15th Exercise 'Vin Blanc' was carried out with 3-tonners representing each glider load. The object was to practise the marshalling, forming-up and landing of gliders in four lanes by night, with specific exercise objectives for Companies and support Platoons on 'landing'. Even the Glider Pilots travelled in the vehicle representing their own glider!

In the late afternoon of 20 June, Exercise 'Eve' was flown over a 100-mile course; 632 men of 1 Border were carried in 73 Wacos towed by RAF Albemarles of 296 Squadron and C-47s of the US 51st Troop Carrier Wing from airfields at Thiersville, Matmore and Froha. All the gliders, which were airborne for about an hour and a half, landed at Thiersville. That night, at 23.45 hrs, 12 Wacos containing representatives of both Battalion and Brigade HQ took off and landed by moonlight on a flare-path at Froha airfield. The operational instructions for 'Eve' in the Battalion War Diary clearly show that the Battalion was organised and loaded and the gliders marshalled and lifted in almost identical circumstances to those that were planned for the operation on 9 July.

Top A series of scenes photographed on an airstrip near Froha, Algeria, in June 1943. In the first a group from 1 Border wait by their Waco Glider as USAF ground staff examine a Mk 1 Bren LMG. *IWM NA3846*

Centre Soldiers from 1 Border unloading a handcart from the cargo bay of a Waco. The whole cockpit has been lifted up and one of the emergency escape doors, just below the edge of the starboard wing, has been removed. Glider chalk No 90 carried men from D Company to Sicily. *IWM NA3854*

Right While members of the Platoon hold the rear fuselage to keep the glider level, others close the front. The cockpit was lifted up by hand and secured by a control wire from the tripod on top to the rear of the cargo compartment. *IWM NA3855*

Top The handcarts are unloaded and the glider front closed. *IWM NA3856*

Centre The soldiers move off with their handcarts. *IWM NA3857*

According to the War Diary, these two exercises were completed without mishap. However, Ronald Hope-Jones recorded in his diary that six of the gliders carrying South Staffords and eight with men of 1 Border crashed, although without any serious injuries, and 14 of 1 Border's gliders failed to arrive back at the airfield, but no other air accidents for this date have been recorded. The IO, perhaps apocryphally, noted that 'One glider in B Company is reputed to have looped the loop 100 feet above the ground and then landed upside down, but no one was injured, though naturally they were all a bit shaken.'

Immediately after the exercises of 14 and 20 June, glider training was halted due to the requirement of the C-47s for paratroop training. The US instructors felt that the British pilots had learned to handle the Waco very quickly, but all the pilots had little night flying experience. Moreover, the Glider Pilots and, perhaps more importantly, the tug pilots had not trained in a mass release of gliders over water off the coast, either in daytime or at night. It was not until the invasion of Sicily that the whole Battalion were lifted and landed under the cover of darkness, together with all their heavy weapons and equipment. With only roughly three weeks training between the British Glider Pilots and the crews of the C-47 tugs, preparations were therefore totally inadequate.

Lt Ron Jack, a Rhodesian who had joined the Battalion in April 1943, was, amongst other duties,

Bottom Four men of 1 Border deploy in front of their Waco during training around Froha in June 1943. *IWM NA3859.*

the Assistant Loading Officer (ALO). He expressed concern over the weakness of the floor between the reinforced wheel treads in the Waco, as several men had put their feet through the floor while practising loading. The hinged cockpit was also a worry because if it was damaged in a crash-landing it was virtually impossible to open the nose and unload anything from a handcart to a jeep.

In the preparation for the operation, Lt Jack 'was charged with working out how we were to load the 6-pounder anti-tank gun. This was very awkward as the barrel got entangled in the control wires at the tail end of the fuselage and we had no really accurate indication as to the centre of gravity of either the glider or gun. In the end I settled for placing a trestle under the tail of the gun and tying the whole thing down. When I asked permission to fly this load, I was refused owing to the shortage of aircraft and was therefore forced to watch them take off [for Sicily] without knowing how they would fly.' (Lt R. R. Jack, ALO 1 Border)

The morale of the Glider Pilot Regiment was raised

A Waco with the front hinged up and a jeep in the cargo area; note the stand for the rear fuselage, used as an alternative to human support while loading, and the reinforced channels on the floor. *BRM*

somewhat by the arrival of Horsa gliders from England. These were flown directly from Portreath in Cornwall to Sousse in Tunisia - a distance of over 2,400 miles - via the USAAF base at Sale near Rabat in French Morocco and Froha in Algeria, using Halifax Bombers of 295 Squadron RAF of 38 Wing as tugs. This was a remarkable achievement, code-named Operation 'Beggar/Turkey Buzzard'. The Horsas arrived between 3 June and 5 July; 27 out of a total of 30 made it to Tunisia, but only eight would be used in the forthcoming operation.

Tony Stafford wrote that 'the Brigade Sappers and Glider Pilots participated with the Companies on training when they were able, which made new ideas and innovations practical propositions and not theoretical fancies. Company esprit de corps became increasingly evident and all had their own peculiar characteristics. The self-assuredness fostered by the Scottish element, Tom Armstrong and Jock Neill in B Company, was matched by the nonchalant carefree spirit that John Gibbon had created in A Company. However, despite company loyalties, pride in the Battalion came first.

'The immediate concern for most was how soon letters from home would begin to arrive. After about six weeks the mail-call was sounded and this was the immediate signal for an outburst of cheering through-

out the camp. Most was out of date, but anything was welcome that voiced sentiments from home. Despite the intense heat and monotonous fine weather, there were few complaints or grouses in the Battalion, and it was generally agreed that Froha was a good spot. Recreation was very limited and Mascara offered little entertainment for the troops, but just as things were becoming organised and settled, preparations were in hand for another move. This complex affair involved the transfer of the entire Battalion transport and equipment by road, rail and air a distance of over 600 miles to Sousse in Tunisia, which would be the forward base for the operation on Sicily.

'Preparations began and training took a back seat. Captain Geoffrey Costeloe and 52 ORs were the first to set off on 21 June east to Algiers, where they were to collect 52 brand new motorcycles and ride them the rest of the way; the Battalion transport was off the road for four days in preparation for the journey, which would take the best part of a week. Trailers were loaded and hitched behind jeeps, rations distributed and finally orders issued. Charles Scruby, the MTO, was in charge of the road party (ten officers and 179 ORs) and the Battalion's column of vehicles that formed part of the Divisional convoy, which set off on 23 June.

'The biggest problem was the disposal of all the baggage and equipment that had to go by rail. First it was moved to the nearest railway station at Perregaux, 60 miles away, and there formed into a dump with the baggage of the 1st Airborne Division; it was loaded by Alan Green's 15 Platoon of C Company. Three trains left Perregaux, the first on 24 June and the other two on the 26th, each carrying a certain proportion of this mass of crates, glider loading gear, 6-pounder and Hispano guns, bicycles and tentage. To prevent anything going missing, a small baggage party - 15 Platoon for the Battalion's equipment - accompanied each train-load to the railhead at Kairouan, and for them it was a journey to be remembered. Battalion transport then collected the equipment, which was taken to Msaken, an Arab village 8 miles south of Sousse.

'After these parties had left, the remaining Battalion personnel were to move by air. On 26 June 29 Officers and 490 ORs marched to Matmore Airfield, about 7 miles from the camp, and, after loading up the Wacos and C-47s, bivouacked the night prior to take-off at 06.45 hrs the following morning. Breakfast was at 06.00, and immediately afterwards each glider load under the command of the senior passenger marched to their respective aircraft and the glider occupants were seated according to their weights.

'With everyone emplaned, safety belts fastened and the two glider pilots checking up on their controls and inter-communication, the nervous composure of all is suddenly interrupted by a violent jerk, which indicates that the tug aircraft is moving forward and that the tow-rope is taking the strain. With the roar of engines that sent up billowing clouds of red dust an aircraft would take off down the runway. Its attendant glider, trailing less than 100 yards behind, would rise daintily from the ground and soar aloft. A little later the towing aircraft too would take to the air. As a result of a succession of take-offs such as this, there is a concentrated dust storm from which the glider emerges shortly after becoming airborne.

'The trip took nearly 5 hours, and as the route eastwards was over country a good way south of the North African coastline, the view seemed an endless succession of barren mountains, relieved by the occasional salt lake. A solitary second-class road partnered by a single-track railway line seemed a dismal link between the remote civilisations of Algeria and Tunisia. Except for odd occasions, when strong breezes or air pockets made the gliders bounce crazily at the end of the tow-ropes, it was not a very bumpy trip and only a few men were affected by air-sickness. The CO, 2i/c, Adjutant and all the Company Commanders constituted the sole passengers of the C-47 tug aircraft. Higher authority decreed that none of these "key" personnel should travel by glider, but should enjoy a safer passage aboard a powered plane.'

However, for most this was to be the last flying before the Sicily operation. And unlike Stafford, Lt Arthur Royall recalled that it was an exceedingly bumpy trip and that he and most of his glider companions were sick during the flight.

Stafford again: 'Owing to the number of aircraft in the convoy and the length of the journey, six landing strips had been prepared for the arrival and they were all located around Gouberine about 10 miles southwest of Sousse. Each airfield was essentially one wide dusty runway strip in the open country. All aircraft and gliders were stored in the open and all accommodation was tented. An assortment of vehicles bearing the familiar sign of the 8th Army, a blue crusader's cross on a white shield, were waiting at each landing zone to transport the troops and their baggage to the new Battalion area, which was to be an olive grove near Msaken.

'Areas had been allotted to Companies by Capt Howard Wilkie, who commanded the Advance Party, and as each contingent arrived so they were directed to their particular plot. The olive grove was divided by a rectangular open space, which was later to become the Battalion parade ground, and on one side were placed the rifle companies and on the other the Orderly Room, QM's stores, MT and the remainder of the Battalion. The only permanent buildings in the whole camp were two Nissen huts, which were immediately earmarked for briefing purposes. A party of Italian PoWs were attached to the Battalion for fatigue duties, and they were invaluable in digging sumps, latrines, etc. On the opposite side of the road were a Company of the Composite Company RASC, while the South Staffords occupied a similar olive grove about a quarter of a mile away. Brigade HQ was also close by just off the main Kairouan road.

'From 27 June until 1 July the Battalion, its transport and equipment were spread over the roads and railways between Mascara and Sousse. Parties kept arriving each day, the last being Capt Morrissey with the Rear Party, which arrived from Froha by road on 4 July. Casualties were remarkably few and, apart from a few men who had fallen off motorcycles, the move was completed without mishap.'

The air move was considered highly successful and of the 85 gliders used there was only one serious accident, in which all the occupants of one glider, South Staffords, were killed when the tail of the aircraft came apart. 'After we had landed at Sousse,' says Wilf Oldham, 'I watched this glider overhead, which suddenly appeared to disintegrate and we could see the men tumbling out. . .'

Tony Stafford takes up the story. '. . .With the arrival of all the Battalion stores, equipment and tentage the camp soon became highly organised. Great rivalry arose between the companies as to who could produce the most luxurious mess or the most efficient cookhouse, and as a result many innovations and inventions were put to good use. Glider loading gear, which until now had been a great encumbrance, took on a new lease of life in the more useful role of furniture. In the troops' mess tents the troughs were so arranged as to form tables and benches, while in the officers' messes an efficient sofa could be erected with the aid of sandbags and camouflage nets for upholstery. Electric light was supplied by lamps connected up to the battery of a 15 cwt truck. A No 21 WT set, fitted with a form of loudspeaker constructed from megaphones, served as a fairly effi-cient means for listening to the BBC 9 o'clock news from home and, occasionally, programmes of dance music. Owing to accommodation difficulties two officers' messes existed. The Battalion HQ group, resplendent in a stores tent sited in a cactus compound and run by the original mess staff, contrasted in many ways with the "slums" occupied by the rifle companies and run by Gordon Welch and John Gibbon.'

Operation HUSKY in its final form involved four separate airborne operations, two British and two American. On 9 July the 1st Air-Landing Brigade would lead off the attack on the night before D-Day in Operation LADBROKE, and were to land below Syracuse. A small force of two Companies of the 2 South Staffords commanded by Major Peter Ballinger, in eight Horsa gliders, was to capture the vital Ponte Grande bridge, a twin-span steel and concrete structure, which they were to hold for the advance by the 8th Army. This bridge carried the main Cassibile to Syracuse road, Highway 115, over the River Anapo and its associated canal, the Canale Mammaiabica, 1,500 yards south-east of the outskirts of Syracuse (see Chapter 5). The landing zone, LZ 3, consisted of two strips of land, half a mile south-west and one mile north-west of the bridge. The Engineers of 9th Field Company were spread between the 'Coup de Main' group and the rest of the force; their vital role was to

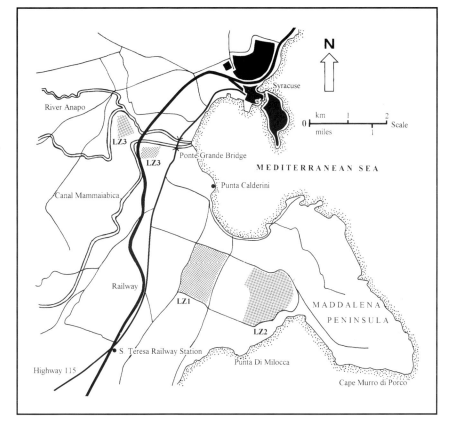

Landing zones and operations area of the 1st Air-Landing Brigade for Operation 'Ladbroke', 9-10 July 1943 on Sicily.

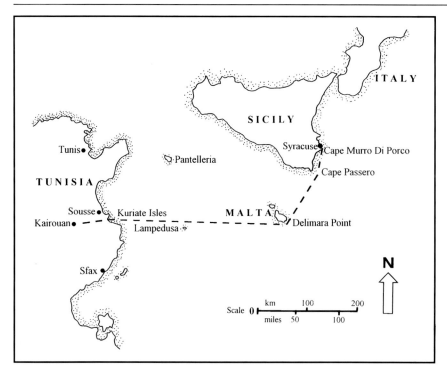

The gliders would be released from their tugs from 22.30 hrs on the 9th, and the attack on the bridge was timed for 23.15 hrs. The link-up by the remainder of 2 South Staffords and 1 Border at the bridge was to be completed by 01.15 hrs. 1 Border were to leave the area of the bridge by 01.45 and to capture and secure Syracuse by 05.30 hrs. The advance into Syracuse would be preceded by Wellingtons of 205 Bomber Group RAF, who would bomb certain targets in the Syracuse area between 02.15 and 02.45 hrs. The final link-up with 8th Army troops was planned for 07.30 hrs on 10 July. The relieving troops would be from 17th Infantry Brigade of 5th Division, commanded by Brigadier Tarleton MC, late of The Border Regiment. After landing, 5th Division was to capture Cassibile, then advance north to Syracuse and Augusta.

co-operate in the attack on the bridge and remove demolition charges. If the bridge was blown, they were to recce for a ford, or detour and prepare for new bridge construction by ground forces, which included clearing the area of mines and booby traps, as well as the collecting and reporting of RE intelligence to HQ.

The remaining glider force would land on two LZs: the other two companies of 2 South Staffords and Brigade HQ on LZ 1 and all of 1 Border on LZ 2. These were in the general area between Punta di Milocca and the Maddalena Peninsula close to the shore-line about 4 miles south of Syracuse. They were to advance and consolidate the hold on the bridge, which with the surrounding area would be held by 2 South Staffords. 1 Border, with a Company of South Staffords under command, were to pass through, advance to and secure Syracuse, including key locations, and deny the approaches to any enemy reinforcements. The Brigade were also required to destroy a coastal artillery battery that could fire on the beaches to be used by the landing forces early on 10 July.

As usual code-names were issued for the operation. The complete exercise was called BIGOT, Kairouan was 'Penarth', Malta 'Finance', the assembly area 'Andover', Syracuse 'Ladbroke', the Ponte Grande bridge 'Waterloo', the railway bridge to the west of Waterloo 'Putney', the sea-plane base near Syracuse 'Calshot', Piazza Foro in Syracuse 'Piccadilly', the bridge linking the old part of the city 'Solent', the railway station 'Bulford', the power station 'Battersea' and the Palazzo Degli Studi 'Eton'.

The second British operation, code-named FUST-IAN, involved Brigadier Gerald Lathbury's 1st Parachute Brigade (1st, 2nd and 3rd Battalions The Parachute Regiment), which would conduct a parachute assault on the evening of 13 July to capture the key Primasole Bridge, a three-span steel and concrete bridge which carried the main road, Highway 114, from Syracuse to Catania 5 miles to the north across the River Simeto. Two hours after the parachute attack, a glider force of eight Wacos and 11 Horsas with artillery, jeeps and other logistical support were to land in two LZs near the bridge; no units of 1st Air-Landing Brigade were involved. The Paras would be relieved by units of 50th Division supported by 4th Armoured Brigade.

To avoid the danger of friendly fire from the Allied task-force, the night airborne operations had to be flown over a long circuitous route to Sicily. The gliders and their tugs were to circle over the departure airfields until they were in for the flight to Sicily. They would then fly east over the Kuriate Islands just off the Tunisian coast towards Malta at a height of 200 feet above the sea. The first checkpoint was Delimara Point on Malta, which would be aided by searchlights on the island. The aircraft were then to turn left and head north-east for Cape Passero on the south-east corner of Sicily, the second checkpoint. At this point the planes carrying 101st Airborne, who were flying on a parallel course to the west, would turn left for their drop zone at Gela, while the British would continue north to the area of Cape Murro di Porco, approaching Syracuse from the south to avoid enemy AA positions. The tug pilots were to take Cape Ognina as their initial point for their final run, and to set a course 1 mile off its tip for the end of Cape Murro di Porco. Approximately 2¹/₂ miles from the promontory, about halfway between the two Capes, gliders would be released from their tugs some 3,000 yards from the shore. The release height for the Wacos to LZ 1 was set at 1,500 feet, for the Wacos to LZ 2 at 1,000 feet, and for the Horsas to LZ 3 at 3,500 feet.

Despite the promise of moonlight, this zigzag course was 450 miles as opposed to the straight flight distance from Tunisia to Sicily of 250 miles. Maintaining tight formation at 200 feet in near black-out conditions would be difficult even for experienced pilots.

It was envisaged that the Wacos would be able to land on their LZs systematically in lanes! The Battalion War Diary actually lists the formation of the Battalion's gliders on landing - four lanes. The operational notes state with unbelievable optimism that 'it will take about 7 minutes to land all the gliders from each take-off airfield', and 'Thus there should be approx 7 mins intervals on LZ 2 after all the gliders from each take-off airfield have landed. This is so designed to give sub-units a chance to pull clear any gliders likely to obstruct the landing of succeeding

machines. This timing will, however, increase the total time required for assembly, and coys must be disposed for all round defence while waiting.' (Appendix D to 1 Border Operational Order No 1 dated 4 July 1943)

Lt Hope-Jones and his Intelligence Section continued with their planning on 25 June, the day after they flew to Sousse. Sgt Burton, the Intelligence Section Sergeant, and Pte Leonard Mein, the best artist in the section, were security cleared and began work on the maps and plans required. 30 June was set aside to brief the Company Commanders in detail, and on 3 July Hope-Jones gave a briefing to the whole Battalion.

A large Brigade Church Parade was held on the morning of 4 July. Lt Arthur Royall, OC 12 Platoon B Company, remembers the hymn 'Eternal Father Strong To Save' with the prophetic line 'For those in peril on the sea'. In the afternoon the Intelligence Office was besieged by officers of the Battalion to study the information. Tony Stafford wrote that 'the heat inside the huts was terrific. The IO bore the brunt of the briefing, while the daily routine of the Battalion was dealt with entirely by the 2i/c, Major Tommy Haddon, and the Adjutant, Lt N. A. H. Stafford. It seemed ironic that the IO should be going to this particular part of Sicily as the spearhead of an invasion force, for as a classical scholar of no mean

Men of the Battalion marching off from Church Parade on 4 July 1943. *IWM NA4006*

repute, one of his peacetime ambitions had been to visit a very famous Greek amphitheatre on the outskirts of Syracuse. His wish was to be fulfilled, but in very unusual circumstances.'

On 6 July everyone in the Battalion was briefed by the IO platoon by platoon until about 14.00 hrs, when a series of explosions occurred as 1st Parachute Brigades stores and ammunition dump and the Glider Pilot Regiment's tents went up in smoke and flames; the bulk of the Battalion rushed off to fight it. The following day was taken up with the second day's briefing. Pte Bert Ingham, who served with the Intelligence Section, recalls that they made a large-scale model of Syracuse from aerial photographs. This model, large-scale maps, aerial photographs and post-card views of the coast and country around Syracuse (see Chapter 5) were studied intently by all ranks.

On landing the roles of the various platoons and groups varied. The Intelligence Section, quite naturally, were to interrogate enemy prisoners. Jimmy Devonport, then a Sergeant in D Company, recalls that his job was to drive a railway locomotive if nec-

essary at one of the Battalion objectives, the railway station. Arthur Royall's 12 Platoon B Company were to capture the Post Office building in the Piazza Foro at Syracuse. Bill George, a sniper in 11 Platoon B Company, was to climb a stone tower, the Pantheon at the north end of Piazza Foro, overlooking Syracuse, and use it as an observation post. Pte Charles Coventry in 16 Platoon C Company recalls that his Platoon were to make for the sea-plane base.

Lt Ted Newport's Anti-tank Platoon were to proceed as quickly as possible from the landing zones with their four anti-tank guns to the bridge. There they were to assist if necessary in the destruction of the pill-boxes if still held by the enemy, and if already in our hands to set up a defensive screen around the bridge as soon as possible. Having moved into Syracuse one gun was to be allocated to each Company to cover various approaches into the city. Ted Newport's main concern was not so much the objectives but flying the guns in separately from their jeeps and ammunition.

For various reasons, principally the lack of gliders,

Lt Ronald Hope-Jones, the Intelligence Officer, recorded in his diary on 8 July 1943: 'Monty turned up this morning, and put on a tremendous show. After talking to Company Commanders he called the whole Battalion around him. First he asked where we came from. Lancashire seemed to win; there was one loud shout of Wigan. He said we had a nice spot for a camp here and that it looked better than Wigan. Did we have any beer? Loud cries of 'No'. Then he said he was glad to have us in the Eighth Army, and hoped we were glad too. We seemed to think so. Finally he wished us good luck, and went off to three tremendous cheers, much louder than those for the King last year.' Here General Montgomery addresses men of the Brigade near Sousse. *IWM NA4062*

Above In the early evening sun of 9 July 1943, half a Platoon of 1 Border, with their Waco/Hadrian glider in the background, stand on one of the airstrips near Sousse, just prior to the Brigade taking off for Sicily. Note the uniform and equipment worn for Operation Ladbroke: except for one man, all wear KD with shorts and 37 Pattern equipment fighting order. Some men wear Sten SMG magazine pouches and others carry a second small pack for extra ammunition and other items. The weapons are mainly No 4 Rifles and Mk 2 Stens. One man carries the Platoon's 'escape axe' and another on the right holds his Airborne helmet, which was to be worn on take-off and landing. The USAF pilot is clearly distinguishable in the right background by his sunglasses, whilst the man in the centre wears a British-issue pair. *IWM CNA993*

Right The same group from 1 Border near their Waco glider on the same evening. An Airborne folding bicycle is in the foreground, and a pack of 2-inch mortar bombs in their cases lies at the feet of the two men nearest to the camera. The man with his back to us carries two small packs and additional 15-round .303-inch pouches fastened to his waist-belt. *IWM CNA992*

certain officers and men were not to go on the operation; according to Shears this was the first-line reinforcement Company of approximately 180 all ranks. These included some men of H Company, from the Anti-tank, 3-inch Mortar and MMG Platoons. Since the combination of a gun with jeep did not fit into the Waco, it was decided to only take four of the eight guns, so one Anti-tank Platoon remained in North Africa. According to the equipment list only four 3-inch mortars were taken and the Vickers MMGs were left. Capt Scruby, the MTO, Lt Barnes, the QM, Lt R Jack, the ALO, and Captains Dickie Stewart MC and Bob Stockwell all had to remain behind, much to their disgust. The latter two officers were detailed for airfield control duties at the depar-

ture airfields, and were to be the first to hear how the Battalion had fared on the way across, for the American tug pilots on their return gave promising reports of how every glider had been released over its correct landing zone. The true situation was not to be known until after the Battalion had returned to North Africa.

At about 15.00 hrs on 9 July everyone donned their battle order, KD with gaiters and boots, and 37 Pattern equipment battle order. The Dennison smock was not worn, but the Airborne helmet was taken, to be worn at take-off and landing. All ranks wore their maroon berets. Each rifleman carried 120 rounds of .303-inch ammunition, of which 50 rounds was in a cotton bandolier; those with Mk 2 Sten SMGs had eight 32-round magazines, and those with .38 pistols 24 rounds each. Each section CO and rifleman carried two Bren mags, and the Section 2i/c six in addition to those carried by the LMG Nos 1 and 2. Each man also carried one or two 36 Grenades and two 77 Grenades. Each Platoon had one Bangalore Torpedo and one Pole Charge, each PIAT nine rounds per gun. Each anti-tank gun had 24 AP and 8 rounds HE. The official report gives the Battalion's operational strength as 43 officers and 753 ORs, and the other equipment as 58 folding bicycles, 55 handcarts, four jeeps, four 6-pounder anti-tank guns, 13 No 18 wireless sets, 10 trolleys and four 3-inch mortars.

Officers and NCOs were furthered encumbered with compasses, maps, binoculars, wire-cutters and other vital equipment. Each glider carried an axe and each man was given a blow-up lifebelt. In operational orders dated 8 July was the instruction that 'on deplaning, all ranks will take their life-belts to Company localities in "Ladbroke" where they will be collected into Company dumps, for use by the Battalion in future operations. These life-belts are irreplaceable.' (Appendix E, War Diary 1 Border, 8 July 1943). In view of what was to take place the following night and during the morning of 10 July, this instruction seemed rather ludicrous.

At 15.20 hrs the men moved off to the RASC 3-ton trucks waiting to take them to airfields C, D and F, and the convoys left at 15.55, 16.45 and 16.55 respectively. The trucks were numbered the same as the gliders to simplify emplaning. The trucks arrived at the airfield at around 18.00. Sgt Victor de Muynck, Platoon Sergeant of 12 Platoon, wrote that as they waited by their glider 'at about 6 pm tea was handed out and we ate our tinned herring sandwich. It was enough to make one sick before setting foot in the plane.'

Lt Ted Newport recalls that it was not an auspicious start to the operation: '. . .having arrived at our airfield and, just as we were about to load our gliders, we witnessed an RAF Albemarle taking off at the same time as an American C-47 was about to land from the opposite direction. The RAF plane saw the American and although barely airborne banked steeply to avoid a collision, but stalled and crashed, exploding in flames. . .'

Lined up on the six departure airfields, the whole force consisted of eight Horsa and 136 Waco gliders, half of which had radio sets hastily installed that afternoon. They would carry 111 Officers and 1,619 ORs of the Brigade including HQ. The Glider Pilot Regiment was reinforced by 20 US Glider Pilots, who volunteered to fly as Co-pilots on the operation. 1 Border were allocated 72 Wacos, numbered 55 to 127: Nos 62, 66 and 70 were allocated to 181 Field Ambulance (Lt Col G. M. Warrack); 105 and Glider Y carried men from 9th Field Company RE (Major Beazley). Four additional Gliders, 101A, 102A, 103A and 104A, carrying men from H Company, were added to the load table at the last minute, but only 101A took off due to the shortage of tug aircraft. All the gliders were arranged in four neat lanes, and each row of four was scheduled to take-off at 1-minute intervals. The 2 South Staffords (Lt Col W. D. H. McCardie) and other sections of 181 Field Ambulance and 9th Field Company were distributed amongst Wacos 1 to 54 and Horsas 128 to 135 on airfields A, B and E. The tug planes comprised 109 C-47s from 60 and 62 Troop Carrier Group USAF, one C-47 from Troop Carrier Command USAF, and 27 Albemarles of 296 Squadron for the Wacos, and one Albemarle of 296 Squadron and seven Halifaxes from 295 Squadron 38 Wing for the Horsas.

As the wind had increased that day, Colonel Chatterton decided to increase the release heights for the gliders a few hours before take-off. For LZ 1 it was now to be 1,800 feet, for LZ 2 1,400 feet and LZ 3 4,000 feet. The men from the Battalion had devoted the previous two days to loading the gliders and ensuring that everything was securely lashed to prevent any movement while airborne or on landing. Everyone knew their role in the operation and there was no undue worry about what might happen during the course of the next 6 hours. At 18.48 hrs the first tug aircraft and glider was airborne; 1 Border's first glider took off at 19.05 hrs and the last was airborne at 20.12 hrs.

Chapter 4

For Those in Peril on the Sea

The gliders and their tugs were still forming up when the first problems began. Two (113 and 127) were pulled off immediately after take-off, and five gliders with their tugs (42, 120, 121, 125 and 126A) turned back. Glider No 125 piloted by S/Sgt Braybrook and Sgt Atkins returned to the airstrip due to an oil leak on their Albemarle tug. The glider had just enough height to scrape over the boundary of the perimeter before it tangled with some power cables and came down heavily; although 3-inch mortar bombs rolled around the floor, none of the Mortar Platoon were hurt.

Lt Pat Stott and 15 men of 14 Platoon B Company were in Glider No 120 piloted by Sgt Read and Sgt W. Gill and towed by an Albemarle. They had only been airborne for some 20 minutes when it was clear that the load would not balance. Despite several men moving from one side of the glider to the other, the problem could not be corrected and, having cast off, the glider landed some 2 miles from Msaken. Another followed when a jeep broke loose from its moorings inside the glider. The remainder headed out towards Malta and the first checkpoint 200 miles away.

The weather had begun to change on the morning of 9 July; the wind began to increase from the southeast as they passed Malta, and at times reached 45 mph. One Horsa and two Wacos broke from their tugs and crashed into the sea. Further on towards Sicily it was difficult for the aircraft to maintain formation. Several tugs began drifting off course, and as they climbed to the prescribed release altitudes landmarks below became hidden by dust storms blowing offshore. The first seven tugs made their runs into the release areas accurately and undetected, their gliders cut loose and the pilots began their descent, eagerly looking for any sign of the LZs.

One of the Wacos that broke from its tug near Malta may well have been Glider No 83 piloted by Sgt Stan Coates and Sgt Vic Perry, carrying A Company's 2i/c, Capt Bill Hodgson, half of A Company HQ, a mortar detachment and a jeep trailer full of kit. The story was recounted to John Gibbon in the Border Regiment Magazine (September 1954) as follows:

'We took off from Sousse and flew for some considerable time in the dark without intercom between the tug and the glider. After a number of hours the Glider Pilot called out that we were approaching an island that looked like Sicily. Yes, he was sure it was Sicily, and the whole place was in darkness. The tug circled round and round, and eventually our pilot said, "Well, here it is," and pushed the button, freeing the glider.

'Down we came and landed most perfectly in the dark on a flat open piece of ground and came to a standstill. Out got the troops, guns at the ready, and pulled out the trailer. Suddenly there was the noise of an approaching vehicle. All the troops got down and waited. A jeep with two men arrived, stopped, and the men got out. Up jumped the troops and dragged the trailer over to hook it on to the jeep. The jeep was pointing in the wrong direction and there was a certain amount of military confusion. No one seemed to be getting anywhere, and least of all the jeep and trailer.

'Eventually I called out, "Stop everyone, stay still - now where are the two men from the jeep?" The two were produced and in a few short sharp words I told them to get their jeep fixed, so that the trailer could be hitched on without further delay, and then all could move off to the Battalion RV. The two protested greatly and said, "Don't give us any more orders, we will now tell you what to do".

'A certain amount of military back-chat went on between us and I kept saying, "Come on, we must get away from here and get to the Battalion RV, and it doesn't matter what unit you are."

'One of the two from the jeep then said, "Look here, old boy, there appears to have been a bit of nonsense. Where do you reckon you are, and what are you doing here, anyway?"

'By now my patience was exhausted, and I explained very tersely that I reckoned I was very near the DZ just outside Syracuse, and that I was now going to take the jeep and move off with it, and if the two owners cared to follow they could do so.

'Unabashed by this, the two said, "We are very sorry to inform you that you are not in Sicily, but on the main airstrip on Malta, and what's more you are blocking one of the runways, and the fighters cannot take off. So please take the jeep, and pull not only the trailer but also this bloody glider 200 yards in that direction."

'This done, the fighters then took off. The glider party was then taken off to a canteen filled with wondering RAF. We were given food, drink and a lot of advice. We also thought we were the only glider off course. We spent the remainder of the night listening to the fighters taking off and drinking ourselves into a depressed coma. . .'

Apart from this glider, only one from A Company landed on Sicily, the other eight crashing into the sea. Another glider landed back in North Africa near the Mareth Line! This may have been Glider No 85 piloted by S/Sgt Stewart and Sgt Guinan, which was one of three that headed back to Africa when the tug pilots were unable to find the release area. The platoon commander related to John Gibbon how they eventually landed, unsure of their position and puzzled by the continuous stretches of sand in all directions as they tried to work out the general direction towards Syracuse:

'. . .I formed an ambush on this straight featureless bit of road and waited for about two hours and then saw in the distance some headlights coming towards us. We had piled sand and a few stones on the road and the whole platoon stood ready. I thought it was strange that there were no signs of firing or bombing, but there it was. The troops had been commenting more and more on what a bloody awful place Sicily must be with this amount of sand, and not what they had expected.

'The vehicle approached and three of us got up. It was going quite slowly and I shone my torch. The vehicle drew up towards me. With my Sten ready, I approached. It was a 15-cwt open truck with two figures in front. A Section ran up to the back. All was well. Then a voice from the driving seat said, "What do you want cock - a lift?"

'Good, I thought, better still, a British unit.

'"Yes," I said, "but I have got about 20 men here."

'"That's alright," said the cheerful driver. "Get them all in - it will be a tight squeeze."

'The platoon gathered round. "What are you on, an exercise?" said the driver.

'"Yes," I said. "What unit are you?"

'The driver replied, "Oh, we are from the mobile bath unit about 8 miles down the road."

'Amazing, I thought, the battle not really under way yet and a mobile bath unit already on shore from the sea-borne landings. All must be going well. I then asked if he had seen any airborne troops.

'"No," he said, "not down here", but he knew that there were some 'around Sousse.

'"Yes," I said. "We were there before we left for the battle."

'"Really?" said the driver. "Didn't you go off with them to the battle then or did you miss the way?"

'I then asked him where we were.

'"About 8 miles from the Mareth Line," the driver replied.

'I was stunned. The Mareth line in North Africa! We had landed back in North Africa and had been rescued by a mobile bath unit. . .!' (Border Regiment Magazine, September 1954)

Alerted by the sound from the engines of the first tug aircraft, the AA batteries, shore batteries and MG positions along the coast and around Syracuse now opened fire as search-lights scanned the sky. The flak, in addition to the wind and other problems, made it even harder for both tug and glider pilots to see their targets. Apart from the two tugs with their gliders who could not find the release area and headed back to Africa, others mistook their position. Six landed between the tip of Cape Passero and Avola, 15 miles south of LZs 1 and 2, six others released in the same area landed in the sea, while one overshot Syracuse completely and the glider landed near Augusta 15 miles north of the city.

Any idea that the glider and tug combinations could maintain formation on their approach, let alone land in sequence, was hopeless; each glider was on its own. More gliders and tugs veered off course and either flew into other areas, flew higher or flew lower to release. However, a large proportion were far beyond the 3,000-yard limit to make landfall, and many crashed into the sea, some very soon after casting-off. Survivors were later to complain bitterly that the tow-plane pilots released them far short of the release area and were too easily put off by the first signs of flak. Ships throughout the invasion fleet were gradually alerted to the problem and troops were rescued from a wide area over the next 12 hours.

Glider No 55, piloted by Major John Place with Major-General Hopkinson as Co-pilot, carried Lt

Arthur Springbett and half a Platoon of C Company. The tug aircraft switched off its blue wing lights as they approached Sicily; these remained off despite repeated requests from General Hopkinson to turn them back on. Arthur Springbett recalled that 'in due course ack-ack fire appeared in the distance and almost immediately we felt a jerk and saw our tow-rope hanging upwards. The American tug pilot had taken evasive action before releasing the glider and we found ourselves almost upside down. With great skill, Major Place kept the glider airborne long enough for everyone to divest themselves of all equipment and weapons and be ready to carry out the ditching drill that had been rehearsed as soon as we hit the sea.' All the occupants escaped safely and remained floating on the wings for about 6 hours before they were picked up by a returning landing-craft.

General Hopkinson's powerful voice was heard by Lt Geoffrey Costeloe, 2i/c of 1 Border's Recce Platoon, as his group huddled on the remains of Glider No 119, piloted by S/Sgt Waldron and Sgt Harris. The group included Lt Bob Coulston, Costeloe's batman, eight men from the Platoon and a Signaller. All emerged from the wreck, but the wings could not support the weight of the men. Six, including Lt Coulston, were prepared to swim for it, leaving Costeloe with the remainder.

As the seaborne invasion began, Hopkinson's voice could be heard shouting repeatedly 'Ahoy there! Airborne troops in distress!' This was eventually answered by a Cockney Royal Marine Sergeant on a landing-craft, who said 'Shut up you — fools, we are doing a — invasion.' At around 05.00 hrs Costeloe's group was picked up by an assault landing-craft, which took them to the Polish ship SS *Sobieski*. The Captain, having assumed from their bedraggled appearance that they were Italian PoWs, told his crew to put them in irons until persuaded otherwise, after which they were treated royally.

The problem with the Waco when ditched soon became obvious. The metal-framed fuselages almost without exception filled with water and sank to up the level of the wings, which, being made of wood, kept the glider afloat. Anyone not quick enough to unbuckle their seat-belts, remove their equipment, or suffering severely as some men had from air-sickness during the flight, could not escape. As the canvas and wood of the wings became saturated, they too began to float beneath the surface. In some cases the weight

L/Cpl E. Barton of Bolton, Lancashire, who was landed on Malta after his glider crashed into the sea on 11 July 1943. He later served with the Battalion at Arnhem. *IWM NA4123*

Pte Thomas Titterington of Preston, Lancashire, on Malta on 11 July 1943. He also was to serve with the Battalion at Arnhem, where he was taken prisoner. *IWM NA4125*

of the fuselage and the heavy seas caused the wings and tailplane to break away. The survivors also had to cope with the cold water and a lifebelt that was little more than a buoyancy aid.

Glider No 91, piloted by Sgt Jack Caslaw and Sgt Anderson, with Padre John Rowell and eight men aboard, crashed in the sea. The pilots warned their troops for landing and all got out, but by dawn two men had been washed away. The survivors were picked up at around 06.30 hrs by HMS *Beaufort* and later transferred to HMIS *Sutlej*, which took them to Malta.

Glider No 90, piloted by Sgt Jack Frampton and Sgt Paddy Cooke, with D Company HQ on board, pulled off on take-off in time to reload in a reserve glider (No R2). They took off again but landed in the sea at about 22.00 hrs and were picked up by HMS *Blencathra*, which also took them to Malta. The cruiser HMS *Arethusa* collected survivors from Glider No 73, piloted by Sgt George Scriven and Sgt Don Watham and carrying part of 8 Platoon A Company; two of the soldiers and Sgt Watham drowned.

Pte Dick Haley of Frizington, Cumberland, then 21, was a passenger in Glider No 75, piloted by Sgt Leadbetter and F/O Dees USAF and carrying Capt Tom Armstong, OC B Company, and Company HQ personnel. He recalled that they were approaching the coast when the pilot of the towing aircraft cast off too early and the glider crashed in the sea. The occupants all managed to get out of the glider, but several men were soon in difficulties and became panic-stricken. Dick rescued and dragged a number of them on to the wings of the glider during the night, until they were picked up by landing-craft, transferred to a supply ship the following morning and taken to Algiers. He was later awarded the George Medal for his gallantry (see Appendix 3).

Another of A Company's gliders crashed in the sea. The survivors who got out clambered on to the wings, then swam towards a warship, which took about 2 hours. Major John Gibbon later related their account: '. . .No one challenged us as we got to the side, found a chain which we climbed up and got aboard. For 10 to 15 minutes we wandered about the ship looking for a hole or doorway. We could not find one and the ship appeared to be deserted. We eventually ended up forward and took shelter, cold and miserable, behind the forward gun turrets. While standing there a door in the back of the gun turret opened and out popped a sailor with a shining bucket in his hand - presumably the man detailed to get the cocoa for the gun turret. He took three steps, saw these 12 bedraggled figures, gave a shout and fell to the deck in a swoon, with the bucket clattering on the deck.

'For a few seconds nothing happened, then the "Silent Service" arrived with shouts and curses and beat the daylights out of the poor, defenceless, unhappy soldiers and carried them, some senseless, through some secret door into the bowels of the ship. Here the soldiers tried to explain who they were and eventually convinced a naval officer that they were in actual fact Airborne troops in the Airborne attack on Sicily.

'The Navy then were magnificent and looked after them in the most lavish way, apologising profusely for the rough treatment they had served out. They said that they hoped they would be forgiven, but the Army must realise that if they said the Airborne troops were to go by air, they must go by air. And if they changed their minds and sent the Airborne troops to swim to Sicily, then they ought to inform HM ships to avoid any confusion. And furthermore avoid inter-service friction, as had just occurred. . .' (Border Regiment Magazine, September 1954)

Private Walter Collings of A Company recalled that his glider, having cast off from its tug, failed to reach the shore and the survivors forced their way out, removing most of their clothing and equipment. Others closer to the shore were fired on by coastal MG and gun positions. Being a non-swimmer, Collings and others clung to their glider for 10 hours, until finally they were picked up by a British naval vessel, which transferred them to the Supply Ship *Reina del Pacifico*, the same ship that carried Major Gibbon and his party.

Sgt Jimmy Devonport of D Company distinctly remembers the conversation over the intercom between tug pilot and glider pilot; the last words from the C-47 pilot as the glider was cast-off were, 'You're on your own, bud'. His glider landed in the sea and he spent 10 hours in the water. He and Provost Sgt Bill Hoyne (Glider No 60) of HQ Company were taken aboard the Dutch ship *Tiedelberg*, which returned them to Algiers. Pte Bert Ingham of the Intelligence Section landed in the sea; he and five others were picked up and taken to RMS *Windsor Castle*.

Private Wilf Oldham, a Bren gunner of 12 Platoon B Company, recalls that his glider, No 92, flown by Sgt Hill and F/O Gunter USAF, took off successfully. 'As we approached Sicily we were rocked by ack-ack fire, then crossed the coast, from where we headed out back over the sea - why, I will never know. Shortly after came the order "Equipment off, prepare for ditching". The glider party included Lt Royall, Cpl John Betts, Cpl Whitton, L/Cpl Jack Heaton, Privates Boyles, T. V. 'Taffy' Jones (Lt Royall's batman), Moss, Taylor and a L/Cpl of the Regimental Police.

'The glider was cast off at about 22.00 hrs and down we came, hitting the sea with an almighty splash. Within seconds the water was chest high and we were unable to open the doors owing to the water pressure. . .others including the two pilots managed to escape, although part of the glider had broken up. . . the group managed to remove most of their clothing and equipment, but conditions remained very difficult due to the strong wind and a heavy swell, which washed us away from the wreckage, and although each man was issued with a blow-up lifebelt, some members of the platoon, especially the non-swimmers, were washed away and drowned.

'Lt Royall and Cpl Heaton became separated from us. By now there were four of us left on what remained of the glider - I think only the wings were still floating. As dawn broke we could see many invasion ships, and shortly an assault boat that had landed men on the shore came alongside and pulled us aboard and then took us to their "mother ship". . .into sick bay. . .and headed for Malta where we came ashore and spent a week in a transit camp and then were transported back by sea to North Africa. . .' (3391058 Private Wilfred E. Oldham, Scout Section, 12 Platoon B Company)

Arthur Royall recalls the same incident: '. . .As Platoon Commander I was in one glider with two sections and Sergeant Victor De Muynck in another with Platoon HQ and another section. I was at the rear of our Waco and after the crash found myself up to my neck in water. I had a commando knife with me; I took this out, cut a hole in the canvas above my head, put my head out and was greeted by a shout, "Here he is!" I was hauled out of the hole, leaving my small pack behind. Later I remembered that it contained a flask of whisky. Corporal Betts reported that his lifebelt would not blow up, he couldn't swim and that he had lost his glasses; he was still with us in the morning due to his mate keeping an eye on him. The majority of our party remained with the wreckage during the night, paddling from one bit of the glider to the other - most of the portions were floating just below the surface.

'I gave permission for two or three of the men to swim for the shore, which was clearly some distance away. I was reluctant to do this; however, I felt that they should have the chance to swim if they could. There was certainly a heavy swell and it was much colder than I ever imagined the Med could be. Our party were picked up by a Greek destroyer. As it came alongside, manned by obvious Mediterranean types, I thought we were about to be captured by the Italian Navy. A lone loud English voice shouted, "It's OK, they are Greeks, not Ities - I'm the only bloody Englishman aboard." He was an RN Signaller. Scrambling nets were lowered and we pulled ourselves aboard; some of the chaps couldn't manage and Greek sailors dived into the sea and pulled them aboard. I had a cut over my left eye which was stitched up by

the ship's MO, then, after egg and bacon, I slept until noon.

'About then we were transferred to the empty troopship *Reina del Pacifico*. Lunch was being served. I was shown down to the 1st Class Dining-Room and the waiter asked "Will you have the lobster, sir?" I acquired a pair of blue silk pyjamas and two silk khaki shirts left behind by a Brigadier, by then fighting ashore on Sicily. Other Border officers and men were on board plus some South Staffords. We were taken to Algiers and joined up with more Border survivors including Major Jock Armstrong, our Company Commander. . .' Arthur Royall spent some time in hospital in Algiers before returning to Sousse by train.

The other half of Arthur Royall's Platoon, under the command of the Platoon Sgt, Victor De Muynck, were in Glider No 96, piloted by Lt Stevens and F/O White. The group included Cpl Clark, L/Cpl Horner, L/Cpl Manley, Ptes Casey, Fairbrass, Gale, Hurley and Richards, plus the Platoon handcart.

L/Cpl Horner: 'We were released from the tug at approximately 22.15 hrs at approx 500 feet. We hit the water nose first, and the fuselage filled up almost

Lt Arthur Royall in 1943. Having joined the Battalion in March of that year direct from OCTU, he commanded 12 Platoon of B Company until taken prisoner at Arnhem on 26 September 1944. *BRM/Arthur Royall*

immediately. One of the emergency doors would not open. A number escaped through the nose, and the remainder through the port door. The Glider Pilot told us to keep on the wings. He said to me that there should be 14 people and that he could only count 13; I checked up and found that the missing person was Pte Hurley. In about 2 hours the aircraft started to break up. The wings broke from the main body, and we held on to the nose as that was all that remained above water. We then had to abandon this support as it was sinking, and transfer to a glider wing that then appeared.

'At this time Sgt de Muynck decided that he and Cpl Nobby Clark should make for the shore as they were comparatively strong swimmers, so as to have more support for the non-swimmers. Five minutes later Pte Richards decided to follow the two NCOs. I shouted to L/Cpl Manley on the other side of the wing - "Is everything alright?" He replied, "Two of them have gone." I knew these two were Ptes Casey and Fairbrass. These soldiers for some time previously had been hysterical. At about 04.00 hrs Pte Gale drifted off from the glider, and we were too exhausted to go for him as we had been doing on several occasions. The last words we heard from Pte Gale were "I've had it, lads". At approximately 04.30 hrs we were picked up by an invasion barge. I reported that Gale had drifted off half an hour previously, but we could not find him. We were then transferred to the *Ulster Monarch*, from which in turn we were taken aboard a Norwegian ship and landed at Malta on Monday morning.' (3603472 L/Cpl T. H. Horner, 12 Platoon B Company)

Richards did make it and Sgt de Muynck and Cpl Clark were picked up by the cruiser HMS *Uganda*; the four men who drowned, as are all those who were lost at sea, are commemorated on the Cassino Memorial.

Glider No 100, carrying Pte Cyril Crickett and others of 13 Platoon B Company and commanded by Lt McCartney, landed in the sea and he was picked up by the transport *Winchester Castle*, which returned him to Suez. 'I cannot recall the number of our glider going to Sicily, but we wrote on the side in chalk BAD PENNY. Unfortunately we did not turn up. We took off about 19.00 hrs and had a fairly good flight, passing close to Malta and flying by the invasion fleet, which was in a large box formation below us. About 21.30 hrs we were told by the tug to cast off. After casting off we were told by the pilot that we would come down in the sea. The glider hit the sea with great force and the whole of the front hinged up and the water came rushing in.

'My next recollection was being under water and feeling for a way to get out. I felt a gap in the top and tried to get through but my webbing snagged on something and was holding me back. I dropped back to the floor, tore off my shoulder straps and tried to discard my webbing. However, this was held by an extra bandolier of ammunition across my chest, but when I took that off the webbing slipped off and I was able to scramble out; I was the last one out.

'Our Pilot was lost [probably F/O Capite USAF]. He had gone through the front when we had hit the water and the other pilot was injured. This was Sgt Worley, and he was placed on the wing and, although the sea was rough, the glider stayed afloat. We inflated our "blow-up" lifebelts and clung to the side of the glider, occasionally climbing on to the wing a few at a time.'

A few of the party decided to swim for it, but the remainder were picked up by a landing craft from the *Winchester Castle*. Crickett's route back to the Battalion took several weeks via Malta, Suez, Port Tewfik and Behghazi! (3531268 Pte Cyril Crickett, 13 Platoon B Company)

Pte Jim Longson, of the same Platoon, in Glider No 104 was rescued by a US Navy frigate, which

Sergeant Victor de Muynck, the Platoon Sergeant of Lt Arthur Royall's 12 Platoon, with his wife Margaret, photographed in Edinburgh probably in the early spring of 1943. Note the woven Airborne title and Divisional patch and the mauve B Company shoulder tab on the epaulette. *BRM/V. G. Murray*

took him and others to Casablanca. Pte Jack Looker, 10 Platoon A Company in Glider No 111, piloted by S/Sgt Arthur Prescott and Sgt Scott, was picked up by the Monitor HMS *Roberts*, which transferred him to the *Reina del Pacifico*. The glider crashed about half a mile off-shore.

The glider carrying Lt Alan Green with half of 15 Platoon C Company landed in the sea several miles off-shore after the Glider Pilot was told to cast off, despite having queried their location with the tug pilot. Pte Harold Frazer, who had opened the side-door of the glider as it sank, was washed away and drowned, despite attempts by Pte Pete Booth to save him. All the other occupants climbed on to the floating section of the glider. The following morning Lt Green and Pte O'Hanlon decided to swim to shore; they eventually made it and contacted some naval officers, who arranged to have the other survivors picked up. Pte O'Hanlon from Liverpool was recommended for and awarded a BEM for rescuing his comrades and maintaining the moral of his group until rescued; the glider party included Pte Eric Blackwell.

Pte Doug Payne, 15 Platoon's Medical Orderly, who was in the Platoon's other glider, recalled that his glider, hit by AA fire, landed in the sea; all got out except Cpl Arthur Pimblott. Doug remembered that at the briefing Major Fineron, OC C Company, had told them, if by chance they landed in the sea, to shine a torch and a tow-plane would drop a dinghy; suffice to say that there were many gliders in the sea, but no dinghies. During the night he swam with Cpl Bob Cox from the band to another glider from A Company to join another bandsman. They were picked up at 08.30 hrs on the morning of 10 July, his 23rd birthday, by a landing craft that took him to the *Winchester Castle*.

Glider No 124, piloted by S/Sgt Iron and Sgt Nelson and carrying the other half of Lt Pat Stott's 14 Platoon B Company, was cast off near the shore, but hit a cliff and fell back into the sea. The Platoon Sergeant, Sgt Gorbells, who was badly injured, Pte George Boardman and a Pte Sanderson were the only survivors.

Pte Bill Thompson of D Company landed in the sea at about 22.15 hrs and was picked up at 07.45 hrs on the 10th by a landing-craft returning to its mother ship after landing troops on the beaches, and was put on board a Dutch ship. Pte Sammy Black of 16 Platoon C Company landed in the sea, was picked up and landed back in Malta.

Glider No 84, piloted by S/Sgt Bridges and Goode and carrying Lt J. G. Louden and 15 men of 11 Platoon B Company, crashed in the sea somewhere between Syracuse and Augusta. Pte Bill George from Farnworth near Bolton in Lancashire remembers the

An unidentified Border Regiment Lieutenant comes aboard one of the invasion ships from a landing-craft, having been picked up in the sea on 10 July 1943. From the coloured tabs on his epaulettes (beneath the pips) it is virtually certain that he is Border Regiment. He still retains the blow-up lifebelt around his waist. *IWM NA4138*

events: '. . .the glider took off. I was sat behind the pilot and we were playing cards as we neared Sicily. The tug plane suddenly veered to the right across the coast and the tow-rope broke, or more likely was released by the tug-aircraft. The Glider Pilot shouted to me "Release that rope, or we'll be down". I released the cable and the pilot shouted "Dinghy Dinghy Ditchy". Within a matter of seconds he had landed the glider flat on the sea approximately a mile off-shore. With the force of the impact the Co-pilot went through the canopy; Sgt David Goode was drowned and his name is on the Cassino Memorial. The rear fuselage section broke from the main part of the fuselage and the young soldier sat on the seat at the rear of the troop compartment was lost from the glider as this happened.' (3860349 Pte William Edgar George, 11 Platoon B Company)

The group emerged from the glider and hung on to the wing sections during the night. Pte Bill Cook from Barrow and another swam to the tail section a few yards away, but returned after about 20 minutes. The aircraft was shot at by MG fire from the shore at least three times during the night, and by the following morning the water had reached waist height as they stood on the wings; an Italian MTB picked the group up. Bandsman Charles Delvoir in the Platoon felt that despite being thoroughly exhausted, they should have attempted to overpower the small Italian naval crew and escape.

They were some of the unfortunate few to be taken PoW by the enemy during the operation. The other members of the Battalion taken prisoner included L/Sgt L. Granville, Cpl J. Ramage, L/Cpl Matthew Campbell, Ptes Norman Backhouse, J. Beddows, John Bell, Harry Buckley, Matthew Gray, J. Moriarty, W. Muggeridge, Henry Naylor, W. O'Donnell, R. Palmer, H. Pratt, Bill Scrogham and N. Simpson. Most were held in the Italian PoW camp PG 66 PM 3400, 30 miles north of Naples, before being moved to Germany. When various officers of the Battalion, who were taken PoW at Arnhem, reached Oflag 79 in

Germany in October 1944, Lt Louden was there to greet them; the ORs were held in Stalag XVIIIA.

In many cases discipline prevailed even in the most trying of circumstances. CSM Albert 'Bish' Pope landed in the sea and ordered the 12 men in his glider to retain their positions. When they were picked up by landing-craft on the morning of 10 July, Pope stood to attention in 4 feet of water, saluted the officer and reported his party present and correct before allowing them to enter the vessel. Pope had been the Drum-Major of the 1st Battalion before the war, and on his return to North Africa was promoted to RSM in succession to George Gardner, who was killed on 10 July. Pope's brother also served with the Regiment and became RSM of the 2nd Battalion. Sadly Pope was to die of his wounds at Arnhem on 22 September 1944.

As these and many others struggled to survive in the heavy swell and cold waters of the Mediterranean, other glider groups managed to swim to shore or actually land on terra firma. With little or no equipment or weapons and, in some cases, little clothing, individuals and groups made strenuous

A Waco glider on the shore south of Syracuse. *US Air Force Photo Collection (USAF Neg No 26827 AC), courtesy of The National Air and Space Museum, Smithsonian Institution*

efforts to reach their objectives and take on the enemy where possible.

Waco Glider No 2, carrying Brigadier Hicks and Colonel Chatterton, who piloted the glider with Lt Harding, was hit by flack and landed in the sea some 100 yards off-shore; fortunately all the occupants made it to dry land. This party linked up with others and, about 150-strong, proceeded inland and attacked strong-points as they found them. Lt Wyatt and 15 men from 19 Platoon were in Glider No 56, piloted by S/Sgt Reg Dance and Sgt Arthur Baker, which crashed near the shore. Wyatt had been terribly airsick during the flight and was unable to get out of the glider.

Lt Col Britten flew in Glider No 57 piloted by Lt Buchan and F/O Rau USAF. The group comprised Capt Stafford, Capt Black RAMC, Lt Hardy RSO, Sgt Burton, Cpl Day, L/Cpl Toman, L/Cpl Smith and Ptes Clark, Ditte, Cull and Gilbert. The glider passed Malta and, as it neared Sicily, the passengers could see the tracer curving up to meet them. The tug cast off and the glider landed in the sea some 200 yards from the shore. The fuselage rapidly filled with water, and Lt Hardy managed to get out through one of the side doors and kicked open sections on top of the fuselage through which the rest emerged. Lt Hardy, together with Capt Stafford and Capt Black, swam for the shore with the object of trying to do something about the MG posts on the shoreline, before the whole glider-load became sitting ducks in the morning. The three, with only three .38 revolvers and 18 rounds between them, made it to the shore only to find that they faced a perpendicular cliff, which could not be climbed in the dark. Tony Stafford recalled that he carried a Union Flag tucked under his shirt, which he intended to haul up the flagpole of the main civic buildings in Syracuse.

As they waited for first light a Wellington bomber taking part in the bombing of Syracuse crashed nearby. Miraculously both Joe Hardy and Godfrey Black were unhurt. Tony Stafford, however, was wounded in the hand and badly across his neck. Joe Hardy then swam to one of the gliders floating off-shore and recovered a first aid kit; the MO applied penicillin powder and a field dressing to the Adjutant's wound.

Having been joined by his CO, Lt Hardy scaled the cliff at first light, clad in KD shirt and shorts and in stockinged feet; as Joe recalls, he looked 'absolutely ridiculous, and on arrival at the top we ran straight into the Italian machine-gunners. They were so surprised to see us appear a few yards in front of them that they just couldn't decide what was best to do, so I shouted in my very best mixture of obscene English,

French and Italian that "La guerra finito, Mussolini kaput". They were very willing to agree to that suggestion, so I immediately relieved one of them of his boots, then demanded that the rest of them should show us how to use their weapons. We took the weapons, explained to them that they were PoWs, to stay exactly where they were and that they would come to no further harm.'

Lt Hardy and Lt Col Britten then set off to find the Battalion. En route they came across another large group of Italian soldiers and civilians. Joe gave them the 'guerra finito' business again, demonstrated how they should destroy their weapons and the bluff worked. Having done this, he and the CO left them to it, and at about 20.00 hrs on 10 July joined Brigade HQ near the bridge, not before Lt Col Britten had remonstrated with Joe about his rather colourful use of French, English and Italian with the Italians they had met! They moved into Syracuse the following day.

Glider No 58 carried Major Tommy Haddon, the 2i/c, Lt Ronald Hope-Jones, the IO, two Sergeants, seven others and a handcart. Ronald Hope-Jones recorded that having emplaned at 18.30 hrs, they took off and 'flew round in circles over Africa for about an hour before finally heading out to sea at the head of the second block of planes. It was dark by the time we reached Malta and soon afterwards Sicily came in sight as a dark strip of land across the moonlit waves. I couldn't recognise the coast and we made a couple of circles before our C-47 sheered out to sea away from the flak and we cast off. There was never a hope of reaching land. We hit the sea hard and went straight under. The sea was around our waists by the time the emergency doors had been jettisoned. Tommy was the last out on one side and I on the other.'

After recovering on the wings for a while, Major Haddon, Lt Hope-Jones and a Signaller decided to swim for shore. Another party of five also attempted the swim. The group included the two Glider Pilots, Lt Connel and Sgt Hill, and Sgt Maurice Marsh RAMC, the Battalion Medical Sergeant, who was the best swimmer in the Battalion. They did not make it and are commemorated on the Cassino Memorial.

After swimming for a while the first group seemed to be making little headway; they had crashed opposite Avola about 4 miles from shore. Eventually they reached the coast near an assault beach, from where an LCI took them to its parent ship. There they were re-kitted and fed and went ashore to 50th Division HQ. That night they moved up from Avola, through Cassibile and on to 'Waterloo', where they found Brigade HQ and the CO.

Chapter 5

The Road to Waterloo

Only two of the eight Horsas made it to LZ 3 near the Ponte Grande bridge; of the others, Gliders Nos 128, 130 and 131 landed in the sea, while Nos 129, 134 and 135 landed dome distance from their LZ. Glider No 132 carried a detachment of the South Staffs and some Royal Engineers of 9th Field Company RE commanded by Major Peter Ballinger, OC D Company 2 South Staffords. Among the

Below Much of the planning for Operation 'Ladbroke' relied on current intelligence and existing photographs or postcards of the Sicilian coastline. This view, showing the cliffs and the lighthouse at Cape Murro di Porco, was used by L/Cpl Chris Thirlwell of the Intelligence section of 1 Border. *Ian Thirlwell*

Bottom A view of Syracuse looking north-east; another photograph used by the Intelligence section. *Ian Thirlwell*

Ved. 32 - *Capo Murro di Porco*, per 310°.

equipment carried were bangalore torpedoes, which were to be used to destroy any wire obstacles protecting the bridge. The glider landed 400 yards west of the bridge and was hit by tracer, which ignited the bangalore torpedoes. The Horsa exploded and only one officer and two ORs, all injured, survived. The second Horsa, No 133, piloted by S/Sgt John Galpin and Sgt Brown, with 15 Platoon (approximately 32 men) of the South Staffords commanded by Lt Louis Withers, landed on the LZ shortly afterwards at 22.45 hrs.

After waiting a short while to see if any others would turn up, Withers decided to attack the bridge from both ends with his small force. He and five men swam the river and approached the concrete pill-box at the north end undetected. On a pre-arranged signal, both groups attacked the bridge at once. The bridge was

View of the old town of Syracuse looking south-west. *Ian Thirlwell*

A black and white trace prepared by Lt Ronald Hope-Jones, the Intelligence Officer (initialled bottom right), of the western half of the city of Syracuse and the main area of the 1st Battalion's operations on 10 July. All the buildings are numbered. *BRM*

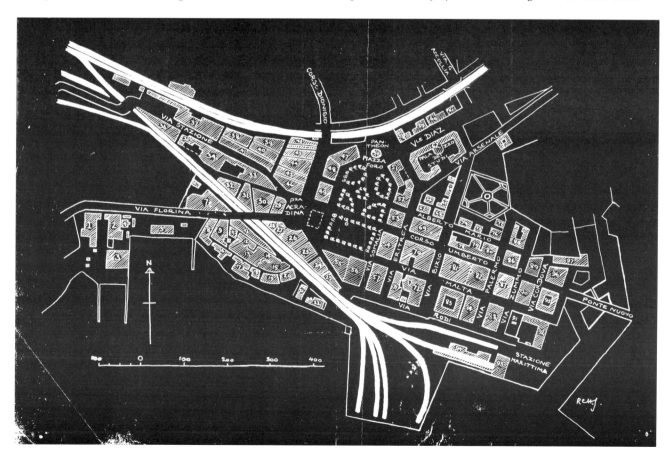

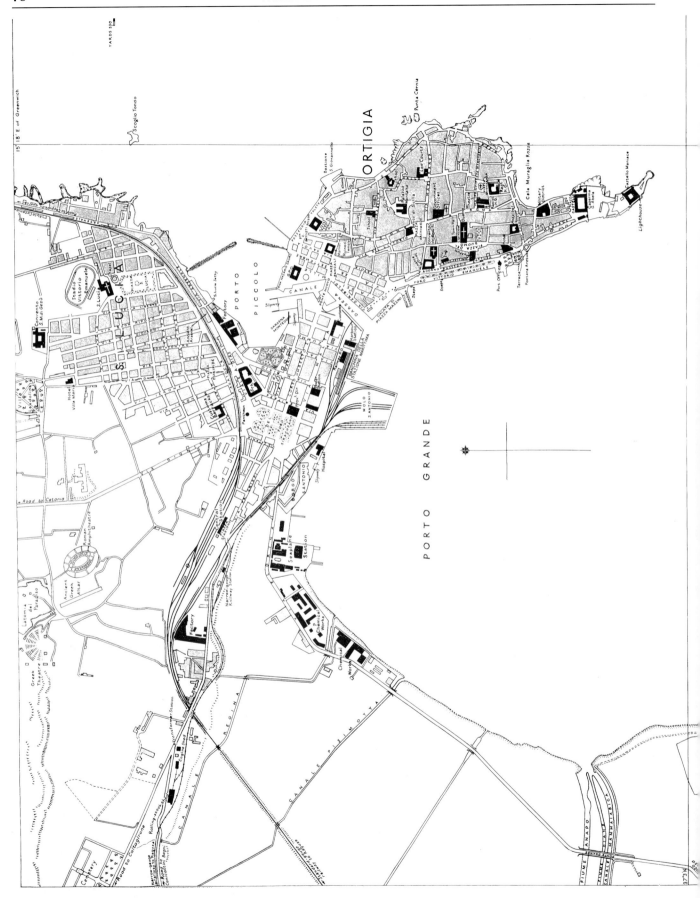

Below left Aerial photograph of the bay of Syracuse, taken on 1 May 1943. Syracuse lies at the top and the Ponte Grande bridge, carrying the main coast road over the River Anapo and its associated canal, can be clearly seen just below the centre of the picture. The railway bridge is further to the west at the edge of the photo, while Italian seaplanes float at anchor in the bay. This and other aerial photographs of the area failed to show one of the major obstacles to the landing of the gliders, the low stone walls commonly used as boundaries in the fields and olive groves. *Taylor Library*

Below Aerial photograph of the same area taken a few days later on 6 May 1943. Compared with the plan, this clearly shows the western half of the city and the various objectives that the Battalion had to take. *Airborne Forces Museum, Aldershot*

Above Plan of the City of Syracuse. The Battalion was to advance up highway 115 from the Ponte Grande Bridge (bottom left) and occupy the western half of the city as far east as the Ponte Nuovo bridge (middle right), and in the north as far as the railway line to Catania. C Company were to deal with the seaplane base 'Calshot' (just left of centre); A Company were to take the station area 'Bulford' and prevent any enemy interference from the west and north-west; D Company were to occupy and cover the Piazza Del Foro ('Piccadilly' - centre of plan) and the approaches to the Ponte Nuovo bridge ('Solent') along the Corso Umberto; B Company were to secure the Pantheon on the north side of the Piazza Foro, the Palazzo Degli Stidi ('Eton' - marked 'Sch.' just to the right of the Pantheon) and the approaches along the Via Arsenale and Viale Diaz (north-east coast road), and the railway line from Catania, which ran parallel with it. *Taylor Library*

secured immediately, as the Italian defenders were taken completely by surprise and the attackers were able to remove the detonators from the Italians' demolition charges and cut the telephone wires. Their prisoners were secured and the victors settled down into defensive positions to await the arrival of reinforcements and the 8th Army.

At around 04.30 hrs on 10 July, the first help arrived in the form of Lt Gordon Welch and seven men of the Brigade Defence Platoon, all from 1 Border. Their glider, No 6, piloted by Lt Barclay and Sgt Owen, had released at 22.15 hrs and had landed on Cape Murro di Porco. They had made their way to the bridge, having dealt with a small Italian patrol on the way. Shortly after arriving, the Italians made a determined attack on the bridge with three armoured

cars armed with MG and cannon. The commander of one was killed and the other two withdrew.

At 05.00 hrs Major Beazley, commanding 9th Field Company RE, fought his way through to the bridge with 15 men. With his batman, one NCO and a Sapper he completed the dismantling of the demolition charges still attached to the bridge. Ten minutes later, Lt Col A. G. Walch, Lt Boucher Giles GPR and men from 1 Border, 2 South Staffords and the Glider Pilot Regiment arrived at the bridge under the covering fire of the defenders. Lt Boucher Giles had flown Glider No 110 with S/Sgt Miller, and carrying Sgt Hodge, two men from S Company and a 6-pounder gun. The Sergeant had been injured in the back by the gun on landing and one of the Privates was left to look after him.

Glider No 86, piloted by Capt McMillan and Lt Halsall, landed rather heavily and crashed into a tree. McMillan badly injured his left leg and the eight passengers were concussed. The group, which included Sgt Irvine, L/Cpl Timmins, L/Cpl Brownlie and Pte Darbyshire of 1 Border, recovered and made their way to the bridge, picking up a Bren gunner from the Mortar Platoon and eight Royal Engineers on the way. En route they were pinned down by an MG post on the coast road. McMillan had to be left because of his injuries. According to an account compiled by Major H. N. Andrews DFM & Bar (then a S/Sgt GPR), Boucher Giles reached the area of the bridge at dawn, and nearby was an RV, where he found a group of Airborne troops, which includ-

Above left The view north across the Ponte Grande Bridge in July 1993. The southern section of the bridge over the Canal is original, but the northern section over the River Anapo has been rebuilt and diverted slightly to the right. The pill-box on the bridge, which was hit by Italian artillery fire, was just above the section of wall on the right. BRM

Left The view across the River Anapo to the original northern buttress of the Ponte Grande Bridge in July 1993. Lt Withers and a small section of his Platoon of 2 South Staffords swam across to the northern side and attacked from both sides the Italians guarding the

ed the party from No 86. All the wounded and injured were left there under Capt McMillan. Sgt Cawood, who piloted Glider No 106 with part of 1 Border's Battalion HQ, also joined Boucher Giles on the way to the bridge. Sgt Gardner-Roberts, Ptes Pooley and Sidebottom and possibly Lt Coulthard from the Mortar Platoon, who had landed in Gliders Nos 125A and 126 made it to the bridge. Another group who had joined the defenders just after first light comprised men from 7 Platoon of A Company, who had flown in Glider No 65 with Sgt D. E. Baker and Sgt Burton. They too had been held up by a pillbox on the way, when three of the men were killed by automatic fire; the remainder wiped out the enemy with grenades.

Colonel Walch took over command at the bridge and had the defences strengthened. At 06.30 hrs Lts Deucher and Reynolds arrived with a mixed group of 23 ORs, which brought the strength of the little force to about seven officers and 80 ORs. Apart from their small arms, rifles and Sten SMGs, the defenders had only one 2-inch mortar with a few smoke rounds, one 3-inch mortar with a few HE rounds, four Bren LMGs and one Sticky Bomb.

To the west the enemy held the railway bridge over the Anapo Canal, where there was also a pillbox. An enemy mortar position to the south-east of the bridge had been knocked out by the defenders' sole 3-inch mortar, which kept its three remaining HE rounds for an emergency. Some time after 07.00 hrs a lorry-load of Italians that approached the bridge was shot up. Sgt Baker GPR recorded the incident, which is also in the Brigade War Diary:

'Everyone watched in amazement as a lorry laden with Italians left Syracuse and came up the road

towards them, rather casually as if they were about to deliver rations. Keeping out of sight the defenders waited and when the lorry got to the bridge it was riddled with small arms fire and a few grenades thrown in for good measure.'

At 08.00 hrs the bridge and forward positions came under heavy and accurate mortar fire. All defenders were withdrawn into positions on the canal, with Lt Welch and two sections on the east side of the bridge and the remainder on the west. An hour later Major Beazley was killed by mortar fire.

Between 10.00 hrs and midday, while the main body of the defenders rested, the sentries returned fire intermittently due to a shortage of ammunition. Further casualties resulted from enemy mortar fire and accurate shelling from a field-gun 300 yards north-

Above right Italian pill-boxes on Punta Castellucio, on the northern tip of the Maddalena Peninsula, in July 1993. Syracuse is in the background. *BRM*

Right An Italian pill-box covering the railway line to Syracuse over the Mammaiabica Canal west of the Ponte Grande bridge, photographed in July 1993. *BRM*

west of the bridge. A shell struck the blockhouse at the north end of the bridge where the Italian PoWs were held, killing them all.

The artillery fire ceased at 12.00 hrs, but mortar and MG fire increased as the counter-attacking force grew to an estimated one battalion strength. At 12.45 hrs the defenders withdrew east of the bridge to a good position astride the canal. This position, could, it was estimated, be held for several hours, provided that the canal end of the bridge remained secure and any flanking move by the enemy north and west of the bridge could be disrupted.

At 14.00 hrs an enemy MG established at the north end of the bridge was firing up the canal. By 14.30 hrs the enemy were within 300 yards of the defenders' position to the north, west and south and were able to mortar the area east of the bridge as far as the shoreline. Casualties increased considerably, and 15 minutes later all the outlying posts had been wiped out. By 15.15 hrs only 15 to 20 unwounded all ranks remained

Left Another pill-box on the northern bank of the River Anapo to the east of the bridge. *BRM*

Below The Ponte Grande bridge action - a painting by C. C. P. Lawson. *BRM*

The present-day view east from across the new northern section of the Ponte Grande bridge. The pill-box on the northern bank is in front of the restaurant with the white roof. On the right is the strip of land between the river and canal, where the final stand of the defenders was made. *BRM*

in a small pocket to the east of the bridge; without cover and with their ammunition spent, they were overrun at 15.30 hrs. Lt Welch, who had been wounded in the hip during a fight with three Italians, and seven ORs including Pte Sam Sidebottom crawled down a ditch running alongside the canal and lay under a small stone culvert, thus avoiding capture.

Welch and his party managed to remain hidden, and at approximately 16.15 hrs saw trucks carrying the leading elements of the 2nd Battalion Royal Scots Fusiliers moving down the road towards the bridge; they crawled inland along the ditch and made contact. Welch explained the situation to the troops and led them back to the bridge, where 2 RSF recaptured and cleared the bridge in the next half-hour. Meanwhile, the main body of the defenders had been escorted due west as PoWs. They comprised about eight officers and 80 ORs, and included other Airborne troops. At around 17.00 hrs patrols of 17th Infantry Brigade released them and took their escorts PoW. Lt Withers and his party collected and evacuat-

ed all the casualties; he reported back to Brigade HQ at 18.00 hrs. Colonel Walch reported back to OC 17 Infantry Brigade and obtained permission to take his party back to the bridge. Among the 1 Border casualties at the bridge were L/Cpl Timmins and Pte Pooley, who were killed, and Sgt Irvine and Pte Darbyshire, who were wounded.

At 21.00 hrs the party again took over the defence of the bridge, arming themselves with captured enemy weapons as Brigade HQ and Battalion HQ of the 2 South Staffords arrived south of the crossing. At 08.00 hrs on 11 July Lt Col Walch handed over command of his party to HQ 1/ALB. Lt Withers is believed to have been recommended for a DSO, but received the MC for his leadership and gallantry in capturing the bridge. S/Sgt Galpin was awarded the DFM, and Lt Gordon Welch received the MC for his part in the operation (see Appendix 3).

Waco Glider No 10, piloted by S/Sgt H. N. 'Andy' Andrews and F/O Morris B. Kyle USAF, and carrying the Brigade's deputy CO Colonel Jonah Jones (formerly the CO of 2 South Staffords), landed at 23.13 hrs on the edge of a cliff. With him were Brigade CRA Lt Col Henniker, DAAQMG Major Tomkins, BRASCO Capt Clarke, Brigade Signal Officer Capt Roberson, Padre Rev Hourigan, some Signallers and

Left A burnt-out Waco glider on Sicily in July 1943. According to the 1st Air Landing Brigade Report, Glider Nos 5 and 10 burned after landing. No 10 carried Col Jonah Jones, 1st Air Landing Brigade's Deputy Commander, and Staff and was piloted by S/Sgt H. N. 'Andy' Andrews and F/O Kyle USAF. *US Air Force Photo Collection (USAF Neg No 25289 AC), courtesy of National Air and Space Museum, Smithsonian Institution*

Below left Another Waco glider in July 1943. The occupants managed to unload this glider, despite the damage sustained to the cockpit section on landing. Later models had additional steel tubing on the cockpit floor, to which wooden skids were added. This gave far better protection to the Glider Pilots, many of whom suffered broken legs and ankles on the Sicily operation, when the gliders hit low walls and other obstructions. *US Air Force Photo Collection (USAF Neg No 26828 AC), courtesy of National Air and Space Museum, Smithsonian Institution*

other Brigade personnel. Soon after the party moved off rifle fire opened up and Rev Hourigan and two Signallers were not seen again. They had been captured, and the Padre was killed on 10 July when an enemy soldier panicked and threw a grenade into the room in which they were confined. The party then reached the Cassibile-Syracuse railway line, where they cut telephone wires.

Glider No 123, piloted by S/Sgt Chapman and Sgt Kelly, landed safely some 2 miles south of LZ 1 at 22.45 hrs, although it had hit a stone wall and two trees, which tore the wings off. This glider carried Lt Bill Budgen with No 2 Section of 1 Border's Recce Platoon including Cpl W. Evans, L/Cpl Otto and Pte William Hill, the Medical Orderly. The party had to tear down part of the wall and smash the front of the glider to get the handcart out. All the noise attracted enemy fire, but the group was able to move away.

They met up with Colonel Jones's group on the railway line at around 02.30 hrs as the RAF commenced the bombing of Syracuse. With the recce section leading, the group advanced towards Santa Teresa railway station roughly 3½ miles south of the bridge. Rifle fire opened up some 400 yards south of the station, but 'the advance continued to a culvert where, by the light of a 77 grenade, three Italians were seen and overcome. Near the station, the main Cassibile to Syracuse road was crossed and a thick barbed-wire fence found. It was decided that the position was too difficult to attack at night.' At 04.00 hrs the party took up defensive positions in a farm and laid up until first light, when the situation could be checked. At 07.00 hrs fire was heard from an artillery battery and a salvo of naval shells landed 100 yards from the farm. The group washed, shaved and breakfasted, and an hour later the position of the battery was approximately fixed; a recce patrol went out and located it and came under British artillery fire. This battery, consisting of five guns, was located to the south of the railway station.

S/Sgt Andrews described the emplacement: 'It was about 100 yards by 40 yards wide. Along the side were dug-outs between the guns interspersed with one or two large marquees that served as sleeping quarters. On the side nearest us was a sand-bagged emplacement, which covered the approach we were taking with a heavy ack-ack machine-gun. The approach was selected because it enabled us to get reasonably close before we broke cover; the last 40 yards were in the open. In front on the sea-side of the emplacement was a large field of tall tinder-dry grass. It would burn well. The emplacement was surrounded by barbed wire with sand-bagged rifle positions at intervals.'

The group was divided as follows: two Bren groups consisting of Capt Clark, a Bren gunner, Pte William Hill, the Medical Orderly, and Pte Cox; a Sten party of Lt Budgen with two British and one American glider pilots; and smoke grenadiers Col Jones and Major Tomkins, with four riflemen of the Recce Platoon forming the second wave. The plan of attack was to fire the grass west of the enemy position and create smoke. The Bren group would then open rapid fire from the south-west, as the assault party threw grenades over the knife-rest on the battery perimeter.

At about 11.15 hrs, as the group advanced, an enemy MG was spotted and one rifleman detailed to neutralise it. The last 100 yards to the position were covered at the double and grenades were thrown, while the Bren group opened rapid fire. The tents and camouflage nets within the position were grenaded; rifle fire from a dug-out was also stopped by grenades. The occupants from this and other trenches surrendered. Six Italians were killed, six wounded and 40 taken prisoner, but the attacking force suffered no casualties.

As this happened, a Company of 2 Northamptons from 17th Infantry Brigade appeared, having been detailed to destroy the battery. A Glider Pilot (two according to Sgt Andrews) being interrogated by the Italians was found in one of the dug-outs; he had been injured in the legs by grenade fragments and was treated by L/Cpl Bill Hill, who also attended to the Italian wounded. Anything that could be destroyed was burned or disabled. The guns had their clinometers removed, and later the ammunition left near them was blown up. At 14.00 hrs the group returned to the main road, where they linked up with men of 2 South Staffords, formed two platoons, marched north and eventually took up a defensive position on the southern edge of Ponte Grande at about 21.00 hrs, prior to moving into Syracuse the following day. Col Jones was later awarded the DSO for this action and Lt Budgen the MC (see Appendix 3).

As Sgt J. Davidson and his group from A Company approached Sicily in Glider No 77, a considerable amount of flak greeted them and their tug immediately banked and headed out to sea. The Glider Pilot made a perfect landing on the water and all the men scrambled out through a hole cut in the top of the fuselage by Cpl Edgar. Sgt Davidson organised his nine swimmers to take care of the five non-swimmers and they headed for the land. Together with Pte Elliott, he made it to the shore, but became separated from the rest. They soon found that they were within yards of an Italian position and had no choice but to surrender, confident that they would be freed the following day. The Italians looked after them well, although they took Davidson's 48-hour rations, water-bottle and compass; he managed to retain his map despite three further searches.

Eventually most of the glider party and other troops joined them. From their group only Pte Eagles lost his life. He was thought to have been drowned, but as he is buried in Syracuse Cemetery it is possible that he made it to shore; the other survivors included L/Cpl Stevens, Pte Birdsell, who had met up with some Staffords and fought with them, Pte Lane and Pte Marriott. They were escorted as PoWs along the main road to Syracuse later on the morning of the 10th and came under accurate Allied mortar fire. Davidson reported that 'we attempted to help the venture by a little fifth column work and started to tell the Italians that the English were all round the island and that they were completely surrounded. This seemed to affect them greatly, and eventually the majority came and surrendered to us; the remainder started waving white flags.' (3600318 Sgt J. Davidson, A Company 1 Border). The prisoners were taken into Syracuse and Davidson's group headed back to the bridge, where they met Col Jones and others from the 1st Battalion.

Glider No 68, piloted by Sgt Ellice and Sgt Bates and carrying 20 Platoon of D Company, crashed within swimming distance of the shore. Those who made it were taken prisoner and marched to a farmhouse near the bridge, where they were later released by a patrol from 2 RSF. Another glider, No 82 carrying D Company's 2i/c Capt Ernie Gaff, seven men and two handcarts, and piloted by Sgt Stan Peacock and Sgt George Cushing, crashed in Syracuse Harbour. Eventually the party, including one non-swimmer, made the shore, where the latter was killed. With Italian troops everywhere, the group hid in a cave until making contact with a party from the SAS; they then moved off into Syracuse.

A group from 16 Platoon of C Company landed in the sea on board Glider No 75 piloted by Sgt Mansfield and Sgt McLeod. After recovering some material from the glider, the group decided to swim for shore, which was estimated by the pilots to be 2½ miles away. Sgt V. McSherry organised the men in groups of threes; the two non-swimmers were accompanied by two men. After swimming for perhaps 4 hours and now some 500 yards from the shore, a searchlight beam picked them out, followed by MG fire. Several men were wounded, and on reaching the shore were taken prisoner and held in a fortified farmhouse until released by a patrol of the Royal Scots the following day.

Sgt McSherry and another man drifted further along the coast and came ashore near a coastal battery guarded by sentries and two LMG posts. They attacked this with their only weapons, two 77 grenades and two 36 grenades. After they threw the former the Italians opened fire; they then hid to see if the remainder of the gun crew would emerge. Later a group of five Italians approached their position, so they threw the two 36 grenades and hid until around 07.00 hrs on 10 July. They then made their way inland to contact anyone from the Battalion, and late in the day found Major Haddon.

As Glider No 88 approached the coast it came under AA fire. The tug pilot took evasive action and released the Waco about 2 miles offshore. It landed some 200 yards inland near Cape Murro di Porco, hitting telephone wires before crashing into a wall. Both pilots, Sgt Richard Martin and Sgt Ken Evans, suffered broken legs; Sgt Martin was seriously hurt and later lost his sight. The group from 11 Platoon B Company included the Platoon Sergeant, Sgt F. Terry, ten men, Cpl J. Waring, the Battalion Signal Corporal, and a handcart. Cpl Coates, and Ptes Lathan, Davison, Jones and Miller received serious injuries in the crash, and the remainder suffered cuts, bruises and shock.

Those capable eventually moved off to locate the LZ, leaving one man to look after the casualties. The group met up with a mortar detachment of the South Staffords and joined forces, but their patrols failed to contact anyone else. They returned to the glider and made the casualties as comfortable as possible, although it was impossible to remove them from the wreckage of the glider for fear of worsening their injuries; the handcart and contents could not be retrieved for the same reason.

At first light they saw another glider 150 yards away, almost certainly No 125A piloted by Lt W. Carn MC and Sgt David Richards, with part of 1 Border's Mortar Platoon on board, which included Lt George Coulthard and Cpl Allen, who was injured together with another Private. The glider had hit a low wall on landing, the force of which broke Richards's ankles, and Lt Carn suffered broken legs. He later recalled that 'Sgt Richards and I had to cut ourselves out because of the mess and damage to the front of the glider. I managed to crawl into a large thorn bush to get some cover, where I lay all night and had a good view of the Wellington bombers bombing Syracuse at about 2 am. They dropped their chandelier flares first of all, then came in quite low on their bombing runs.'

Enemy troops were seen approaching down the beach and were fired on, at which point they retired to a blockhouse on the beach. L/Cpl Morgan and Cpl Waring reconnoitred it for a possible attack, but there was no cover and they returned. Then another blockhouse about 1,000 yards down the beach to the left opened up. The Italians were contained by rifle and LMG fire as a Sergeant and four men from the South Staffords joined the group with their 3-inch mortar and set it up in a house nearby. As they began to mortar the two enemy

positions, further enemy fire came from the right and rear. Fired on from several sides, with little cover and unable to return fire effectively, a 77 smoke grenade was thrown to obscure the position and allow the group to move towards the house and better cover.

Unfortunately the grenade ignited the stubble in the field to their front, where Lt Carn was lying. Cpl John 'Pongo' Waring, one of the Battalion Signallers, went out under fire and brought Lt Carn into the

Right A general view of LZ 2 in July 1993, where the gliders of 1 Border were to land. *BRM*

Below One of the 2 South Staffords gliders, chalk No 29, in a tomato field in July 1943. *US Air Force Photo Collection (USAF Neg No C 26827 AC), courtesy of National Air and Space Museum, Smithsonian Institution*

house. He then returned for Sgt Richards before the glider, containing the mortar ammunition, caught fire. According to Lt Carn, 'Waring brought in seven Air Landing troops that morning, all wounded or injured, as well as three Italian prisoners, a Bren gun and ammunition. . . I did not know that he had several broken ribs and his lung was damaged from the glider crash. He deserved more than the MM that he was awarded'. (See Appendix 3)

Another little group comprising two Glider Pilots, a Medical Orderly and five Royal Engineers joined them. The Orderly proceeded to Sgt Terry's glider to deal with the injured, who were still inside. As shots were hitting the glider he placed a white flag on top of it and turned it into an aid post. Three German FW 190s strafed the position, but later the casualties were recovered from the glider and moved to the house.

At about 17.00 hrs on 10 July, due to the fire of the South Staffords mortar, the enemy fire had practically ceased, and later the Italians surrendered. Despite all the enemy fire the group had suffered no further casualties since landing. Ptes Davison and Smith from B Company 1 Border, who had swum ashore, joined them. The injured, wounded and Italian PoWs were left under the command of Lt Carn, with Ptes Miller, Jones, Bennet and Davison, who were all walking-wounded, to guard them. The remainder formed three sections and headed off towards the bridge; one was composed of the South Staffords with their Sergeant, another of Sgt Terry with men from 1 Border, and the third of Sappers and Glider Pilots with L/Cpl Morgan. They later contacted men of the Battalion and came under the command of Lt Joe Tate of D Company.

Lt Ted Newport landed safely in his glider, No 109, some 4 miles from the LZ, hitting a farm wall. His fears about carrying the gun and jeep separately were proved well-founded. In fact, only one other gun made landfall, and only one of the four towing jeeps with the ammunition supply. The group managed to get the gun into action, but with only a limited

supply of ammunition its effect was limited, and after man-handling it for over half a mile, they decided to spike and conceal it. After several encounters with the enemy, Newport's small group managed to get a lift to Syracuse late that day. They crossed the Ponte Grande bridge, the damage and enemy dead evidence of the intense fighting.

Small groups from 1 Border and 2 South Staffords eventually found their way inland. Alan Fisher, a Private in 21 Platoon of D Company commanded by Lt Sainty, had a dry landing about 5 miles west of LZ 3. With about 11 others he headed off to the objective, collecting three other injured bodies on the way. After covering about 5 miles the group met stiff opposition at dawn from an Italian platoon. With the little group's Bren gun out of action and most of the members wounded, Pte Fisher surrendered his party, but they were released later in the day.

Pte Andrew Hartshorn of 10 Platoon A Company,

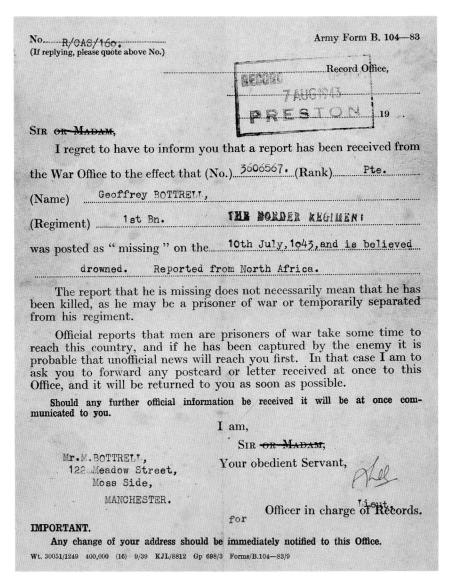

No. ... R/CAS/160.
(If replying, please quote above No.)

Army Form B. 104—83

.... Record Office,

RECORD
7 AUG 1943
PRESTON ... 19 ..

Sir or Madam,

I regret to have to inform you that a report has been received from the War Office to the effect that (No.) 3606567. (Rank) Pte.

(Name) Geoffrey BOTTRELL,

(Regiment) 1st Bn. THE BORDER REGIMENT

was posted as "missing" on the 10th July, 1943, and is believed

drowned. Reported from North Africa.

The report that he is missing does not necessarily mean that he has been killed, as he may be a prisoner of war or temporarily separated from his regiment.

Official reports that men are prisoners of war take some time to reach this country, and if he has been captured by the enemy it is probable that unofficial news will reach you first. In that case I am to ask you to forward any postcard or letter received at once to this Office, and it will be returned to you as soon as possible.

Should any further official information be received it will be at once communicated to you.

I am,

Sir or Madam,

Mr. M. BOTTRELL,
122 Meadow Street,
Moss Side,
MANCHESTER.

Your obedient Servant,

for　　Lieut.
Officer in charge of Records.

IMPORTANT.
Any change of your address should be immediately notified to this Office.

Wt. 30051/1249　400,000　(16)　9/39　KJL/8812　Gp 698/3　Forms/B.104—83/9

in Glider No 107, made dry land a considerable distance from the LZ. Seven men in all were fit enough to proceed, but they did not meet any Allied troops until 16.00 hrs on 11 July, when they met a party from the SAS. Pte Bill Campbell, with another section of the Recce Platoon, landed near two Italian barracks and were in action immediately. Two haystacks near their position were set alight and the group were forced to surrender, but managed to escape and rejoin the battle the following day.

Jimmy McDowell recalls that their glider, probably No 126 piloted by S/Sgt Chandler and S/Sgt Torrance, crashed into a wall of an olive grove on landing; both glider pilots suffered leg injuries in the crash. However, his party, which included Ptes Logan, Jacob and Trevor Dawson of Appleby, all from the Mortar Platoon, moved off with their handcart (one of the collapsible examples that apparently lived up to its name). Moving up a road the group encountered a number of Italians who mistook the party for Germans; both groups shot off in opposite directions, leaving the handcart in the middle of the road. McDowell then reconnoitred ahead alone and found a large group of Italian soldiers; he then found himself illuminated by a flare between this group and three pill-boxes.

'I was subsequently taken prisoner and marched off under escort by two Italians, one of whom carried my rifle. A little while later I saw two red berets appear above a wall, both apparently of the Staffords. One ordered me to bring my prisoners forward whereupon I told him to have another look and see who was carrying the rifle. I was told to break for it and jump over a wall, which I did and received a bullet in the chest as the Italians guards were disposed of.'

One of the Staffords was a Capt Foote, who was awarded an MC for various actions during the operations on Sicily. Jim was patched up by an RAMC Orderly and exchanged his No 4 rifle for Capt Foote's .38-inch revolver. He was taken down to the beach and evacuated by hospital ship to No 2 General Hospital at Tripoli, then to a convalescent home at Homs before rejoining the Battalion at Msaken.

In dribs and drabs individuals and groups from the Battalion made their way into Syracuse. Following the capture of the city late on 10 July by Brigadier Tarleton's Brigade, the remnants of 2 South Staffords and 1 Border moved in on 11 July, where Major-General Hopkinson took the salute. They then took up defensive positions, 1 Border being in the St Lucia area north of the railway line to Catania. By 12 July Battalion strength stood at 15 officers and 199 ORs. They worked as salvage and burial parties throughout the day on the landing areas and equipped themselves with any available Allied and enemy clothing and weapons. The Battalion was ordered to embark the following day.

Naturally, as all the tow-planes returned successfully to North Africa those left behind there were given optimistic reports of the out-

News of events on Sicily unfolds between August and October 1943 for the father of Pte G. Bottrell, killed in action during the Sicily operation. *BRM*

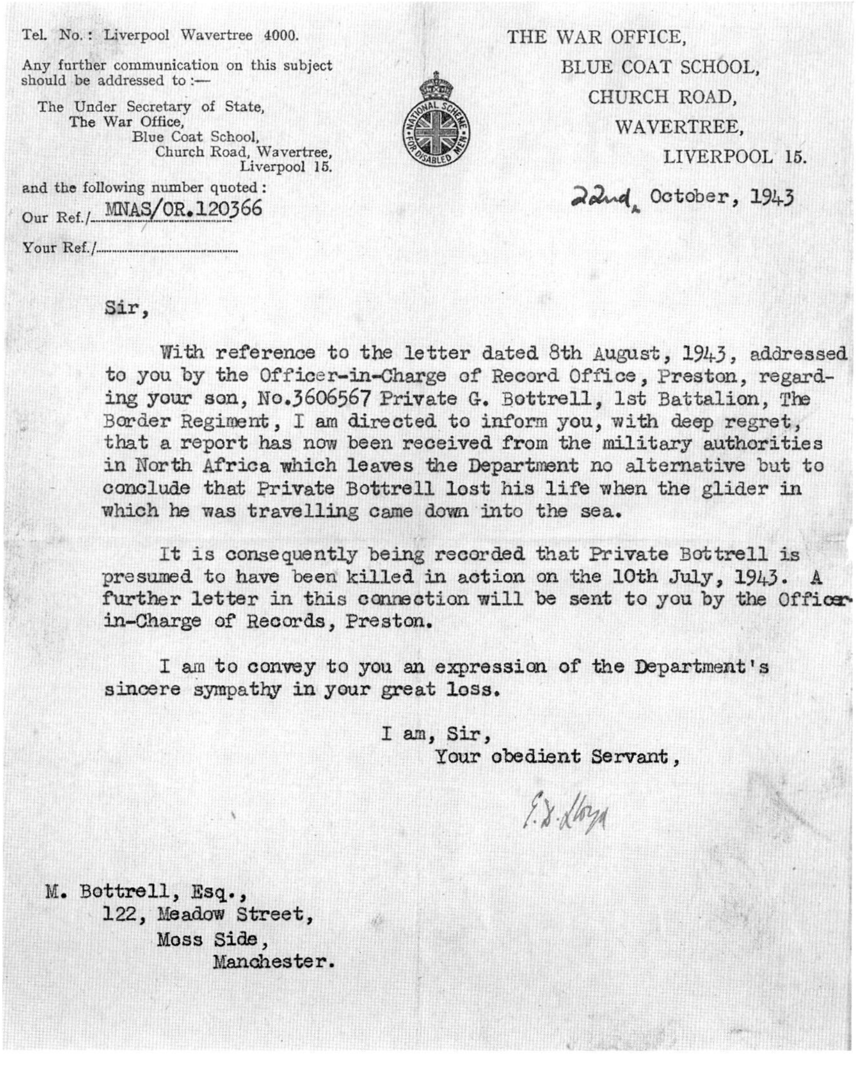

Tel. No.: Liverpool Wavertree 4000.

Any further communication on this subject should be addressed to:—

The Under Secretary of State,
  The War Office,
    Blue Coat School,
      Church Road, Wavertree,
        Liverpool 15.

and the following number quoted:

Our Ref./ MNAS/OR.120366

Your Ref./.................

THE WAR OFFICE,
BLUE COAT SCHOOL,
CHURCH ROAD,
WAVERTREE,
LIVERPOOL 15.

22nd October, 1943

Sir,

    With reference to the letter dated 8th August, 1943, addressed to you by the Officer-in-Charge of Record Office, Preston, regarding your son, No.3606567 Private G. Bottrell, 1st Battalion, The Border Regiment, I am directed to inform you, with deep regret, that a report has now been received from the military authorities in North Africa which leaves the Department no alternative but to conclude that Private Bottrell lost his life when the glider in which he was travelling came down into the sea.

    It is consequently being recorded that Private Bottrell is presumed to have been killed in action on the 10th July, 1943. A further letter in this connection will be sent to you by the Officer-in-Charge of Records, Preston.

    I am to convey to you an expression of the Department's sincere sympathy in your great loss.

        I am, Sir,
        Your obedient Servant,

M. Bottrell, Esq.,
  122, Meadow Street,
    Moss Side,
      Manchester.

come of the operation, and this optimism was reflected in the initial newspaper reports of the Sicily landings. However, of the 136 Wacos that took off, 11 pulled off, returned, or did not cross the North African Coast, 75 landed in the sea, and only 50 landed on Sicily. Of these 50, only two landed inside LZ 1 and one in LZ 2. Of the eight Horsas, three landed in the sea and five on land; of the latter, two landed on LZ 3 by the bridge and one was lost immediately.

Of the 72 Waco gliders that carried men of 1 Border, one landed on Malta, seven in North Africa, 44 in the sea and only 20 on Sicily; of the latter, five landed in Sicily within 5 miles and 15 within 8 miles of their correct LZs. The Battalion officially began Operation 'Ladbroke' with 43 officers and 753 ORs. Four officers and 84 ORs either returned to base or failed to take off; 28 officers and 478 ORs landed in the sea; and only 11 officers and 191 ORs actually landed in Sicily. Of those who landed in the sea, 14 officers and 91 ORs made it to shore. The total for killed, wounded, injured and missing was nine officers and 180 ORs, of which two officers, Major Fineron and Lt Wyatt, and 108 ORs lost their lives; of these 89 were lost at sea (see Appendices 1 and 4).

However, the official report concludes that. . . 'Glider loads were too widely dispersed to reach any pre-arranged RVs. Enemy posts and batteries in the area were numerous, and many small parties of the Bn, 5-10 strong, did a very useful and necessary job of work in neutralising or destroying these. Confusion and dismay, leading ultimately to surrender, was spread amongst the Italian troops. The Recce Platoon played a part in the capture of a battery and a glider load of D Company assisted in the defence of Ponte Grande against Italian counter-attacks.'

Casualties for the Air Landing Brigade and the Glider Pilot Regiment were given as 605 officers and men, of which over 300 were drowned. This was a terrible blow to the Air Landing Brigade and the Glider Pilot Regiment as a whole, as all had trained long and hard for their operational role. Most did not even get the opportunity to fight. For 1 Border it meant the loss of many who had been with the unit for a long time, were highly trained and part of a very strong Regimental Family.

Chapter 6

Italian Interlude

The remnants of the Air Landing Brigade, some 800 strong, moved down to Syracuse Harbour on the afternoon of 13 July, where at 20.30 hrs they embarked in four landing-craft and sailed for Sousse. Fifteen officers and 214 ORs of the Battalion arrived at around 21.00 hrs on the evening of 14 July and returned to camp that night, where they met those who had been forced to land back in Africa and others who had returned from Sicily by other means. Three days later Major Haddon, the 2i/c, succeeded Lt Col Britten as Commanding Officer. According to Tommy Haddon, Britten had made such a fuss about having to leave equipment behind when they were evacuated by landing-craft from Sicily that he was relieved of his command and moved to a Staff appointment in Algiers.

The immediate task was to recover and rebuild the Battalion to sufficient operational strength. The Battalion was re-organised on the basis of four rifle companies, brought up to strength by men from R and H Companies, plus HQ and S Companies. The first training instruction, issued on 16 July, was quick to reflect lessons learned on the recent operation, and included training with enemy weapons, attacking of strong-points and obstacles by platoons and sections, and, perhaps most significant in the light of the previous week's tragedy, the instruction by CSMI Connett that 'all ranks will be taught to swim'.

Officers and men returned to Sousse from ports along the length of the North African coast from Gibraltar to Egypt; seven officers and 73 ORs arrived from Malta on 16 July, five officers and 134 ORs from Algiers on the 21st, and nine ORs from Tripoli on the 29th. The Adjutant, Capt Colin Douglas, who had taken over from Capt Stafford, and the IO, Lt Ronald Hope-Jones, spent long hours until the end of the month trying to list and assess the casualties. Major

John Gibbon, who returned from Algiers, recalled that he had organised as many senior surviving representatives from the gliders as possible to write reports, which were submitted by him when the *Reina del Pacifico* returned them to North Africa.

Two entries in Hope-Jones's diary sum up the work at this time. On 26 July he wrote: 'By 10.00 I really did feel that my job was pretty well complete - I cleared everything up, preparing to start on grave locations. Then Edward Balmer came in and asked for a return of numbers who proceeded on operation, took off, landed in Africa, landed elsewhere than in Africa or Sicily, reached Sicily, killed in crash, wounded in crash, killed in action, drowned, missing believed drowned, missing on land, missing at sea, wounded at sea and killed at sea. There may have been other categories that I've forgotten. We were also asked to provide full stories of 20 gliders. . . Colin and I had a rather late supper. . .' (For the full analysis see Appendix 4.)

Then, on 27 July: 'I spent an utterly gloomy morning packing up Mein's kit [Pte Leonard Mein from the Intelligence Section], and wondering what on earth to write to his wife. There's no man in the Battalion whom I'd be sorrier to lose, both for his own and his wife's sake, because though he's almost as bad a soldier as you could possibly imagine, he really is devoted to his home and lives for his return. Then in the evening of course he turned up, along with more of 69 and 99 gliders. He'd kicked his way out of his glider after drinking pints of sea, hung on to the glider pilot's rubber cushion, transferred on to a submerged wing with seven others and stayed there for $8^{1}/_{2}$ hours until picked up by a Greek destroyer. A non-swimmer, but he has too much to lose to get himself drowned or anything like that.'

In August the 1st Airborne Division were placed in

readiness for a seaborne landing in Italy in anticipation of the Italians capitulating, which they did on 9 September. The Battalion was still short of equipment, exemplified by the issue to all ranks of the 'Battle-Jerkin', an item designed for and normally used by the Commandos and other special forces. They would also have to rely on local resources and captured enemy equipment and transport on landing. On 11 September the Battalion embarked at Bizerta for Taranto on two cruisers; HMS *Sirius* carried 25 officers and 438 ORs under the command of Lt Col Haddon; and HMS *Dido* carried 11 officers and 204 ORs under Major Gibbon. One of the sights that many recalled was passing the Italian Fleet sailing to Egypt to surrender as part of the Armistice agreement. The landing at Taranto was marred by the tragic sinking of HMS *Abdiel*, which hit a mine in the harbour with the loss of 129 officers and men of the 6th Battalion Parachute Regiment and 2nd Air-Landing Anti-Tank Battery.

The Division was ordered to pursue the retreating German forces up the Adriatic coast. 1 Border took up positions astride the Taranto-Bari road - the enemy were thought to hold Bari on the Adriatic coast. The road had previously been held by 156 Battalion The Parachute Regiment of 4th Parachute Brigade, who had moved forward. Ronald Hope-Jones recalled that Tommy Haddon some years later maintained that he nearly caused a diplomatic incident 'on our arrival by obeying Brig Hicks's instruction to me to requisition the best car (a Fiat) in the town for him. He was delighted with what I brought back, but only for a few hours, as the Bishop of Taranto stormed in livid with rage and demanded his car back.'

Sadly, on 12 September Major-General Hopkinson, CO of the 1st Airborne Division, was killed near Taranto; he was succeeded by Major-General E. E. Downs. Drummer John Pulford of the 1st Battalion played the 'Last Post' and 'Reveille' at Hopkinson's funeral on the following day, for which he received the thanks of his Divisional Commander and the 8th Army's Commander General B. L. Montgomery, who wrote personally to Lt Colonel Haddon.

Patrols were regularly sent out but reported little contact with the retreating German forces, then on the 18th 1 Border moved to a new location between S Basilio Mottola and Gioja Del Colle. Hope-Jones recorded that the first contact with the enemy was made by a patrol led by Lt Pat Baillie on the 19th. This was followed by a move on 23 September further north by road and rail to Gioja and then via Bari, Trani, Andria and Canosa to just south of Cerignola on 25 September, where 4th Armoured Brigade were harassing the retreating enemy.

SAS patrols reported that Cerignola was free of Germans, who were retreating north towards Foggia; further patrols failed to make contact. The mood of the Italians was generally welcoming throughout. On the 27th the Battalion entered Foggia; this was an important rail junction and the location of several large airfields, which were of great strategic importance to the Allied advance towards Naples. Lt Col Tommy Haddon and Lt Ronald Hope-Jones were the first to enter the town, guided by a local on a motor-bike wearing a bowler hat!

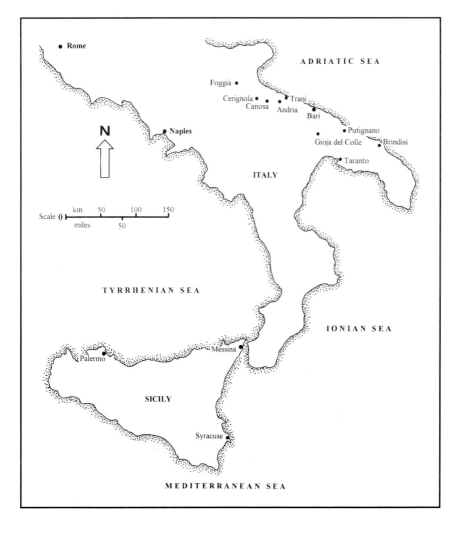

Locations of the 1st Battalion in Italy, September-November 1943.

The town was largely deserted, ruined and in a filthy state due to Allied bombing, a sight made worse by the pouring rain. Lt Joe Hardy had taken a small detachment to the north-west side of the town. When a jeep-like vehicle with five soldiers on board approached, a little old Italian lady yelled 'Tedesci, Tedesci' at him and pulled him off the road. As the vehicle passed he saw that there were Germans in it and radioed back to HQ warning them of this. This was probably one of two vehicles shot up by Cpl Thirlwell and the Intelligence Section; two officers were taken PoW and the other three escaped. After establishing defensive positions in the area, the Battalion, less C Company, moved by road to Andria on 1 October and then on foot and by MT to Putignano, where they arrived late on the 7th. C Company later joined from Foggia, while A and B Companies left for Taranto on the 15th for internal security duties. By the 23rd C and D Companies were in Taranto, B at Brindisi and A at Putignano. The 78th Division relieved the Airborne Division and the Battalion enjoyed a fairly comfortable existence until their return to North Africa.

Captain Graham Jones RAMC, who had succeeded Capt Godfrey Black as MO at the end of July, recalled that they were expected to help the local populace as well as deal with the Battalion's medical needs. In Italy 'our facilities had been enhanced by a gift from Major John Gibbon of a crystal ball on a black velvet cushion "to help your diagnosis, doctor", and Sergeant Thompson was speaking fluent Italian, making it a great delight to hear him taking the medical history from a local farmer. "Come-o in-o. What-o is your trouble-o? How long-o have you had it-o?" (Capt Graham Jones, MO 1 Border July 1943-September 1944)

On 17 November the Battalion embarked from Taranto for North Africa, disembarking at Philippeville on 21 November, where they met the rear party that had been left at Sousse. The Battalion waited in a transit camp until they boarded the *Duchess of Bedford* on 27 November, which sailed late on the evening of the following day as the 1st Airborne Division left for home. The ship was known

Capt Graham Jones RAMC at Putignano, Italy, October 1943. Having served as a Section Commander with 181 Field Ambulance and taken part in the Sicily landings, he joined the Battalion in late July 1943 as MO in succession to Capt Godfrey Black, who moved to 181. With him as Battalion Medical Sergeant came Sgt Thompson RAMC; he succeeded Sgt Maurice Marsh, who had been drowned on 9-10 July. Capt Graham Jones was taken prisoner at Arnhem on 26 September 1944.

Left Two aerogramme letters sent home by Pte John Pulford of HQ Company and Pte Wilf Oldham of 12 Platoon B Company. Pulford's and almost certainly Wilf Oldham's were illustrated by Pte Leonard Mein of the Battalion's Intelligence section, who drew cartoons for members of the Battalion in exchange for a couple of cigarettes. *BRM*

Below left Colin Douglas joined the Battalion in 1942 and served as an MMG Platoon Commander until July 1943, when he was appointed Adjutant in succession to Tony Stafford, who had been wounded in the Sicily landings. He served the Battalion and Lt Col Tommy Haddon very well. Being an actor by profession, he quickly learned to imitate his CO in actions and on paper, so much so that Tommy Haddon was never sure whether it was him or Colin that had drafted a particular letter. He continued as Adjutant to Lt Col Charles Breese.

Colin enjoyed a long career as a character actor, but is perhaps best remembered for his patriarchal role in *A Family at War*, the Granada TV saga of the wartime travails of a Liverpool family. He died in December 1991, aged 79. *BRM/Joe Hardy*

as the 'Drunken Duchess' because of her inclination to roll. During the voyage home she developed a steering problem and was unable to alter course when the ships in the convoy started to zigzag as part of their anti-submarine precautions. Capt Graham Jones recalled that she 'had specially strengthened bows to cope with the ice encountered on the winter runs to Canada. This was to prove of some importance when the Adjutant tempted fate. He and I shared a cabin, and as Colin Douglas the actor he would entertain me from time to time with excerpts from parts he had played, warning me that anything was acceptable except *Macbeth*, which actors considered brought bad luck. A few days out from Philippeville, having returned to our cabin after lunch, he could not resist giving an impassioned speech from the dreaded play, and after about a dozen lines there was an almighty bang as the whole ship shuddered and began to slow down.'

The *Monarch of Bermuda* had crossed her bows from the port side and was rammed by the *Duchess of Bedford* amidships just below the bridge. Port-holes were stoved in and some lifeboats, swung out according to practice, were shattered. The *Monarch* had to put into Gibraltar for repairs. Pte Sandy Masterton of S Company recalled that for many of the men below decks it was a terrifying experience, as the watertight doors were closed at the time of impact. Fortunately, the *Duchess* was able to continue with a solitary destroyer escort, the problem was corrected and eventually she caught up with the convoy, arriving at Liverpool at 15.00 hrs on 9 December 1943.

Chapter 7

Home and the Long Wait

The Battalion disembarked the following day and proceeded on two trains to Woodhall Spa in Lincolnshire, arriving in the early hours of 11 December. They were warmly welcomed by the advance party of 6th Airborne Division, who had been stationed in the area, and 7th Battalion The King's Own Scottish Borderers, who were to bring the 1st Air-Landing Brigade up to strength. Most members of the Battalion were able to get away on a fortnight's leave before Christmas. Thirty ORs from the Divisional rear party arrived home on Christmas Eve, followed on 5 January 1944 by Capt Howard Wilkie, three officers and 62 ORs of the Battalion rear party.

The Battalion settled down in its new home. All Companies were located in and around Woodhall Spa, except B Company, who were billeted nearby in the small village of Bardney. On 21 January they were visited by Major-General Roy Urquhart DSO, who had succeeded Major-General Downs as GOC of 1st Airborne Division, followed two days later by the Colonel of The Regiment, Brigadier Hyde Harrison DSO. Three former AA officers were posted to the Battalion on 28 January after completing a conversion course, and several small drafts of men arrived during February. The Battalion re-organised on similar lines, but S Company now comprised two Mortar Platoons, each with six mortars, two Platoons of four 6-pounder anti-tank guns and two of four Vickers MMGs. At the end of February the Mortar Platoons went to Hardwick Hall in Derbyshire for a Divisional mortar concentration.

The C-in-C, Field Marshal Montgomery, visited the Battalion on 14 March, followed two days later by HM King George VI. At the beginning of April the Battalion departed for Bulford, where they would be under canvas for three weeks training, which began with the airborne exercise 'Dreme'. Gliders were loaded at Tarrant Rushton and Harwell airfields and took off in the early evening of 4 April. All flew successfully apart from the Horsa carrying 12 Platoon of B Company under Lt Arthur Royall, which crash-landed near Steyning without any casualties. On the 10th and 11th the MMG and Anti-Tank Platoons went on shoots at Larkhill and Netheravon. The final

Above right Officers of the 1st Battalion at Woodhall Spa on 23 January 1944, during a visit by the Colonel of the Regiment.
Front row, left to right: Major John Gibbon, Major Tom Armstrong, Major Stuart Cousens (2i/c), Brigadier-General Hyde Harrison DSO, the Colonel of the Regiment, Lt Colonel Tommy Haddon (CO), Capt Colin Douglas (Adjutant), Major Dennis Morrissey, Major Dickie Stewart MC.
Middle row: Capt Barnes (QM), Major Jock Neill, Capt Bill Hodgson, Capt Gordon Welch MC, Lt Joe Hardy (RSO), Lt Law, Lt Cox, Lt Pat Baillie, Capt Barry Ingram, Capt Graham-Jones RAMC MO, Capt Ronald Hope-Jones (IO), Capt Bob Reese.
Back row: Capt Ingram Cleasby, Lt Ted Newport, Lt Coulthard, Padre John Rowell, Major T. E. Montgomery, Lt Mike Holman, Lt Joe Tate, Lt Bob Crittenden. *BRM*

Right 23 Mortar Platoon (handcarts) at Chesterfield in February 1944.
Back row, left to right: Pte A. Hughes, Pte Green, Cpl Bates (later PoW), Pte Joe Coupe, Pte K. Egerton, Pte J. Fosbrooke, Pte Dixon, L/Cpl Ronnie Lord, Cpl McInnes, Pte J. Middlemiss, Pte Fred Seed (KiA 21.9.44), Pte J. Dunne, Pte Turner, Pte Arthur Smart (KiA 24.9.44).
Centre row: Pte Edward Mason (PoW), Pte M. Chalet, Pte McLaughlin, Pte Robert Price, Pte John Hart, Pte Syd Cringle (PoW), Pte Ernie Westerman, Pte Jack Hardwick, Pte F. Mcgarr, Pte Denton, Pte Ron Tierney, Pte Searson, Pte Latimer, Pte Wilson, Pte Robert Ellery (KiA 21.9.44).
Front row: Pte Ramshaw, Cpl Jim McDowell, Cpl Eric Tebay, Pte Joe Hutchinson, Pte Dennis Cooper (PoW), Pte Norman Knight, Lt Mike Holman, Sgt Fred Price (KiA 22.9.44), Pte Johnny Gordon, Pte Quinn, Pte Oakley. *BRM/Bill Homer and Jack Hardwick*

days at Bulford were taken up with another Glider exercise, 'Mush', between 20 and 22 April.

Everyone returned to Woodhall Spa on 23 April, and the following day three Canadian officers, Lts Comper, Colbert and Crabbe, joined the Battalion as volunteers under the 'Canloan' scheme; in 1944 the Canadian forces had a surplus of junior officers, many of whom volunteered for service with British units. Crabbe was tragically killed in a PIAT accident on 4 June. Several more Canadians were to join the Battalion in July, and four, Lts Aasen, Boville, Comper and Wellbelove, would serve at Arnhem. Yet another exercise involving comprehensive field firing took place in North Yorkshire in early May.

On 7 June, D-Day plus one, the Battalion moved to Bulford. While 6th Airborne Division had been committed to operations in

Top Men from the Mortar Platoons in the Derbyshire hills in March 1944. From the left: Joe Quinn, Ronnie Lord, Dixon, unknown, Ron Tierney, Norman Knight, J. Hart, Joe Ramshaw. *BRM/Bill Homer*

Centre Field Marshal Montgomery inspects men of the Battalion during a visit to the 1st Airborne Division at Woodhall Spa, Lincolnshire, on 14 March 1944. He is accompanied by the Commanding Officer, Lt Col Tommy Haddon, and behind him is Major-General Roy Urquhart DSO, the Divisional Commander. *IWM H36653*

Bottom HM King George VI inspects the rations issued to Airborne Troops on a visit to the 1st Airborne Division at on 16 March 1944. On the King's right is Lt Col Haddon and to his left General Frederick 'Boy' Browning DSO, GOC Airborne Forces, and Brigadier Pip Hicks, commanding the 1st Air-Landing Brigade. Tommy Haddon later wrote that during the King's visit to the Battalion he ventured to describe what HM was to see with the display and was afterwards told in no uncertain terms by Browning that he should speak to His Majesty only when spoken to! *IWM H36728*

Normandy, it was the lot of the 1st Airborne Division to remain prepared for deployment at short notice for future operations. Thus the major theme for the Battalion was training, training and more training.

On 24 June two Bren carriers were added to Battalion transport for use by the Mortar Platoon; these would be carried in the large Hamilcar glider on operations. Lt Ron Jack, who was Battalion MTO at the time, recalled that the Battalion's transport establishment included 70 jeeps, both Willys and Ford, 12 Bedford QL

Right Lt Col Tommy Haddon bids farewell to HM King George VI watched by men of the Battalion on 16 March 1944. *BRM/Mrs C. Haddon*

Below Men, possibly of A Company, loading folding bicycles into a Horsa, probably for Exercise 'Mush', 20-22 April 1944. The officer standing at the right of the door may be the Adjutant, Capt Colin Douglas. *BRM/Tony Stafford*

Left Members of A Company practising the loading of a jeep into the front of a Horsa. The glider is named 'Gibbon's Goofers', presumably named after Major John Gibbon, the Company Commander. Exercise 'Mush', 20-22 April 1944. *Taylor Library*

Below left Soldiers from the 1st Air-Landing Brigade, possibly 1 Border, man-handling equipment from a Horsa during Exercise 'Mush'. *IWM H37688*

spares), Fitter Sergeant (maintenance), S Company Sergeant and 61 ORs; the latter included a Corporal Clerk who was responsible for the Platoon's paperwork. All aspects of training continued at Bulford throughout June, and the Battalion returned to Woodhall Spa on 5 July. Two more exercises, 'Bones' and 'Frolic', were held around Strensall and Scarborough in Yorkshire in July and early August, after which the Battalion returned to Lincolnshire. HQ, A, B, C and D Companies went to Well Camp near Alford, and S and R Companies to Woodhall Spa.

Following the break-out of the Allies from Normandy, the pace of operations was extremely swift. From the time of D-Day onwards many Airborne operations were planned, but did not progress beyond that stage. Those that resulted in active preparations by the Battalion will be mentioned in brief, since in the six weeks up to Operation 'Market' the Battalion was perpetually in readiness for active duty in Europe. On 11 August all personnel were recalled from leave and the Seaborne Tail prepared to move. It left for France the following day with the other Seaborne elements of 1st Air-Landing Brigade. The Tail consisted of Capt (QM) Harold Barnes, Capt C. H. Baker and Lt Bill Baldock, with 88 ORs, including C/Sgts West, Morrison and Cook, Armourer Sergeant F. Salmon REME, Sgt W. Lound ACC, Cpl (shoemaker) F. Cook RAOC and the MT Sergeant, Sgt Kelly (see Appendix 6 for full composition). Major W. E. Balmer from the Battalion was in overall command of the Air-Landing Brigade's Seaborne Element. Capt Baker had replaced Lt Ron Jack as MTO within the Seaborne Tail, when Ron was diagnosed as having acute appendicitis and sent to hospital.

3-tonners, eight Bedford 15 cwt trucks, 100 10 cwt trailers, 30 500cc Matchless motorcycles, around 20 125cc Enfield motorcycles, a few PU 8 cwt trucks, six Norton motorcycles with sidecars, and the CO's Humber staff-car.

Ron Jack recalled giving Tommy Haddon and Colin Douglas a demonstration of the Bren carrier, but their interest soon waned as Ron drove the carrier at speed descending Beacon Hill! The MT Platoon was a sizeable organisation that came under HQ Company. All drivers were part of the Platoon and were allocated with their vehicles to the Companies. Those attached to S Company were under an MT Sergeant but were considered to be more permanent in their attachment to this Company than to others. The Platoon consisted of one officer, a Transport Sergeant (discipline), Technical Sergeant (stores and

17 Platoon of C Company, photographed at Woodhall Spa on 3 June 1944.
Back row, left to right: Ptes Peacock, Norman, Lowery, Braithwaite, — , Scott, — , Moss.
Middle row: Ptes Darbyshire, Coulson, Lomax, Lee, — , Curtis, Thompson, Syrett.
Front row: Sgt Gardner-Roberts MM, L/Cpl Harrison, Cpl Simpson, Lt Crittenden, Major Neill, Cpl Sandham, L/Cpl Payne, Cpl Smith, Pte Smith. *BRM/Doug Payne*

The Tail travelled to London by road, entered the docks and left on 14 August on an LST for Normandy. Bill Baldock recalled that they docked at one of the Mulberry harbours and initially bivouacked in a field near Bayeux after coming ashore. They remained in this area for about ten days, where, under the guidance of Sgt Kelly and his MT fitters, they managed to get a number of German vehicles working, including a 10-ton diesel load-carrier. The group then travelled north via Amiens, Douai and Tournai to the outskirts of Brussels.

The remainder of the Battalion prepared to move to Harwell for Operation TRANSFIGURE, a landing by 1st Airborne Corps to close the Paris-Orleans gap, thus preventing the German retreat. The main body left on 15 August for the transit camp at Harwell, on 48 hours notice. On the 16th Lt Col Haddon attended Brigade HQ to be told that the operation was scheduled for 18 August. At 09.30 hrs glider loading

began at Welford and Aldermaston, then the same day the operation was postponed until the 19th. It was cancelled at 10.30 hrs the following day, and the gliders were unloaded on the 18th. Members of the Battalion then proceeded on a short 48 hours leave.

On 30 and 31 August the CO attended O Groups at Brigade HQ for Operation LINNET, which was to seize a secure base in the Tournai area, secure and hold a bridgehead over the River Escaut and control the main roads leading north-east from the front through Tournai-Lille-Courtrai to cut off the German retreat. Plans and flight plans were prepared, Company commanders were briefed on 1 September, and glider loads were adjusted. The final briefing for all ranks was held on the 2nd and the Battalion stood by for take-off as the Glider Pilots checked all the loads. However, events on the ground overtook the planners. LINNET II was prepared for execution no earlier than 3 September, with a target area in the Aachen-Maastricht region. This was cancelled on 5 September, the day that the Battalion moved from the rather soggy camp-site at Harwell into billets in the Cotswold village of Burford.

LINNET II was followed by Operation COMET, the seizure of the bridges over the Rhine from Arnhem to Wesel by the 1st Airborne Division and the Polish Parachute Brigade - 4th Parachute Brigade were to land at Grave, the Divisional HQ, 1 Air Landing and

Polish Brigades at Nijmegen, and the 1st Parachute Brigade at Arnhem. This was scheduled for 10 September, with take-off at 06.00 hrs. Lt Col Haddon went to HQ for briefing on 6 September. Briefing was completed during the next day and the Battalion stood by. A 24-hour postponement on 8 September was followed by another of 48 hours on the 9th, and the cancellation of the operation on the 10th.

The plan was rapidly revised to involve the whole of the 1st Allied Airborne Army as Operation No 16, MARKET; what had been planned for one Division now became the objective of three, 1st British, US 82nd and 101st Divisions, together with the Polish Parachute Brigade. The US 101st Airborne Division would secure the canal bridge at Son and the bridge at Grave over the River Maas, the 82nd Airborne the bridge at Nijmegen over the River Waal, and the British 1st Airborne Division with the Polish Parachute Brigade the road bridge over the Rhine at Arnhem. Each Division would form a defensive perimeter around each objective. They would be relieved by troops and armour of 30 Corps, who in Operation GARDEN would force a corridor along the main road from the Dutch-Belgian border to Arnhem.

The landings at Arnhem would take place 8 miles to the west, where the only suitable areas for massed glider landings were available. On D-Day the 1st Air-Landing Brigade, less half the 2 South Staffords, would land and secure the LZs and DZs for the 1st Parachute Brigade and other Divisional troops. 1st Parachute Brigade would advance into Arnhem, secure the road and, if possible, the rail bridge, and set up a defensive perimeter, whilst the Air-Landing Brigade would remain on the LZs and DZs to secure these areas for the landing of the 4th Parachute Brigade and the remaining glider forces on D+1. 4th Parachute Brigade would then proceed into Arnhem and take up positions in the perimeter. The Air-Landing Brigade would then move east into Oosterbeek on the western side of Arnhem to secure approaches from the west and north and protect the LZ for the gliders of the Polish Brigade due on D+2. The main body of the Polish Brigade would land on D+2 on the south bank of the Rhine and reinforce the perimeter over either the road or the rail bridge. It was estimated that the force would be relieved in two to four days. (For the full Battalion Operational Order for MARKET see Appendix 7.)

The Battalion's gliders were re-loaded at Broadwell and Blakehill Farm airfields, all ranks were briefed by the 16th and the camp sealed for security reasons that night. They had practised their loading and unloading until it was second nature, they knew their objectives and now everyone was ready to go.

Bandsmen of the Battalion at Woodhall Spa on 25 July 1944.

Front row, left to right: Pte A. Thorn, Cpl Titchener, Pte Geoff Powell (PoW Arnhem), Pte Jake Turner (PoW Arnhem), Pte Francis 'Buster' Yapp (KiA Arnhem).

Middle row: Pte Bill Fenwick (Medic 16 Platoon, wounded and PoW Arnhem), Pte Peter Tunstall, Pte Joss Elliott (from the Isle of Man and at 42 probably the oldest member of the Battalion to serve at Arnhem, where he was taken PoW), Pte 'Nobby' Donald Clark (PoW Arnhem), Pte John Dixon (PoW Arnhem).

Back row: Sgt Tom 'Pop' Ferguson (RAP), Cpl Bob Cox (RAP), Pte W. 'Marmy' Windross, L/Cpl Doug 'Jack' Payne (wounded and PoW Arnhem), Pte George Curtis (Medic 17 Platoon, wounded and PoW Arnhem), Pte Paddy Flynn (Medic 18 Platoon, PoW Arnhem). *BRM/Doug Payne*

Chapter 8

Operation MARKET

The story of 1 Border and its toughest test of the war over the ten days from 17 to 26 September is related here by Canon Alan Green, who commanded 20 Platoon of D Company.

Sunday 17 September

The early hours of the morning of Sunday 17 September saw a great deal of activity within the Battalion lines at Burford. After a good breakfast the Battalion embussed for the airfields at 07.00 hrs; the next meal would be in Holland. The main body of the Battalion was to fly from Broadwell Airfield in 44 Horsas (chalk Nos 161-184 and 243-262) piloted by G Squadron of the GPR and towed by Dakotas of 512

and 575 Squadrons RAF. C Company and 24 Mortar Platoon (jeeps) were to be lifted from Blakehill Farm in 12 Horsas (chalk Nos 196/8, 207/9 and 211-218) piloted by F Squadron GPR and towed by C-47s of 437 Squadron RCAF. The Battalion's two Bren carriers would be flown in one Hamilcar from Tarrant Rushton. 19 Platoon of D Company under Lt John Bainbridge was to fly out on the second lift the following day from Down Ampney, together with five glider loads of the Transport Platoon and the Battalion Reserve of ammunition; they were in Horsa gliders (chalk Nos 799, 799A and 800-803) piloted by

Horsa gliders ready for the off, 17 September 1944. *Taylor Library*

E Squadron GPR and towed by C-47s of 48 Squadron RAF.

At Broadwell the C-47s were arranged alongside the runway ready for take-off, their Horsa gliders positioned on the runway with the tow-ropes neatly arranged between glider and tug. They were so arranged that as each tug and glider combination took off, the next aircraft could move on to the runway and commence its tow. Each man was allocated a specific seat, and in the loading manifests even his operational weight was noted.

The troops debussed alongside the glider in which they were to fly. There was, as always on these occasions, much hilarity with ribald commentary, some subtle and some not so, and suitable epitaphs were inscribed on the sides of the gliders. Outwardly it was for all the world like any one of those many other occasions when the men were off on an exercise, but now deep down they were wondering what was going to happen and if they would be coming back. Medical Orderlies came down the line of gliders handing out small white benzedrine capsules, three for each man. They looked like small sweets, like old-fashioned liquorice torpedoes.

'What are they for?'

'Well, if you're frightened take one half an hour beforehand,' came the reply.

Some took them, others like Private Bernard Murphy, a Signaller, refrained, wanting to avoid the headache that was rumoured to accompany them. Others, like Cpl Jim Swan of C Company, thought that they were probably made from some innocuous substance and were given out for the psychological rather than the medical effect!

The order came to emplane, before long the men were all strapped in and very soon airborne. As the aircraft combination moved forward, there was a jerk as the tow-rope took the strain and within seconds the glider was airborne. Once the Stirling tug itself became airborne the Glider Pilot endeavoured to keep his aircraft either above or below the slip-stream of the tug. Glancing out through the cockpit window there was always the doubt in some minds as to whether the heavily laden combinations of aircraft and glider, hurtling towards the boundary fence of the airfield, would ever become airborne.

The first glider took off at 09.45 hrs. It was a pleasant day, warm with some cloud that cleared after crossing the English coast. Cpl Jim McDowell of 23 Mortar Platoon recalls looking down after take-off and seeing people going to church. The men knew that they had fighter escort - some 44 Squadrons were involved and it was pleasing to see these aircraft around the great armada of tugs and gliders. The route had been skilfully planned to avoid those areas known to have strong AA locations, giving the invading force as much protection as possible.

However, there were some glider casualties. One glider carrying the 6-pounder anti-tank gun 'Suvla Bay' and its detachment under the command of Sgt Tom Bate failed on take-off. The soldiers were able to take-off in another glider, but the gun had to be left in England, the only one of the eight not to arrive in Holland. Three gliders came down due to poor visibility in thick cloud between tug and glider, which prevented the Glider Pilot from seeing his tug; it was necessary for the pilot always to keep the tug in view in order to maintain position and avoid problems.

One such was the glider carrying Lt Col Haddon, the IO, Lt Ronald Hope-Jones, L/Cpl Nolan, Ptes Kearn, Kelly, Longton (the CO's driver), Manley and Chapman was the second to take off from Broadwell. The weather was fine and still, but the morning mist had not lifted and, after flying for some ten minutes, the glider ran into thick mist and the tug became invisible. Now the Glider Pilot, Major Blatch, had to fly keeping station on the tow-rope. Unfortunately the glider's instruments were not working properly, and Major Blatch could not hold the same course as the tug. After climbing, diving and turning in the most terrifying way, he finally cast off just as the tow-rope broke. They made a perfect forced landing, unloaded the jeep and trailer and by midday were back at Broadwell arranging to reload in another glider and fly in with the second lift.

The glider carrying Lt Pat Stott, the acting 2i/c of B Company, his driver with a jeep and two trailers of Company HQ also came down due to poor visibility between glider and tug. It landed safely, although narrowly missed some power lines. 13 Platoon of B Company commanded by Lt Wellbelove ('Canloan') came down when the engines of their Albemarle tug overheated; Cpl Cyril Crickett recalls that it was something of an anti-climax. They landed safely near Hatfield, watched the air armada pass overhead, gathered mushrooms and waited for transport, which flew the glider-load back to Broadwell ready to take-off with the second lift.

Lt Crittenden with 17 Platoon of C Company came down near Braintree due to the poor visibility and their tow-rope breaking. Capt King, the Glider Pilot, tried to release the tow-rope from the glider, but only one side fell free, while the length on the other side swung up and tried to hammer its way through the plywood skin of the glider. However, King and his co-pilot managed to put the glider down; it landed heavily, crossed two fields, tore through a hedge and eventually came to rest in a cornfield with its undercarriage skid, fencing posts and wire in a beautiful tangle inside it. Fortunately no one was hurt and the platoon unloaded the handcart containing equipment, ammunition and compo rations. Cpl Doug 'Jack' Payne wrote of how they watched the other gliders and aircraft passing overhead with great despondency.

Then an official of some kind arrived on the scene and arranged for the local Home Guard to watch over the glider while he with Capt King and Lt Crittenden went off. It transpired that they had landed close to an US Air Force base. Here they were offered dinner by the American Colonel, but Bob Crittenden refused this, insisting that they had to get back to base as soon as possible. Doug Payne did not let his platoon commander forget this when they were in Oosterbeek, as he believed that they had indeed been given a meal. The American Colonel arranged for them to be flown back to their start point in Marauder bombers that were stationed at this airfield. The handcart was slung in the bomb-bay of one of the aircraft and the platoon was split up between several aircraft for the flight home. At the base every man was examined for injury and only one was unable to fly out the next day.

The main party was now approaching the Dutch coast, and as the aircraft crossed it they could see spread out below the flooded countryside, the water

shimmering in the sun. It all looked so peaceful. Soon the Rhine could be seen and the troops knew that the first part of the journey was nearly over. What would

Right Horsas with their tugs crossing the Rhine, viewed from the cockpit of a glider on 17 September 1944. *BRM*

Below An aerial view of LZ 'S' looking east on 17 or 18 September 1944; Reijer's Camp Farm is in the top centre. The 1st Battalion's gliders landed in the lower half of the LZ bordering the railway and the Battalion rendezvoused in the south-west corner before moving across the Ede-Arnhem railway line to deploy to their Phase I positions. Some of the first PoWs were captured at the western end of the LZ near Buunderkamp. *Taylor Library*

be meeting them in the next few minutes? Conversations between the RAF and Glider pilots confirmed their positions. Any moment now the LZs would be in sight. Messages of thanks were passed from the gliders to their tugs. Promises between aircrews were made of 'I'll buy you a drink at the end of the week when we return'.

LZ S was soon spotted. In the warm sunny afternoon, smoke could be seen rising and circling lazily skywards from the ground markers, and there was also a large letter 'S' that had been laid by the Pathfinders of 3 Platoon 21st Independent Parachute Company, who had landed some 30 minutes before. It was now 13.00 hrs.

There was, as always, a bang as the tow was cast off and the nose of the glider dropped momentarily as the forward speed slowed and the Glider Pilot took control again. Almost at the same moment he had to select his flight-path into the LZ - flaps down, and hopefully it would be a landing without incident. Some gliders had already made their decision as to their approach and were committed. There was little opportunity to make any change, or come round again for a second try. Some gliders had been unable to avoid others already down and there were some collisions; several ended up in the trees at the western end of the LZ.

As the glider carrying Lt Green and 20 Platoon of D Company came in over the edge of the LZ, there was a burst of automatic fire from the ground and the nasty sound of bullets winging their way through the body of the glider. There was an awful moment while everyone wondered what damage had been done; then came a surprise comment from Pte Ron Stripp: 'I've been hit in the arm.' Everyone else gave a sigh of relief; no one else was injured and the glider still

answered its controls. Nothing could be done for Pte Stripp until the glider had landed. The pilot made a perfect landing well up the LZ, leaving plenty of room for those who were to follow. Pte Stripp's wound was dressed by Pte Danny Fowler, the Platoon's Medical Orderly, and he departed for the RAP. The glider was quickly and expertly unloaded and, together with other members of the Battalion, the Platoon headed for their Company rendezvous on the edge of a field.

The warmth of the sunny day was tempered by a very gentle breeze, but there were the usual complaints from the men about everything in general and nothing in particular. It had all been said before, and as usual on this occasion it was all ignored. The weight of the platoon handcart, which had to be man-handled, the state of the ground and the amount of kit that had to be carried, were all grounds for good-natured banter and griping.

Lt Pat Baillie commanding 7 Platoon of A Company found, as did everyone else, that LZ S was a field on which the crop had been grown and harvested, so it was fairly level but very dusty. His glider came in at about 80 mph and was heading straight for the wood at the west end of the LZ. The pilot put on full flaps, brought the nose up and stalled the glider on to the ground. There was a mighty crash as it hit, the undercarriage broke off and the glider slid into a barn on the edge of the field. Fortunately the occupants suffered only slight grazing.

The Platoon emerged to find, as had others, that there was spasmodic fire across the area of the LZ, which was more irritating than dangerous. Due to the bad landing of the glider, they had difficulty in removing the platoon handcart; this was a lidless metal cube about 4 feet square with motorcycle wheels and inflated tyres and a handle with which to pull it along; a towing eye enabled the cart to be hitched behind a jeep, if one was fortunate enough to be offered a tow. The cart carried the platoon reserve of ammunition, spades, pick-axes and boxes of compo rations for the men while they were mobile, before the company cooks could set up their kitchen. It was an essential part of the platoon's equipment, so it was imperative to unload it from the glider. They could be easily unloaded by being quickly emptied

A view taken looking west to the corner of **LZ S in October 1993. 1 Border** rendezvoused in the trees at the far corner. *BRM*

of their contents, then re-loaded on the ground. If the glider's load was a 6-pounder anti-tank gun that had perhaps become entangled in the debris of the crashed glider, then the task was more difficult.

Lt Ted Newport, one of the two Anti-Tank Platoon commanders, found his glider coming to rest in an awkward position. He took one look at the stranded craft and told his men to leave the gun 'Cambrai' and its equipment and make for the rendezvous. Shortly after reporting to Major Dickie Stewart MC, OC S Company, he was told in no uncertain terms to return to the stranded glider and retrieve the gun together with all the other useable equipment. Not one of them relished the job as they were now under sporadic fire. Eventually, after a great struggle, they managed to get the gun and jeep out of the glider and rejoin the Company. As he remarked later, 'Once again experience succeeded where rash and immature decisions proved wrong. Newport learned the hard way!'.

An interesting insight into the loading and unloading of the gun and jeep combination is given by Pte Alexander 'Sandy' Masterton. Sandy was No 2, the loader, in the crew of the gun 'Scimitar Hill' commanded by Sgt Johnny Molloy. As loader he flew with the gun and jeep, which were securely held by chains and quick-release shackles to metal channels bolted to the floor of the glider. The gun was hitched to the jeep ready to be towed out of the glider, and the jeep was laden with stores, equipment, petrol and 6-pounder shells, which were strapped in boxes to the bonnet and the top of the front bumper. Had the glider been hit by small arms fire or flak, the results would have been spectacular to say the least. The gun and jeep were loaded in by ramps through the large door on the port side of the glider behind the cockpit. The jeep was loaded first, then the gun, which was manhandled into place. There was very little clearance within the fuselage so the operation proved somewhat difficult. As the steering wheel of the jeep would strike against the frames of the glider, it was removed by releasing the butterfly nut that held it in place and laid on the passenger seat. The two steel loading ramps were carried in the glider and were also fixed down to prevent unwanted movement.

All the preparations were done beforehand. One of Sandy's crew went AWOL before the operation, but had been returned to the Battalion on Saturday evening. However, before daylight he had disappeared again, so Sandy's crew flew into Holland one man short. Their glider landed safely, and without opposition they began unloading and were soon joined by the rest of the crew, who had flown in another glider with a jeep and trailer carrying more equipment and ammunition. Together the men quickly removed the four bolts that held the tail-section of the glider in place. The removal of the bolts should have allowed the tail to drop free, but Sandy recalled that the whole unit jammed and had to be freed using an axe. The tail section was rolled away, and the steel channels un-shipped and put into position; this allowed Pte George Haskins, the driver, to move the jeep and gun forward and clear of the bulkhead before replacing the steering wheel. Then came the tricky operation of driving the jeep and gun down the ramps, endeavouring to avoid driving off them and overturning. Thankfully all was managed safely and they took up position to assist in the guarding of the LZ.

Pte Johnnie Peters of 14 Platoon B Company, commanded by Sgt Thomas Watson, related how when their glider, No 161, piloted by Lt Col John Place and Lt Ralph Maltby, was crossing the Dutch coast it came under fierce fire from enemy flak. There was a cry from the rear of the glider: 'The tail's coming off'. This message was relayed up to Johnnie, who was sitting just behind the cockpit. Sgt Watson had not heard what was said, and Johnnie related the message to Lt Col Place, who sent Lt Maltby back to investigate. He returned from the tail end with a cheerful grin on his face and reported that it was only flak and that no damage had been done.

He had just returned to his seat when there was a loud explosion in the cockpit and he slumped sideways in his seat. Sgt Watson went forward to help him, despite the fact that had also been wounded in the head. Ralph Maltby died before the Medical Orderly could reach him, as Johnnie Peters realised from the look on Sgt Watson's face. A sudden fear gripped him. What if the pilot should receive a fatal injury? Who would pilot the glider then? The truth was that there was no one capable, and if this should happen then they would all be killed. Soon they were over the LZ and, nose down, dived towards the ground. Bullets ripped through the fuselage and Pte Hughes, the Bren gunner of the scout section, was wounded in the knee by a single bullet that came up through the floor of the glider. The landing was otherwise uneventful; prayers had been answered.

L/Cpl Albert 'Ginger' Wilson, 11 Platoon B Company, saw that his glider had halted 10 yards away from a group of large trees, and, looking up into them, saw that another Horsa had smashed into them 40 feet above the ground. The pilots were dead in the branches of the tree; the anti-tank gun that the glider was carrying had smashed through the bulkhead into the cockpit. Sgt Hewitson, the Platoon Sergeant, was carried away wounded, and Ginger and Pte Frank Aston were ordered to take a PIAT and cover the railway line with the object of firing at any locomotive that approached the LZ from the west.

An aerial view looking south-east across LZ S towards Wolfhezen, probably taken on 17 September 1944. *BRM*

The LZ was now littered with gliders; some still airworthy, others with their tails removed to permit the unloading of heavier equipment. Some had crashed into each other or into fencing and trees and were reduced to matchwood. However, there was not a great deal of time to notice too much as one had to make the Company rendezvous, ready to push on to the next stage of the operation, the forming of a defensive perimeter around the LZs and DZs ready for the second lift on Monday.

The loose surface of the ploughed fields was now blown up as dust as troops and vehicles raced across it. Soon all the Companies were on the move to their appointed areas to form the necessary defensive positions. As they moved off the LZ, gliders were still coming in. Now it was the heavier Hamilcars with their more cumbersome loads - 17-pounder anti-tank guns and Morris 15 cwt towing vehicles, and airborne artillery with their 75 mm pack howitzers. At about 14.40 hrs the C-47s carrying the 1st Parachute Brigade made their long procession over DZ X, the men spewing out of the aircraft.

What could go wrong when one could see all this

going on? The Dutch people themselves thought as the troops did that nothing could falter and that in a few days they would have pushed on allowing the local people to pick up the threads of life under the watchful eyes of the Allies, and the Germans would be falling back. They poured out to welcome the Allies and offer the hand of friendship. They gave the troops a terrific welcome, and cigarettes and chocolate were handed out by the men. The Dutch for their part, even though they were short of food, brought out bread and milk for the troops. Some with an eye to the future salvaged the silk parachutes. There must have been many items of clothing made from them in the following weeks.

The Battalion Administrative Officer, Lt Doug Skilton, recalled that B Company picked up the first PoWs shortly after landing. Three German Marines were captured at Buunderkamp just beyond the edge of the western end of LZ S.

Capt Ingram Cleasby remembered the drop of the 1st Parachute Brigade: 'We had thankfully moved away from our gliders and were taking up our pre-determined positions. Then we heard the roar of approaching aircraft coming in from the south-west. As wave after wave passed over us, the sky was filled with bursting parachutes. Moments later it was empty as the paratroopers reached the ground and almost

Above An aerial view looking roughly north, with C-47s dropping 1st Parachute Brigade over DZ X on 17 September 1944. The farm in the top centre is Jonkershoeve, which was the Phase I location for 1 Border's Battalion HQ and RAP. The track ran north though the farm area to the north end of DZ X, where A Company took up their first positions. *Taylor Library*

Right The farmhouse at Jonkershoeve, located centrally between DZ X and LZ Z, photographed in October 1993. Battalion HQ, S Company HQ and the Battalion RAP were based here on 17-18 September. The track leads south into Heelsum and north to the edge of the DZ and A Company's first-day position. *BRM*

immediately the great open polder was like a field of mushrooms with parachutes scattered all over it. It was an amazing sight. And then within minutes local men and women came running across the near empty field, appearing as from nowhere to greet us. Such high hopes soon to be disappointed.'

The Battalion moved to the south-west corner of LZ S and crossed the railway line to move quickly to their allotted positions. B Company under Major Tom Armstrong moved off first as they had the furthest to go. The Company set off down Telefoonsweg towards Heelsum for the village of Renkum, where they were

Above LZ Z with gliders being unloaded, while men of the 1st Parachute Brigade land, 17 September 1944. *BRM/IWM BU1163*

Below An aerial view looking north over DZ X and LZ Z, with LZ S across the railway line, 17 September 1944. *BRM*

to block the main Utrecht road heading toward Oosterbeek and Arnhem. D Company, commanded by Major Charles Breese, accompanied them part of the way as far as the crossroads on the north side of Heelsum to block the road from Bennekom. A Company, commanded by Major Montgomery, remained in the north-west corner of DZ X/LZ Z covering the railway line between there and LZ S. C

Right The north-west corner of DZ X looking south in October 1993. The road on the right is Telefoonsweg, down which B Company travelled to Renkum and D Company to Heelsum. This area was occupied by A Company until the early evening of 18 September. *BRM*

Below Soldiers of B Company on the Utrechtseweg in Renkum on the afternoon of 17 September. This photograph was taken by a Dutch civilian, J. H. A. Barents, a local dentist. One man approaches the gateway, while another two make their way along the inside of the garden hedge, watched, no doubt delightfully, by the owner of the house. *Airborne Museum, Oosterbeek*

Company under Major Jock Neill were across to the east, south-west of the village of Wolfhezen, to provide protection from a possible attack from the Arnhem area. Battalion HQ was in the centre of DZ X/LZ Z at a farm called Jonkershoeve in a central position to the rifle companies. It was here that S

Company, commanded by Major Dickie Stewart MC, had its headquarters. In the area was 23 Mortar Platoon under Lt Mike Holman, to give support to A and C Companies, which were closest to them. The other Mortar Platoon, 24, commanded by Lt George Coulthard, and whose mortars were jeep-hauled, provided two mortars each for B and D Companies. Two anti-tank guns, 'Ypres' and 'Somme', and a section of two Vickers MMGs, were also sent off with B Company.

Here also at Jonkershoeve Captain John Graham-Jones set up the Regimental Aid Post (RAP). There were fortunately few casualties to attend to during the day. Lt Alan Roberts, OC 15 Platoon of C Company, was sent out to recce the Mental Hospital at Wolfhezen, which was close to their position. He found that it had suffered damage and casualties due to Allied bombing. During the night they were warned to look carefully before they opened fire as some of the inmates had left the home and were wandering about.

On the way to Renkum, B Company captured four Germans and two MG 34s. The prisoners were made to ride on the trailer belonging to the MMG section

Left One of S Company's 6-pounder anti-tank guns and jeep, its bonnet stacked with shells, travels along Dorpsstraat in Renkum on the afternoon of 17 September 1944, accompanied by a Dutch civilian on his bicycle. This must be 'Ypres' or 'Somme', one of the two guns attached to B Company, which were spiked and abandoned when the Company evacuated the brickworks on the afternoon of 18 September. The photograph, looking east, was taken by H. Hoefsloot, a local resident. *Airborne Museum, Oosterbeek*

Below The brickworks at Renkum on the north bank of the Rhine, occupied and resolutely defended by B Company until the afternoon of 18 September, when it was captured by Naval Manning Battalion 10 of Kampfgruppe Von Tettau. Photographed in 1947 *BRM/Arthur Royall*

so that they could be watched. This still annoyed the gun crews, who were not allowed to ride on them. Having arrived in Renkum, B Company were moving down the main street when a German lorry with an MG mounted on it suddenly appeared. The lorry was shot up and prisoners taken by the Company, which then moved towards the river, where they dug in and prepared defensive positions. 11 Platoon under Lt Barnes moved into the brickworks and dug in on the eastern side. Lt Arthur Royall's 12 Platoon were in the area of the ferry facing west and north-west. 14 Platoon commanded by Sgt Watson covered the north side of the road; here a small group of Germans guarding the ferry surrendered to 12 Platoon.

It proved impossible for Battalion HQ to get wireless messages through to B Company. However, the Dutch Resistance managed to relay messages by using their own secret line to telephone the local Police Station in the nearby village. This was very useful as the Signallers had soon found that the 18 wireless sets would not work properly in the wooded country and built-up areas. As Battalion HQ could not radio B Company directly, all wireless messages had to be relayed through D Company at Heelsum, when conditions allowed. The problem with the sets would occur frequently. Most of B Company took up their position for the night in the brickworks buildings or slit trenches.

Johnnie Peters recalled how they dug in within the grounds of the brickyard and during the night heard the sounds of someone approaching. Holding their fire, they waited in nervous anticipation and could hear someone climbing over the barbed wire fence that separated the field to the front. A Very light went up and they saw several German soldiers in front of them. The order to fire was given, then everything was quiet until morning.

L/Cpl Albert 'Ginger' Wilson, a Section Commander in 11 Platoon dug in by the brickworks, was sent by Lt Barnes with his section to lay an ambush on the road. A party of some 60 German troops on bicycles had been seen approaching by members of the Underground. It was, he said, about 21.00 hrs and they chose a house with a good view of the road. The house was occupied by two elderly gentlemen who had retired to bed. When the section burst in on them they were wearing nightshirts and long pointed caps, much to the amusement of the men. Ginger Wilson tried to explain that they should get dressed and take shelter in the cellar. The language barrier proved too great, but eventually with many antics and contortions they eventually made them understand what they were to do; finally they managed to them dressed and into the cellar. The Bren gun was sited at the window, 36 grenades laid

out and preparations made to ambush anything that came up the road. They were there until 23.00 hrs, when they were recalled to the main Company position, as the enemy had turned down another road.

Battalion HQ realised that B Company were likely to have the first contact with the enemy, being on a main road leading to Arnhem and forward of the rest of the Battalion. However, since the Company was under strength due to the failure of Lt Wellbelove's 13 Platoon and part of B Company HQ to arrive with the first lift, it was essential that there should be direct communication between the Company and Battalion HQ if at all possible. Lt Joe Hardy, the RSO, and his Signal Platoon Sergeant, Jock McCluskie MM, drove off in a jeep from HQ, laying a telephone line as they went. This was a simple job, done many times before, and within a couple of hours it was done, with the line working perfectly.

They set off to return to Battalion HQ, but as they topped a slight rise, they were surprised to see what appeared to be two soldiers silhouetted against the skyline. As they got closer they realised that they were indeed soldiers, and not men of B Company either. Lt Hardy leapt from the passenger seat over the bonnet of the jeep, his Sten gun in his hands, landed at the feet of the two Germans and said 'How's about it, chums?'. As he recalled later it sounded very stupid, and had he come out with a sentence in Arabic, Swahili or Cantonese the effect would have been exactly the same. They must have been even more frightened than he was. They dropped their SMGs and were bundled into the back of the jeep. Lt Hardy and Jock McCluskie did a rapid U-turn and headed back rapidly whence they had come.

Back in the B Company area the two PoWs were questioned by a Dutchman. It appeared that had Joe Hardy and Sgt McCluskie arrived a few minutes earlier, they would have found themselves in the middle of a German Company. It was obvious that they could not return to Battalion HQ, so they remained with B Company and Lt Hardy took over as Company 2i/c to Major Tom Armstrong in the absence of Lt Pat Stott, who was due to land the following day with part of Company HQ.

At Battalion HQ Major Stuart Cousens, the 2i/c, took over temporary command as Lt Col Haddon had failed to arrive. Major Charles Breese, OC of D Company, took over as Battalion 2i/c either late on the following day or on the 19th, and Capt Bill Hodgson, Breese's 2i/c, took over D Company from him. S Company HQ remained at Jonkershoeve, and there Major Stewart organised those sections of the Company not allocated to the Rifle Companies with his 2i/c, Capt Ingram Cleasby, OC MMG group, Capt Bob Reese, OC Anti-Tank group, and Capt Barry

Lt Joe Hardy MC, Signals Officer 1st Battalion, photographed in 1943. Born at Annan in Dumfriesshire in 1917, Joe was one of eight brothers who served in the forces during the Second World War. Three of them, including Joe, served in The Border Regiment, which they joined before the war. Joe enlisted in November 1933 and was posted to 1 Border, then stationed at Holywood Barracks on the outskirts of Belfast, where his brother Fred was serving. He qualified as a Signaller and joined the Signal Platoon, with which he remained for most of his service. Having served in Palestine, he was promoted to Sergeant at Aldershot before the outbreak of war. In 1942 he was sent to OCTU at Dunbar and was commissioned. After a short period serving at a recruit training camp at Ballykinlar in Northern Ireland, he was posted back to 1 Border as Signals Officer in February 1943; it was extremely rare for a man to return to the unit with which he had served prior to commissioning. He remained with the Battalion until he left the Army in the summer of 1945, having served in North Africa, Sicily, Italy, at Arnhem (where he was awarded the MC for his part in B Company's action at the Renkum brickworks) and in Norway. After serving in the Durham County Fire Brigade, he emigrated with his family in 1956 to Australia, where he still lives. *BRM/Joe Hardy*

Ingram, OC Mortars. He then made a round of the Company positions.

A Company were in a much more open position in the north-west corner of DZ X/LZ Z and had good visibility over the area, but with little cover from the air. D Company were in a small urban area on the north side of Heelsum where Telefoonsweg crossed the Benekomsweg. The Platoons dug in quickly in the gardens of the nearby houses. 20 Platoon, commanded by Alan Green, were on the south-east looking towards Heelsum. Here the ground dropped away and overlooked some open ground to a row of house on the edge of a wooded area. 21 Platoon under Lt Philip Holt were on their right facing in the general direction of Renkum and 22 Platoon under Lt George Brown were on the north side facing the LZ. As the Company came into their positions they surprised a German lorry coming along the Heelsum road, killed two of the occupants and captured the remainder. The Battalion position was otherwise quiet for the remainder of the day and night, for which the men were thankful, being able to get a meal and some rest. The Dutch in the vicinity kept their heads well down, no doubt wondering, as we all were,

An October 1993 view looking northeast from Telefoonsweg, just north of Heelsum, across DZ X towards Jonkershoeve in the woods on the far side. *BRM*

Above Dutch civilians welcome Airborne troops at the south end of DZ X near Heelsum on 17 September. The 'X' marker laid out by the Pathfinders of No 1 Platoon 21st Independent Parachute Company is clearly visible on the extreme left of the photograph. The jeep belongs to 24 Mortar Platoon, whose six mortars were divided between B and D Companies. Pte Vernon Smith of Carlisle, the driver, was killed five days later. Also in the jeep are Pte Don Cawood and Cpl Davison. *Wilf Oldham/IWM BU1125*

Right Pte J. O'Dowd, batman to Major Charles Breese, OC D Company, with an SCR-356 radio set at the crossroads at Heelsum where Telefoonsweg and Benekomsweg meet, on 17 September 1944. *BRM*

Right The same crossroads looking north in October 1993. The three Platoons of D Company were positioned around this area until the early evening of 18 September. Pte O'Dowd was photographed near a milestone, which stood on the other side of the roundabout. *BRM*

Airborne soldiers, almost certainly men from D Company, questioning German PoWs in the grounds of a house on the east side of the Telefoonsweg/Benekomsweg crossroads at Heelsum on the afternoon of 17 September. Although most of the original buildings survive from 1944, the house in the photograph was demolished in the 1980s. *Taylor Library/IWM BU1127/28*

what the following day would bring. Over towards Arnhem the sounds of firing could occasionally be heard. Lt Pat Baillie, commanding 7 Platoon of A Company, wrote in his diary that a red glow could be seen in the sky over the town.

During the night all Companies had small patrols out in front of their positions, but generally all was quiet in front of the Battalion. Everywhere that night there was 50 per cent stand-to; that is to say that in every trench there were two men, so that one could keep watch while the other slept, turn and turn about. This was to be, in so far as it was possible, the way of life throughout the whole operation, and indeed on some occasions no one slept for hours on end.

Monday 18 September

Monday dawned warm and bright. Everyone stood to, but there was no real enemy activity. Tea was brewed and a meal eaten from the rations the men had with them. It was a good morning, or so it seemed - very quiet. The weather for the second lift was looking good. In a few hours time we would be moving from these positions to form the perimeter around Arnhem itself.

The Germans opposing 1 Border from the west were part of 'Kampfgruppe Tettau', one of the hastily formed groups comprising a variety of units that would take on the British. To the north of the Ede-Arnhem railway line was Helle's Dutch SS Surveillance Battalion 3, which had already received a bloody nose from 7 KOSB to the north on the previous day. It was to be supported by SS-Battalion Eberwein. In the centre was Fliegerhorst Battalion 2 (a Luftwaffe unit converted to infantry), which would link the northern units with SS-Battalion Schulz from Colonel Lippert's NCOs School 'Arnheim' Regiment and Naval Manning Battalion 10, which had been reinforced by men from two other similar units. In reserve was 184 Artillery Regiment fighting as infantry.

In D Company positions the near neighbours in the houses were still keeping low and out of the way. Occasional glimpses could be seen of them through the windows as they moved about inside, no doubt wondering what was going to happen next as they prepared their breakfasts. The whole area was clean and tidy - spotless houses and gardens. But all too soon the area was to be ravaged by fighting.

Down in the B Company area, when dawn broke there was a dead German soldier in front of their position. The others, wounded in the action the night before, had managed to withdraw, perhaps with those more fortunate who had escaped injury. At about

07.00 hrs it was observed that the enemy had established some sort of position in one of the houses on the northern side of the main road about 200 yards immediately opposite the Company. It was quite obvious that they were ignorant of the location of our troops. Lt Joe Hardy explained the situation to Battalion HQ over the line laid the previous evening. Having explained that B Company was surrounded, the curt response was 'Fight your way out!'.

SS-Battalion Schulz had moved into Renkum and cleared it by early morning, before moving east into Heelsum. The task of clearing B Company from the brickworks and the factory to the west was assigned to the Naval Manning Battalion 10. As Major Armstrong and Lt Hardy discussed how they should break out and rejoin the Battalion, a German motorcycle and sidecar arrived with three soldiers on it. It parked in the courtyard of the house and in full view of our troops German soldiers poured out of the house and gathered around the motorcycle. No doubt they were all interested in learning what was going on. This did not take long. With such a target presented to our men, it was too good to miss. Lt Hardy gave the order to fire and two or three Bren guns and 10 or 12 rifles opened up on the sitting target.

As Lt Hardy later said, 'War is a filthy, rotten business. The two boys who had been captured the previous evening looked exactly the same as our own men, except that they wore field grey and we were in camouflaged smocks over our battledress. They were probably two nice young fellows. The crowd that clustered around the motorcycle were probably much the same, but at that moment they had no parents, brothers, sisters, wives and children. They were just a target, for this was war!'

The burst of fire was the signal for all pandemonium to break loose! It took a while for the Germans to re-organise themselves, but when they did start to return fire, it was obvious that there were a large number of them in the area. A number of fire-fights and minor attacks took place all round the Company perimeter. The two prisoners were killed by the first burst of enemy fire.

Pte Jim Longson, a Vickers machine-gunner of S Company, had one of the two guns with the Company set up in the hay-loft over the stables of the brickyard. A column of Germans advanced from the direction of Renkum, led by an officer who appeared unsure of his route, as he made constant reference to a map that he was carrying. He pointed in the direction of the brickworks and led his men towards it. The target was again too good to be true. Fire was opened at 200 yards and the dead and wounded were left in the road as the remainder managed to take cover in nearby houses alongside the road.

The sound of breaking glass could be heard as the Germans broke windows to give firing positions. Joe Hardy recalled that the situation became hectic as the enemy opened fire on them and appeared to bring up reinforcements. An attack from the direction of the paper-mill to the west was repulsed with heavy losses caused by the Vickers and 3-inch mortars. However, shortly afterwards a sniper was firing on the Vickers section in the hay-loft. His first shot hit the tripod of the gun and apparently split in two, as both Jim Longson and his No 2 were hit, Jim in the face and his companion in the shoulder. Jim climbed out of the hay-loft as another bullet flew past him. He reported the situation to Lt John McCartney, his MMG Platoon commander, and was ordered to bring his gun out and remount it on the river bank to cover the ferry.

Under sniper fire the gun team managed to remove the gun and equipment out of the loft over the roof of an outhouse. With one box of ammunition still to retrieve, a tracer round set fire to the hay in the loft. The team then realised that there were three horses in the stables beneath, but they could not get them out as the stable-door was on the side of the building facing the sniper; sadly the horses were burned to death. After having their wounds dressed by the Company Medical Orderly, the team were soon back on their gun. The question that had been occupying their minds was 'Why had the stable been set on fire?'. The answer was soon obvious as enemy mortar and artillery rounds ranged in, using the smoke from the burning building as an excellent marker.

After some initial success it became apparent that the Company was heavily out-numbered and the decision was taken to pull back. The action lasted until after 14.00 hrs, by which time all the Company vehicles and those of the Mortar and Anti-tank detachments had been badly damaged and the buildings in which they were positioned had been set on fire by heavy enemy mortaring. The order for the gallant Company to retire was now passed via D Company, the direct line from Battalion HQ having been cut by mortar fire. B Company were ordered to retire along the main road to D Company's position at Heelsum. However, this proved impossible as the Company were virtually surrounded.

The first problem was how they were to withdraw. The Company HQ was at the rear of a house with its back to the river. It was only a short distance to the water's edge and it was noticed that the river was some 12 feet below the top of the bank, thereby providing excellent cover for the men; it was an ideal way out. The next problem was how to disengage from the enemy. Major Armstrong quickly organised a rear-guard consisting of men from 11 Platoon under Lt Barnes. The final section to withdraw was Ginger

Wilson's. This section was placed to engage the enemy, while the main body withdrew a few men at a time down to the river and into the dead ground below the bank; from there it was possible to walk towards Arnhem completely out of sight of the enemy.

Lt Hardy and Sgt Hank Burr, one of the two Anti-tank gun detachment commanders, remained with the rear-guard, and it was here that Sgt Burr was killed. As soon as it was practical, the rear-guard was withdrawn back behind the house, which had been the Company HQ, and then down to the water's edge. From the amount of enemy fire being put down on the now empty positions, it was obvious that there

S Company Anti-Tank Platoon NCOs. Back row: Sgt Hank Burr (left), who was killed at Renkum on 18 September, and Cpl B. Lever, commanding the detachment of 'Gallipoli'. Front row: Cpl Tom Bate (left), who commanded the detachment of 'Suvla Bay', and Sgt George Fisher from Bermuda, the Platoon Sergeant of Lt Tony Howe's 25 Anti-tank Platoon. *BRM and Tom Bate*

A view looking west down the Rhine towards the Renkum brickworks, taken by Arthur Royall in 1947. On 18 September 1944 B Company withdrew from the brickworks along this path towards Castle Doorwerth, before heading north to rejoin the main Utrechtseweg east of Heelsum. *BRM/Arthur Royall*

was a full-scale attack going in. L/Cpl Wilson, on hearing the noise, climbed up the river bank to have a quick look at what was going on. In his words, he nearly had a heart attack at the sight of the force attacking their last position at 15.00 hrs. They must have been surprised to find it empty.

The withdrawal was very successful, and although the Company had sustained casualties, they had inflicted far more on the enemy. When the party were well clear of the brickworks, they clambered up on to the bank and followed the path that led towards Noerdberg and Castle Doorwerth and advanced with fixed bayonets towards the Battalion's main position. The theory was that if there were any enemy between them and their own troops, the enemy would have their backs to them as they would be facing C, D or A Companies, and the sight of fixed bayonets would give them a surprise.

With no transport left, the Company had to carry out as much ammunition as possible. The two Vickers guns were carried out, but the mortars and the two anti-tank guns 'Ypres' and 'Somme' were spiked and

left; it would have been impossible to man-handle them back to the main position now being established some 4 to 5 miles to the east. Small packs were also left behind in lieu of extra ammunition. Cpl Ian Hunter recalled that one of the battered jeeps was driven out. It was only with the inspired leadership of Major Armstrong and the courage of the officers, NCOs and men that the Company were able to achieve their successful withdrawal. Lt Hardy later received the MC for his part in the action.

In D Company's area there had been some enemy activity during the morning as small probing attacks were made by the enemy to locate them; SS-Battalion Schulz had cleared through Renkum and advanced into the outskirts of Heelsum, and the Soesterberg Fliegerhorst Battalion were on the western side of DZ X, both supported by MG and mortar fire. Pte Fred Hodges spotted the enemy moving into position in front of 20 Platoon to the south-east and warned L/Sgt Stan Sears, who was close by. As the section opened fire, so did the enemy, and as a result Pte Joe Walker, in a forward slit trench with a Bren gun, was killed. The bullet struck the change lever on the left-hand side of the gun and ricocheted off, striking him in the centre of the forehead.

This section position was on the edge of the small orchard of a house, which formed the centre of the

Sgt Hugh Pinkney, from Whitchurch, Hants, who served as a Corporal in 14 Platoon B Company during the battle and was taken prisoner, with one of the two guns attached to B Company at the western end of the brickworks at Renkum. The photograph was taken during a visit made by members of the Battalion to the Oosterbeek area in late 1945 while stationed at Hann Munden, near Brunswick in Germany. *BRM/Pat Stott*

Platoon position and overlooked a field that fell away to some houses on the other side of the valley. The Germans were in these houses and fired a burst at the section position. Sgt Stan Sears was pointing out the enemy position to Lt Green when another burst of fire struck him, killing him instantly. Lt Green and his runner, Pte Len Powell, threw themselves to the ground behind a convenient greenhouse as another burst ripped through the wooden building above their heads. It was a fascinating sight to see the clean white wooden splinters being torn away from the tarred side of the building. Shortly afterwards 21 Platoon under Lt Holt was attacked by a section of ten Germans who approached No 1 section commanded by Cpl Alan Fisher of Blackburn. They came towards the position under cover of a hedgerow, quite oblivious of the section's position and more concerned to remain unobserved by other sections of the Platoon.

There was a nail-biting period until the enemy were about 100 yards away, then the order was given to fire. The first burst from the Bren gun went over their heads; the next did not. Most were wounded by this burst, or the subsequent rifle fire. A little later a stronger force was seen to be approaching from the direction of a line of trees. It was reported that 21 Platoon had been driven from their position, and Capt Hodgson ordered Lt Green to retake it with his Platoon, but as an O group was being held, word came through that Lt Holt's Platoon had reversed the situation. The enemy had infiltrated into a wooded area known as 'Laura' to the east of D Company's position. The Airborne Light Battery targeted this area and provided fire support, which helped D Company repulse all attacks.

Lt Ted Newport of S Company remained with one of his guns, 'Cambrai', whose detachment was commanded by Cpl Iveson; the gun was in D Company's position near the crossroads. Ted recalled that 'we had just managed to dig our gun in, camouflage up and were thinking we might have a bite to eat, when a German tank appeared at the edge of a wood to the right of the Company position, followed by what I estimated to be a Company of the enemy. There was a lively engagement in which I joined by turning a Bren on a group of about 20 Germans advancing towards our positions - they went to ground after losing some men. Meanwhile Cpl Iveson attempted to have a go at the tank, but it retreated after firing a single round. He told me afterwards that he looked upon this action as a good rehearsal for further activities as the battle developed.' The tank was probably a French Renault Char B of Tank Company 224.

The anti-tank guns carried a supply of some HE rounds, but most of the ammunition was armour-piercing. The main supply was carried in the towing jeep with two spare rounds on the inside of the gun-shield. Ted Newport added that 'those of us in the anti-tank fraternity were not a little aggrieved back in the UK to be issued with the new ammunition called 'Sabot'. This was a solid shot of high-quality tungsten encased in a hard plastic, the shot being somewhat smaller than the bore of the gun. When the shot was fired bits of the plastic fell away and the velocity was increased by some 35 per cent. The trouble was that the bits of plastic falling away were often mistaken by the gun-layer for the fall of shot, and corrections were made with totally inaccurate results. We had been issued with this ammunition only a week before Arnhem and had only one day on the ranges to practise with it. The gun-layers had reached a high degree of efficiency with the old ammunition and to send us to war with this new ammunition we all believed was an error of judgement.'

At about 11.00 hrs the LZs and DZs were attacked by 30 German ME 109 fighters, which came over and machine-gunned the area. A Company suffered casualties because the men at first thought that the aircraft were our own, and they had stood out in the open waving their yellow celanese triangles used for ground-to-air recognition. The triangles were of two types; one was tied round the neck and tucked into the Battle Dress blouse or smock, while the other was pinned into the trouser pocket and could be pulled out and expanded. Lt Pat Baillie of 7 Platoon believed that some seven men were killed and a further 14 wounded during this attack, and that two enemy aircraft were brought down by small-arms fire.

As the planes came over, Pte Sandy Masterton, with his anti-tank gun crew, threw himself into a slit trench for cover. Here he bumped into a fellow Scot, Jake Turner of C Company. Jake had a premonition that he was not going to come out of the action alive and persuaded Sandy to take a letter to give to his girlfriend, a WAAF at Coningsby. Sandy duly delivered the letter at a later date, but was not aware of Jake's fate; he was in fact taken prisoner on 24 September. Pte Syd Cringle from the Isle of Man, 23 (Mortar) Platoon, recalled that he and others thought the aircraft were RAF Typhoons, so extensive had been the air cover on the way over.

An attempt was made to get a patrol led by Alan Roberts of C Company through to B Company during the afternoon. As they went along the road a coach-load of soldiers passed them driven by a civilian driver, but a mile or so further on they came across the coach with all its occupants killed. Shortly afterwards they met B Company coming along the road towards them. Both A and C Companies came under intermittent fire during the morning as the enemy fired at anything that moved on the DZ and LZ.

The second lift, which had been expected to arrive during the morning, eventually came in at about 15.00 hrs. The delay was caused, it was learned later, by heavy mist in England, which prevented the aircraft from taking off. This resulted in the Battalion having to cover the landing areas for longer than planned, thus delaying the move towards Arnhem. It is arguable that even this short delay in the plan had some effect on the final result of the Battle, as it allowed the Germans to infiltrate through the widely scattered positions. A typical example of this occurred when the Battalion moved to Phase II positions.

As the second lift came in, there was increased enemy activity and LZ Z came under fire from MG 34s in the area of 'Laura' to the east of D Company's position; the Vickers section and mortars with C Company managed to silence much of this. The firing that continued seemed to be aimed at the empty gliders from the first lift. Nevertheless there were some casualties among the incoming troops. All the Battalion glider loads that were due on the second lift, together with those that had failed to arrive with the first, arrived safely, with the exception of that of Lt Col Haddon.

His party was among the last to take off from Broadwell. There was no problem with visibility, but somehow they missed the rest of the Airborne convoy, and although they made every effort to rejoin the main body, they saw nothing of the other gliders. Having left the North Foreland, they crossed the North Sea, made landfall near Dunkirk, then flew along the coast as far as Ostend before eventually turning inland. Soon another glider appeared below them, and they flew together for some time, but this glider turned north and they were alone again. This was not a problem as they were flying over Allied-held areas, and after some 45 minutes they reached the front line at Herenthals on the Albert Canal. This meant that they were some 3 or 4 miles north of their correct course. The tug made a final attempt to make the proper course heading by cutting another corner, which proved disastrous.

Herenthals was still enemy-held, and the Germans opened up with everything they had. Lt Ronald Hope-Jones, who had trained as an AA gunner before joining the Battalion, leaned forward to Lt Col Haddon and remarked that they had only to hold the same course and they would be hit. As it happened only a few shots hit the glider, but the tug was hit in its port engine and shortly afterwards reported over the intercom that the First Pilot had been killed and the Second Pilot was flying the aircraft. With only one engine the tug began to lose height. Then Sgt Lester, who was flying the glider at this point, reported that the port ailerons had been shot away and were not answering the controls. Major Blatch, the pilot, took over and at once cast off. The glider went into a steep diving right-hand turn and landed very fast. Fortunately there were no obstacles, and after two or three nerve-racking hops the glider crashed with its nose in the ground and tail in the air; the skill of Major Blatch saved the day. The occupants were out of the glider in seconds and down on the ground under the wings.

A wildly gesticulating but, as it turned out, friendly Dutch farmer arrived on the scene, and in his best Dutch Hope-Jones asked where the Germans were. He was told that they were about 3 kilometres away. However, before they could ask anything else, a jeep with three gunners arrived and they discovered to their great relief that they were among their own troops.

It proved extremely difficult to unload the jeep and trailer with the tail of the glider in the air. Eventually, however, they managed to right the glider and get both jeep and trailer out. The party of 11 men all piled on to the transport and they set off in search of 30 Corps. At that HQ they traded the Sunday newspapers, which they had brought from England, for the loan of a 15 cwt truck. They soon found the Seaborne Tail of the Battalion encamped in a wood near the small village of Lilo; they had come north from Brussels and through Louvain. The QM, Capt 'Uncle' Barnes, made them welcome, fed them and gave them a tot of whisky each and everything else that they needed; eventually they bedded down for the night at about 01.30 hrs.

At Jonkershoeve Capt Barry Ingram of S Company recalled watching a large Hamilcar glider landing on fire: 'Here they come. Christ! Why don't they throw the kitchen sink at them? Six hours late and now they've bought it. I've never seen a Hamilcar in flames before. Its going to hit those trees. Over and over and over; three somersaults with two Bren carriers inside.'

Having taken off again in the morning from Broadwell, Lt Pat Stott with B Company transport and part of Company HQ made an uneventful landing and reported to Battalion HQ. Lt Wellbelove and 13 Platoon also made a good landing, although Cpl Cyril Crickett thought for one awful moment that they would have to fight their way out of a haystack that they appeared to be approaching too fast for comfort; fortunately the glider stopped within a short distance of it. Not so lucky was the glider that landed after them; it had insufficient space to stop and ploughed into a group of trees resulting in some casualties. 13 Platoon remained on the LZ until the evening assisting the Medical Orderlies by giving covering fire as they tried to aid the injured.

Lt John Bainbridge with 19 Platoon D Company, who had flown in from Down Ampney, also arrived safely and, although under light fire from time to time, made the 2-mile journey to the Company position without casualties. Lt Bob Crittenden with 17 Platoon C Company recalled that he received a hell of a wigging from Major Jock Neill, his Company Commander, for not arriving on the first day. They had not been there long when they were ordered to go and assist B Company at Renkum. Pte Bob Lee remembered that on the way to Renkum they met some men from B Company who told them that the Company had withdrawn. An exchange of fire between the Platoon and some Germans then followed. Cpl Doug Payne recalled that the few prisoners that were taken appeared very bewildered and quite happy to be taken prisoner. The Platoon

returned to C Company taking their PoWs with them.

Battalion HQ called an O Group as the move to Phase II positions was about to take place. Company Commanders, supported by a section from C Company, were to recce their allocated positions, which were located to the west of Oosterbeek. The move began at about 19.00 hrs, but was very slow. Lt Baillie's Platoon of A Company was the lead, and they had to move off across a ploughed field that offered no cover at all. Ahead of them was woodland on the western side of Wolfhezen. The Company moved off across this large field with its leading Platoon in an arrowhead formation, but when they were within 40 yards of the wood a shot rang out and one of the men fell, killed instantly. Unfortunately the position from which the shot came could not be located, so they did not return fire.

The Platoon moved forward again, but 10 yards further on they were met with heavy fire from all along the edge of the wood. Sgt Kerr, the Platoon Sgt of the leading Platoon, could see a couple of badly sighted MG 34s just in front of him. He leapt to his feet and tried to fire his Sten, but it jammed, so with a 36 grenade in each hand he ran shouting at the guns and the crews and threw both grenades, killing the crews and putting the guns out of action. The Company were held up for about an hour in this position, out in the open without cover, and every move meant that mortar fire would be brought down on them. Eventually the firing died down, and by now it was becoming quite dark. The Company were ordered to reform on a track at the edge of the field, where a quick check revealed only one casualty with some very close shaves.

This delay caused the Battalion, who were following up behind, to be late getting into the new positions. There were only some 3 miles to go, but this short distance took some $5\frac{1}{2}$ hours to cover. Eventually A Company reached their positions near Kasteel de Sonnenburg, a large house north of the Utrechtseweg, and a wooded area, Graftombe. The house, on slightly higher ground, was in an area of thick woodland and small open fields.

B Company, having moved along the bank of the Rhine, had reached the track running directly east to Noordberg and Doorwerth. After passing Noordberg, they turned north along a broad track into Heelsum at about 17.00 hrs, where they were held up by mortar fire. The Company rejoined the Utrechtseweg, eventually passed through C Company and turned off south down the Van Borsselenweg to a position in woodland bordering the Oosterbeeksche Weg between Heveadorp and Westerbouwing. Lt Pat Stott recalled following the main road with the Company

Oosterbeek, Kasteel de Sonnenberg

Above The Kasteel de Sonnenberg, Oosterbeek, seen in about 1935. A Company were based around the house and in its grounds from the late evening of 18 September until the end of the Battle. *Gemeente-Archief, Renkum*

Right The view south-east down Sonnenberg Laan towards the Utrechtseweg in October 1993. Late on 18 September 1944, A Company occupied this area as their Phase II positions, which they held until 25 September; on the right, in and around Sonnenberg, and in the woodland to the left up to an area known as Graftombe. *BRM*

transport and meeting up with his Company on the way.

As they moved up towards Oosterbeek along the Utrecht-seweg, they saw at the Wolfhezen crossroads a German staff-car, its four occupants lying dead beside it. One was Major-General Kussin, the Commander of the Arnhem District; the car had been ambushed the previous day by 3rd Battalion The Parachute Regiment. C Company then moved directly south to the Utrechtseweg, rather than down Wolfhezen Laan, if the map reference in the War Diary is correct. The Company finally took up positions on either side of the Utrechtseweg at the Wolfhezen road junction, with Battalion HQ in a house a few hundred yards behind them; the positions were taken up during the night and some effort was made to dig in. Lt Alan Roberts's 15 Platoon had the General and other German casualties as near neighbours during this period.

The area into which the Battalion was to be

deployed was heavily wooded, principally with beech, and the distance between the Companies meant that it was difficult for them to keep in touch with one another. The men wondered whether there would be friend or foe next door by the following morning. 23 Mortar Platoon managed to get itself dug into a suitable area ready to give support to the rifle Companies as they moved back, should this be necessary, and waited for the Rifle Companies to move.

From what could be seen in the dark, the position allocated to A and D Companies did not appear to be favourable. In the darkness the countryside appeared heavily wooded with little to offer in the way of fields of fire. D Company were below C within the heavily wooded Hoog Oorsprong estate, west of the Italiaanseweg towards an area known as Zilverenberg.

Just to the rear of D Company's position was a large house, Hoog Oorsprong, which if occupied by the enemy would be the very devil to clear. It proved very difficult to allocate Platoon and section positions in the dark with anything like a sensible order, so that each group could give covering fire to the others should it be necessary. Digging in also had its problems, as noise might attract unwanted attention from the enemy.

Top General Kussin, the Military Commandant of the Arnhem District, whose car was ambushed by men from the 3rd Battalion Parachute Regiment in the late afternoon of 17 September at the junction of the Utrechtseweg, Wolfhezen Laan and the Italiaanseweg. Following their move off LZ Z south-west of Wolfhezen, C Company occupied this area as their Phase II position from the evening of 18 September until the early evening of the following day, when they moved east to the area of the Koude Herberg crossroads. *Taylor Library/IWM BU1155*

Centre The site of Kussin's ambush photographed in October 1993, looking west along the Utrechtseweg with the road to Wolfhezen to the right and the Italiaanseweg off to the left just behind the speed limit sign. *BRM*

Bottom The view looking roughly south-west in the heavily wooded Hoog Oorsprong estate/Doorwerth Woods and down the Italiaanseweg just off the Utrechtseweg, October 1993. D Company occupied this area late on 18 September 1944. The dense woodland was one reason why the Company pulled back to a better position on the Van Borsselenweg the following day. *BRM*

Tuesday 19 September

The Battalion was dug in by 05.15 hrs in the positions taken up late the previous night. At Battalion HQ it was obvious that wireless communications between the Companies were still going to be difficult in the heavily wooded country. Pte George Attenborough, a Signaller attached to Battalion HQ, spent most of his time as a runner, carrying messages to various Companies. Under Battalion command were five anti-tank guns of the 2 South Staffords and two 17-pounder anti-tank guns from Brigade HQ. However, at 11.15 hrs the 2 South Staffords requested that the guns be returned to their command, and they did so.

The situation was generally quiet throughout the day. At 09.45 hrs reports were received from civilian sources via Brigade HQ that large numbers of the enemy had passed through Heelsum and Noerdberg to the west and that some had crossed the Rhine opposite Doorwerth, where there was a small ferry; this was later confirmed by the Recce Corps. These troops were on roads that led directly towards the positions of B, C and D Companies. At 11.00 hrs Brigade also received a report from a Sergeant of 156 Battalion Parachute Regiment that he had been pinned down close to a railway crossing where he could

observe a self-propelled gun and an armoured car at a point close to A Company's position; the gun was able to fire south or west as required. He had been close enough to hear the words of command.

C Company were coming under mortar fire and in Lt

Above right A section of 2 South Staffords, who came in on the first lift, marching towards Oosterbeek along the Utrechtseweg at around midday on 18 September 1944. Note the handcarts stacked high and most men wearing their equipment around their waists. *Taylor Library/IWM BU1090*

Right One of the 2 South Staffords 6-pounder anti-tank guns being towed east along the Utrechtseweg late on the morning of 18 September 1944. Like all the jeeps of the anti-tank gun teams, the vehicle was piled high with weapons, kit and ammunition of all kinds. Several of the 6-pounders were attached to 1 Border on the morning of 19 September. *IWM BU1091*

Robert's position his batman and L/Cpl King were killed and a number of men wounded. The latter were taken into the nearby houses on the north side of the Utrechtseweg for protection and were well treated by the local Dutch people. Later in the day he lost contact with the rest of the Company and eventually withdrew south-west to D Company area, from where he eventually discovered his own Company position and returned to it under cover of darkness.

Battalion HQ and A Company were strafed at 15.00 hrs by 12 ME 109s. As always there was a state of fear caused by the sound of roaring engines as aircraft dived to ground level - the crack of bullets and having to cower in slit trenches or cling to the earth as close as possible and hope that no one would be hit. This time there were no casualties. As the action was taking place, a plan was organised whereby Major Montgomery and Lt Baillie of A Company would arrange for a patrol to stalk the self-propelled gun and armoured car in their area and destroy them. The patrol left, and at about the same time the third lift of gliders carrying Polish troops began to arrive on the nearby LZ, which was being covered by 7 KOSB. The Poles fired on both 7 KOSB and on Major Montgomery's patrol, so the stalk was called off, but it was later learned that both gun and armoured car had moved from the area.

An hour later, at 16.00 hrs, the RAF carried out the first re-supply drop and many panniers and containers were collected in the Battalion area. L/Cpl Doug Payne, 17 Platoon C Company, recalled that the last time he saw the Platoon handcart was in the morning. The great regret was that it was hit by a mortar bomb in the

Supplies being dropped by RAF Stirlings, possibly on 19 or 20 September. *Taylor Library/IWM BU1092 & BU1106*

early afternoon, destroying the Platoon's ammunition reserve and boxes of compo rations. During one of these attacks he was sent with Pte Braithwaite and a Bren gun to cover the Company's flank, as they were told that the enemy might infiltrate from that direction. They went into a garden where there were two or three large greenhouses and took up their position in a boiler-house, knocking bricks out of a wall to obtain a field of fire. It was than that they heard the sound of aircraft engines and all hell was let loose as two containers of arms and ammunition with red parachutes came crashing into the greenhouses. But before they could get to them, they were called away to take up a new position where they could fire down the road to give covering fire as an attack was going in to clear a crossroads to their front. However, the Company came under heavy fire and the plan was cancelled.

At 19.00 hrs light probing attacks were made on all Company positions as Von Tettau's units moved from the west towards Oosterbeek. These attacks were repulsed without difficulty.

It was becoming clear that the Battalion line had to be shortened and thereby strengthened, as a determined attack would allow the enemy through. Without the ability of Companies to give each other supporting fire, each one could be isolated and in theory be taken out of the action. Late that afternoon and during the evening the Battalion re-adjusted the positions, which it was now to hold until the end of the Battle, as part of the Divisional perimeter around Oosterbeek, which was formed that night and consolidated the following day.

Above right No 3 Van Lennepweg, the house where Battalion HQ was located from 19 to 25 September 1944, photographed in late 1945 or 1946. *BRM*

Right The Koude Herberg Cafe cross-roads looking west along the Utrechtseweg in October 1993. Valkenburg Laan runs off to the right and the Van Borsselenweg to the left. 17 and 18 Platoons of C Company occupied this area late on 19 September 1944, 17 Platoon on both sides of the main road and 18 Platoon below them in the houses and gardens on the south side. Providing their main anti-tank support were two 6-pounders, Sgt Bill French's gun 'Hellespont' and Sgt Johnny Molloy's 'Scimitar Hill'. *BRM*

At about 17.30 hrs Battalion HQ had moved to a detached house on Van Lennepweg, just off the Utrechtseweg. C and D Companies also began to move back to new positions. C Company now had 17 and 18 Platoons forward occupying the Koude Herberg Cafe, crossroads and houses on Wolterbeek Weg and along the Van Borsselenweg, which ran directly south to the river. The other two Platoons, 15 and 16, with Company HQ were 200 yards further back on the Van Lennepweg facing west. 15 Platoon covered the lower part of Van Lennepweg and part of a track running south-east to the Hoofdlaan. 16 Platoon were above them and in the gardens along the line of the main road. A section of 16 Platoon with two Vickers MMGs were on the opposite side of the Utrechtseweg, covering both the main road and the open ground north of it and up to the Valkenburg Laan. The section also provided a link towards A Company's position around the Sonnenberg area, which was later strengthened by Royal Engineers and Paras. C Company HQ was initially located on the west side of the corner of Van Lennepweg, where a track ran towards Van Borsselenweg.

In support of C Company were two mortars from 23 Platoon, located in woodland below Battalion HQ on the south side of Van Lennepweg. Moreover, there were three 6-pounder anti-tank guns; 'Scimitar Hill' commanded by Sgt Johnny Molloy and 'Hellespont' commanded by Sgt Bill French were located in gardens bordering the Utrechtseweg near the crossroads. Further back near the Van Lennepweg was a third 6-pounder, 'Gallipoli II', commanded by Cpl Lever. All covered the main road and approaches from the west.

D Company had moved back through C Company's position and turned right down the Van Borsselenweg. About halfway down the Company took positions around a farmhouse and in woodland facing west and south. To the north on the western side of the road was an open field, between their position and 18 Platoon C Company on their right. From the road to the west was woodland. This also stretched south before opening out on to fields down towards B Company's position. The farmhouse with an attached barn stood on the east side of the road and became Company HQ and Aid Post. Just below it was a brick cottage, No 36 Van

Top Looking north from the edge of D Company's positions across the field separating them from the left flank of 18 Platoon C Company, in October 1993. The Van Borsselenweg is on the right. *BRM*

Centre The farmhouse at 34 Van Borsselenweg, D Company's HQ and Aid Post from 19 to 26 September 1944, photographed in October 1993. *BRM*

Bottom The estate keeper's cottage on Van Borsselenweg just below the farmhouse in October 1993. Lt Philip Holt's 21 Platoon were dug in in front of the cottage facing towards B Company, while 20 and 22 Platoons were dug in amongst the woodland on the west side of the road. *BRM*

Borsselenweg, where the estate keeper of the Hoog Oorsprong estate lived. There were gardens and some open ground around the buildings and more woodland further east. As the Company moved down the road, fighters flew overhead; it was thought that these were Allied planes, but they were soon recognised as being enemy aircraft. There was great disappointment at this as the men had at least been expecting close support from the RAF. The Battalion were not to know at this stage that the wireless communication with HQ across the Rhine and with 30 Corps was non-existent.

When the move took place it was still light, but by the time Platoon positions then section positions had been allocated it was getting dark. As 20 Platoon D Company dug in, their standing patrol reported that there was an enemy patrol in the area. 21 Platoon under Lt Holt were on the east side of the road facing south; there was open ground to their front and woodland to their left. 20 Platoon were on their right on the other side of the road on the edge of the woodland; they faced south-west and west. 22 Platoon under Lt Brown were on their left on the edge of the wood overlooking the field separating them from C Company and covering a track that ran from the road to a barn on the western edge of the field. With

Top In October 1993 this was the view south towards B Company's positions from those of 21 Platoon D Company. The White House owned by the Van Daalen family is just visible in the distance beyond the pond. *BRM*

Centre Looking west from the northern edge of D Company's position on either side of the Van Borsselenweg in October 1993. *BRM*

Bottom Looking north up the Van Borsselenweg towards D Company's positions from the White House crossroads, also in October 1993. *BRM*

them were two anti-tank guns, 'Cambrai' and 'Arras III', one facing south towards the river and the other facing west along the track that ran between the wood and the open field. 19 Platoon under Lt Bainbridge were a kilometre further west in a rather isolated position in woodland covering a junction on the road at Heveadorp.

The Battalion's line of defence now stretched from Sonnenberg in the north with A Company down through C and D Companies to B Company at Westerbouwing overlooking the north bank of the Rhine. Below these heights was the Driel Ferry, which remained operational until at least the 20th and which B Company were required to hold.

On the Westerbouwing heights overlooking the Driel Ferry and the Rhine was a restaurant, surrounded by woodland. Below it to the east the ground sloped gently down over an open field towards the crossroads, where Van Borsselenweg met Benedendorpsweg. At the bottom of the field was an orchard, a farmhouse and another house. Immediately to the south was a steep cliff, which was wooded, the

woodland extending east along the edge of the field as the cliff was reduced to a gentle slope. Between the cliff and the lower river road to Heveadorp, the Veerweg, was open ground. There was woodland to the north side of the restaurant up to the main road and also to the west, where it was broken by open stretches of ground and pathways or rides. Like many other areas of the Battalion front, the enemy's approach could not be easily observed.

There was not a great deal of activity in the early hours. Lt Pat Stott, the 2i/c, took a patrol out towards Heveadorp, but there was no sign of the enemy. Shortly afterwards tanks or other motorised vehicles could be heard in the direction of Heelsum.

According to the Battalion War Diary, late that evening B Company had deployed one Platoon on the high ground around the restaurant. The other three Platoons were established with Company HQ between the crossroads and river road. Company HQ and the Aid Post were established in the farmhouse at the bottom of the field. Later that night or during the following day Major Tom Armstrong decided to adjust the Company positions.

11 Platoon under Lt Barnes dug in north of the restaurant in woodland along the edge of the Oosterbeeksche Weg, the road from Heveadorp. Some of 14 Platoon under Sgt Watson were dug in above the buildings facing west and 13 Platoon covered the southern edge of the restaurant area and

The present-day view looking south across the Rhine from Westerbouwing, with the Driel Ferry moored on the far side. The Veerweg to Heveadorp runs below the slope beyond the line of the trees in the foreground, and the access road to the ferry from the Veerweg can just be seen in the right centre; Cpl Cyril Crickett, Ptes Hulse and McDonald were dug in on this access road. *BRM*

woodland parallel with the Veerweg. A section of 13 Platoon comprising Cpl Cyril Crickett, Pte Hulse, a Bren gunner, and Pte McDonald, a sniper, dug in along the small road from the Veerweg to the Driel Ferry. Some 500 yards to their front was a paper-mill on the eastern outskirts of Heveadorp. 12 Platoon under Lt Royall dug in at the bottom of the field in an orchard near the crossroads on the left of Company HQ, while a section of 14 Platoon under Cpl Ian Hunter covered the corner of the Veerweg in line with the gas-works.

L/Cpl Wilson remembers that they found a warehouse with a store of brand new German MG 34s in the farmhouse; these were cleaned and put together, but no ammunition could be found. Two 3-inch mortar teams were allocated by Capt Barry Ingram to the Company to replace those left at Renkum; one was dug in on the south side of the restaurant, the other near Company HQ. However, as there were no 6-pounder guns spare, the Company had to rely on their PIATs for any anti-tank support.

During the night Lt Hardy with a party from the Signals Platoon laid a line from Battalion HQ along the Van Borsselenweg to B Company. C Company had dug in amongst the gardens and hedgerows around the Koude Herberg Cafe crossroads. Beyond the gardens to the west the country opened out. The Van Borsselenweg remained the fast link between Battalion HQ and D and B Companies; it was also the road along which casualties were evacuated by jeeps fitted with special carriers to which stretchers could be fastened. However, this was only possible during the early part of the next day, as from then on the road was under enemy fire.

Captain Graham-Jones had set up the Regimental Aid Post in 'Geldershof', a house at the corner of the Hoofdlaan and the Utrechtseweg. 'Geldershof' was a fairly new two-storey building with a large cellar standing in its own grounds and with modern sanitary facilities. Here he could deal with casualties in ideal conditions, whence they would be returned to duty or evacuated to the Dressing Station (DS), which was located in the Hotel Schoonord with a surgical annex at the Hotel Tafelberg. Dr Graham-Jones recalled that 'the

Battalion's medical organisation was designed to fit in with the Brigade plan centred on 181 Field Ambulance RAMC. Companies had their own Medical Orderlies. The RAP included the MO, batman, RAMC Sergeant and two trained Orderlies and was located as close as possible to the Companies in action. 181 Field Ambulance had two surgical teams capable of resuscitation and surgical treatment of serious casualties and provided a DS located conveniently for the whole Brigade. The battle plan envisaged continuous evacuation of casualties from the RAP to the DS during the action, which was expected to be for three days or so before being relieved by 30 Corps. The medical supplies, which had to be easily transportable, were calculated to cover this period with a small reserve. Medical training within the Battalion concentrated on rescue and handling of casualties, immediate first aid, more detailed treatment in the RAP and transport to and from it.'

During the night of the 19th patrols were active along the Battalion's front. Pte George Smith of 17 Platoon was a member of one such patrol, which also included Pte Ron Cruickshank, returning to Company lines during the night. As they came down the drive of a house he noticed the muzzle of an MG 34 protruding from under a camouflaged sheet. The gun was pointing directly at the Company positions. He lifted the sheet and there was a German soldier fast asleep. The man had quite a shock when he was woken up. He was taken to Company HQ where Major Neill tried to interrogate him. Little progress was made, then the prisoner made a dash for freedom. He did not get very far and was shot and killed, paying the price for his rash effort. Cpl Jim Swan recalled that just as the German made his run for it,

'Geldershof' at the junction of the Hoofdlaan and the Utrechtseweg. The Battalion RAP was based here from 19 to 25 September. *Dr J. Graham-Jones*

Lt Roberts was coming up the path to Company HQ and was nearly killed, with all the flying bullets!

In front of D Company the enemy made probing attacks, but there was no exchange of fire. The country was so heavily wooded that it was always possible that the two sides could get within 10 yards and neither be aware that the other was there. The woods contained lots of dense cover provided by shrubs and tall grasses and weeds; it was only by being constantly alert and keeping good observation that anyone could be aware of what was going on in front of the Company.

Capt Barry Ingram, OC of the Mortar Platoons, was also having difficulties due to the nature of the countryside. His problem was that he could only do shoots by map reference, as it was impossible for the fire controllers to see the fall of shot. Ingram therefore had to rely on wireless communication with the Companies, which had already been found to be difficult because of the lack of suitable wireless sets to operate in wooded country. He now had ten mortars left out the 12, two having been left behind at Renkum, but by judicious scrounging he later managed to increase these to 16, which were allocated to the Companies. Ingram later wrote that he had severely chastised Lt George Coulthard for abandon-ing the two guns at Renkum, and that in retrospect it was very unfair. Ingram remained in the A Company area.

Wednesday 20 September

Once more the day was bright and sunny, but from 06.00 hours all the Company positions were mortared and shelled, and this continued throughout the day. The casualties caused by shells striking the branches of the trees and exploding in the air were mounting. Two of the 6-pounder crews attached to C Company suffered casualties from this mortar fire. Amongst the crew of the gun 'Hellespont' at the Koude Herberg crossroads, Pte Jimmy Wells was killed, Pte Jock McKinley wounded in the leg and Sgt Bill French wounded in the head. Later, when things quietened down, the gun was moved to another position.

Two dead German soldiers in front of the positions occupied by 15 and 16 Platoons of C Company on the Van Lennepweg on 20 September 1944, having tried to infiltrate the positions during the previous night. The location is at the bend of the Van Lennepweg and the track running west along the bottom of various gardens towards Van Borsselenweg a few hundred yards away. C Company HQ was just off the track to the right. *Taylor Library/IWM BU1104*

During the day Von Tettau's units advanced to contact with 1 Border's positions, supported by armour from 224 Company's Renault tanks. North and along the Utrechtseweg were SS-Battalion Eberwein, which had advanced from Wolfheze and reached the Koude Herberg crossroads by early afternoon, and the Fliegerhorst Battalion 2. South of the Utrechtseweg to the Rhine was SS-Battalion Schulz, the Naval Manning Battalion 10 and the Worrowski Battalion of the Hermann Goering Training Regiment, which had just arrived.

The whine of the bombs from the German Nebelwerfers, their six-barrelled mortars, became more insistent and the men counted the explosion of the bombs. After six there would be a short respite. How these things were loathed. Then the counter-fire of the Allies' 75 mm pack howitzers and the discharge of their mortars added to the general noise. This, together with the crack and whine of bullets ripping through the trees, was altogether most unpleasant.

At about 08.30 hrs a direct hit on 1st Air-Landing Brigade HQ killed four officers, two of whom were from the Border Regiment, Capt William Burns, the Brigade Intelligence Officer, and Lt Anthony Thomas, the Brigade Defence Platoon Commander. A number of other personnel were wounded. Lt George Coulthard from 24 Mortar Platoon left the Battalion at 15.30 hrs to go to Brigade as Intelligence Officer.

To the north of the main road leading to Arnhem, around the area of Graftombe just north of the Sonnenberg in A Company's position, the enemy began an attack at 10.00 hrs. Infantry, supported by a self-propelled gun and a tank, pushed through the woods using the paths and rides. Cpl Walter Collings commanding the Scout section of 10 Platoon had his section covering two such paths. They heard the noise of the armoured vehicles approaching, took the PIAT and positioned themselves in the cover of a small cottage; it was at this moment that everything happened. Just as the tank broke cover, Lt Eric Scrivener, the Platoon commander, and Sgt John Hunter, the Platoon Sergeant, who were on their way to visit the section, came round a corner on the path into the full view of the tank, which immediately opened fire; Sgt Hunter was killed. Pte Jack Crawford opened up with a Bren gun to give covering fire for Lt Scrivener and Cpl Collings, and in doing so killed the tank commander. The action was swift and brief. 10 Platoon dug into the north of the position and found that they had a large house to their front, which was continually being occupied by the enemy, only to be driven out by the Platoon.

In the C Company position on the Utrechtseweg at the Koude Herberg crossroads, an attempt was made

Cpl Walter Collings of 10 Platoon A Company, photographed in 1945. *BRM/Walter Collings*

to evacuate the wounded from Lt Roberts's Platoon, who were in houses close by the Company position. Only the walking wounded were able to be got out, and as the party were moving back to the Company lines they were fired on and mortared, suffering further casualties. This was the prelude to an attack on the Company position. First a tank came forward, and a patrol from 16 Platoon with an RE officer went out against it, but all the time the enemy fire was increasing and the Platoon's casualties were mounting.

This first attack on C Company was driven off, as was a second, which developed soon after. L/Cpl Doug Payne recalls that 17 Platoon had dug in around the crossroads and sustained a lot of casualties due to the shelling. It was in one of these attacks that the Signaller lost a foot. It seems, he says, that from this time onwards they were moving from one crisis to another, trying continually to hold the crossroads and the houses nearby, being pushed out of these positions then retaking them in order to consolidate the Company line. Various houses in the area with

Above Perhaps the most famous 3-inch Mortar team of the Second World War: Corporal Jim McDowell in the foreground, Pte Norman 'Jock' Knight and Pte Ron 'Ginger' Tierney (facing the camera), all of Lt Mike Holman's 23 Mortar (Handcarts) Platoon of S Company. This was one of the two 3-inch mortars attached to C Company, photographed by Sgt Smith on 20 or 21 September. This team was also filmed by Sgt Lewis, and L/Cpl McInnes can be seen on the film footage shouting 'Fire!'; he is just off camera to the left in this picture. Jim McDowell said that he could not recall the filming; had he known, he would have turned round and smiled! One mortar position was located at the edge of woodland to the south of Van Lennepweg below Battalion HQ, with the second further back nearer the road itself. Note the ranging rods at the front of the mortar pit, the site of which was still visible in 1993. Jim McDowell as a Sergeant revisited the site in 1946 with a group from the Battalion, then stationed

at Ochtrup in Germany. Two of the crew of the second mortar, Jack Hardwick and Ernie Westerman, even rediscovered the tube of their mortar. *BRM/IWM BU1098*

Below left The 3-inch Mortar team viewed from the other direction on 20 or 21 September. Now Ron Tierney's back is to the camera, with Jim McDowell on the far side. Jim's No 4 rifle lies on the side of the pit; he had originally carried a Mk 5 Sten, but exchanged it early on in favour of a rifle. The mortar pit measured roughly 8 ft x 8 ft x 4 ft deep, the picks and shovels to dig it being carried in the handcart. At this stage they were firing at very short ranges, hence the almost upright angle

of the mortar tube, and were not using any secondary charges on the bombs, which meant that they landed well within the 'safety' zone; the majority of the rounds fired were HE. Jim recalls that they hardly ever left the position, had little or no hot food and only the 24-hour ration packs that had been issued. They provided fire support both for C and D Companies. All three men made it back across the Rhine on 25-26 September 1944, Jock Knight being wounded during his journey to the river. *Taylor Library/IWM BU1099*

Above The same mortar just after Pte Jock Knight had put a round down the tube. *BRM/Jim McDowell*

thatched roofs were set alight with tracer rounds. Some had people trapped inside and, despite their screams, our men were powerless to help. For the second time that morning C Company had fought off another attack.

CSM Les Fielding of HQ Company was responsible for the distribution of the Battalion Ammunition Reserve to the various Companies. On one occasion, going forward to C Company with the scarce bandoliers of .303-inch ammunition, he was confronted by two geese, 'bloody but unbowed', which made a vigorous attack on his ammunition party. Despite the intense mortar fire they were far more intimidated by these birds than the enemy.

During this particular day it became no longer possible to evacuate D Company's casualties back to the RAP. The jeep that was being used to bring the stretcher cases up Van Borsselenweg to the RAP had not gone far when it was hit in the front differential by an anti-tank shell. This caused the front wheels to tilt in at the top and the vehicle could only be steered with difficulty. Nonetheless, the driver managed to bring the vehicle and the wounded back to the Company lines, where they were placed in the cellar of the farmhouse acting as Company HQ. From this time onwards no wounded were evacuated and the Platoon Medical Orderlies looked after all the wounded with great care and compassion.

19 Platoon under Lt John Bainbridge had been detailed to act as a standing patrol on a crossroads just north of Heveadorp near the junction of a minor road and Oosterbeeksche Weg, nearly a mile from D Company's main position. Their task had been to report any enemy movement eastward along the main road. They managed to get there on the evening of the 19th without any trouble and dug in a defensive position. There was the usual problem of not being able to confirm by wireless with Company HQ that they were in position; the 18 set proved useless in the heavily wooded country. The Platoon Signaller was Pte Ron Graydon, who carried the set and was assisted by Signaller Ernie Hamlet.

The detachment of 19 Platoon meant that D Company had more ground to cover on its front, and, with only three Platoons, it proved difficult to provide supporting fire between the Platoons and to neighbouring Companies. During the morning there was the sound of voices coming through the wood - a German patrol had managed to infiltrate the position and destroy the two jeeps used for towing the two anti-tank guns 'Cambrai' and 'Arras III'. The patrol had then been able to withdraw without casualties and before anyone in the Company had realised what was happening. It had managed to get into a position between 22 and 20 Platoon where there was a fall in the ground, providing dead ground for them to move in. This resulted in 22 and 20 Platoons having immediately to re-organise their positions to prevent this happening again. However, it also meant that now there was no visual link between 20 and 21 Platoon, who were lower down and on the other side of the road below the cottage. For the rest of the day the Company had a quiet time.

Later in the afternoon an enemy armoured car supported by infantry approached 19 Platoon's position from the west. They advanced along the road to where the Platoon was dug in, quite oblivious of what lay in wait for them. The armoured car was soon destroyed by a PIAT round, and Bren gun fire dispersed the infantry into the woods on either side of the road. Sgt Tom Northgraves, the Platoon Sergeant, recalled that one of the armoured car crew was killed outright and the other, who was wounded, was lifted out and patched up and left for his own side to pick him up. Lt Bainbridge now realised that his Platoon could no longer provide information on enemy movements along this particular road and, as he had no radio communication with Company HQ, decided on a phased withdrawal to the main D Company position.

The Platoon was divided into two groups, Lt Bainbridge leading one and Sgt Northgraves the other. Signallers Ron Graydon and Ernie Hamlet made a dash for it down the road and eventually arrived at C Company positions from where they moved back to their own Company, arriving later in the day. During the night in the thickly wooded country, now heavily infested with the enemy, contact between the two groups became difficult. They became intermingled, and some men were lost, killed or captured when the groups ran into enemy patrols. Pte Hugh Riley was among those captured; he was eventually moved to Apeldoorn with other PoWs, where he later met up with Lt Col Haddon after the Battle was over.

On one occasion during the night Sgt Northgraves, together with Lt Bainbridge and Cpl Atherton, were lying in thick undergrowth when they heard a patrol coming through the wood. They did not know whether it was friend or foe, and did not dare look up, but the sound of German voices convinced them that they were not among friends. The enemy patrol was now so close that they could have touched their boots. The three spent two days in the woods without detection and eventually spotted a red beret some 80 yards away. They decided that they must therefore be near the Company lines, and when the coast was clear they made a dash for it.

They ran like mad with shots ringing out and around them, then a German suddenly appeared from behind a tree in the path of Sgt Northgraves. Lt Bainbridge, following behind the Sergeant, hit the man full in the face, thus certainly saving Northgraves's life. This sadly depleted little group found that the Company was in a similar state, but Lt Bainbridge was able to give information that enabled fire to be brought down on enemy positions.

In the B Company area some probing attacks were made on the forward position of 13 and 14 Platoons, but the ground was held. There were, however, the ominous sounds of tracked vehicles approaching the Westerbouwing area. This encouraged members of the Company to spend their time during the day in preparing and perfecting their defensive positions. During the day Cpl Cyril Crickett and his section by the ferry escorted a couple of Sappers as far as the paper-mill near Heveadorp; the Sappers were scouting possible crossing points over the Rhine and the availability of any boats. A Capt Walker RE came through their position that night to cross the river and report to 30 Corps; how he crossed the Rhine is not clear, but it may have been over the Driel Ferry. Lt Arthur Royall said that during the day three Germans on bicycles, probably from the Hermann Goering Regiment, rode down towards his position at the crossroads, much to everyone's surprise; one was shot and killed and the other two were taken prisoner.

At about 15.00 hrs C Company were heavily

attacked by infantry supported by two flame-throwing tanks and a self-propelled gun. Sergeant Hanson was killed almost immediately. Fighting was heavy and the Company were pushed off their position; some of the men came down into D Company's position, obviously worried by the flame-throwers, but an angry Lt Roberts followed them and took them back to their positions. The Company, having been rallied by Major Neill, retook their positions. The Germans, however, were not beaten and attempted to turn the Company's flank. This manoeuvre was spotted by Cpl Freddie Webster with a PIAT, who with Bren gunner Pte Eric Blackwell and Pte Frank Fitzpatrick attacked the tanks, but they still came on and were attacked with grenades.

The Army Film Unit photographers, Sergeants Lewis, Smith and Walker, were in the house at eastern corner of Van Lennepweg and the Utrechtseweg and were able to film and photographs actions of C Company during the day. Sgt Walker filmed the gun 'Gallipoli' as it knocked out the self-propelled gun only some 80 yards away; only a couple of seconds of his original film survive. The Company ammunition reserve was set ablaze by a mortar bomb, but CSM Gerry Stringer dashed into the flames and rescued many boxes of ammunition. It was during this action that L/Cpl E. Mead, the Company Medical Orderly, distinguished himself by his bravery in going out under fire to attend the wounded and recovering those unable to walk.

Major William 'Jock' Neill, OC C Company, and Lt John McCartney, OC MMG Platoon, in their foxhole in C Company's area on Van Lennepweg on 20 September 1944. McCartney had commanded 13 Platoon of B Company on the Sicily operation prior to transferring to S Company. Jock Neill joined the Battalion in 1942 and served with it throughout the war; for his leadership of the Company he was awarded the DSO. He later served with the African Police and eventually emigrated to live in Tasmania. He returned for the 40th Anniversary in 1984 and sadly, one week after returning home, he died. His medals are in the Regimental Museum in Carlisle Castle, having been presented by his widow. *BRM/IWM BU1102*

Left Men of 15 and 16 Platoon, C Company, dug in along the Van Lennepweg on 20 September 1944. Two sections of 16 Platoon were on the Van Lennepweg, with 15 Platoon to their left. The other section of 16 Platoon was across the Utrechtseweg with a section of two Vickers MMGs. C Company HQ was just off camera to the left. The beech hedge marks the edge of the garden of 14 Van Lennepweg, and the view has changed little to this day. *BRM/IWM BU 1103*

Below left Van Lennepweg, looking south, in October 1993. C Company were dug in along and on either side of the road, and the hedge shown in the previous photograph is at the bottom of the road on the right. In the centre is the driveway of No 16; the photograph on page 139 shows a section recovering ammunition boxes from this garden on 20 September 1944. *BRM*

Above right A view of Van Lennepweg from the north side of the Utrechtseweg in October 1993. 16 Platoon, with 15 platoon below them, were dug in along this road and in the adjacent houses and gardens from late on 19 September 1944 until the withdrawal on the night of the 25th. The house on the left-hand side of the road was occupied by the three AFPU Sergeants, Lewis, Smith and Walker, from 19 to 22 September 1944, when the thatched roof caught fire. *BRM*

Below The three AFPU Sergeants, (from the left) Sgt D. M. Smith, Sgt G. Walker and Sgt C. M. Lewis, photographed at the AFPU HQ at Pinewood Studios on 28 September 1944. Lewis had jumped in with 1st Parachute Brigade, while Smith and Walker had flown in by glider with their jeep and equipment. Historically, the Border Regiment is very fortunate to be covered by both stills and cine footage taken by them on the 17th and during the three days that they were based in C Company's area. Sgt Walker wrote on his dope sheet that on the night of the 21/22 September 1944 'we had to get out in a terrific hurry and we have lost most of our kit. All I have is my Eyene and 200 feet of Plus X. When the situation clears up, if the house we were in is not completely destroyed, perhaps we may be able to salvage my 16 mm and film. There is also a roll of exposed 35 mm there so I am hoping it is OK.' Sadly the film was never recovered. *Taylor Library*

Above The 6-pounder anti-tank gun 'Gallipoli II' ('Gallipoli I' was lost en route to Sicily) engaging a German SP some 80 yards away along the Utrechtseweg on 20 September 1944. From the left: unknown, L/Cpl Eccles, Pte Taffy Barr and Pte Joe Cunnington. The photograph was taken by Sgt Lewis and the gun was filmed from a slightly different position by Sgt Walker. The original film footage taken by Sgt Walker is very short and ends abruptly when the gun fires. Walker commented on his dope sheet: 'I managed to get a shot of the 6-pounder before it knocked out the SP and used the rest of the roll on re-supply by parachute. This is a very important thing as it is the only means of keeping what is left of the div. going. We are with 'C' Coy 5th Batt. The Border Regt. and they have held the western tip of the perimeter all the time. They are magnificent.' Walker got the Battalion's number wrong, but his comments are well worth noting.

The gun is clearly located in C Company's area and is probably in a garden bordering the Utrechtseweg between the Van Lennepweg junction and the Koude Herberg Cafe crossroads; the typical chain-mesh fencing used in this area can be glimpsed to the right of the muzzle. The enemy engaged was probably a STUG III or more likely one of the flame-throwing Renault Char B tanks of 224 Tank Company. Tom Bate, the gun Sergeant of 'Suvla Bay', recalls that the gun NCO wore body-armour plates as he was usually the most exposed member of the crew. *Taylor Library/IWM BU1109*

Left A Renault Char B tank, probably of 224 Tank Company, knocked out on the Utrechtseweg near the Koude Herberg Cafe crossroads. It is likely to have been a victim of one of the 6-pounder anti-tank guns attached to C Company. One shell strike can be clearly seen on the lower edge of the front glacis-plate. *Bundesarchiv Koblenz*

Top Men from 15 Platoon C Company recover .303-inch ammunition boxes from a wicker pannier in the garden of No 16 Van Lennepweg on the west side of the road. In the centre is Cpl Freddie Webster (smoking a cigar), who was later awarded the US Silver Star. Helping him carry the ammunition box is Pte Eric Blackwell from Carlisle, the section's Bren gunner, and behind them is Pte Boow. According to Jim Swan, the two men to the left of Freddie Webster are probably himself, wearing a beret, and CSM Gerry Stringer. Sgt Walker, the cine cameraman, had earlier filmed this section running across the road and down the drive of this house. The house, which had been built in 1939 by a Mr Koenraad Moolhuizen, was destroyed during the Battle and a new one now stands on the site. This pannier was probably one of those dropped at around 17.30 hrs on 20 September 1944, as recorded in the 1st Air-Landing Brigade War Diary. *Taylor Library/IWM BU1107*

Centre An ammunition container being recovered by an Airborne soldier. *Taylor Library/IWM BU 1113*

Bottom Looking north from Van Lennepweg across the Utrechtseweg to the position taken up by one section of 16 Platoon and two Vickers MMGs. They covered the open ground towards the Valkenburg Laan and provided a link up to A Company's position around the Sonnenberg, which was later reinforced by Sappers from 9th (Airborne) Field Company RE, 4th Parachute Squadron RE and 261 (Airborne) Field Park Company RE. *BRM*

An aerial photograph of Oosterbeek and the area covered by the 1st Airborne Division's perimeter from 19 to 25 September 1944 - compare with the colour map on the right.

1 - The Sonnenberg, A Company; 2 - Koude Herberg crossroads, 17 and 18 Platoons C Company; 3 - Utrechtseweg; 4 - Van Lennepweg, 15 and 16 Platoons C Company; 5 - Battalion HQ; 6 - RAP; 7 - D Company on Van Borsselenweg; 8 - Westerbouwing; 9 - B Company; 10 - Veerweg; 11 - Road to Driel Ferry; 12 - Gasworks; 13 - Oosterbeek Church. *BRM*

Right Arnhem - the Perimeter. Locations as at 23.59 hrs on 20 September 1944. This is sketch R1 as prepared for the report to the Cabinet on Operation 'Market', with locations overlaid on a Dutch 1:25000 map (divided into approximately 1 km squares). Key: a - Lonsdale Force; b - C Sqn, 2 Wing GPR; c - 10 Para Bn; d - 156 Para Bn; e - 1 Airborne Recce Sqn; f - 7 KOSB; g - 21 Indep Para Sqn; h - 2 Wing GPR; i - A Coy, 1 Border; j - RE; k - C Coy, 1 Border; l - D Coy, 1 Border; m - B Coy, 1 Border; '+' - MDS. *Crown Copyright; reproduced with the permission of the Controller of Her Majesty's Stationery Office*

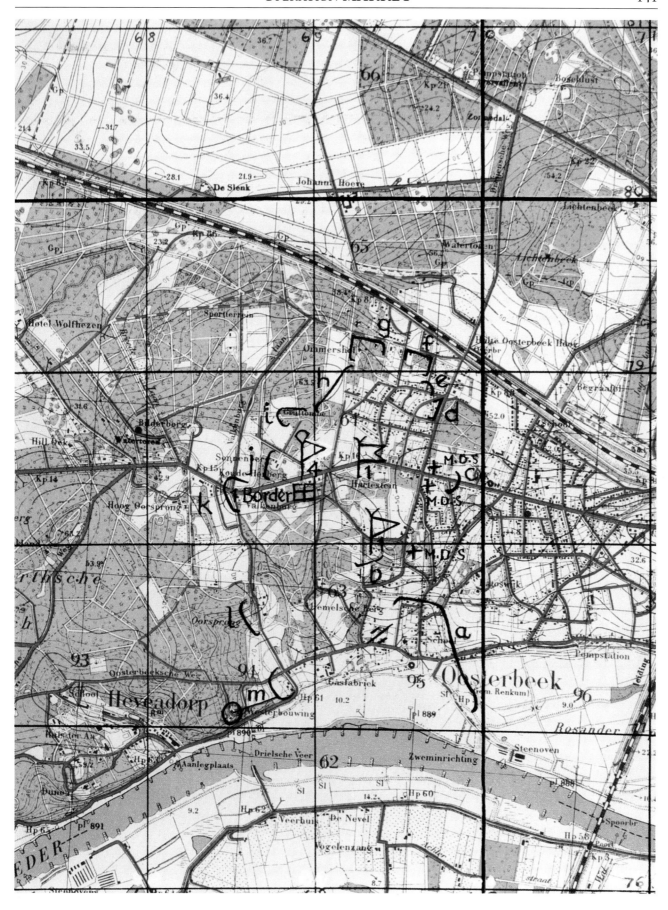

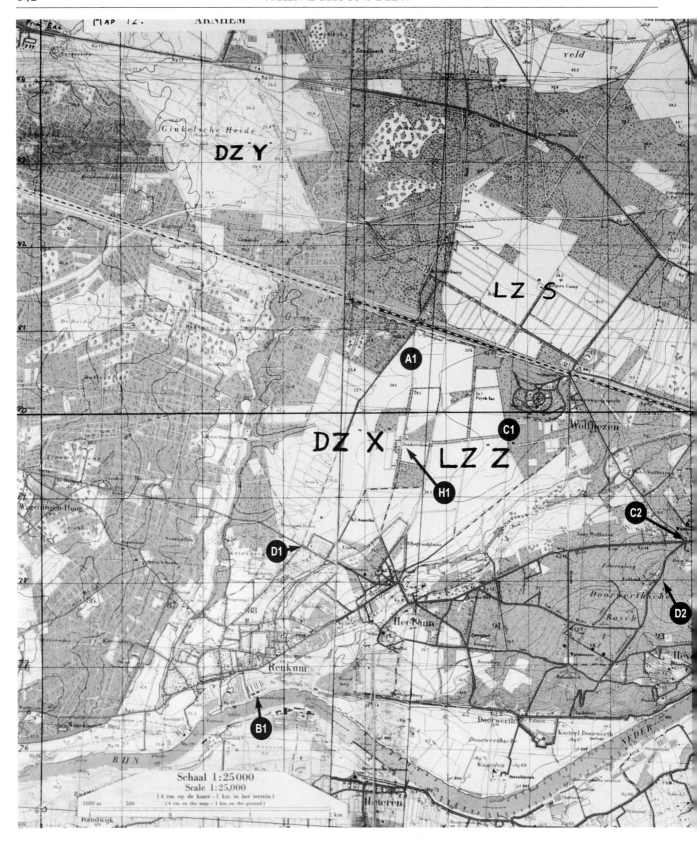

A Dutch 1:25000 map marked with the DZs and LZs for Operation MARKET, from the report to the Cabinet.
A1, B1, C1, D1 and H1 - positions of the Rifle Companies and Battalion HQ/RAP, 17-18 September; C2, D2 and H2 - C and D Companies and Battalion HQ, 18-19 September; B2 - B Company, 18-21 September; C3, D3 and H3 - C and D

Companies and Battalion HQ, 19-25 September; B3 - elements of 11 and 12 Platoons B Company, 21-25 September; BR - 'Breeseforce', 22-25 September; M - RAP, 18-25 September.

Crown Copyright; reproduced with the permission of the Controller of Her Majesty's Stationery Office

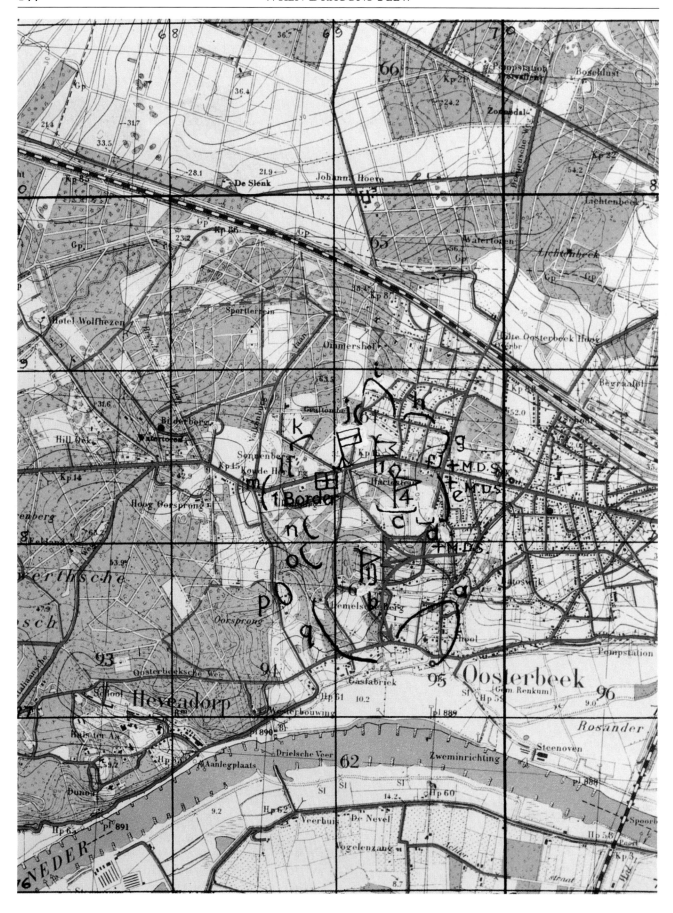

Left Arnhem - the Perimeter. Locations as at 14.00 hrs on 25 September 1944. This is sketch R2 as prepared for the report to the Cabinet on Operation 'Market', with locations overlaid on a Dutch 1:25000 map (divided into approximately 1 km squares).
Key: a - Lonsdale Force, 2 S Staffords, RA and GPR; b - HQ 1 Air-Landing Bde and GPR; c - GPR (Div reserve); d - 4 Para Bde Defence Pl; e - 21 Indep Para Coy; f - 10 Para Bn; g - GPR and Poles; h - 156 Para Bn and 2 troops 1 Airborne Recce Sqn; i - 7 KOSB; j - 2 Wing GPR; k - A Coy, 1 Border; l - RE; m - C Coy, 1 Border; n - Poles; o - C Sqn, 2 Wing GPR; p - D Coy, 1 Border; q - Breeseforce; '+' - MDS. *Crown Copyright; reproduced with the permission of the Controller of Her Majesty's Stationery Office*

Above right A Vickers MMG team in the western perimeter. They may be from 1 Border, but the area they are covering suggests the open ground to the north of the Hartenstein Hotel. *Taylor Library/IWM BU1149*

Below Ptes L. 'Taffy' Jury and Malcolm, both of C Company, with a Bren gun in a garden, probably that of the house on the east corner of Van Lennepweg and Utrechtseweg, where the AFPU Sergeants were based, 20/21 September 1944. *BRM/IWM BU1108*

In the early evening sun the RAF brought in the day's re-supply. The drop commenced at about 17.30 hrs. The aircraft came in quite low and the flak that followed them was extremely heavy; the men on the ground marvelled at the courage of the aircrews and the dispatchers, with aircraft flying a steady course only some 2-300 feet up and a sitting target for the gunners on the ground. Dakotas were being hit and bursting into flames, but still the aircraft flew a straight course as the dispatchers, who could be seen in the open doorways of the aircraft, pushed out panniers and containers to which were attached parachutes. Panniers that fell in the Brigade area were collected by the Divisional RASC unit, but many were lost as they fell in enemy-controlled areas.

Once more the message was passed around the Platoons that our friends would be with us the next day. That simply meant that the men would be relieved and with luck would be on their way home again in a few days. The message raised the morale of everyone, and so the evening drew to a close with the enemy fire dying down. Patrols were set up and some reported that the enemy had withdrawn from their daytime positions. After stand-to all companies had a quiet night.

In the RAP the MO, together with Capt John Rowell, the Padre, worked with their team of Orderlies to give what relief they could. There had been a steady steam of casualties throughout the day, with an increasing number of serious cases being evacuated to the DS. The RAP was suffering, as were the Companies, from the mortar and shell fire; minor damage meant that all casualties had to be treated on the ground floor or in the cellar. The one good point was that there was still some capacity to offer shelter and the team were still operating with reasonable efficiency.

From now onwards, for most men, the remaining days rolled into one long endless day. Because of tiredness, lack of food and water and forever having to be alert, it became almost impossible to distinguish one day from another.

In retrospect, 50 years on, most remember the constant bombardment by the enemy and by their own guns and mortars, because whenever an enemy attack erupted the only way that fire could be brought on to the enemy was to call it down on to their own position first to spot the fall of shot, then to lift the fall on to the enemy. All this added to the unpleasantness and danger, as many of the shells burst on impact with the tree branches and trunks, giving the effect of air-bursts, thus causing many more casualties. There was also the ever nearness of the enemy and the firing of personal weapons at close quarters. Hardly ever was a gun fired at more than 50 yards range, and very often it seemed that the enemy were sitting on the muzzle of each rifle or Sten gun. Each day every man hoped that the troops of 30 Corps would be with them during the night, or early the following morning, so that they would have the much needed support of heavy weapons and armour. If that support had been forthcoming every man would have been more than willing to move forward with the armour.

Thursday 21 September

At first light, about 05.30 hrs, the enemy once more brought down the morning hate on all positions. This was especially heavy in the areas of A and C Companies and Battalion HQ. Mortar bombs and shells exploded in the air as they struck the trees, or, if they missed the trees, on contact with the ground. Whichever way, there were casualties and it was becoming more and more difficult to evacuate the wounded; moreover, even if they could be taken to the RAP or Divisional DS, there was no guarantee that there would be room for them, or that they would receive any treatment other than the application of a simple field dressing. The number of dead was mounting and it was impossible to bury them. As one man remarked: 'We would be digging our own grave'. Snipers were active too, and it proved very difficult to pinpoint them and winkle them out. No one stayed in the open longer than was absolutely necessary. Telephone lines were laid to the Companies from Battalion HQ where possible, but due to the shell fire constantly cutting the lines they were as much of a problem as the wireless sets.

On this day the Germans launched a concerted attack from about 08.00 hrs all around the Divisional perimeter. Von Tettau had re-organised his forces the previous day and placed the more experienced troops forward. From the Rhine northwards, the units were the Worrowski Battalion and the SS Battalions Schulz, Eberwein and Helle under the command of Colonel Lippert and supported by the Renault Char B tanks of 224 Tank Company.

The attacks on C and A Companies the previous day having proved abortive, the Germans turned their attention to B Company down at Westerbouwing. It is difficult to know whether or not the Germans appreciated or were aware of the strategic importance of the high ground there, but possession of it would give them the Driel Ferry, a good FOP and the chance to force a route along the Benedendorp-sweg into the Divisional perimeter from the south, thereby cutting the Division's route to the Rhine. The desperate action that followed has been pieced together from the accounts of various members of B Company, whose experiences of this particular day differed widely.

At 09.00 hrs the Worrowski Battalion attacked B Company's position in force from the west and north-west with infantry supported by four French Renault Char B tanks of 224 Tank Company. Shortly after the attack started, Cpl Cyril Crickett, who led the Scout Section of 13 Platoon, was ordered to assist the other sections of his Platoon, which was located in woodland on the slope between Westerbouwing and the Veerweg, the road to the Driel Ferry and Heveadorp. As he and Ptes Hulse and MacDonald reached the top of the slope leading from the road, they could see the enemy infantry

Top Looking north from the area of the Driel Ferry in October 1993. The Westerbouwing Restaurant is in the wood at the top left, and 13 Platoon were positioned in the woodland on the slope when the Germans attacked on 21 September. *BRM*

Centre A 1945 view looking east from below Westerbouwing towards the gas-works. The ruins of the Company HQ are at the bottom of the field where 12 Platoon had their positions. Some of B Company's wounded had to be left in the buildings when the perimeter was pulled back. *BRM/Pat Stott*

Bottom A similar view taken in October 1993. The gasworks have been demol-ished since the war, but the Van Daalen house at the crossroads is clearly visible on the left. *BRM*

and tanks. At this moment there was an explosion close to Cyril and he was blown down the bank. As he regained the top he saw one of the tanks hit by a PIAT bomb fired by either Pte Ainsworth or Pte Savage of 13 Platoon. The tank burst into flames and the crew spewed out of the turret cupola. The man with the PIAT then changed his position, taking up a new one behind a dead cow. From here he attacked a second tank and disabled it. A third tank approached 12 Platoon's position near the crossroads, and it too was knocked out by PIAT fire. The fourth tank withdrew with its supporting infantry. The enemy were by this time well within the Company area and many were killed within this perimeter.

L/Cpl Ginger Wilson recalled that some of the first to meet this attack from 11 Platoon were Lt Barnes, himself, and Ptes Davidson and Harry Bragg. When they first saw the enemy they opened up with everything they had. The Bren gun jammed and, despite desperate efforts to hammer the cocking lever back with the base of a 36 grenade to free it, they could not clear the gun. As they worked on it Pte Bragg was hit and killed. By now the enemy were only 40 yards away and the group decided to run for it and attempt to rejoin the Company. As they went back up the hill they came across an officer with a wireless set calling for the lifting of the barrage that had been put down on the Company position by Allied guns; this had been requested by Major Armstrong. The first salvo landed slap on the enemy, but now the salvoes were landing among the Allied troops. At this moment a shell landed near the officer with the wireless set and he was wounded in the shoulder. He completed the sending of the message and the set was destroyed to prevent it falling into enemy hands.

One, possibly two, sections of 14 Platoon were already dug in near the restaurant. The third section under Cpl Ian Hunter, located down by the corner of the Veerweg facing the gasworks, was ordered up the hill by the Platoon commander, Sgt Watson, as the Germans were attacking. Halfway up the hill he met Major Armstrong, who told him that he would find some mortarmen on the right. In the confusion of battle he made for some slit trenches that he had previously occupied, but finding no men there decided to take up position

in them. They had not been there long when a burst of MG fire killed the L/Cpl and put the section's Bren out of action. A smoke grenade was thrown and the section made a rush to rejoin the Platoon on their left. When Cpl Hunter reached them he was unable to find anyone from his section. As he lay there he was aware that he was being fired on by a tank up on the road above him, and armour-piercing shells were bouncing off the bank above his head.

As the remaining enemy tank and infantry withdrew, Cyril Crickett recalled that 13 Platoon with Sgt Terry decided to pursue the enemy back to their positions. Lt John Wellbelove of 13 Platoon was in the forefront of the action and it was here that he was mortally wounded. Pte Jarvis, who was alongside Cyril, was also killed. The group came under heavy MG fire as they approached the German position and took cover behind a rise in the ground. So intense was the fire that they decided to withdraw to their original Platoon position.

When the tank that had fired at him was knocked out, Cpl Hunter also joined in the same counter-attack as Cyril Crickett. As he ran with his Platoon Sergeant, Sgt Watson, he found a couple of German stick grenades, which he picked up and gave to the Sergeant. In front of him was a German soldier who was running away from him. From time to time the man turned and threw a grenade, and each time Cpl Hunter found cover. His Sten gun would not fire, and as he tapped the bottom of the magazine with the palm of his hand, all the 9 mm rounds shot out into the bottom of a slit trench. His only hope now was a grenade. The German turned to throw yet another, but Hunter's grenade fell at the man's side and exploded, killing him instantly and he fell back with

Cpl Ian Hunter (front left) of 14 Platoon B Company with L/Cpl Jack Heaton and L/Cpl Joe Southwood (rear left and right) and L/Cpl Murray (front right), all of B Company. *Ian Hunter*

his grenade still in his hand. Hunter now rejoined the remnants of the Company and, as he picked up a PIAT to load it, was hit in the back and legs by mortar bomb fragments. Sgt Watson was killed during this action.

Before the Germans attacked, Lt Pat Stott, B Company's 2i/c, had been sent by Major Armstrong to Battalion HQ to deliver personally a situation report, since the wireless sets were not working and the telephone line laid by the Signal Platoon had been cut. He was away from the Company for less than 2 hours, but on his return to the Company position there was no one in sight, so he assumed that 11 and 12 Platoons had been redeployed. As he moved forward to Westerbouwing to assess the situation, he was surprised to see two tanks visible near the top of the field, one of which was moving towards the farmhouse used as Company HQ. He jumped into a slit trench and prayed hard that the tank would pass him by. After what seemed like an interminable length of time, but which was probably only a few minutes, the engine seemed to falter; it had been hit. This was the last tank to be knocked out in the action; Pat Stott later believed the marksmen to have been Pte Fitzgerald and Pte Jock Devlin of 14 Platoon, who were firing from the wood at the side of the field. In fact Devlin and Fitzgerald probably knocked out the tank nearer the top of the field, while the one approaching Company HQ was hit by 12 Platoon's PIAT fired by Pte Everington.

Pte Syd Cringle from 23 Mortar Platoon was dug in with his mortar close to the restaurant to cover the ferry area. He recalled that as the attack came in 'we turned our mortar on to the woods, removed all the secondary charges from our bombs and elevated the barrels until they were nearly firing perpendicular to reduce the range. Eventually we were forced to abandon the mortar as the tanks broke through. . .took up defensive positions with a Platoon on the edge of the cliff above the river. . .and were then ordered to cross the driveway of the restaurant and fight our way through the woods.' Syd was among a group of about six who came under heavy fire from one of the tanks as they fell back to the main Company position. Having reached the area of Company HQ, he was wounded by mortar shrapnel, joined the other wounded in the Aid Post, and was taken prisoner later that day.

Lt Stott realised that the high ground had been taken by the Germans, so without delay he made the journey back to Battalion HQ to report the new situation. The capture of the Westerbouwing heights had given the enemy an excellent position from which to observe a large area. However, as he moved by the quickest route along the Van Borsselenweg and D

Private Francis 'Jock' Devlin of 14 Platoon B Company, who knocked out one of the three German tanks during the attack on B Company on 21 September. He was taken prisoner during the Battle and subsequently rejoined the 1st Battalion after the war. He was tragically killed in a PIAT accident in Germany on 26 January 1946. *BRM/Johnnie Peters*

Company, he missed B Company in their new positions near and around the gasworks and north of the Benedendorpsweg.

Lt Arthur Royall recalled that as the first German attack developed, 14 Platoon were ordered to strengthen the forward position. 12 Platoon were then ordered up, but before he got there the remnants of the Platoons had fallen back and two tanks were moving down the field towards their positions, but both were knocked out by PIAT fire, one by his Platoon. In view of the numbers left, they were ordered to retire.

Meanwhile Cpl Hunter, now wounded, rolled down the bank and was carried by another soldier towards the Aid Post and finally brought in by Cpl Brett and a stretcher party. He found himself with other wounded, including Pte Cranswick, in the kitchen of the Company HQ farmhouse. L/Cpl Dunne, one of B Company's Medical Orderlies, re-dressed his wounds and gave him a morphia injection. All those fit

The Van Daalen house at the Van Borsselenweg and Benedendorpsweg crossroads photographed in 1947. Arthur Royall's Platoon was dug in among the orchard in the fore-ground at the edge of the field facing towards Westerbouwing. Royall and the remnants of 12 Platoon withdrew through the house and its garden towards the gasworks on 21 September. Several of B Company's wounded had to be left in the house, which was taken over by the Germans the same day and used as an Aid Post by them. *BRM/Arthur Royall*

enough eventually left as the Company pulled back; Pte Ryding was one of the last to leave, and as he grabbed a first aid satchel he said to Hunter, 'Sorry Jock, we have to leave you'. The Dutch family later emerged from the cellar of the farmhouse and informed the Germans that wounded men were in the various rooms. Cpl Hunter and the other wounded had to endure another day before they were moved by the Germans and taken to St Antonius Hospital in Utrecht, where he was operated on by the MO of 156 Battalion The Parachute Regiment.

Cpl Cyril Crickett recalled that they were ordered to evacuate the position around the Westerbouwing restaurant and together with others from the Company retired initially to the area of Company HQ, then beyond the crossroads into woodland on the north side of the Benedendorpsweg. Many of the Company's wounded were in the farmhouse or in the White House at the crossroads, which belonged to

the Van Daalen family. At some point during the afternoon Cyril recalled that Major Armstrong, the Company Commander, came up to him and said, 'You can take out a patrol, can't you?' and walked away.

Whether Tom Armstrong realised the significance of Westerbouwing, or Battalion HQ ordered that the ground be recovered, is unknown. Perhaps it was just on his own initiative and motivated by the desire to recover lost ground that made him change his mind about a patrol and lead instead a group of about 50 men from the Company back up towards the original B Company positions. Among the group was Cpl Crickett and Sgt Terry, the Platoon Sergeant of 13 Platoon, together with men from the Platoon. They had covered a fair bit of ground and were crossing an L-shaped clearing when they came under machine-gun fire. The group suffered a number of casualties including CSM Ernest McGladdery, who was killed. Cpl Crickett was badly wounded in the hand, and remembers sitting in the middle of the clearing putting a shell dressing on it.

Sgt Terry, who was nearby, had been hit in the chest and appeared to be in a bad way. At this point Major Armstrong dashed past. Cpl Crickett crawled away to the cover of the woods where he found Cpl Brett, who had been wounded in the throat, and Pte Swarbrick, who was wounded in the arm. Major Armstrong had also been wounded and, together with

Left Capt Pat Stott (centre) with Sgts Johnnie Peters and Hugh Pinkney in the ruins of what was B Company's HQ from 18 to 21 September 1944 in the farm buildings on the west side of the Veerweg and at the bottom of the field that runs down from Westerbouwing. The photograph was taken in 1945 when they re-visited Oosterbeek. *BRM/Pat Stott*

Below left The ruins of the Westerbouwing Restaurant, which B Company fought desperately to hold on 21 September, photographed by D. Renes in 1945, looking south-west across the Rhine. *J. van der Zeyden, Gemeente-Archief, Arnhem*

those who could not withdraw, was eventually taken prisoner later in the day. Major Armstrong was also wounded and taken prisoner. Later, on Friday 22 September, Cpl Crickett was operated on at the St Joseph's Hospital in Apeldoorn for the amputation of his arm as gas-gangrene had set it.

Meanwhile Lt Royall gathered the remnants of 12 Platoon and others and moved back through the Van Daalen house and garden at the crossroads towards the gasworks, where they dug in on its western side. Down to the river was open ground. The Platoon did not receive any orders to participate in the counter-attack and when the fumes from the gasworks made the buildings untenable, they withdrew to the east side. 12 Platoon then dug in along a track that led from Benedendorpsweg down to the footpath that ran from the Veerweg to Oosterbeek Church. At the end

of the track was a small farmhouse, which they occupied during the day. Near them was an Airborne Light Battery. Here, as everywhere else, they were subject to heavy mortar and MG fire. The casualties were taken to the house at the rear, which was being used as an Aid Post, and from time to time members of the Red Cross would come out and ask for a truce while they collected the wounded of both sides. The house rapidly overflowed with casualties and there were no medical supplies with which to treat the wounded, but the people of the house cared for them as best they could.

Lt Barnes and some men from 11 Platoon eventually found themselves in front of a house called Dennenoord. From here, with a group of some 30 men, he was given the task of neutralising an enemy MG post located in the summer-house in the gardens

The gasworks viewed from the Veerweg, looking east in 1947. Cpl Ian Hunter's section of 14 Platoon covered this corner. A path, the 'Kerk Pad', runs from the Veerweg along the hedge and wall of the gasworks, past the small farmhouse (right centre) to the Ter Horst house and Oosterbeek Church on Benedendorpsweg. 12 Platoon dug in at the front of the gasworks on the 21st, then moved beyond it to occupy the farmhouse by the path and the area above it until the evacuation. One of the escape routes taken by the remnants of the Division on 25/26 September crossed the path between the farmhouse and the Ter Horst house. *BRM/Arthur Royall*

of the house. They approached this with great caution, but casualties mounted so quickly that they withdrew to the house. They dug in behind the boundary fence of the tennis court some 25 yards away from the house, which seemed to offer protection against any assault.

Meanwhile, back at Battalion HQ Lt Stott had reported the situation at Westerbouwing to Major Cousens, the acting Battalion CO. It was decided to form a fighting patrol led by Major Dennis Morrissey of HQ Company and Capt Bob Reese, the Anti-Tank Group Commander, who were to work south through the woodland around Hemelsche Berg and eventually counter-attack the enemy holding the former B Company positions. The patrol was about 18 strong and included Lt Stott and Lt Joe Tate, one of the MMG Platoon commanders from S Company. As the patrol moved in a line across the first area of woodland, a German soldier moved out from behind a tree with his arms held upwards. Then without hesitation he fired from less than 15 yards and Lt Tate was killed

instantly. Someone in the party reacted quickly and shot the German. Further on there was another brief encounter when they were held up, but a grenade despatched three enemy soldiers who were screened behind some thick undergrowth.

The final sweep through the wood towards Benedendorpsweg and the B Company farmhouse met with very strong opposition from the enemy, who now held the crossroads area. As no further advance was possible, it was decided to withdraw and reform. Major Morrissey had been badly wounded in the back, but they managed to get him to an Aid Post. The force was reformed under Major Dickie Stewart of S Company and continued to patrol through the woods, eventually making contact with a group of Glider Pilots.

Capt Cleasby had also been detailed by Major Breese to gather up any stray soldiers to support B Company and were probably part of the group commanded by Major Stewart. Capt Cleasby was hit and taken back to the DS at the Tafelberg Hotel by his batman, Pte R. Sawyers; he was later taken prisoner there. During the action ammunition became very low, and Pte Alfred Knott volunteered to take a Bren carrier to re-supply the group. Despite heavy mortar and shell fire he forced his way through with the ammunition and eventually returned with eight pris-

A view looking east along the Benedendorpsweg taken in 1947. The white house known as Dennenoord stands on a narrow road between the Benedendorpsweg to Kerk Pad and the farmhouse where 12 Platoon were based. Lt Barnes, L/Cpl Ginger Wilson and the remnants of 11 Platoon were dug in near the house, which was also used as an RAP. BRM/Arthur Royall

oners. On the return journey the carrier was hit and destroyed, but Pte Knott escaped injury and volunteered to return for more ammunition and food. He was justifiably recommended for an MM for his gallantry, but received a C-in-C's Certificate.

After the attack on B Company had finally petered out and stragglers who had lost touch with their sections and Platoons made their way to D Company lines and Battalion HQ, it was now D Company's turn to be attacked. The whole position came under heavy mortar bombardment and 21 Platoon came under heavy fire. Their casualties were severe and the Platoon commander, Lt Holt, was killed; he was later buried by the estate keeper, Herr Beumer, whose cottage was adjacent to 21 Platoon's position. Those of the Platoon who could still fight were withdrawn to the area of Company HQ to form a reserve.

During the late morning at least two heavy armoured vehicles could be heard moving about in the woods to the Company's front. At about the same time the first hot meal for some days was being distributed to the men. There had been an issue of compo rations and the cooks had made a stew of sorts. Lt George Brown, OC 22 Platoon, who was acting Company 2i/c, was overseeing the distribution when he was caught in the open as he moved between slit trenches. A tank opened fired with its machine-gun and he was killed instantly.

This tank now moved down the edge of the wood on the field side of the boundary fence. It was moving slowly towards 22 and 20 Platoon positions, firing short bursts from its machine-gun as it came. A second tank could be heard moving across the front of the position towards a ride in the wood, which came directly into the Company lines in front of 20 Platoon. For a few brief moments there was hectic action. L/Cpl Bill Beck ran forward firing a Bren gun from the hip at the tank. Pte Parker and another soldier ran forward with a PIAT and took up position in a hedgerow. Almost immediately they were presented with a target, but the PIAT bomb did no serious damage to the tank and it could still move.

The 6-pounder anti-tank gun sited on the edge of the wood nearest to the approaching tank could not be turned to come into action as it was pointing at right-angles to the tank's line of approach. The gun crew under Lt Tony Howe, one of the Anti-tank Platoon commanders, raced to the second gun at the rear of the position. They rapidly man-handled it round to face the tank, which by now was only 20 yards away, but was still obscured by the trees and the bushes of the hedgerow. As they did so there was another burst of fire across the position and Cpl Tommy Langhorn, who was on the barrel end of the gun, was killed and Pte Fred Hodges was seriously

wounded in the arm. There was a cry of 'They've got the Corp, let 'em have it!', and the gun was quickly loaded with SABOT armour-piercing shot. The crew were ordered to hold their fire and there were some anxious moments as they waited until the tank broke from behind the cover of the hedge. Heavy enemy small arms and mortar fire was falling on the position, but by now no one seemed to notice.

The tank broke cover and as soon as it did so the gun-crew fired six rounds into it in a matter of as many seconds. The tank halted after the first hit, then burst into flames. The crew must all have been killed instantly, or been seriously wounded, as no one escaped. The gun crew were so incensed that Corporal Langhorn had been killed that they had to be pulled off the gun to stop them firing. As this incident developed Lt Alan Green had taken two men with a PIAT to lay an ambush for the second tank, which sounded as if it was also going to come down the ride into the Company position. As the party were taking cover there was a barrage of mortar and shell fire from Allied light artillery, who had to fire directly on to the men's position to observe the fall of shot. The effect of the barrage, the loss of the tank and the rapid rate of fire put down by the Company deterred any further enemy action and the second tank withdrew. The attack was thwarted.

Lt Green was wounded while trying to find a suitable site for the PIAT; fortunately he was still able to move about and direct activities in the firing line. This meant that of all the Company officers, only Capt Bill Hodgson was still unharmed. Lt Howe was also wounded, and along with other casualties had to be moved during a lull in the battle to the Company Aid Post in the cellar of the farmhouse. Here they had some protection from the mortaring and shelling, though in one of the neighbouring rooms there was an unexploded mortar bomb, which had come through the roof and the floor of the bedroom!

C Company were again attacked with the enemy trying to turn their flank. This move was spotted by Cpl Jim Swan who, leading a party of six men, attacked and dispersed the enemy platoon with bayonets and grenades; he received the MM for his leadership in this action (see Appendix 3). During the day C Company asked Battalion HQ to clear the wood between them and HQ as they were being sniped at from the rear. CSM Les Fielding, with a party of Signallers, Pioneers and anyone else who was available, was given the task. Their efforts were successful in that they flushed out and killed two snipers; but the Company was again attacked in the evening.

A Company had a fairly quiet day, although as in all Companies and units, ammunition was running short, there was no food and worst of all no water.

Cpl James Swan of the Scout Section of C Company HQ, who was awarded the Military Medal for leading a charge on 21 September. The photograph was taken outside Buckingham Palace on 6 December 1944, after he had been invested with the MM by HM King George VI. Four other members of the Battalion received awards on the same day. *BRM/Jim Swan*

The dusty ground aggravated the situation, as with every shell or mortar burst dust was thrown up into the air adding to the problems of thirst. Everywhere casualties were mounting and the worst was that most of them had to suffer in silence, as there was no way of getting them to the RAP and to surgical teams behind the lines. In any case there was no defined line and nowhere was safe even in the perimeter. In many cases it was impossible to bury the dead; they were laid out in buildings and in the open behind the Dressing Stations, in the open elsewhere, or where they fell.

Information and communications were still almost non-existent, though later in the morning some communication to 30 Corps was made by Pte Joe Maguire, a Signaller with D Company, due to freak weather conditions. Later some communication was made with 30 Corps by 1st Air-Landing Brigade HQ and

units were asked to select targets for 64 Medium Regiment RA of 30 Corps. Re-supply was falling regularly into enemy hands, as it was impossible either to indicate to the RAF where they should drop, or because recognition triangles and other signals shown by the troops on the ground were ignored.

Lt Pat Baillie recalled how the morning started strangely quietly for A Company compared to the previous day, but during the morning they received a message to be prepared to be attacked at some time during the day. In the early afternoon the enemy did make their attack, and to boost their spirits the Germans came forward making an awful noise. For the men of A Company the suspense and the tension mounted as they stood in their slit trenches watching the enemy come closer. As ammunition was in short supply, the order was that no man was to fire until the enemy were 30 yards away. When the order came there was hot lead flying everywhere and the enemy were taken completely by surprise. Three times they attacked and three times they were repulsed with heavy casualties, but there were also casualties amongst the Company that could be ill-afforded. Later during the night the Germans made another attempt, but were again repulsed.

Capt Ingram found it difficult to remember how long the Battalion had been in action. Something he thought must have gone terribly wrong. He had a total of 16 mortars, but there was no ammunition. The supplies brought with them were rapidly being used, although he felt that they were doing great work, for every mortar round seemed to kill 20 or more of the enemy. The noise of the battle had been going on for days and it was now quite impossible to reach B and D Companies even though they were less than a mile away, and extremely difficult to reach HQ and C, who were close at hand. There was an awful walk to Brigade HQ, always undertaken by two men at a time, and sometimes neither came back. Ingram walked around the mortar positions to keep the men informed and sang as he went to keep morale up. Yet he found the men always smiling. How they managed it he just did not know.

He suffered the common problem with his wireless sets and had 29 in all among his two Platoons, none of which worked properly. No one knew for sure where the other units of the Division were, and his position was fired on from all directions. What he disliked most was the relaying of messages from the command post to the individual mortar teams. Messages were received from the Companies asking for fire and these were called out to Ingram, who stood in the open at the bottom of the garden; he then relayed them to Lt Mike Holman, who was also standing in the open some 25 yards away, and who was in turn relaying messages to the teams. Both were being sniped at, and enemy shells were falling all around them.

During the evening B Company were ordered to attempt to recapture the Driel Ferry, from which position they had been earlier driven off. Lt Barnes called for volunteers and they set off in the dark. They went down by the greenhouses, over a dyke and out across open ground. In open formation they moved steadily forward until they came to the dyke running from Westerbouwing to Oosterbeek Church and beyond. As they reached the western end of the dyke, the Germans spotted them and brought down heavy fire. The rate of machine-gun fire was incredible, recalled Ginger Wilson. Some of the men took cover in the dyke, which was full of water. Eventually, when the firing died down, the survivors made their way back to Company lines.

As L/Cpl Wilson walked along the dyke, he could hear the squelch of mud and water underfoot. It seemed so loud that he thought the enemy would hear it and mortar the area. Passing the gasworks he approached Dennenoord by crawling across open ground. He was horrified to see four men crawling towards him in the darkness. He immediately thought that they were Germans, but all was well as they were friends from the Company.

As dawn broke on Friday 22 September there were shouts of 'Don't shoot, we're Poles!' coming from their right flank. Everybody held their fire and they were joined by some 20 men who had crossed the Rhine during the night. Sadly, by the middle of the morning 16 were to become casualties.

Friday 22 September

The night was reasonably quiet, but as usual in the early morning the enemy heavily mortared and shelled the Battalion area. At about 09.00 hrs the Battalion ammunition dump received a direct hit, which did considerable damage in the area and destroyed all but two of the remaining serviceable Battalion vehicles. The explosion caused a fire, which set ammunition exploding in all directions, yet RSM 'Bish' Pope and CSM Fielding and a party of men managed to salvage mortar bombs and .303-inch ammunition before the fire reached the plastic high explosive. Everyone managed to reach cover before this went up with a deafening roar, the loudest, said Les Fielding, that he had ever heard. Trees within a radius of hundreds of yards were stripped of leaves and small branches. The fire caused by the explosion became the registration point for the enemy mortars, so any movement from the slit trenches would result in casualties. It was during this incident that RSM

Pope, who had served with the Regiment since 1927, was fatally wounded. He was taken to the RAP, where, even as he lay dying, he joked with a Medical Orderly about getting his hair cut. He died shortly after, a much respected and well-loved father figure. CSM Les Fielding took over his duties.

At about 12.00 hrs Major Breese, the acting Battalion 2i/c, with Lt Stott gathered a small force together to go and support the remnants of B Company down towards the river and the force commanded by Major Stewart. The enemy had attempted during the morning to force a way through by the river road and deny use of the Driel Ferry. It became imperative that the ferry be regained, as 30 Corps were now moving their attack round to the west and 129 and 214 Brigades of 43rd (Wessex) Division had been ordered to take all risks to establish a link across the river.

Major Stewart had been wounded and there had been numerous other casualties. 'Breeseforce', as Major Breese's group came to be known, consisted of two depleted platoons of A Company commanded by Lt Bob Coulston and his Platoon Sergeant, Sgt Davidson, and Sgt S. Clark respectively. Remnants of B Company and a mixed force of Paratroopers also came under their command. Their orders were to prevent the enemy from out-flanking the Brigade position along the Benedendorpsweg. Lt Coulston and the A Company group dug in on the north side of the main road in woodland several hundred yards east of the White House crossroads, which was part of the Hemelsche Berg estate. Major Breese and Lt Stott were 20 yards away.

To the east of the gasworks and directly south of this group, Lt Royall and 12 Platoon were still defending the approaches from the west and inflicting enemy casualties, having shot up a German patrol that came down the path alongside the gasworks towards their farmhouse. Having discovered 'Breeseforce' on the other side of the road, Royall went across from time to time to exchange information. The enemy continued to attack on all the Company fronts throughout the day, but now artillery support was available from the medium and heavy guns of the 2nd Army across the Rhine.

In C Company's area Lt Roberts took out a patrol and returned with two German MGs, having killed the crews in the process. The Company's wireless link with Battalion HQ failed, so L/Cpl Gavaghan of the Signals Platoon, the only Signaller available at HQ, volunteered to lay a telephone line through enemy positions to restore communications. He duly restored the link, which enabled HQ to lay on artillery support for C Company as they were being attacked. Gavaghan was recommended for the MM, but only

Above The 'Kerk Pad', which led from Veerweg to Oosterbeek Church, photographed looking east in 1947 from the rear of the gasworks; 12 Platoon's farmhouse is in the centre. *BRM/Arthur Royall*

Left Men of C Company in their foxholes in the Van Lennepweg area, 21/22 September 1944. Note the light sandy soil, which is characteristic of the whole area, and the woodland, which afforded only limited visibility to both defenders and attackers. *Taylor Library/IWM BU1133*

received an MiD. Sgt Thompson also distinguished himself on patrol work.

All Companies were subjected to heavy and constant shelling, suffering more casualties, despite inflicting heavy losses on the enemy and 30 Corps artillery assisted in breaking up their attacks. At one stage, in D Company's position, a mortar bomb fell through the trees above Lt Green and Pte Len Powell, dropped behind Lt Green, struck him on the back of the knee and landed in the bottom of the trench. Pte Powell picked it up and threw it out of the trench. Fortunately it did not explode when it hit the ground for a second time. At 16.00 hrs the Company reported to Battalion HQ that it was almost surrounded and that the fighting strength of the Company was now down to two officers and 35 ORs.

However, there was no withdrawal from the Company's position; despite all attacks and the casualties, everyone was still in good spirits. The casualties did not complain and bore their problems very stoically, ever hopeful that 30 Corps would arrive and that they would be hospital-bound. The cellar of the farmhouse was now very overcrowded and it was becoming difficult to find suitable accommodation. Pte Danny Fowler, one of the Medical Orderlies, did

Ptes Fred Hodges (*below*), Harold 'Skip' Ennis (*above right*) and John Ranger of 20 Platoon D Company. Harold Ennis and Fred Hodges, who was from Coventry and was severely wounded, were both taken prisoner and held in Stalag XIB. *Fred Hodges and John Ranger*

what he could for them, but he was running short of dressings and antiseptics. Men needed the attention of a doctor, but there was no means of taking them to the RAP, even though it was only half a mile away.

Capt Graham-Jones found that the heavier mortar and shell fire on the Battalion HQ area caused further damage to his building, although no personnel were injured. The treatment areas were now restricted to the hallway and cellars of the house. He too was experiencing a shortage of food and medical supplies, and matters were made worse by a message from the ADMS of the Division, which stated that there was to be no further evacuation of casualties to the DS, since the treatment was now no better than that at the RAP. The risks of transporting the injured was unacceptably high, and another message informed the MO that there were no vehicles left to transport the injured anyway.

The day drew to a close, with re-supply still falling anywhere, except to where the troops were actually fighting in the ever-smaller perimeter. The battle on the ground was one in which everyone knew that they had fought gallantly and gloriously, with a great deal of bravery from all ranks, but the men marvelled at the bravery of the aircrews and the dispatchers working behind them as they flew at such a lazy pace over the battlefield and at such low altitude. Despite continual AA fire at point-blank range, they held to

their course, dropping containers by parachute and throwing panniers out of the doors of the aircraft. Sometimes aircraft were hit, but the crews continued their work. Often when they were dropping panniers they flew so low that it seemed almost possible to reach out and touch the crews working at the open doors. The casualties to RAF crews and RASC dispatchers testify to their outstanding courage. One C-47 was seen to have fire streaming from an engine nacelle with flames reaching back almost to the tailplane. It was obviously going to crash, yet the crew were still shoving the panniers out. The crash was eventually heard above the noise of battle.

The most valuable piece of property that anyone could have was a slit trench, which provided cover from mortar bombs, shells and ricocheting bullets. These were usually shared by two men; one could crouch in the bottom in an endeavour to get some rest, while his companion could keep watch. Never were two men allowed to sleep at the same time in any trench.

As in all battles there was a continual flow of rumour and gossip, which passed from trench to

Soldiers signalling to the supply aircraft with their yellow celanese recognition triangles. The photograph was probably taken in the grounds of the Hartenstein. *Taylor Library/IWM BU1097*

Airborne soldiers searching a ruined building in Oosterbeek, probably around 21 September 1944. The location is unknown, but may be the stable-block of the Hartenstein Hotel. Syd Cringle, who served in 23 (Mortar) Platoon, recalled that years later he met the son of the man on the left; he identified his father, who served with 1 Border. *Wilf Oldham/IWM BU1121*

trench. It came from many sources: a visit to Company HQ, or perhaps from someone who had managed to get through to Battalion HQ, or from a straggler from another company or unit. 'So and so has been killed', 'A section on patrol has been wiped out', 'Such a Platoon or Company is being attacked by tanks and overrun', or 'The 2nd Army is on its way and will be with us tonight'. But always the men smiled and kept in good spirits, cursing, as only soldiers can, the slowness of the 2nd Army.

Lt Joe Hardy related how they were short of food, just as everyone else was. Into their lines came a hungry-looking chicken, and a small, poor bird it was. A soldier quickly cured its hunger with a bayonet. The feathers were taken off, its innards removed, and it was then thrown into an old-fashioned galvanised bath-tub. Each man contributed a small amount of water, bits of broken hard tack, bits of bully and pieces of concentrated oatmeal, most of which was well peppered with sand and thickened up with grass from the shell and mortar fire; the lawns, he recalled, had been good in Oosterbeek that year. The fact that

sand came up with the grass seemed to be unimportant as there was the quite distinct ring of dried soap-suds around the upper edges of the bath; however, as there was only sufficient water to reach half-way up the bath, this little item was of no consequence. Eventually all was cooked and to hungry men the resulting concoction was really the epitome of home cooking.

Saturday 23 September

During the night at 02.00 hrs a small party of men from the Division's reserves were sent to strengthen A Company, who had sent two platoons to 'Breeseforce'. On their left were small parties of Royal Engineers and Paras, who formed a link with C Company on their left.

With the dawn came the usual morning hate, and again it was a case of keeping heads low and a very watchful eye all round the area, which by now was beginning to look devastated with the constant heavy fire. This heavy fire continued until around noon, when both A and C Companies were attacked by infantry, self-propelled guns and flame-throwing tanks. The north flank of A Company was turned during the furious fighting. At Battalion HQ Capt Ingram arrived in time to hear a wireless message from the Company: 'Flame-throwing tank in the area, and shelling Company HQ - all officers and NCOs killed or wounded - what shall we do?' Ingram thought what a good type the Signaller was. A flame-throwing tank some 30 yards away and the Signaller sounding as calm as anything.

Sgt Herbert Burton from the Intelligence Section then appeared with ten men from A Company, and Capt Ingram was ordered to go to the Company area to see if he could do anything. He took Pte J. Gordon, 23 Mortar Platoon's Range-Taker, and the Sergeant and his men. As they approached the area they met with the Royal Engineers on the south flank of A Company's position. Leaving the party behind, Ingram and Gordon carefully went forward under the shelter of a wall. As they peered round the end of the wall an amazing sight faced them. Men were throwing grenades at a tank and running around in the trees, and shells and mortar bombs were still raining down; all in all there was incredible noise and confusion. Ingram sent Pte Gordon to fetch Sgt Burton and his men, and as they came up the tank burst into flames. However, the MG fire was intensifying. The question was, were the infantry going to attack?

At this point Capt Charles Wilson, the 2i/c of A Company, appeared. This was a surprise as it was understood that all the Company officers had been killed or wounded; among these was A Company's commander, Major Montgomery, who was to die of his wounds later in a German hospital. Capt Wilson led the way down to the cellar where the Signaller was, warning Barry Ingram to be careful as they went through the door into the house, as there was a sniper about. As they went through the door two shots missed him by inches. As Wilson was about to explain the situation to Ingram, he was hit and severely wounded by a shrapnel burst.

Ingram assessed the situation. There were 60 or 70 men of various units, one Vickers MMG, two Brens and one PIAT with three rounds. Company HQ was in a house with a sparse fir plantation about 30 yards wide on two sides of it. The enemy were some 40 yards away along a hedgerow, which followed two sides of the Company position. Beyond them were two or three small cottages. He assumed that the German HQ was in the cottage that had a thatched roof and that the sniper, with a fixed line on the door of Company HQ, was in one of the others.

He thought that they could hold off an attack of up to 100 infantry as they had 40 yards in which to see an attack coming; as for a tank attack, he thought that if he could let them get into the woods, they would have a good chance of knocking them out. The men were duly briefed on what action to take, then the long wait began. When the Germans attacked they came in shouting and screaming as if trying to frighten the Allies. The Company held their fire, then opened up

Lt, later Capt, Baldwin 'Flip' Wilson. He served as 2i/c to Major Tui Montgomery with A Company at Oosterbeek and was wounded on the 23rd and later taken prisoner. The photograph was taken in Italy in 1943. *BRM/Baldwin Wilson*

at point-blank range, resulting in an instant massacre. The men ran out and collected urgently needed arms and ammunition from the debacle in front of them; two MG 34s, two Luger pistols and a rifle with ammunition were recovered, which was all very useful as they were running short of ammunition for their own weapons. Captain Ingram returned to Battalion HQ to report on the situation. There he found Lt Lawrence Withers MC of 2 South Staffords, who joined him as his 2i/c. The year before Withers had won his MC for the action at Ponte Grande bridge on Sicily. Ingram also found Sgt Rogers and a 3-inch mortar with nine HE and three smoke rounds.

Ingram decided to try one HE round as a ranging shot on to the thatched cottage, followed by one round of smoke on to its roof, then, if the roof was hit, another HE round. The scheme was an instant success; the roof caught fire, then flames engulfed the cottage and the enemy ran in all directions only to suffer numerous casualties as the Vickers MMG opened up on them. So it went on: heads down between attacks, then when the noise of the shelling stopped they knew that an attack was coming in, so they popped up and opened fire, then out into the open to collect enemy weapons and ammunition.

Twice a day Ingram reported personally to Battalion HQ and over the radio every hour, and each time he went through the cellar door the sniper got in two shots. There were four attacks that day on the Company. Capt Ingram was recommended for the MC for his leadership, gallantry and devotion to duty as both the Mortar Group Commander and as A Company's acting OC; he received an MiD.

During the engagements the Company signalled urgently for 82 Grenades (Gammon Bombs) to deal with the tanks and SP guns. None were available in the unit reserve, but L/Cpl James Steele remembered having seen a container of ammunition dropped in the woods in No Man's Land. Hoping that it might contain some grenades, he set out at once to recover it. Several men had already been killed trying to bring supplies back from these woods, which were under continuous fire of all kinds. Without a thought for himself, L/Cpl Steele went out and brought in the container, which was full of anti-tank grenades; he duly assembled them and carried them to the Company under heavy fire from the tanks, thereby enabling the Company to beat off the attack. For his gallantry he was recommended for the MM; he received a C-in-C's Certificate.

CSMI Fred Connett APTC, attached to the Battalion and based with Battalion HQ, volunteered to go for a badly needed supply of wireless batteries from the Divisional dump via a route that was under fire and had already claimed lives. He successfully completed the task, then helped to bring ammunition forward to A Company; thereafter he continued to organise and lead ammunition-carrying parties from the Divisional dump to Battalion HQ. Lt Doug Skilton, HQ Company's Administrative Officer and also the acting Intelligence Officer, moved between A and C Companies and Battalion HQ, gathering information, and organising and conducting carrying parties for ammunition and supplies. These men were duly recommended for the MM and MC respectively; they received a C-in-C's Certificate and an MiD. Their gallantry played no small part in restoring the grave situation in A Company's area. (It is interesting to note that many of the recommendations for awards must have been watered down or refused at a higher level, since no gallantry medals were awarded to any rank from the Battalion who was taken prisoner.)

CSM Fielding took some of the meagre reserves of .303-inch ammunition over to A Company, and when he arrived he spoke with the Vickers MMG section attached to the Company. They too had a water problem; the supply for the water jackets of the guns necessary to cool the barrels had run out. There was nothing for it; all ranks had to produce a 'wee pee' to fill the 2-gallon condenser can so that the gun could continue firing. The Platoon Sergeant concerned gravely thanked them for their assistance and then went off with CSM Fielding and a PIAT to mortar a German tank crew, who were outside their tank trying to repair it. They were too far away to be really effective, but the shot scared them off.

In the lulls between attacks, the drill was for one man to stay on watch and for the other to sleep in the bottom of the trench. Capt Ingram, who was sleeping thus, was kicked awake by his companion, Lt Withers. There was a near disaster as a shell had landed on some dud ammunition, setting it alight. The fire had also set one of the trees on fire, which had to be put out before it spread to the rest. Ingram, Withers and a couple of men set about putting the fire out, silhouetted by the flames. The enemy opened up, but amazingly no one was hit.

At one point during his busy day, the CO asked Ingram to withdraw his men to a position nearer the Battalion HQ. The chosen position seemed to be the focal point of enemy barrages, so he was not particularly pleased with the idea. Under duress he agreed to the move, but first requested that the wounded in the nearby RAP be evacuated. For the first time since the action had begun, Ingram visited the RAP to arrange for the removal. It was a particularly horrible and poignant sight. Wounded were everywhere and the smell almost too much to bear. No one seemed to know where the MO was. As Ingram descended the flight of stairs to the cellar, an evil smell of unwashed bodies, dirty dressings and fetid air met him. He trod on the Padre, John Rowell, who told him that the MO was out on his feet and it was doubtful whether it would be possible to wake him. By dint of much shaking and pummelling, Graham-Jones was woken, and Ingram asked for his wounded to be evacuated. The MO grunted 'impossible' and fell asleep again. Ingram returned to Battalion HQ with an apology that the Company could not move and leave the wounded to be taken prisoner; he therefore refused to move and was threatened by Major Cousens with an eventual court martial. In the ensuing exchange Ingram told Major Cousens that his order was unreasonable and that it was not worth leaving such a large number of wounded men to certain death or imprisonment, to say nothing of the 50 per cent casualties they could expect in moving back to the new position. The two officers eventually parted on the worst of terms.

Meanwhile C Company were holding firm against repeated attacks, as was D Company, who were by now completely surrounded. The enemy were continually trying to infiltrate through the perimeter at this point; shelling and mortaring was almost continuous and patrols trying to reach the gallant Company were repeatedly driven back. The only communication between D Company and Battalion HQ was by wireless, and this was precarious as the batteries for the sets were running down and there were no spares. During the night further patrols were sent out, but could not get through to the Company.

Down on the Rhine some Polish troops had managed to cross the river and join up with B Company, but the position was soon to be the centre of a fierce 'hate' by the enemy. The Poles were soon reduced to 50 per cent of their number; for some reason they would not dig slit trenches for cover. Lt Robert Coulston, OC 9 Platoon A Company, was killed and the Platoon taken over by Sgt Davidson, the Platoon Sergeant. His one great worry at this time was the

A Bren-gunner in C Company's area photographed during the battle. *BRM/Sammy Black*

shortage of cigarettes. Nevertheless he kept up a constant patrol of the Platoon positions, keeping the men under his command cheerful. Cpl Edgar was another great example, always in the thick of the fighting; if he thought there were Germans near, he would go off on his own and always come back with a good bag.

At one stage the Company DS was overrun. This was located in the house known as Dennenoord, whose Dutch occupants had made it their responsibility to care for the wounded. Cpl Edgar re-loaded his Sten and entered the house, where he killed the majority of the enemy and chased the remainder out of the back door. Sadly, later in the day a wounded German officer managed to raise his pistol as he died and shot Cpl Edgar, who was killed instantly.

It was now imperative that B Company area be held at all costs. Lt Stott had attended a briefing at Brigade HQ, where it was announced that 30 Corps would attempt to make a river crossing at that point. Lt Mike Holman had managed to keep his 23 Mortar Platoon working all day, but some were knocked out through accurate counter-battery fire from the Germans, and those that survived had little or no ammunition. He continued to direct the fire of his mortar teams and encourage them, then, when the ammunition ran out, he formed his remaining men

into a rifle section and fought on. Like Barry Ingram, he too was recommended for an MC, and eventually received the award of the Dutch Bronze Lion.

During Saturday evening C Company were attacked, the enemy trying to infiltrate through their positions. Despite being wounded four times during the day, Major Jock Neill rapidly organised a counter-attack, and his leadership and courage were a key factor in driving the enemy out of the Company lines. Not content with this, he led a patrol from 17 Platoon and Company HQ support group through into enemy lines; the group included Cpl Jim Swan, Pte Freddie Matthews, Pte Joe Rainford and Cpl Freddie Webster. As they approached their objective, the houses near to the Koude Herberg Cafe cross-roads, they came under fire. The patrol took cover, and Major Neill rested a Bren on the shoulder of Pte Bob Lee and fired at the objective.

L/Cpl Doug Payne was close to a building when the enemy started mortaring the area. A bomb falling between Payne and the building severely wounded him down his left side and face, and the patrol, having left him for dead, continued their attack, driving the superior enemy force from their own position and captured their HQ. L/Cpl Payne eventually regained consciousness and, as he made his way back to the Company lines, was wounded by MG fire on the way, which broke his left leg! He called out, was dragged in by Cpls Swan and Webster, and was taken to the Company Aid Post, where L/Cpl Mead and Pte Murphy RAMC patched him up. He was then driven in a jeep by Pte Bob Syrett of 17 Platoon to the Tafelberg, where the doctors saved his leg, but he lost his left eye. Major Neill was later awarded the DSO for his leadership (see Appendix 3).

Capt Graham-Jones could no longer evacuate casualties to the DDS at the Schoonoord. By now the RAP was filled with men from every unit in action in the area together with a large number of civilians. Fortunately the building had suffered no further damage despite the shelling, but there was little food and a shortage of medical supplies. The staff now had to move as many of the severely wounded cases into some sort of bomb-proof shelter, making them as comfortable as possible and devising means of keeping their spirits up.

Back over the river, Lt Col Haddon, the CO, and Lt Ronald Hope-Jones, the IO, together with the small party of men from their glider, had heard that the Poles were to attempt a night river crossing opposite the Divisional area. Having been fed and looked after by their own Seaborne Tail, Haddon thought that they ought to attempt the crossing with this force. As he put it, 'However hairy a party it might be, we ought to have a shot at it with them'.

They set off after dark, and an hour or so later reached the Polish forces in the village of Driel, just south of Oosterbeek across the river. For 2 or 3 hours they waited outside Polish Brigade HQ, getting colder, then at last drove down a succession of small lanes, the only landmark being a single burning farm. Eventually they reached the position from which the crossing was to be made; here they found unrelieved chaos. A Sapper officer was trying to unload his boats and get them down to the river, but the Poles did not seem to have any idea where they were meant to go, what they were meant to do, or when they were meant to do it. Lt Col Haddon's party could do nothing except wait.

Before long they put the finishing touch to the evening by ditching their jeep. This was pulled out backwards on to the road, then machine guns on fixed lines opened up and fairly heavy mortar fire was put down on the bank; the latter protected them from the MG fire, but the mortar fire was unpleasantly accurate. They spent 2 hours in this position, awaiting their turn to cross the river and in complete ignorance of what was going on. Part of the plan had been as absence of supporting fire to assist the crossing in order to 'safeguard surprise'. This was already lost.

No fire plan was subsequently put into effect by the Allied forces, and by the time the 1st Battalion party had moved down to the embarkation point to take their place in the queue, they had concluded that it was indeed a 'hairy party' - there was no doubt about it. The party waited at the embarkation point under continuous and accurate fire for what seemed ages, until the Polish General who was in charge decided that no further crossings were practical that night. So the whole crossing was called off and, as dawn broke, the party climbed back into their jeep and drove back to the local Brigade HQ, cold, tired, dispirited and hungry.

The members of the Battalion's Seaborne Tail had remained with the Brigade Group in the lying-up area near Eindhoven. At 20.00 hrs that night, the group, together with other Seaborne elements of the Division, began the journey north as the situation for the Division became critical. They travelled throughout the night, passing through Grave and reaching a bivouac area near Nijmegen just before midday. During the journey north the column became divided by an enemy attack and progress was impeded by other units with priority cutting into their column.

Sunday 24 September

The river crossing by the Poles during the night had been partially successful, since a small part of a Battalion, less HQ Company, had managed the crossing. Of these some 200 were allotted to 4th Parachute Brigade to strengthen the north-east part of the perimeter, and the rest to 1st Air-Landing Brigade; some of these came under the command of the Battalion, being allocated to B Company.

Overall it was a fairly quiet day, and there was still hope that 30 Corps would get across the river and relieve the Division, or what was left of it. Despite all the problems and difficulties imposed by casualties, shortages of food, water and above all ammunition, morale was high. The previous night the re-supply had dropped all over the area. In D Company's area there was great rejoicing as a pannier came crashing through the trees. It was quickly retrieved and opened only to disappoint everyone with its contents of PIAT bombs - everyone had hoped that there would be some food at last. This was typical of the whole Battalion area. The Battalion ammunition reserve was down to 2,500 rounds of .303-inch, and C Company reported that they were using up to 50 per

cent captured weapons and ammunition. This was true of all Company areas.

'Breeseforce', down by the river, had found that two tanks had penetrated their position and Sgt Sidney Clark, Platoon Sergeant of 7 Platoon A Company, destroyed one of them single-handed. Later, when he was leading his Platoon in clearing the enemy from a wood, they came under fire from a tank in a hull-down position. Using the covering fire of his Platoon, he stalked the tank, rushed it and, having climbed on to it, raised the turret-hatch and dropped grenades inside. The firing ceased as the tank became a blazing wreck. For this action Sgt Clark was awarded the DCM (see Appendix 3).

Lt Stott was ordered by Major Breese to take a severely wounded man to the nearest RAP. At this time they still had a jeep available, and the wounded man was placed on a stretcher strapped to the vehicle. The journey was over rough tracks through the woods of the Hemelsche Berg estate, and the man must have suffered acutely. Lt Stott had his own head wounds dressed and returned to 'Breeseforce' positions in the jeep. There was no opposition on the way, but he recalled quite clearly that the enemy were openly moving around the RAP. At 19.35 hrs there were attacks on D Company and the Battalion area to their

CSM Sidney Clark DCM (left), photographed at Sezana, Italy, in 1946 with CQMS Bulmer of D Company, who had joined the 1st Battalion from 4 Border after Arnhem. CSM Clark, as a Platoon Sergeant in A Company attached to 'Breeseforce', won his DCM for destroying a tank single-handed on 24 September 1944. *Jim Swan*

Private John Hamer of the MMG Platoon (centre) with a Polish Glider Pilot and a Para in the grounds of the Hartenstein Hotel towards the end of the Battle. *Jim Longson*

right. All the attacks were repulsed, although D Company had to report that they were now reduced to 19 all ranks, but were still holding out. Capt Bill Hodgson and Lt Alan Green, although wounded, were the only two officers still mobile. Efforts to get a two-man patrol through to Battalion HQ were again thwarted, Lt John Bainbridge being wounded at about this time.

In C Company's area the attack was developing quite strongly, so Lt Hardy, who was passing messages to the Light Battery after the Artillery FOO had been killed, called for close fire support along the Company's front. Thinking he would get the message to which he had become accustomed, that there was no ammunition, he was surprised to hear his call answered by a deep American voice, telling him that he had a Regiment of 'Long Toms' (US 155 mm Howitzers) under his command. Joe Hardy had no idea of what a 'Long Tom' was, but assumed correctly that it was heavy artillery and situated possibly somewhere near Nijmegen. Above all, the voice said, they were not short of ammunition. Lt Hardy asked the voice to lay a barrage in front of the Company. The response was dramatic and effective and no doubt shook the enemy in no uncertain terms. To know that

these guns were only some 12 miles away was a great relief, for it meant that the relieving force must be only just over the river. This thought and a continued determination to resist enabled the tired and hungry men of the Battalion to carry on.

During the day an O Group was called at Battalion HQ and orders were given concerning the reception of the relieving force, which was to cross the river during the night and was to take over Battalion positions. Immediately spirits and hopes rose on receipt of this news.

The IO, Lt Hope-Jones, and the CO, who were still trying to cross the river, had arrived back with the forward troops on the south bank of the Rhine. He says that after breakfast they heard that the 4th Battalion Dorset Regiment were to make a full-scale crossing during the night of the 24th, properly supported with artillery, mortars and MMGs. They were to establish themselves on the high ground to the west of the Airborne Division and thus secure a bridgehead through which supplies could be passed. The decision to reinforce them or to evacuate the position would be taken by the Corps Commander on the following day.

On the whole this looked a more promising party than the shambles of the previous night, and the party was considerably cheered by what they had heard. Once again they set off in good time and reached the rendezvous on the north side of Driel by

20.00 hrs. Once more, however, they had to endure a long wait. At about 01.00 hrs they moved off through the woods to the river bank. There was some mortar fire, but by this time 30 Corps were providing heavy supporting fire, which gave everyone more confidence than on the previous night. Soon after arriving at the start point the crossing began, but Lt Col Haddon's party had to wait for the second lift; this meant another hour's delay. When they eventually set off there was very little fire coming from the north bank and the crossing was much less nerve-racking than expected. Unfortunately, they were a little too far upstream, and after turning round in a complete circle they finally reached the far bank, upstream of the Driel Ferry. Everyone was soon out on the bank, but in front of them was a steep and thickly wooded slope, from which the occasional shots were being fired.

Almost immediately the party was split up. Lt Hope-Jones was at the rear with a couple of Signallers, one of whom had had to return to the boat for a battery; by the time he found it the rest of the boatload had moved off. Since there was firing immediately to the front, Lt Hope-Jones went along the bank to the east, where he ran into a rather frightened platoon of the Dorsets. They looked on him as a gift from heaven, obviously expecting to be led safely through the enemy lines into the arms of their Battalion. Lt Hope-Jones says that he hardly felt qualified to do the job, but he went to the front and began to lead them up the bank through the tangle of undergrowth. It was extremely steep and the sandy soil made him slip back 2 feet for every 3 he climbed. After struggling through the brambles for what seemed to be an eternity, he heard a movement a few yards in front and above him, and at once challenged 'British or German?'. The only answer was a remark in German, passed from one man to another. Throwing a couple of grenades and shouting 'Charge!', he tried to rush the position up the slope. By the time he reached the Germans they were either dead, or feigning so. By now some of the Dorsets had struggled up to him and there was more small arms fire being aimed at the party, both from the right and the left; he fired back with his Sten. At this point he discovered that there was a Platoon Officer with them, so he felt that he had no further obligation to shepherd them.

Lt Hope-Jones's task was now to work east in the general direction of Arnhem. Occasionally he was fired on, but nothing came too close and as dawn broke he found himself on one side of a clump of bushes in the centre of quite a large clearing. Then he heard someone moving on the far side of the clump. The two stayed there, conscious of each other's pres-ence, for at least 5 minutes. Then he could stand it no longer and shouted 'I'm British, what are you?' There was a short pause, then he saw a very little man in German uniform scuttling across the clearing as fast as his little legs would carry him. There was plenty of time to shoot, but by now he had no ammunition left. Anyway, Hope-Jones said that he did not think he could have brought himself to shoot him.

It soon became clear that there was no hope of get-ting through to the Battalion or anyone else, and the best he could do for the time being was to join up with the Dorsets and try to link up with the Air-Landing Brigade later in the day. Some 10 minutes later he located the Dorsets' main position and found them digging in furiously. Selecting a suitable spot for a slit trench, he plied his entrenching tool as never before. Having managed to get down about a foot, the bullets started cracking over his head and he became acutely conscious that a slit trench 5 feet long, 1 foot wide and 1 foot deep provided remarkably little cover for a man over 6 feet tall.

The machine-gun and mortar fire became more intense, and in the distance the rumble of tanks could be heard. This went on for an hour or two, then to everyone's astonishment there was a cry of 'Cease fire!' from behind them. Two officers, one English and one German, came down to the position and told the men that the CO of 4 Dorsets had surrendered the Battalion. Hope-Jones was never more surprised in all his life, but there was a feeling of relief, for it was obvious that with no fields of fire and up against a superior enemy force, they had little option. When he fell in with the others he found Pte Kelly and L/Cpl Nolan, Lt Col Haddon's batman, who had been badly wounded in the stomach. They carried him up the road, where he was given morphia by Hope-Jones. A stretcher was fetched for him and he was carried off by Kelly and some other men to a dressing station. Lt Col Haddon, who had left the Dorsets fairly early on, was captured later that morning while trying to find the Battalion.

So Sunday passed into Monday 25 September, the fateful day for the final decisions.

Monday 25 September

Monday morning came at last, and with it the usual cacophony of mortar and shell fire, followed by attacks on all Company fronts. These were all beaten off with the aid of medium guns from across the river, laying down fire in front of all the Company posi-tions. D Company were still holding on, despite being reduced to 19 all ranks the day before. It was during one of the attacks in the morning that Capt Bill Hodgson, the Company commander, was hit and severely wounded. Signallers Ron Graydon and Joe Maguire tried to get through from Company to Battalion HQ, but their efforts were in vain; wireless traffic was out of the question. Capt Hodgson suggested that the set be taken out into the open to make a contact from there. As the Signallers bent down to pick up the No 18 Set, Capt Hodgson went out into the courtyard of the farmhouse. At that moment the enemy began mortaring the area and the building and the immediate vicinity were heavily bombarded. Caught in the open and with buildings on two sides, the effect was devastating. As the bombs exploded pieces of metal ricocheted around the area and Capt Hodgson received fatal wounds. During this attack Signaller Joe Maguire was also caught in the open, but his friend Cpl Larry Cowin, another Signaller, was killed by a mortar round that landed squarely on the slit trench where he was sheltering.

Major Breese went to Brigade HQ during the morning and learned of the impending withdrawal. He was told that the Division would withdraw through his lines and that they would be remaining until the evacuation of all the other areas was complete. Across the river at Nijmegen the Seaborne Group was informed of the evacuation of the Division and instructed to prepare for their reception. Capt Barnes and his fellow Quartermasters from 7 KOSB and 2 South Staffords were given the responsibility for feeding, re-clothing and accommodating the troops. Brigadier Roger Bower of the Divisional Staff and a former CO of the Battalion arranged for the setting up of various hostels; and Sgt Lound and his cooks from 1 Border prepared meals for unknown numbers.

At 13.30 hrs orders were issued from Divisional HQ at the Hartenstein for Operation 'Berlin', the withdrawal of the Division across the Rhine that night. The O Group was attended by Major Cousens and the Adjutant, Capt Colin Douglas. At the RAP the MO, Padre Rowell and the Medical Staff prepared the walking wounded for evacuation that night. There were some 70 casualties in the RAP; those who were not attempting the break-out had their dressings changed so that they could remain undisturbed for several days, and were made as comfortable as possible. The walking wounded would be accompanied to the river bank and seen into the boats by the Medical Staff, who would then return to be with the more seriously wounded and to go into captivity with them.

An hour later Cpl Alan Fisher from D Company arrived at Brigade HQ. He had been given the task of attempting to get through to Battalion HQ to report the situation in D Company as wireless communication had failed; this was the first contact for two days with the Company. He was sent back with a note from Brigadier Hicks to order the immediate withdrawal of the Company, and as he arrived the enemy laid down a mortar barrage. He was under the false impression that the Company had been overrun, and called out to the men nearest to him that they were to follow him; he then returned and led them back to Brigade HQ.

What had happened in the D Company area was that there was concern for the more seriously wounded men and it had been decided, after a discussion between the surviving officers and senior NCOs, who were all wounded, that an attempt should be made to obtain a temporary cease-fire between themselves and the Germans, to evacuate these men. It fell to Lt Alan Green to attempt this, but as he made his way to the German positions he came under fire as the enemy laid down another mortar stonk. Lt Green was wounded four more times and had to withdraw. The situation was now becoming very serious as there was no food, no water and only a few medical supplies for the Orderly, who had carried out his work magnificently. As there seemed to be nothing else to do, the few remaining men under Lt Green's command manned their slit trenches for as long as possible.

At 16.00 hrs Captain Ingram was called to Battalion HQ for an O Group. The news of the previous day that the Battalion would be relieved was countermanded and the order given to withdraw. He could hardly believe his ears. A Company was to cover the withdrawal on the north of the perimeter, having taken over the area to their left covered by the Sappers. The wounded would be left behind with the Medical Orderlies. Where possible sandbags were to be wrapped around feet to reduce noise. The Company would finally pull out at 23.30 hrs, then move down to the river in parties of 14, which was one boatload. Having crossed the river, there was a 12-mile march to be faced before reaching the final assembly point.

Back at Battalion HQ Lt Joe Hardy still had one of the two pigeons he carried as part of his personal load. An RAF officer, who had flown in with the Signals Platoon, asked early on during the battle if he could send one of them back to ADGB (Air Defence Headquarters Great Britain) as wireless communications had failed. The message was duly written and the bird released on 19 September, but it was never discovered whether or not it returned safely.

The second bird was given its chance to escape in the late afternoon. Food for the pigeon had become scarce, so it was decided to give it a chance of life, although there were some covetous eyes cast on the small bird, as some could see it as a meal. The acting CO, Major Cousens, was approached as to what message should be sent. 'Anything you like,' was the astonishing reply. So Joe Hardy wrote:

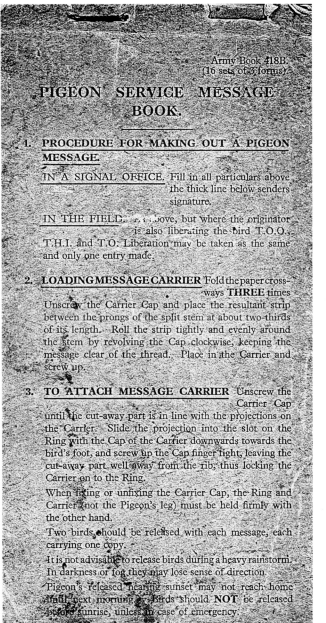

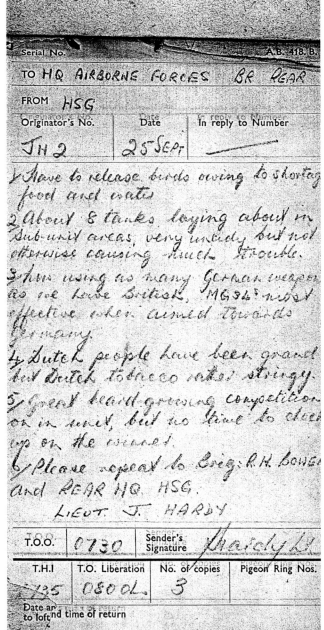

The cover of Lt Joe Hardy's Pigeon Service Message Book, and his message of 25 September. *BRM*

'1. Have to release bird owing to shortage food and water.

2. About 8 tanks laying about in sub-unit areas, very untidy but not otherwise causing much trouble.

3. Now using as many German weapons as we have British, MG 34s most effective when aimed towards Germany.

4. Dutch people have been grand but Dutch tobacco rather stringy.

5. Great beard-growing competition in our unit, but no time to check up on the winner.

6. Please repeat to Brig R. H. Bower and REAR HQ HSG.'

The message was written at 07.30 hrs and the pigeon released at 08.00 hrs. The bird miraculously got back to Corps HQ and became a nine-day wonder.

In the B Company/'Breeseforce' area, close to the river bank, Lt Royall had been repelling many attacks for most of the morning and afternoon. To the north of their position tracked vehicles and SP guns could be heard moving about, and their position was under almost constant mortar and shell fire. Lt Barnes and L/Cpl Wilson left their muddy slit trench to shelter

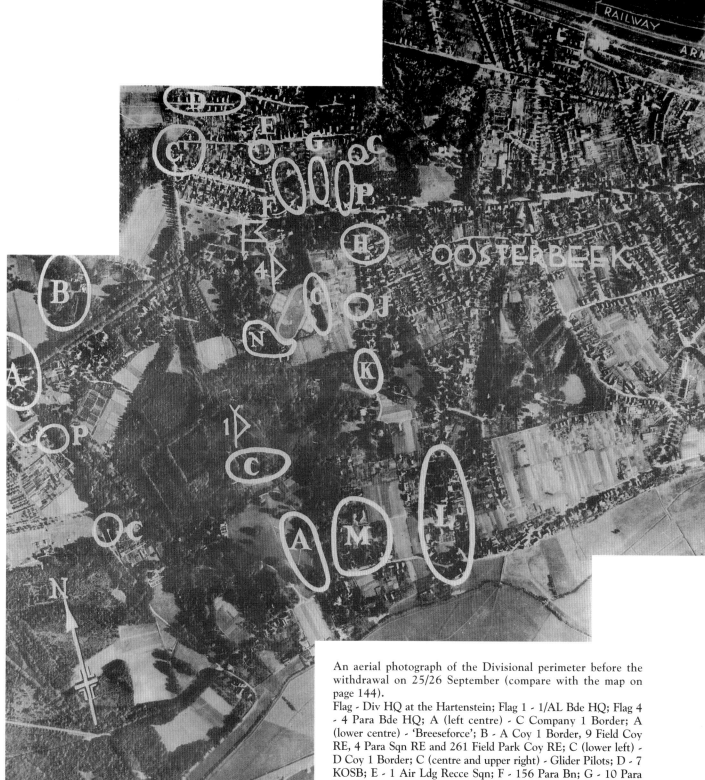

An aerial photograph of the Divisional perimeter before the withdrawal on 25/26 September (compare with the map on page 144).
Flag - Div HQ at the Hartenstein; Flag 1 - 1/AL Bde HQ; Flag 4 - 4 Para Bde HQ; A (left centre) - C Company 1 Border; A (lower centre) - 'Breeseforce'; B - A Coy 1 Border, 9 Field Coy RE, 4 Para Sqn RE and 261 Field Park Coy RE; C (lower left) - D Coy 1 Border; C (centre and upper right) - Glider Pilots; D - 7 KOSB; E - 1 Air Ldg Recce Sqn; F - 156 Para Bn; G - 10 Para Bn; H - 21 Ind Para Coy; J - 4 Para Bde Composite Pl; K - RASC; L - Lonsdale Force (elements of 1, 3 and 11 Para Bns); M - Div Artillery; N - Div HQ Troops; P - units of 1 Polish Para Bde. *BRM*

for a time in the garage at Dennenoord, from where they could cover their position. As they stood there in the garage leaning on the car, four other men came in and stood just inside the door. Then there was a loud explosion as a shell landed in the doorway. The four men were killed and Lt Barnes was badly wounded in the foot; miraculously Ginger Wilson was

unscathed. Lifting Lt Barnes on to his shoulders, Wilson managed to get him into the cellar at Dennenoord, where the Company Aid Post was situated. With the help of a Medical Orderly, Wilson cut off Lt Barnes's boot and put shell dressings on the wound. The bleeding would not stop so an airborne smock was tied round the wound.

Towards the end of the day, at around 20.00 hrs, a reconnaissance party moved down to the river to establish a Battalion RV. At about the same time A Company came under heavy shell-fire and were attacked by infantry.

Lt Stott reported to Brigade HQ for further orders and was told that they were to remain in their positions until midnight, although the evacuation of units was to commence as darkness fell. Tapes had been laid through the trees down to the river and each man was to hold the tail of the smock of the man in front of him. The idea sounded simple and easy to follow, but in reality there were problems. If a man stumbled in the dark and let go of the man in front of him, it was almost certain that he would not find the man again and would become lost.

Capt Barry Ingram says that there was no elation at the thought of withdrawal. The humiliation of having to do so seemed to be stronger than the joy of being home again. At 21.00 hrs A Company was 42 men strong plus 28 wounded; that was three boatloads of unwounded men, and the wounded would be staying behind, although they would not be told this fact. The noise seemed to have redoubled. The gunners over the river were putting down a heavy barrage to cover the withdrawal and the Germans, expecting no doubt an attempt at reinforcement, were also joining in.

A final burst from the Vickers, and A Company moved out in single file to take over their new positions. They arrived at the appointed place only to find that it was the focal point for a great deal of fire. In the dark, made darker by the rain that had now begun to fall, it was almost impossible to recognise anything. They saw some slit trenches and everyone piled into them. By now it was 21.30 hrs and the Company, squeezed six to a trench, was supposed to remain there for 2 hours to cover the withdrawal. Capt Ingram managed to find Lt Withers and discovered that of their 42 men, only 22 were still unwounded, but they were all under cover. To remain would be suicidal, so he decide to ask Battalion if they could move off earlier.

Leaving the party with instructions to Lt Withers that, if he was not back in 45 minutes, they were to withdraw to the river, Ingram and Pte John Kerwin, his batman, crossed the 300 yards of ground to Battalion HQ. It seemed, he said, like 10 miles. He himself was very shaken, but Pte Kerwin seemed quite imperturbable. The CO was not there, and he found Lt Joe Hardy and Lt Mike Holman in charge. Capt Ingram managed to contact Major Neill, who was preparing to withdraw the remnants of C Company, and requested that A Company retire to Battalion HQ to cover C Company out. The journey back to A Company was a nightmare, and they had difficulty in

locating the men in the dark before starting the journey down to the river.

On the northern flank of B Company all troops capable of movement had made their withdrawal, so it was decided to withdraw Battalion HQ, S Company and all the walking wounded from the RAP. This move was to take place at 22.40 hrs, with A and C Companies holding their positions until 22.50 and 23.00 hrs respectively. The first men left their positions around the Van Lennepweg, across the Hoofdlaan and made their way down the Kneppel Houtweg through 'Breeseforce's' positions, across the Benedendorpsweg and down through 12 Platoon towards the river. The MO recalled that he helped to bring the walking wounded down to the river, had laid down and fallen asleep, waking the following morning as a PoW.

A Company found that it was almost impossible to act as a rearguard, since there were Germans all round the place and there was some chaos. They reached the end of a queue - a long line of men waiting along a track without any idea as to what was going on. Capt Ingram tried to find out what was happening, but no one seemed to know. So, calling A Company to follow him, he led them on down to the river, sometimes up to their waists in water as they stumbled into dykes; on one occasion they fell over a dead cow. Near the river they found the Brigade Major, reported to him and were moved on. The ground became very flat, soft and swampy. Here they found a long serpentine queue four abreast, for all the world like a cinema queue. Mortar bombs were falling around them, but as the ground was so soft they did little damage. C Company put in an attack on enemy positions at 23.00 hrs and then smartly disengaged and withdrew to the river 10 minutes later, forming the Battalion rearguard.

Major Breese had to report to Brigade HQ at 22.00 hrs and, as he had not returned by midnight, Lt Stott visited all the men of 'Breeseforce' and ordered them to make their way to the river. There had been no sound of men moving through the position for some time, but shortly after Stott returned to the command slit trench, Major Breese arrived and ordered him to get the men back into their positions because they had to remain for another hour. The majority returned, but it was impossible to get all the men back in the pitch-black night. In due course they made an orderly withdrawal at the appointed time. They also found themselves at the end of a long queue waiting for transport across the river.

D Company were still sitting and waiting for the arrival of Allied troops from across the river. Surely they would come up the Van Borsselenweg; it was the only road up from the river leading into the Divisional position, and the barrage being put down must surely mean that 30 Corps were crossing in

Above An aerial photograph of the Rhine looking north from the west of Heveadorp to the east of Oosterbeek. During the night of 25 September 1944 many of 1 Border and others of the Division withdrew from their positions in the perimeter across the Benedendorpsweg and the 'Kerk Pad', the footpath between the gasworks and Oosterbeek Church, across the wide expanse of open polder to the north bank of the river.

1 - Heveadorp; 2 - Westerbouwing; 3 - Driel Ferry; 4 - Benedendorpsweg/Van Borsselenweg crossroads; 5 - gasworks; 6 - Kerk Pad; 7 - Oosterbeek Church and the Ter Horst house. *BRM*

Left The view looking south from the Kerk Pad across the open polder to the Rhine in October 1993. Many men from the Battalion came via Kneppel Houtweg and across Benedendorpsweg down to this track to reach the river. *BRM*

strength. The rain made it difficult to spot movement amongst the trees. However, on this front the enemy were not seeking to get wet on such a night. Meanwhile, in the cellar of Company HQ the wounded were heartened by the noise of the barrage - tomorrow the Company would be relieved.

Fortunately the enemy did not appreciate that the withdrawal was in progress and made little attempt to interfere. Even so there were many casualties as the troops waited to cross and crossed the river. The assault boats ferrying them across were hit by MG fire and many were sunk with loss of life. Men were hit in the boats, on the bank and as they tried to swim the Rhine. There were cries for help coming from the water. Tracer criss-crossed the river, and the number of boats able to take the troops became less and less as they were sunk or damaged.

Capt Ingram attempted to bring some order to the situation. Lt Withers was no longer with them, but Lt Stott and Lt Royall appeared and tried to help. Arthur Royall recalled Major Charles Breese's specific instructions to him that 'one of the routes to the river will pass through your position, the evacuation will take place tonight you and your men will cover the withdrawal and will remain in position until just before first light'. Just before first light Lt Royall duly ordered the remnants of his Platoon to make their way down and attempt to cross. However, as dawn broke there were still some 500 men on the north bank of the river, and they were ordered to disperse and lie low until the following night, when they would make another attempt to cross - to be caught on the bank in daylight would have been sheer madness. They might then be able to swim across the river, or perhaps find a friendly Dutchman or woman who would help.

Major Breese collected together the remaining wounded into the last boat and Sgt S. Clarke rallied the remainder of those in his area and swam with them across the river. Pte Wilf Oldham of 12 Platoon found himself with Cpl Nobby Clark and about 12 other men. The situation at the bank was such that they decided to try and find some other means of getting across. They walked along the river bank for about a quarter of a mile and found a boat. Climbing in they pushed off and made for the other side, but the current was strong and they were carried out beyond the lines of tracer being fired across the river to mark the area where our troops were on the southern bank. They eventually managed to get ashore in the right area and were taken care of by Canadian troops.

Pte Norman Antwistle from the Signals Platoon was part of a crocodile of men making their way through the woods when a Very light went up. Everyone froze, and when the light died away Norman realised that the man in front of him was dead. When he reached the river he found an orderly queue, but he was too late to get aboard a boat. He and his friend, Pte Charlie Meachin, therefore decided to swim across the river. They stripped off and slipped into the water. About halfway across Charlie Meachin called out that he wasn't going to make it, and when Norman turned round to speak to him he had disappeared. Finally Norman made the south side and climbed over the top of the bank into its shelter. Here he heard a voice calling him - Charlie had made it after all.

Pte Eric Blackwell was among about nine men - some wounded, including himself - from 15 Platoon C Company who made it to the river. The group found a boat full of dead Dorset Regiment men. The bodies were removed and laid on the bank and the group embarked using their rifle butts and the few paddles to fight the current and make it to safety. When they landed on the other side they climbed up the bank and through an orchard before realising that they were in the British lines. As a walking wounded case, Eric Blackwell refused to ride in an ambulance, which carried one of his comrades, Pte Frank Fitzpatrick. The road was under fire and the ambulance carrying Fitzpatrick was hit and he and the other occupants was killed.

Lt Alan Roberts eventually made the river bank having taken four walking wounded with him. They came to a wall that they could not climb, but soon found a hole in it through which they could crawl and in doing so fell into a stinking ditch. Following this ditch they soon found the river, where two of the men were taken by a boat. Lt Roberts and the other two men walked down the bank where Alan fell into the water. As he was wearing a German cloak, he was in danger of sinking, but one of the men seized a piece of wood and managed to pull him out. They eventually crossed the river at about 02.00 hrs. According to the War Diary, the last known man from the Battalion swam the river at 05.15 hrs on Tuesday morning.

The discipline of the Battalion stood the test - and it was tested to the utmost. As one senior officer said later, 'The discipline of the Battalion was beyond praise'.

Tuesday 26 September

Before it was daylight the last boat had left and some men attempted to swim the river. Those left on the bank made their way to find suitable cover, hopefully to attempt the crossing again that night. Soon, however, there were Germans everywhere, rounding up those men who were still seeking a hiding place and taking in the wounded.

Capt Ingram, Lt Stott and Lt Royall set off together to find a hiding place. They dumped most of their kit, keeping their pistols, torches and compasses. They had to climb fences as they looked for a suitable house that would offer a hiding place for the day. Before they had gone very far an MG 34 opened up on them from about 20 yards away. In the halflight the gunner's aim was poor and they were not hit, but they were separated and a couple of hours later both Lt Stott and Lt Royall were taken prisoner. As it was getting lighter, Capt Ingram entered the first house he saw. On the floor lay a dead Gunner Captain, with his small pack nearby. In it Ingram found, much to his joy, 50 cigarettes, an emergency ration, a toilet kit and a Sunday newspaper. He deduced from this that the officer had come in with the second lift, for the paper contained news of the landings the previous week. Upstairs in a bedroom he found some pyjamas, so he undressed and went to bed. This was heaven!

He awoke feeling like a new man. On looking out of the window he discovered that the house next door appeared to be a German Company HQ. This was annoying, for it meant that extra care had to be taken. Nothing, however, appeared to be happening, so he relaxed, cut his finger and toe nails, had a shave and then, wrapped up in a civilian overcoat, ate the emergency rations and smoked a cigarette reading awhile the *Sunday Express*.

Down below some Germans wandered in but did not attempt to investigate the upper floors of the house. Now he had to make a decision. If he waited until the evening and then attempted to leave, he would no doubt be shot on sight, so he decided to make a bold bid in daylight. In this way he hoped to bluff his way through the lines and perhaps make contact with the Dutch Resistance. The suits in the wardrobe were all too big for him, but by putting one suit on over his uniform, he managed to fill it out. A pair of shoes and a hat fitted perfectly, and a pair of lady's silk pyjamas wrapped around his neck as a scarf made him look a very odd civilian indeed.

With a friendly wave to the Germans in the house next door, which they answered, he set off down the street, Weeverstraat, moving in the general direction of the town. To passing Germans he spoke a mixture of French and, as he called it, 'Edward Lear'. It was

so easy. He seemed to be getting away with it. However, a patrol then appeared that seemed to have a more purposeful air about it. He was stopped, and as he stood speaking to them one of the men brushed into him and felt something hard in Ingram's coat pocket; it was the torch. There and then he was searched, the torch and compass were found and he had to admit that he was a British Officer. At that moment a Propaganda Korps type arrived in his Volkswagen, gave Ingram a cigarette, took some photographs and in due course the photograph, together with an article concerning 'the Brave British Officer' appeared in a German newspaper.

Capt Barry Ingram, the OC of the Mortar Group, with his captors on Weeverstraat, Oosterbeek, on 27 September 1944. Ingram had managed to get hold of civilian clothes and get past several German patrols until he was eventually stopped. He was photographed by a German press team and the article was published in *Die Westfalische Neueste Nachrichten* of 23 October 1944; the caption read: 'An English Officer dressed in civilian clothing and belonging to the 1st Airborne Division has been un-masked by our troops'. The full story of Barry Ingram's capture was revealed in 1984 after he had made a visit to the Airborne Museum at Oosterbeek. *Airborne Museum, Oosterbeek*

The experiences of all the men differed. In D Company the end of the fighting was signalled by the appearance of Sapper Stan Holden of the Royal Engineers and several others, who informed the incredulous survivors that the Division had withdrawn during the night and that all the wounded had been surrendered to the enemy, together with Medical Staffs and Padres who had remained behind to care for the casualties. Pte Hugh McGuiness of

Below Wounded being driven by the Germans for medical treatment after the Battle. The officer on the stretcher is possibly Lt Tony Howe, one of the Anti-Tank Platoon commanders of 1 Border. 26 September 1944. *BRM*

Bottom PoWs from the Division being marched into Arnhem on 26 September. Fred Jackson, who served in 14 Platoon of B Company, recognised himself as the man on the right with a field dressing on the back of his neck. *BRM*

Whitehaven later wrote in a letter to Brigadier Breese: 'When we couldn't fight any more, we just sat and waited for the Hun to come, but he still wouldn't come until we told him we had no more ammunition. . .the SS Captain asked me where my commander was. I took him to Capt Hodgson, whom he saluted. . . Capt Hodgson was mortally wounded and could not respond. . . The German thanked him and us for an honourable fight; they treated us with great respect and said we were the finest soldiers they had come into combat with. When he found out how many of us were left capable of fighting he said that had he known, he would have taken the position two days ago.'

As the Germans moved into the positions, the more seriously wounded were taken away on jeeps, while the walking wounded were led away to hospital, first to St Elizabeth's Hospital on the western outskirts

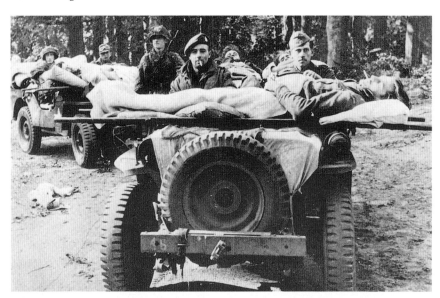

Above right Survivors photographed on 26 September at the Missionary College, Verlengde Groenestraat, Nijmegen.
Back row, left to right: Pte Jack Cohen (Ox & Bucks LI, 1st Airborne Division Defence Platoon), Pte Poule, Pte Johnnie Peters (14 Platoon B Company, 1 Border).
Middle row: L/Cpl McInnes (23 Mortar Platoon S Company, 1 Border), Pte D. Doran (1 Border), unknown.
Front row: Cpl Jim McDowell (23 Mortar Platoon S Company, 1 Border), unknown officer, Pte Danny Shaw (9th Field Company RE), L/Cpl Thomas McKewan (18 Platoon 10 Para), unknown (1 Border), Pte A. R. Morgan-Lewis (Royal Signals, 1st ALB), unknown, Trooper Jim Cooke (1st Recce Squadron), L/Cpl Ronnie Lord (23 Mortar Platoon S Company, 1 Border), WO Terry Armstrong (unit unknown), L/Cpl S. 'Judy' Wright (Ox & Bucks LI, 1st Airborne Division Defence Platoon).

Jim McDowell recalls a photographer asking if there were any northern lads around, and he took this photograph, which was published in the *Daily Express* on 29 September. A neighbour of his wife back in Bothel, Cumberland, brought the paper to show her. She recalled that, although surprised by his appearance, she at least recognised Jim by the ring on his finger. Johnnie Peters put his helmet on, he recalled, just to be recognised. *Taylor Library*

Right Men of the 1st Airborne Division being re-equipped and clothed from their Seaborne Tail at Nijmegen on 26 September 1944. There are Glider Pilots in the foreground. *BRM*

DRIED APPLE RINGS
Dried to perfection with A1 SALT
Made crushed or in blocks
At grocers in packets & drums
Palmer Mann & Co., Ltd., Sandbach, Cheshire

Daily Mail
NO. 15,103 PRICE 2 FR. 50 CONTINENTAL EDITION THURSDAY, SEPTEMBER 28, 1944

LATE WAR NEWS

Bear Brand Stockings
We'll meet again.

THE NEWSPAPER FOR THE ALLIED FORCES IN FRANCE

EPIC OF SKY MEN

THE AGONY OF ARNHEM

TO-DAY The Daily Mail is able to print pictures taken from the inside that show the Agony of Arnhem. The photograph above—radioed from a neutral source last night—is of exhausted and wounded parachutists captured after their great fight against odds.

PARATROOPS in action, firing on the nearby enemy with a 3-inch mortar, while themselves are under heavy fire. The Airborne men brought this picture back with them when the survivors were finally withdrawn. Other pictures on BACK Page.

ONE of the airborne photographers wrote: "We are completely surrounded. Our perimeter becomes smaller every hour. Now it is a matter not of taking pictures, but of fighting for our lives. If the land forces don't contact us soon, then we've had it."

230 HOURS OF HELL

From RICHARD McMILLAN, B.U.P. War Correspondent

WITH BRITISH ARMY BEFORE ARNHEM, Wednesday.

STRUGGLING through a hurricane barrage of fire from 88mm. guns, tank cannon, and machine-guns, the last survivors of the noble band of British Airborne troops who held the Arnhem bridgehead for nine days were ferried over to our lines during Monday night.

I saw the tragic but heroic cavalcade of bloody, mudstained, exhausted, hungry, and bearded men flood up from the river bank into our lines after going through 230 hours of hell.

Many were stretcher cases. Many were wrapped in blankets. Some hobbled with sticks. All were so completely exhausted that they could hardly keep their eyes open. They were beaten in body, but not in spirit. "Let us get back again; give us a few tanks and we will finish the job," they said.

Every one of them had a story to tell of terror by day and by night, of ceaseless enemy attacks with flame - throwers, tanks, and self-propelling guns firing high explosive and armour-piercing shells.

Captain Bethune Taylor, of Landsdowne-place, Cheltenham, wearing a beard like a French poilu's, told me his story of the tragic adventure as he struggled against sleep.

"Most of the division dropped on Sunday," he said. "I—a gunner—dropped on Monday. It was easy. A bit of flak hit our glider, but we landed west of Oesterbeek, and took up positions.

"There were odd snipers, but they did not cause much trouble, and we started moving towards the bridge. One brigade began to move down the railway lines.

"It ran into the first tough opposition. Eighty-eight millimetre guns were at the road and rail crossing and they forced this section back.

FIREWORKS BEGIN

"That was the beginning of the fireworks. The next day the situation began to deteriorate. We were forced to take up new positions.

"We scooped out some earth in a cabbage patch and got our guns going. We took a bit of a bashing that day—from 88mms., from tanks, and machine-guns.

"We were told to withdraw, and at nightfall we did so, with tanks following us up. We then got into a field in the middle of a wood. The German tactics were to send in tanks followed by infantry. The tanks fired then turned away, leaving the infantry.

"We usually managed to clean up the infantry, who were not too good. But then the Germans brought in flame-throwers and self-propelling guns. They gave us more than we gave them. They also sent over fierce fire from mortars.

"The weather was fine, with odd spots of rain. We had two days' food, with an extra day's food for the whole division. The resupply seemed to work well.

"We marvelled at the amazing

BACK PAGE—Col. FIVE

'Break-out' Order to Survivors

From ALAN WOOD, Representing the Combined Press

WITH ARNHEM AIRBORNE FORCE, Tuesday.

THIS is the end. The most tragic and glorious battle of the war is over, and the survivors of this British airborne force can sleep soundly for the first time in eight days and nights.

Orders came to us yesterday to break out from our forest citadel west of Arnhem, cross the Rhine, and join up with the Second Army on the south bank.

Our commander decided against a concerted assault on the Germans round us. Instead, the plan was to split up into little groups, 10 to 20 strong, and set out along different routes at two-minute intervals, which would simply walk through the German lines in the dark.

Cheeky patrols went out earlier tying bits of white parachute tape to trees to mark the way. To hinder the Germans waking up to what was happening, Second Army guns laid down a battering box barrage all afternoon.

The first party was to set off at 10 p.m.; our group was to leave at 10.4 p.m. They went round distributing little packets of sulphanilamide and morphia. We tore up blankets and wrapped them round our boots to muffle the sound of our feet in the trees.

Waited for Boats

We were told the password—"John Bull." If we became separated, each man was to make his way by compass due south until he reached the river.

Our major is an old hand. He led the way, and linked our party together by getting everyone to hold the tail of the parachutist's smock of the man in front of him, so our infiltrating column had an absurd resemblance to some children's game.

It was half-light, with the glow of fires from burning houses around, when we set out. We were lucky; we went through a reputed enemy pocket without hearing a shot except for a stray sniper's bullet.

Another group met a machine-gun with a fixed line of fire across their path. Another had to silence a bunch of Germans with a burst of Sten fire and hand grenades.

Another had to pause while a German finished his evening stroll

BACK PAGE—Col. FOUR

'Jet' Planes Beat the Fly-bombs

BRITISH jet-propelled aircraft fought "with success" against the flying bombs, it was announced last night.

This is the first statement about our jet-planes since January last.

Reports from the south-east coast areas during the heavy flying-bomb attacks stressed that the two fighters most successful against them were the newest Spitfire and the secret Tempest.

The statement last night was issued simultaneously in Britain and America.

It added: "Details of the jet-propelled aircraft and their engines must still remain secret, but research scientists, aircraft technicians and workers in both Britain and America may take pride in their work."

About Germany's jet-planes, the Ministries say: In spite of their high speed and rate of climb, they have shown themselves to possess poor manœuvrability.

'Hot Gospeller' Dies

OAKLAND, California, Wednesday. —Aimee Semple MacPherson, the "hot gospeller" evangelist, died at Oakland to-day of heart disease. She was 53.

She had a temple of her own and her services had stage settings and theatrical lighting. She visited England in 1926 and 1928.—B.U.P.

Arnhem Gave Us Nijmegen

2,000 Men Safe Out of 8,000

TWO thousand troops of the First British Airborne Division were evacuated from the Arnhem bridgehead out of 7,000 to 8,000 dropped in the area, according to an American broadcast from Paris last night.

The speaker said the figure may be higher. About 1,200 wounded were left behind in the care of the Germans and British doctors who stayed with them.

The Germans claimed that they held 6,450 prisoners, including 1,700 wounded, and that British killed numbered 1,500.

At SHAEF last night it was emphasised that the Arnhem operation must not be regarded as a failure.

Without it we could never have hoped to capture the even more vital Nijmegen bridge, where the Waal is twice as wide as the Lower Rhine at Arnhem.

The British troops prevented the Germans from moving south at speed to Nijmegen, and forced them to send their reinforcements by a roundabout route through Emmerich. When they reached Nijmegen they were too late.

Two to three days is regarded as the fighting span of airborne troops. The First Division held out for nine days.

Bad weather eventually made withdrawal necessary.

★

A correspondent with the British Second Army has given his reasons for the failure of General Dempsey's spearhead to relieve the airborne forces.

After the weather he blames the difficult, canal-intersected Dutch countryside, where our tanks had to keep to elevated roads and were consequently good targets for hidden German 88mm. guns.

The epic of the airborne invasion of Holland began on Sunday, September 17.

While American formations were securing the bridge at Nijmegen, British troops, dropped 10 miles deeper behind the German lines, fought their way into Arnhem and for a time controlled the bridge there.

But the Germans, acutely sensitive to this grave threat, rushed up some of their best units and finally the gallant little band controlling the bridge was overcome.

From then on the rest of the British force held out grimly on a stretch of wooded high ground about three miles to the west of Arnhem.

General Dempsey's men struck north from Nijmegen in a determined effort to relieve them, but only a few patrols and limited quantities of supplies got across the Rhine.

German troops lining the north bank in strength prevented an effective link-up.

Enemy Retreat in Holland Begins

BRITISH 2ND ARMY H.Q., Wednesday.

MORE than 100,000 Germans in West Holland are in process of organising a mass getaway. They are attempting to withdraw north and then eastward through the 25-miles gap between Arnhem and the Zuider Zee.

The gap is their only hope of escape.

The British corridor from Eindhoven to west of Arnhem bars all other west-east routes to the Reich.

The Luftwaffe yesterday made an all-out attempt to aid the withdrawal by an attack on the great Nijmegen span bridge, across which all Allied transport must pass to Arnhem.

From five o'clock onwards last night the German planes used everything, from bullets to a pick-a-back glider bomb, in the attack.

Allied traffic was halted for a short time while débris was cleared round a 20ft. hole near one of the approaches.

The British corridor continues to broaden. General Dempsey's forces are making steady progress in the two-flank advance west and east of it.

Canal Line

British and Canadian troops on the west hold a firm line along the Antwerp-Turnhout canal.

They have mopped-up a six-mile stretch of territory.

Farther north on this flank there is very stiff fighting in the woods to the west of Oedenrode—where 48 hours ago the Germans momentarily cut the corridor highway.

The Germans are fighting well to hold this flank to make possible the general withdrawal from West Holland.

East of the corridor two re-equipped German divisions, the 107th Panzers and the 10th S.S., have had 150 of their 200 new tanks smashed by the British armour, and opposition to our thrust is diminishing.

Meanwhile, in their offensive against Calais the Canadians have cleared the whole area west and south-west of the town.

The Germans have withdrawn into the town itself and, protected by water inundations, are offering heavy opposition.—*Reuter.*

Throughout the British south-east "hell-fire" area bills were posted yesterday carrying this message from Mr. Herbert Morrison to the townspeople: "Every sympathy with the gallant citizens in the concluding stages of their ordeal. Hold on! I am assured by the competent military authority that the end of your trial will not be long delayed."

Everybody In Insurance For Injuries

By Daily Mail Political Correspondent

EIGHTEEN million people are affected by the Government's revolutionary plan for reforming the laws on workmen's compensation which have been in existence in various forms for the past 50 years.

Complete details of the Government's proposals are issued as a White Paper to-day.

All who work for their living and receive wages or a salary are eligible for all benefits. They will be placed on the same footing as ex-Service men.

Disability will be assessed by medical boards, and compensation will be awarded on the basis of medical reports without recourse to the law courts.

Once an award has been made it will be permanent and will not be varied not even should the recipient earn extra money.

A new principle is introduced whereby compensation will not only be paid, as in the past, to those who lose their earning power, but also in future to those who "lose their health, strength, and power to enjoy life."

Outline of Scheme: Page THREE.

Rainstorm in the Strait

Sea.—Little disturbance.

Weather.—Fine until 8 p.m., when there was a rainstorm. Maximum temperature, 60 deg., 52 deg. at 7.30 p.m. Visibility fairly good. Wind west, light; sky overcast.

Barometer.—Steady.

THE 'CARPET BAGGERS'

Commons Question

Mr. J. H. Wootton-Davies (Con., Heywood and Radcliffe), in a Parliamentary question to the War Secretary next Tuesday, will ask:

"What principles are being applied by the Supreme H.Q. of the Allied Expeditionary Force with regard to granting permission to business men of Allied nationality to go to France for the purpose of re-establishing their trade connections, and whether he can give an assurance that British business men will be given facilities in this respect not less favourable than those accorded to other Allied nationals."

'Civil Air' is to Have a Minister —But a Junior

By COLIN BEDNALL

THE Government, I am reliably informed, is more or less agreed on the appointment of an Under-Secretary for Air (Civil Aviation).

As the title implies, it is intended that this junior member of the Government should devote himself exclusively to the needs of the future Merchant Air Fleet—but still under the ægis of the Air Ministry.

The announcement is intended to convince the reassembled Parliament of the Government's good faith.

Parliament's reaction, it is expected, however, is more likely to follow the first thoughts of those already aware of the new proposal.

★

IT is thought, in fact, that only one of two reasons can really be responsible for the appointment now of an Under-Secretary for Air (Civil Aviation).

The first is that the Lord Privy Seal, Lord Beaverbrook, at any moment will show himself to be weary of the frustration involved in representing the present Government on Civil Aviation. Some sort of ready stop-gap for the exasperated Lord Beaverbrook may, therefore, be considered desirable.

The other more cynical explanation advanced is that the appointment is a convenient way of ensuring political suicide for some gentleman not held in very great affection by his colleagues.

Nowhere in aviation circles is it now expected that Parliament will tolerate the continued administration of Civil Aviation by the Air Ministry. Many reasons for this view are being advanced. Some of them are considered to be a little unfair to a Ministry which after all won the aerial Battle of Britain and the aerial Battle of Germany.

One fact, however, is not disputed. If the Air Ministry is to continue with its task of ensuring superiority in military aviation, it cannot, and will not, give a fully sympathetic attention to a serious rival. The rival, of course, is Civil Aviation.

★

THE Government's failure on Civil Aviation is known to be much more the result of high Cabinet policy than the inadequacy of any one of the confusing number of Departments now charged with responsibility for it.

To blame the Air Council, for instance, for the lack of the air-liners wanted for the peace or even for insufficient numbers of British military air transports is a waste of breath.

The Air Council — and this apparently may be something of a revelation—is not constituted to deal with Civil Aviation.

Aviation circles fear, in fact, that astute political organisers might be delighted to see Parliament launch itself once again into an endless discussion around such "red herrings."

The Government has an embarrassing list of specific charges to answer. They can be listed in their full array, if necessary.

ALBANIA FORCES PRESS ENEMY

Partisans Link

From EDWIN TETLOW, Daily Mail Special Correspondent

SOUTH EUROPEAN H.Q., Wednesday.

ALBANIA, pocket kingdom on the Adriatic, occupied by Mussolini five years ago, is the newest war front.

Picked Allied troops have landed secretly in a sea and air invasion, and are already fanning out on a wide stretch of country.

Partisans have linked with them and the joint forces are now engaging the Germans, prodding them on into a general withdrawal from the south-west Balkans.

The landing is the fruit of months of "cloak and dagger" stabs at enemy garrisons on the Adriatic seaboard.

British and Allied troops have been ashore for weeks, living in caves and in mountain hideouts, training Partisans and leading them in resistance and sabotage against the Germans.

The Allied invasion has come as the climax to their operations.

In addition to the landings on the Albanian mainland troops are ashore on the islands off Yugoslavia. No Allied mention is made of operations in Yugoslavia itself, but the Germans report landings along the whole Dalmation coast.

The Allied troops now in Albania can count on the help of some 20,000 Albanian guerillas. In addition, Yugoslav Partisans of Marshal Tito's command have been operating with the Albanians in recent weeks, and it is possible that these forces have been strengthened.

General Tolbukhin's Russian troops in Bulgaria are also only 165 miles from the northern Albanian coast, and an Allied drive inland might result in a link-up which would cut off the five German divisions in Greece.

Heavy fighting is already raging in Macedonia, west of the Belgrade-Salonika railway, the Germans' main escape route from Greece, and between Leskovac and Nigh, farther up the line, between Yugoslav Partisans and the enemy.

FRENCH GOVT. TAKE RENAULT WORKS

The French Government have decided to requisition the Renault works at Billancourt as part of the policy of purging firms which aided the Germans. —Reuter.

RIGA: NEW SOVIET ADVANCE

Soviet communique announces more progress in the drive on Riga. Over 200 places captured.

A.T.S.

It is because you wear this badge—or that of some 'sister' Service—that we, the makers of Diana Shoes, send you this personal message. We recognise that while you are serving you have no need of us, but to lose touch would be a pity. Duty may postpone a renewal of old acquaintance with Diana Shoes or delay your first introduction to their comfortable stylishness — enjoyed to-day by thousands of women on the 'home front'—but the day will come. Meanwhile . . . here's to you and your splendid Service!

Diana
Shoes for Women

DIANA SHOEMAKERS
LEICESTER

The *Daily Mail* Continental Edition of 28 September 1944.
BRM/Jim McDowell

of Arnhem, then to Apeldoorn to the north. Those still mobile were given the job of gathering together the debris of war, the weapons, personal kit and other impedimenta strewn around the area. Of the Company, only those five who went with Cpl Alan Fisher made it across the river.

L/Cpl Ginger Wilson found that when he reached the river bank with Lt Barnes, his wounded Platoon commander, the situation was such that they had no chance of crossing. They decided therefore to make their way back to Dennenoord, where they arrived at dawn. At the door to the cellar a tall Dutch lady told him to leave his machine-gun at the door. Shortly afterwards they heard German voices. The Dutch lady went out first followed by Ginger Wilson with his hands up. He found a German Sergeant and eight men there. They searched him and then gave him a cigarette. The Sergeant looked into the cellar and told Ginger Wilson to go with a couple of Germans to look for wounded. They found a CSM of 2 S Staffords and took him on a stretcher to St Elizabeth's Hospital.

From there Ginger was taken to the Hartenstein Hotel, where he was again searched then taken to the rear of the building, where he found some more men of the Division. He was pulled across the lawn and made to stand there; then the others were brought across and made to stand at intervals of about a yard apart. They all thought at this moment that they were going to be shot. However, they were made to get down on their hands and knees and the SS man bent down and picked up pieces of paper; he indicated that they were to do the same. There was a mass of these torn-up bits of paper, which were the documents destroyed by Divisional HQ before they pulled out of the Hotel. Now they had to pick the lot up. Ginger remarked afterwards, 'If only General Urquhart knew what we had gone through'. Later they were marched off and given a piece of bread and put into a house overnight, before being marched off to captivity. So the remnants of the Battalion, who had failed to cross the Rhine, became prisoners-of-war.

The Battalion had fought well and had maintained the high standards of courage, discipline and honour with which the Regiment had always prided itself; it had also left, as in other wars, many sons of the Regiment on the battlefield. The wounded were taken to a Dutch Army Barracks at Apeldoorn, where the more seriously wounded were taken to local hospitals for treatment, and the rest were eventually moved to Germany as PoWs, where they had to endure six months of misery and deprivation before release.

The losses were dreadful, the fatal casualties being the highest of any Battalion. However, 1 Border managed to evacuate more than any other Battalion and came out of the Battle as a Battalion. The Battalion War Diary noted that 41 Officers and 754 ORs went to Arnhem. However, Regimental records list 44 Officers and 775 ORs, including RA, RAMC, REME, AAC and other attachments; the total also included men serving with 1st Air-Landing Brigade's Defence Platoon, which was formed entirely from 1 Border. In addition there were two officers attached to 1st Air-Landing Brigade HQ and another serving with 21st Independent Parachute Company. Only ten officers returned across the Rhine, including Major Breese, who had been wounded; another 27 were PoWs, of whom 15 were wounded and ten had been killed or died of their wounds - these were Lt Brown, Capt Burns 1st ALB HQ, Lt Coulston, Capt Hodgson, Lt Horsley 21 Ind Para Coy, Lt Holt, Major Montgomery (DoW later in hospital), Lt Tate, Lt Thomas 1st ALB HQ, and Lt Wellbelove. Of the 775 ORs, 115 had been killed or later died of wounds and sickness as PoWs, 391 were PoWs, of whom 151 were reported as wounded (this can only be taken as an estimate, since others regarded their own wounds as insignificant and not requiring formal medical aid or attention), and 269 were evacuated, of whom 17 were recorded as being wounded (see Appendices 1 and 2).

For those fortunate enough to have crossed the Rhine, the day was completely different. Eric Blackwell with others was taken to a school in Nijmegen, a reception area for what was left of the Division. He recalled that there the QM, Capt 'Uncle' Barnes, issued a rum ration to everyone. He was a man that Blackwell had known from childhood; he and Blackwell's father had served together as Sergeants in the peacetime Border Regiment. Quartermaster Barnes, a man of many years service in the Regiment and very much a father figure to many in the Battalion, just said 'Young Eric'. From there Eric travelled with the other wounded to Brussels, but saw no one from The Border Regiment.

Chapter 9

Rebuilding the Battalion and Norway

The survivors of the Battalion, nine officers and 241 ORs, spent most of the 26th resting. The QM, 'Uncle' Barnes, made meticulous efforts to reclothe all ranks before they were taken to Louvain and then to Brussels, from where most were flown directly to the airfield near Woodhall Spa. According to the War Diary they arrived at 17.40 hrs on 27 September. Some had managed a change of clothing after they had crossed the Rhine, others stripped off on the tarmac and changed on Lincolnshire soil. Those not requiring hospital treatment were accommodated in Roughton Moor Camp. The Seaborne Tail returned by road and sea, but Lt Bill Baldock, together with his batman, Pte Mick Bugler, and a driver, Pte Paddy Ward, remained until early October, having been delegated to check and log each plane-load of Airborne survivors as they departed for England. The three then travelled home via Ostend.

Over the next few days the Battalion settled into

Right Three more of the Battalion from the Leeds area photographed by Herbert Dewhirst at Louvain on 27 September. From the left they are Pte Joe Coupe from Chapeltown, Pte Ken Chambers from Beeston, and Pte John Pulford from Burley. This photograph was published in the *Yorkshire Post* and *Leeds Mercury* on 29 September 1944. *BRM/Ray Brown*

Below right The Mayoress of Liverpool entertaining members of the 1st Airborne Division to tea at Liverpool City Hall in late 1944. Cpl John Rannard of A Company is on the extreme right. *Mrs J. Rannard*

camp and underwent long debriefings to establish the nature of the casualties and details of the Battle. The kits and personal effects of those who had not returned were packed. 1 Border was re-established with HQ, S, A and C Companies, together with a small Reinforcement Company; at this stage there were serious doubts as to whether or not the unit and other parts of the Division, which had suffered such severe losses, would survive or be disbanded.

On 4 October the Battalion moved to Well Camp near Alford in Lincolnshire, and went on 14 days block leave the following day. At the end of the month the awards of the DSO to Major Neill, the MC to Captain Hardy, the DCM to Sgt Clark, and the MM to Cpl Swan and Pte O'Neill were confirmed, and all were congratulated by Brigadier Hicks when he visited the Battalion on 28 October. On 9 October RSM Paddy Kearns arrived with a party of men from 6 Border, who had been disbanded in August 1944

Left Men of the 1st Battalion at Louvain on 27 September photographed by Herbert Dewhirst, the *Yorkshire Post* War Photographer prior to their return to the UK.
From the left: Sgt Tom Bate from Warrington, Cpl W. Clarke from Leeds, unknown, Pte H. Blakeley from York, Pte Cyril Pryke from Ossett, Pte Sandy Masterton, Pte Paddy Quinn, Pte Harold Spink from Seacroft, Leeds, Pte C. Stones from Seacroft, unknown (2), Pte Ernie Westerman from Holbeck, unknown (2), and Pte Wilf Pridmore from Keswick. This photograph was published in the *Yorkshire Post* on 2 October 1944. Members of the Battalion were flown back in C-47s from Brussels direct to the airfield at Woodhall Spa in Lincolnshire later that day. *BRM*

after operating as with a Beach Group in Normandy since D-Day.

At the end of November Major Charles Breese was appointed to command the Battalion, taking over on the 24th from Major Cousens, and the process of selecting and receiving replacements for the Battalion continued. A draft of 28 ORs was selected for the Investiture Parade in London on 6 December, when HM King George VI presented gallantry awards for Arnhem to members of the Airborne Division at Buckingham Palace. Four days later a Divisional Memorial Service was held at St Wulfram's Church in Grantham, during which Bugler John Pulford played Last Post and Reveille.

The progress of rebuilding and re-training the Battalion was very slow, with a strength of only around 25 officers and 500 ORs. Small drafts had been received, including 25 former Royal Artillery AA Sergeants and Bombardiers, who had converted to infantry and who arrived on 1 January 1945.

However, Lt Col Breese was overjoyed on 6 January, when 157 assorted 2 Border and 4 Border personnel joined, many of whom had returned home from the Far East under the 'Python' scheme, whereby men who had completed over three years overseas service were repatriated. Not only were they already trained,

Above Men of the Battalion with others members of the 1st Airborne Division at Wellington Barracks, London, on 6 December 1944. Detachments representing every unit of the Division went to London for a parade and medal presentation at Buckingham Palace. Major Jock Neill DSO commanded the 1 Border group, which included Capt Joe Hardy MC, Sgt Sidney Clark DCM, Cpl Jim Swan MM and Pte J. O'Neill MM, who were to receive their awards from HM King George VI, Capts Colin Douglas and John McCartney and a party of 28 Other Ranks. *Bill Homer*

Left Men representing the various units of the 1st Airborne Division parade in Buckingham Palace after the inspection and investiture by HM King George VI on 6 December 1944. A Border Regiment Sergeant is on the front row, fourth from the right. The lack of publicity of this event caused one correspondent to a newspaper to refer to it as the 'ghost march'. *IWM H40979*

Lt Col C. F. O. Breese leads the Battalion in a march-past at Alford, Lincolnshire, on 21 January 1945. Brigadier Hyde Harrison DSO, Colonel of The Regiment, took the salute, accompanied by Major-General Roy Urquhart CB DSO, GOC 1st Airborne Division, and Brigadier Roger Bower CBE, commanding 1st Air-Landing Brigade. Following behind Lt Col Breese are Capt Colin Douglas, the Adjutant, RSM Paddy Kearns, Major Howard Wilkie, OC HQ Company, Capt Ron Jack and Lt Percy Boville (CAN-LOAN). *BRM*

but most had already seen active service in Burma. These men were housed at Bilsby Camp nearby, where S Company were based, and were quickly sorted out and posted to Companies within a few days. A second Python draft of 32 ORs arrived from 18 Holding Battalion at Formby on 13 January. Training was developed, despite the cold weather and snow, and on 29 January a drill Horsa glider fuselage arrived for loading training; this was finally completed by 16 March.

Among various visitors to the Battalion was the former CO of 4 Border, Lt Col Johnnie Burgess OBE, who visited the Battalion on 2/3 February to interview Arnhem survivors with a view to writing a lengthy article in *The Cumberland News* and for the Regimental Museum. The former AA NCOs received their maroon berets in mid-February, followed by the remaining recruits in mid-March. On 13 March the Battalion was at War Establishment strength (less 1st Line Reinforcements) and re-organised on the basis of four Rifle Companies, S Company and HQ Company.

In April 13 officers joined the Battalion, which then went to Keldy Castle in North Yorkshire for two weeks of exercises, training and field-firing on the ranges at Fylingdales. On 28 April the Battalion moved again to Shudy Camp near Bartlow in Essex. With constant rumours that the war was over, the Battalion was involved on a glider exercise 'Amber' from 3 to 5 May, for which they returned to Shudy. The German unconditional surrender was announced on the 8th, and the Battalion was briefed for a landing in Norway.

The Airborne Division (less the two Parachute Brigades) was ordered to Norway on VE Day, 10 May. The role of the Allies was to control, disarm and evacuate the German occupation forces; to receive and repatriate Allied PoWs; and to assist the Norwegian authorities to restore order and government. The operation was code-named DOOMSDAY.

The Seaborne Tail elements were shipped from Leith in Scotland, while the bulk of the Battalion was flown from Barkston Heath, South Grove and Rivenhall airfields in 43 RAF Stirling and four Halifax bombers to Gardemoen airfield, 30 miles NNE of Oslo. En route the aircraft encountered bad weather, principally fog, and were recalled to England. Johnnie Peters, by now a Sergeant in B Company, recalled that one of the aircrew in his plane dropped an orange phosphorous flare, the recognition signal for aircraft to return. However, for some reason a number of planes did not respond to the signal and four crashed, killing all on board.

One of these was Stirling LK147 of 196 Squadron, which carried six aircrew, Lt Saville and 12 men from HQ Company 1 Border, mainly from the Pioneer and Signal Platoons; some of the men were veterans of the Sicily landings and Arnhem, and others had served in the Far East (see Appendix 1). Capt Bill Baldock, Rev John Rowell and a small party recovered the bodies from the wreckage of the plane about a week after the Battalion had arrived. Each body was carefully recovered and buried near the crash site in a small cemetery that the party had prepared; the burial service was read by the Padre. Later the Commonwealth War Graves Commission moved them to Oslo Western Civil Cemetery.

The Battalion took off again on 11 May and landed at 18.00 hrs at Gardemoen airfield, directed in by a combined team of RAF and German controllers! The German forces in Norway had surrendered unconditionally on 7 May and representatives had flown to Scotland with details of the dispositions of their forces; the Wehrmacht alone numbered in the region

Top Officers, WOs and Sergeants at Well Camp, Alford, Lincolnshire, in March 1945. *BRM*

Centre B Company at Well Camp in 1945. *BRM*

Above C Company at Well Camp, also in March 1945. *BRM*

Left The original cemetery near the airfield where the Stirling carrying Lt Saville and 12 men of the Battalion crashed on 10 May 1945. After the wreckage was located, a party from S Company 1 Border led by Capt Bill Baldock, Padre John Rowell and Sgt McNamara went to recover the bodies on 23 May; they virtually pulled the wreckage apart to be sure that they found everyone. As each body was identified by the dog tags, it was carefully sewn into a blanket, then all were buried in this small cemetery made by the burial party near the site. Padre Rowell read the burial service and each grave was marked with a simple wooden cross. The bodies were subsequently moved to a permanent Commonwealth War Graves Commission plot in Oslo Western Civil Cemetery at Vermork. *BRM/Bill Thompson*

of 364,000 personnel, and there were vast quantities of ordnance, weapons, equipment and vehicles throughout the country. Despite the surrender, the Division landed prepared for anything.

The Battalion was driven in German Army lorries with armed German drivers to the nearest station, then a train took them into Oslo. Lt Alan Roberts, now commanding 18 Platoon C Company, recalled that 'all the way through to Oslo, the train slowed down as we passed through stations and we were pelted with flowers and cheered. We arrived in Oslo at about 23.30 hrs to a terrific reception, then marched to the barracks through cheering crowds. For the first few days we were ordered to go around in twos as there were a number of Quislings still around.' Initially the Battalion was billeted in Norwegian Army barracks in Oslo, then towards the end of May they moved to Smesstad in the northern suburbs of the city.

Lt Col (later Brigadier) Breese recalled that after five years of occupation the Norwegians were naturally ecstatic in their welcome to the Allies and 'two or three days after we arrived the Oslo City authorities gave a civic reception for the senior officers of the British Forces. I was driven down into Oslo for this by L/Cpl Robertson (ex-4 Border) and the crowds to see us arrive were so dense that we crawled along and at times were stationary; the cheering was deafening. At one of our halts a little girl aged about 10 or 12 nipped on to our running-board, threw a posy of flowers into the car and said "God bless your King". I have seldom been more touched.'

On 11 May Crown Prince Olaf boarded HMS *Apollo* at Rosyth and landed at Oslo on 20 May. He was greeted by a Guard of Honour of 100 officers and men from each of the Air-Landing Brigade Battalions; 1 Border's Guard was commanded by Lt Col Breese. King Haakon VII returned to his country on 7 June with the rest of his family on board HMS *Norfolk*. On 24 June a huge Allied Nations Day parade was held in Oslo where the people of Norway paid tribute to the forces of Britain, the USA and Russia; King Haakon

Below The setting in Oslo for the return of Crown Prince Olaf in May 1945. *BRM/Bill Thompson*

Right The Battalion party for the return of Crown Prince Olaf, Oslo, May 1945. Note that they are carrying the No 5 Jungle Carbine rather than the normal No 4 rifle. *BRM/Bill Thompson*

Below right Crown Prince Olaf, with Lt Col Breese behind, inspecting men of the Battalion in Oslo. *BRM/Bill Thompson*

Top Lt Alan Roberts with 18 Platoon for the demonstration exercise carried out by C Company for the Milorg on 25 June 1945 at Ovrevoll. *BRM/Alan Roberts*

Centre and bottom A Vickers MMG team and a group with a 2-inch mortar during the demonstration by C Company on 25 June 1945. *Bill Homer*

took the salute on the steps of the Royal Palace. At the end of June the Milorg, the Norwegian Military Resistance Movement Forces, asked if the Battalion could carry out a demonstration for them of equipment and basic infantry tactics. On 25 June C Company under Major Jock Neill DSO obliged, and the event made front-page news in the local paper.

The Battalion left the Oslo area on 9 July to move north to Aarnes (Kongivingen) from where they mounted the Lillehammer operation. Brigadier Breese later wrote that it was 'a cordon and search task because military intelligence suspected that the German HQ in a large hotel in Lillehammer might be plotting something nasty. This dawn raid gained a mention in the national dailies, which reported that The Border Regiment had caught two senior German Commanders in bed with their Norwegian mistresses.'

On 24 July the Battalion left for Bergen on the west coast. Battalion transport, which principally comprised jeeps and trailers, was supplemented by hired buses, which moved the Battalion as far as a fjord some 70-80 miles from Bergen. As the jeeps and then the troops were being ferried across, Lt Col Breese and Capt Douglas caught sufficient mackerel to provide breakfast for the Officers' Mess. The Battalion then marched in stages to Bergen, the QM and transport setting off each day to find a bivouac some 15-16 miles ahead, finally arriving in Bergen on 1 August. Football matches

The Liberation Certificate awarded to all ranks of the 1st Battalion who served in Norway. *BRM*

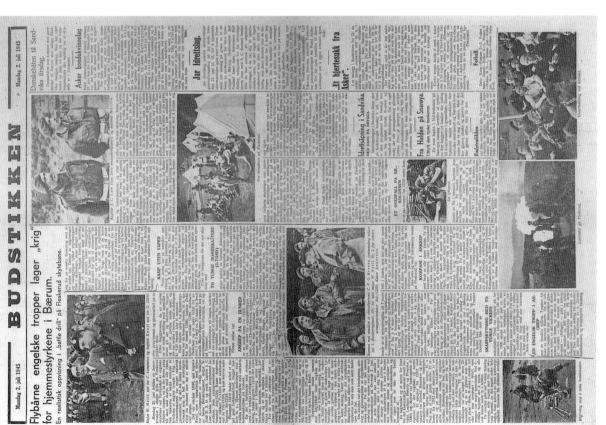

A Norwegian newspaper recording the exercise carried out by C Company. *BRM/Alan Roberts*

against the local villages were a great success, but the Battalion's main role was the guarding and repatriating of German PoWs and Russians.

The stay in Norway was an extremely happy one. The Norwegian Government produced a coloured 'Freedom Certificate' for every member of the Allied Forces who took part in the Liberation.

On 3 September 1 Border embarked at Oslo on the SS *Stratheden*, arrived in Liverpool on 6 September and travelled by train to Perham Down and Fowler Barracks near Ludgershall, where a number of officers, NCOs and men who had been taken prisoner at Arnhem re-joined the Battalion.

In October the Battalion received orders to move overseas, and on 18 October Lt Col Breese left for HQ 5th British Infantry Division at Brunswick in Germany to await their arrival. As the men returned from embarkation leave they held a ceremonial parade for a farewell visit from Major-General Urquhart CB DSO on 22 October, and the same day every man received a signed copy of the Order of the Day from Brigadier R. H. Bower CBE, Commanding 1st Air-Landing Brigade, who also visited the Battalion. After nearly four years the Airborne role was at an end; the Pegasus patches, AIRBORNE title and the universal symbol of the Airborne soldier, the maroon beret, had to be given up and replaced by a khaki beret and the 'Y' badge of the 5th Infantry Division. As the Battalion prepared for their journey to Hann Munden, a significant chapter in their history had come to an end.

To Lt.-Col. C. F. O. Breese and All Ranks of 1st Bn. The Border Regiment.

ORDER OF THE DAY
BY
BRIGADIER R. H. BOWER, C.B.E.
Comd. 1st Air Landing Brigade.

It is almost exactly four years since the 1st Bn. The Border Regiment became an airborne unit. At that time the fortunes of this country were not very bright and the Army was somewhat indifferently trained and equipped. However, even in those days preparations for offensive operations were being started and the 1st Airborne Division came into being.

For the succeeding fourteen months I had the honour of commanding the 1st Bn. and I shall always remember your splendid and cheerful response to our efforts to carry out the experimental and sometimes hazardous glider training of those early days. Many of you will remember the day early in 1942 when "B" Company carried out the first glider exercise ever undertaken by the British Army, and that Mr. Churchill was present to see it.

Based on long regimental traditions and on unsurpassed esprit de corps, the 1st Bn. has lived up to the high standard of courage, discipline and military training which it has set for itself. As a result of this the Battalion has acquitted itself with honour and distinction in the battles of Sicily, Italy, and finally at Arnhem.

You have now finished with great credit the airborne role that was assigned to you, and you can hang your red berets on the peg at home with the knowledge that your duty was well and truly done and that you have added a worthy chapter to the famous history of your Regiment.

I wish most sincerely to thank all ranks for their prolonged and whole-hearted co-operation in carrying out the various tasks that have faced us, and I wish you all the best of luck for the future.

22nd October, 1945.

R.H.Bower
—Brigadier.

Appendix 1

Battalion Roll of Honour

This is based principally on information from the Commonwealth War Graves Commission (CWGC) Cemetery and Memorial Registers, the Regimental Roll of Honour and information from other regimental records, contemporary newspapers and veterans. The pre-1974 county names have been used.

Abbreviations

D	Died
DoW	Died of Wounds
FB	First burial location
KIA	Killed in Action
(M)	Mother; (F) Father; (S) Sister; (W) Wife
P/N	PoW number
R M	Date reported missing
R W/M	Date reported wounded and missing

UK

BARKER 4753861 Pte Edward Charles, 12.4.43. Born and domiciled in Essex. Accidently killed during exercise at Swanage. Waltham Holy Cross New Cemetery, Essex (UK3656), Section 0, Grave 181/182/195/196.

BATES 3596259 Sgt Simeon, 4.6.40. DoW received in France aged 29. Born Bolton, Lancashire, son of Simeon and Primrose Bates, husband of Norah Bates of Bolton. Bolton (Heaton) Cemetery, 3.0.8 CE 7.

CRABB Lt Allen Peter CDN1140, CANLOAN A Company, 4/5.6.44. Killed due to PIAT accident at Woodhall Spa, Lincolnshire, aged 29. Son of Charles Pyatt and Ethel Crabbe, husband of Eliza Waters Crabb of Johnstown, Pennsylvania, USA. Brookwood Military Cemetery, Woking, Surrey (UK4156), 61.D.7.

ECCLES 3053202 Pte Frederick John, 15.1.42, aged 29. Born in Cumberland, son of Richard and Mary Elizabeth Eccles of Workington, Cumberland. Workington (Salterbeck) Cemetery (UK190), Section 2 Div M 18.

FELTON 3602947 Pte Lewis William, 19.12.41, aged 25. Born in Gateshead, Co Durham, son of Robert and Isabella Felton of Pelaw, Gateshead. Heworth St Mary Churchyard, Felling, Newyard, Co Durham (UK352), D.61.

GLENN 14401972 Pte John, 24.10.45, aged 21. Born Manchester, son of Hannah Carr of Chorlton-on-Medlock, Manchester. Phillips Park Cemetery, Manchester (UK 715), H NON/CONF grave 206.

HARRISON 4530282 Sgt Harry, 19.12.41, aged 31. Born Carlisle, son of Herbert and Christina Harrison, husband of Doris Ann Harrison of York. Southern Cemetery, Manchester (UK717), Q Column GR 231, screen wall panel 4.

HORNBY 3595375 Pte Henry G., 19.12.41, aged 32. Born in Bolton, Lancashire, son of Nicholas and Catherine Hornby, husband of Lilian Rosa Hornby of Longford, Coventry. Exhall St Giles Churchyard, Bedworth, Warwickshire (UK6895), Section E Grave 29.

IVESON 3593644 Pte Leonard, 4.8.40, aged 34. Born Burnley, Lancashire, son of Richard and Margaret Iveson, husband of Agnes Iveson. Burnley Cemetery NE 1517.

KEOGH 3598424 Pte George M., 19.12.41, aged 22. Born in Preston, Lancashire, son of Fred and Alice Keough, husband of Olive Margaret Keough of Ovington, Northumberland. Southern Cemetery, Manchester, Section Q Column GR 225, screen wall panel 5.

MARSHALL 3603533 Pte Richard Foster, 19.12.41, aged 24. Born and domiciled in Burnley, Lancashire, son of John William and Mary Marshall of Nelson, Lancashire. Nelson Cemetery 12 206.

O'MALIA 3600614 Pte Thomas, 17.4.42, aged 23. Born in Gateshead, Co Durham, son of Thomas and Catherine Ann O'Malia and husband of Sarah Jane O'Malia of Gateshead. Gateshead East Cemetery (UK332), Div 3 Grave 514.

PILKINGTON 3595364 Pte Matthew, 19.12.41, aged 40. Born Lancashire, husband of Agnes Pilkington of Haslingden, Lancashire. Haslingden (Holden Hall) Cemetery G.410.

POOLE 228662 2/Lt James Carey, 13.4.42, aged 21 Born in Wolverhampton, son of Stephen Carey and Elsie May Poole of Shipley, West Yorkshire. Bradford Crematorium (UK981A), panel 2.

SCOTT 3594989 Pte Edward, 8.7.41, aged 35. Born Manchester, son of Alec and Helen Scott, husband of Florence Scott of Clayton and Manchester. Phillips Park Cemetery, Manchester (UK715), Section K NON/CONF 339.

SCOTT 774819 Cpl, 13/14.7.41, aged 32. Died in Crickhowell Hospital, South Wales. Born in Cumberland, son of John and Jane Scott of Maryport, Cumberland, husband of Hannah Lizzie Scott of Flimby near Maryport. Flimby Cemetery, Maryport (UK142), Section D Grave 826.

BEF - Belgium and France

FCC: Froyennes Communal Cemetery (B137); TCC: Tournai Communal Cemetery Allied Extension (B160); DCC: Douai Communal Cemetery (FR44)

BECKETT 3593932 Sgt William James, 21.5.40, aged 38. Born in Carlisle, Cumberland, son of Capt W. and Margaret Beckett, husband of Margaret Beckett of Lancaster. FCC 2.15.

BENSON 3598603 Pte John Thomas, 21.5.40, aged 20. Born and domiciled in Manchester. FCC 3.21.

BOWE 3597059 Pte James, 24.5.40, aged 27. Born in Bolton, Lancashire, son of Thomas and Lizzie Bowe of Bolton. FR125 2.F.1A.

EARLEY 3600518 Pte Martin, 20.5.40, aged 20. Born in Salford, Lancashire, son of John and Georgina Earley of Cheetham, Manchester. TCC VI.C.4.

EASTON Lt Francis John, 21.5.40, aged 26. Born in SE London, son of Rowland W. and Elizabeth Easton of East Dulwich, London. FCC 3.28.

FIELDING 6769325 Pte J., 19.11.39. Born in SE London, son of James & Sarah Fielding of Wandsworth, London. DCC K.6.

FITZGERALD 2/Lt Desmond Kildare, 21.5.40, aged 20. Domiciled in Surrey, son of W/Cdr Cyril and Betty Fitzgerald. FCC 2.13.

HAMNETT 3598495 Pte Bernard, 21.5.40, aged 19. Born in Lancashire, son of Arthur and Florence Hamnett of Todmorden, Yorkshire. TCC VI.B.3.

HEAVEN 3596449 Cpl Harry, 21.5.40, aged 27. Born in Manchester, domiciled in Belfast. FCC 3.20.

HUMPHREYS 3594129 Pte Reginald, 23.10.39. Died as the result of a motor accident. Born and domiciled in Liverpool. DCC K. 13.

LAYTHAM 3596788 Pte Joseph Eric, 21.5.40, aged 26. Born in Lancashire, son of Tom and Elizabeth Laytham of Heysham, Lancs. TCC VI.B.1.

O'HARE 3599011 Pte Henry, 20.5.40, aged 20. Son of Annie O'Hare, husband of Doris O'Hare of Raffles, Carlisle. TCC VI.B.11.

O'NIELL 3596267 Pte Fergus, 21.5.40, aged 28. Born and domiciled in Co Armagh. FCC 1.5.

SAVAGE 6630602 Pte Frederick H. C., 21.5.40. Born in London, domiciled in E London. FCC 3.40.

SWINDELLS 3595890 Sgt Herbert, aged 27. Born Rochdale, Lancashire, domiciled in Bury, Lancashire. FCC 3.27.

TAYLOR 3382702 L/Cpl Thomas, 21.5.40, aged 31. Born in Rochdale, Lancashire, son of John and Letitia Taylor, husband of Mary Alice Taylor of Crawshawbooth, Lancashire. FCC 2.17.

WALLWORK 3595302 Cpl George Harold, 23.5.40, aged 30. Born in Salford, Lancashire, son of Nathan and Alice Wallwork, husband of Elizabeth Wallwork of Swinton, Lancashire. FR119 3.A.12.

WHALLEY 3595298 Pte Nelson, 21.5.40, aged 30. Born in Cumberland, husband of Ellen Rosina Whalley of Bath, Somerset. FCC 2.20.

WISE 3599490 Pte Leslie, 23.5.40, aged 22. Born and domiciled in Cumberland. TCC VI.A.6.

WRIGHT 3448890 Pte Clifford, 21.5.40, aged 19. Born in Bolton, Lancashire, son of Moses and Jessie Wright of Bolton. FCC 2.12.

SICILY

SWC: Syracuse War Cemetery, Sicily; CWC: Catania War Cemetery, Sicily; CASM: Cassino Memorial, Italy. P7 indicates Panel 7

BAINBRIDGE 3600449 Pte Thomas William, 10.7.43, aged 24. Born in Cumberland, son of Isaac Ernest and Helena Annie Bainbridge of Skelton, Cumberland. CASM P7.

BASTIMAN 3059845 Pte John James, 18 Pl C Coy, 9.7.43, aged 25. Born and domiciled in Bradford, West Yorkshire. CASM P7.

BATEMAN 3603956 Pte Charles Harry, 9.7.43, aged 22. Born in Manchester, son of Charles Harry and Catherine Bateman, Clayton, Manchester. CASM P7.

BELL 3602775 L/Cpl Ralph William, 9.7.43, aged 27. Born in Newcastle-upon-Tyne, son of Harry and Emily Eugene Bell, husband of

With the famous Monastery of Monte Cassino behind them, the official wreath bearers, including two men from the 1st Battalion, represent the British and Commonwealth Forces and the Italian Army at the unveiling of the Cassino Memorial on 30 September 1956. *BRM*

Lena Bell of Seaton Delaval, Northumberland. CASM P7.

BLACKHURST 3392008 Pte Robert, 9.7.43, aged 21. Born in Stockport, Cheshire, son of Percy and Rosa Blackhurst of Davenport, Stockport. CASM P7.

BOTTRELL 3606567 Pte Geoffrey, 10.7.43, aged 20. Born in Manchester, son of Mark and Anna Bottrell of Moss Side, Manchester. CASM P7.

BRETT 3605419 Pte Tom Talbot, 10.7.43, aged 21. Born in Manchester, son of Robert and Ellen Brett of Swinton, Lancashire. SWC II H 12.

CALDWELL 3606563 Pte Douglas Henry, 9.7.43, aged 21. Born in Lancashire, son of John and Bertha Caldwell of Cheetham, Manchester. CASM P7.

CANNON 3606845 Pte Harold, 9/10.7.43, aged 20. Born in Oldham, Lancashire, son of Harold and Annie Cannon of Wallasey, Cheshire. CASM P7.

CANNON 4207070 Pte Raymond, 10.7.43, aged 22. Born in Lancashire, son of Joseph and Ada Cannon of Ulverston, Lancashire. SWC II D 3.

CASEY 3595345 Pte John, 12 Pl B Coy,

Major W. N. R. Scotter MC escorts Field Marshal Lord Alexander of Tunis, accompanied by Field Marshal Sir Gerald Templar, as he inspects the Guard of Honour of the 1st Battalion at the unveiling of the Cassino Memorial on Sunday 30 September 1956. 120 men from the Battalion, commanded for the second time by Lt Col Tommy Haddon OBE, had travelled to Italy from Gottingen in Germany; 48 men from A Company formed the Guard, the Regimental Colour was carried by 2/Lt H. F. Rogers and the Band were under Acting Bandmaster Sergeant T. Cunnel. A wreath was laid on behalf of the Border Regimental Association and former members of the 1st Battalion by Mr Herbert Thyer, formerly CSM of D Company, who served at Sicily and Arnhem. On the marble columns are the names of 4,068 servicemen who lost their lives on Sicily, in Italy and in the Mediterranean, and who have no known grave. Among these are 89 from the 1st (Airborne) Battalion The Border Regiment, who drowned during the invasion of Sicily. Major Bill Scotter later commanded the 1st Battalion King's Own Royal Border Regiment and, as General Sir William Scotter, was the Regiment's Colonel from 1971 until his death in 1981. *BRM*

10.7.43, aged 30. Born in Durham, son of Joseph and Mary Casey, husband of Dorothy Laura Casey of Derby. CASM P7.

COLEMAN 3598837 Pte George, 9.7.43, aged 25. Born in Salford, Lancashire, son of Fred and H. Coleman, husband of Mary Coleman, Salford. CASM P7.

COLLINS 3606362 Pte Ronald, 14 Pl B Coy, 9.7.43, aged 20. Born in London, domiciled in Surrey. CASM P7.

COULTON 3603435 Pte Alexander, 10.7.43, aged 26. Born in Preston, Lancashire, son of William and Elizabeth Coulton, husband of Kathleen Coulton of Fulwood, Preston. CASM P7.

COUSINS 3602791 Pte Lawrence, 10.7.43, aged 28. Born and domiciled in Co Durham, son of John and Elisibeth Cousins. CASM P7.

COXHILL 3597014 Sgt Walter, 9.7.43, aged 29. Born in Accrington, Lancashire, husband of Sarah Coxhill of Currock, Carlisle. CASM P7.

CROW 4469780 Pte Thomas William, 9/10.7.43, aged 20. Born in Co Durham, son of John and Margaret Crow of Sunderland, Co Durham. CASM P7.

CUNLIFFE 3603466 Pte Arthur, 9/10.7.43, aged 29. Born and domiciled in Lancashire. CASM P7.

CUNNINGHAM 3127983 Sgt Richard, 9.7.43, aged 29. Born in Cumberland, son of John and Jean Cunningham of Parton, Cumberland, husband of Elizabeth Drummond Cunningham of Dumbarton. Recalled as a reservist in 1939. CASM P7.

EAGLES 3772549 Pte Albert E., A Coy, 10.7.43. Born and domiciled in Liverpool. SWC II D 1.

ECCLES 3709614 Cpl Andrew, 10.7.43, aged 28. Born in Barrow-in-Furness, Lancashire, husband of Sarah I. Eccles of Belfast, NI. CASM P7.

EMMERSON 3602810 Pte William, 9/10.7.43, aged 27. Born and domiciled in Yorkshire. CASM P7.

EVERITT 3603202 Pte Frank Cornelius, 10.7.43, aged 34. Born in E London, son of Frank and Rebecca Everitt, Stepney, London. CASM P7.

FAIRBRASS 3602814 Pte Thomas, 12 Pl B Coy, 9.7.43, aged 26. Born in Middlesbrough, Yorkshire, son of John and Ada Agnes Fairbrass of Redcar, Yorkshire. CASM P7.

FINERON Major Frederick William, OC C Coy, 16.7.43, aged 34. Born in York, son of Edward and Elsie Fineron, husband of Teresa Fineron of York. SWC II B 16.

FITZPATRICK 3535515 Pte Nicholas, 9.7.43, aged 21. Born in Eire, domiciled in Stockport, Cheshire, son of Nicholas and Elizabeth Fitzpatrick. CASM P7.

FRASER 4394430 Pte Gordon Anderson, 15 Pl C Coy, 9.7.43, aged 20. Born in Yorkshire, son of George Anderson and Annie Fraser of Darlington, Co Durham. CASM P7.

FRAZER 3604116 Pte Harold, 9.7.43, aged 28. Born in Cumberland, son of Mr and Mrs M. A. Frazer, husband of Mary Elizabeth Frazer of Penrith, Cumberland. CASM P7.

GALE 3605063 Pte Dennis Kewley, 12 Pl B Coy, 10.7.43, aged 21. Born on the Isle of Man, son of May Gale, foster-son of Mrs A. Sayle of Ramsey. CASM P7.

GAMMON 4982654 Pte Albert, 9.7.43, aged 20. Born in Lincoln, son of Alfred and Ellen Gammon of Northampton. CASM P7.

GARDNER 3594958 WO1 (RSM) George Walter, 10.7.43, aged 37. Born in Lancashire, son of Thomas and Mary Eleanor Gardner of Bowness-on-Windermere, Westmorland. SWC II C 6.

WO1 RSM George Gardner, Syracuse Cemetery, Sicily. *BRM*

GEDYE 3602825 Pte William Henry, 9.7.43, aged 23. Born in N Ireland and domiciled in Yorkshire, son of Samuel and Mary Ann Gedye. CASM P7.

GRAHAM 3392010 Pte Thomas Stewart, 10.7.43, aged 21. Born in Eire, son of James Joseph and Elizabeth Graham of Thornton, Lancashire. CASM P7.

GREAVES 3602735 Pte John, 10.7.43, aged 26. Born in Cumberland, son of John C. and Ada Jane Greaves of Parton, Cumberland. CASM P7.

GREEN 3598828 Pte James Alfred, 9.7.43, aged 28. Son of Clara Green, husband of Edith Green, Rochdale, Lancashire. CASM P7.

GREENWOOD 3600685 Pte Arthur, 9.7.43, aged 24. Born and domiciled in Westmorland, son of William Wright and Elizabeth Ann Greenwood. CASM P7.

HANSON 3595094 Pte Alwyn Roy, 12.7.43. Born in Yorkshire and domiciled in Hull, East Yorkshire. CASM P7.

HARVEY 4698641 Pte Maurice George, 9.7.43, aged 20. Born and domiciled in Yorkshire, son of Joseph Charles and Eleanor Harvey. CASM P7.

HEAD 3603844 Pte Richard Berkeley, 10.7.43, aged 29. Husband of Elizabeth Ellen Head of Walker, Newcastle-upon-Tyne. CASM P7.

HENDERSON 3130815 Pte James, 10.7.43, aged 26. Born in Ayr, son of Mr and Mrs H. Henderson of Minishant, Ayrshire. CASM P7.

HOLCROFT 3718823 Pte John, 9.7.43, aged 19. Born and domiciled in Lancashire. CASM P7.

HULME 3451927 Pte Herbert Henry, 10.7.43, aged 24. Born Wigan, Lancashire, son of Robert and Hilda Hulme, husband of Ellen Mary Hulme of Haslingden, Lancashire. SWC II F 5.

HURLEY 3607729 Pte John, 12 Pl B Coy, 10.7.43, aged 28. Born and domiciled in Newcastle-upon-Tyne. CASM P7.

JOHNSON 3603540 Pte William, 10.7.43, aged 28. Born in Wigan, Lancashire, son of William and Nancy Johnson of Standish, Lancashire. CASM P7.

JONES 3597006 Pte Alexander McNeil, 9.7.43, aged 28. Born in Cumberland, son of Robert and Leah Jones, husband of E. Jones of Workington, Cumberland. CASM P7.

JONES 3606141 Pte Maurice Rock, 9.7.43, aged 20. Born in Bolton, Lancashire, adopted son of Mr and Mrs C. Pace of Harwood, Lancashire. CASM P7.

KEENAN 3606493 Pte Joseph, 10.7.43, aged 20. Born in Manchester, son of Elizabeth Keenan, Denton, Lancashire. CASM P7.

KENNETT 3595612 Sgt Eric Henry Tyson, 9.7.43, aged 32. Born in Cumberland and domiciled in Carlisle. CASM P7.

KERVIN 3604122 Pte Rupert, 9.7.43, aged 28. Born in Preston, Lancashire, son of Peter and Bridget Kervin, husband of Marjorie Kervin of Cleator Moor, Cumberland. CASM P7.

LACK 3602853 Pte Ernest, 9.7.43, aged 23. Born in Middlesbrough, Yorkshire, son of Ernest and Martha Lack, Great Ayton, Yorkshire. CASM P7.

LANE 4465294 Pte Harry, 10.7.43, aged 30. Born in Yorkshire, husband of Mary Lane, Rawtenstall, Lancashire. SWC III G 13.

LEIGHTON 3604097 Pte William John, 10.7.43, aged 28. Born in Co Durham, son of William and Mary Ellen Leighton, husband of Evelyn Leighton of Denton Holme, Carlisle. CASM P7.

LITTLE 7371966 Pte Alfred, RAMC att'd 1 Border, 9.7.43, aged 23. Son of Arthur and Annie Little, husband of Madge Little of Ingrow, Keighley, West Yorkshire. CASM P12.

LOMAX 3605003 Pte John, 10.7.43, aged 28. Born in Blackburn, Lancashire, son of Robert and Margaret A. Lomax, husband of Annie E. Lomax of Astley Bridge, Bolton, Lancashire. CASM P7.

McCANDLISH 3606427 Pte Wilfred, 10.7.43, aged 21. Born in Stockport, Cheshire, son of William and Ann Jane McCandlish of Dukinfield, Cheshire. CASM P7.

MALONEY 3596101 Sgt John, 9.7.43, aged 31. Born in Lancashire, son of John Thomas and Mary Ellen Maloney, husband of Edna Maloney of Leigh, Lancashire. CASM P7.

MALONEY 3603015 Pte William, 9/10.7.43, aged 27. Born in Manchester, husband of May Maloney of Harpurhey, Manchester. CASM P7.

MARSH 7517611 Sgt Maurice Bertram, RAMC att'd 1 Border as Battalion Medical Sergeant, 9.7.43, aged 23. CASM P12.

MATHER 3660834 Cpl Joseph, 9.7.43, aged 29. Born and domiciled in St Helens, Lancashire, son of Joseph and Annie Elizabeth Mather. CASM P7.

MAUGHAN 3604761 Pte Edmund/ROH Edward, 10.7.43, aged 24. Born in Northumberland, son of Henderson and Elizabeth Maughan, husband of Ellen Maughan of Bedlington, Northumberland. CWC IV.J.49.

Pte Edmund Maughan, Catania War Cemetery, Sicily. *BRM*

METCALFE 3606149 L/Cpl Thomas, 9.7.43, aged 20. Born in Colne, Lancashire, son of Ida and George Metcalfe of Colne. Commemorated on Colne War Memorial. CASM P7.

MOLLAN 3602982 Pte Thomas William, 10.7.43, aged 28. Born in Eire, son of Walter E. and Margaret M. Mollan of Selloo, Co Monaghan, Eire. SWC IV D 7.

MONK 3605605 Pte Matthew Henry, 9.7.43, aged 36. Born in Gateshead, Co Durham, son of Margaret E. Monk of Bensham, Co Durham. CASM P7.

MOORE 3606349 Pte Leslie Hughes, 10.7.43, aged 21. Born in Cheshire, son of Amy Moore of Nantwich, Cheshire. CWC IV.J.48.

MOUNSEY Lt Nigel D. W., Border Regt att'd 7 Green Howards, 18.7.43, aged 21. Born in India and domiciled in Carlisle, son of Lt Col Walter S. Mounsey. CWC I.B.27.

NELSON 3601246 Pte Stanley, 9/10.7.43, aged 24. Born in Cumberland, son of John and Ada Nelson, husband of Mary Nelson of Workington, Cumberland. CASM P7.

O'BRIEN 3657761 L/Cpl Norman, 9.7.43, aged 27. Born in Liverpool, son of Matthew and Daisy O'Brien, husband of Dorothy O'Brien of Sale, Cheshire. CASM P7.

O'CONNOR 3776202 Pte Herbert Francis, 9.7.43, aged 26. Born in Eire and domiciled in Manchester. CASM P7.

PARKER 3602870 L/Cpl Peter, 10.7.43, aged 23. Born and domiciled in Yorkshire, son of Lily Parker, stepson of Alfred Sturman, husband of Mary Parker. SWC II C 16.

PARTINGTON 3607120 Pte Alfred Owen, 10.7.43, aged 20. Born in Bolton, Lancashire, son of Mr and Mrs E. Smith of Bolton. SWC III H 11.

PATTERSON 14298041 Pte James Laurence, 10.7.43, aged 19. Born in Gateshead, Co Durham, son of James and Mary J. Patterson of Gateshead. CASM P7.

PHILLIPS 3594593 Pte Charles John, 9.7.43, aged 35. Born in E London, son of Charles and C. Phillips, husband of Sarah Elizabeth Phillips of Crook, Co Durham. CASM P7.

PIMBLOTT 3600560 Cpl Arthur, 15 Pl C Coy, 10.7.43, aged 26. Born and domiciled in Cheshire. CASM P7.

POOLEY 4547101 Pte Derek, 10.7.43, aged 19. Born in Yorkshire, son of Albert Edward and Evelyn Alice Pooley of Shildon, Co Durham. SWC II B 3.

Pte Derek Pooley, killed in action at the Ponte Grande bridge on 10 July 1943, Syracuse Cemetery, Sicily. *BRM*

POPE 3598823 Pte Frederick John, 9.7.43, aged 23. Born in Manchester, son of Frederick John and Emily Pope, husband of Winifred Pope of Newton, Manchester. CASM P7.

PRITCHARD 3523632 Cpl Samuel Ernest, 9.7.43, aged 31. Son of James William and Sarah Pritchard, husband of F. Pritchard of Manchester. CASM P7.

PRYOR 3606368 Pte William Joseph, 10.7.43, aged 19. Born in Lancashire, son of Herbert and Annie Pryor of Bury, Lancashire. SWC I G 1.

RAWCLIFFE 3597300 L/Cpl Robert, 9.7.43, aged 29. Born in Preston, Lancashire, son of Richard and Jane Ann Rawcliffe of Preston. CASM P7.

REEVES 3606772 Pte Vincent, 9.7.43, aged 20. Born in Manchester, son of William Thomas and Mary Flora Reeves of Cheetham Hill, Manchester. CASM P7.

RIGBY 3394002 Pte Walter 9.7.43, aged 21. Born in Rochdale, Lancashire, son of George

Harry and Martha Rigby of Firgrove, Lancashire. CASM P7.

RIMMER 3607096 Pte John, 9.7.43, aged 19. Born in Southport, Lancashire, son of John and May Rimmer of Marshside, Southport. CASM P7.

RISELEY 3606249 Cpl Tom, 9.7.43, aged 20. Born in Cheshire, son of George and Ellen Riseley of Macclesfield, Cheshire. CASM P7.

SHAW 3598879 Cpl Norman, 9.7.43, aged 21. Born in Westmorland, son of W. W. and Esther Shaw of Staveley, Kendal, Westmorland. CASM P7.

SHERWOOD 3602730 Pte Leonard, 9.7.43, aged 26. Born in Dorset, son of Jim and G. Sherwood of Poole, Dorset. CASM P7.

SIMMONS 3605190 Pte Frederick, 9/10.7.43, aged 23. Born in N London and domiciled in Cumberland. CASM P7.

SIMPSON 3596388 Pte Edwin, 9.7.43, aged 30. Born in Barrow-in-Furness, Lancashire, husband of Elizabeth Simpson of Barrow-in-Furness. CASM P7.

SMITH 3603369 L/Cpl Benjamin, 9.7.43, aged 28. Born in Stoke-on-Trent, Staffordshire, son of Harry and Nelly Smith, nephew of Mrs G. Callear of Tunstall, Stoke-on-Trent. CASM P7.

STAIT 3603338 Pte Thomas, 10.7.43, aged 23. Son of Joshua and Ann Stait, husband of Frances E. Stait of Kirkdale, Liverpool. CASM P7.

STUBBINS 3603399 L/Cpl John Arthur, 10.7.43, aged 28. Born in Manchester, son of John Arthur and Jessie Maud Stubbins of Rusholme, Manchester. SWC II C 14.

SWIFT 3597225 Pte James, 9.7.43, aged 33. Born in Lancashire and domiciled in Wigan, Lancashire. CASM P7.

TAYLOR 3603538 Pte Richard 'Dad', 12 Pl B Coy, 10.7.43, aged 28. Born in Lancashire, son of Mrs M. A. Taylor of Adlington, Lancashire. CASM P7.

TAYLOR 3604566 Pte William John, 12 Pl B Coy, 10.7.43, aged 21. Born in Walsall, Staffordshire, son of Mr and Mrs W. A. Taylor of Laxey, Isle of Man. CASM P7.

THOMAS 3783781 Pte Thomas, 9.7.43, aged 22. Born in Bootle, Lancashire, son of Cornelius and Jesse Thomas, husband of Elizabeth A. Thomas of Bootle. CASM P7.

THORNTON 3602713 L/Cpl Arthur, 9.7.43, aged 29. Born in Burnley, Lancashire, son of Walter and Henrietta Thornton, husband of A. Thornton of Burnley. CASM P7.

TIMMINS 3595791 L/Cpl Albert Hewitt, 10.7.43, aged 30. Born in Cumberland, son of Morrison and Harriet Alexandra Ernestine Timmins, husband of Isabella Timmins of Whitehaven, Cumberland. SWC II.B.1.

TODD 3606904 Pte Joseph Bradley, 9.7.43, aged 20. Born and domiciled in Birkenhead, Cheshire. CASM P7.

TOMLINSON 3598428 Pte John William, 9.7.43, aged 26. Born in Manchester, son of R. H. and Annie Tomlinson of Higher Crumpsall, Manchester. CASM P7.

WALLBANK 3603757 Pte William, 9.7.43, aged 23. Born in Preston, Lancashire, son of William and Ellen Wallbank of Barton, Preston. CASM P7.

WALMSLEY 3783911 Pte John, 10.7.43, aged 19. Born in Blackburn, Lancashire, son of Mr and Mrs J. W. Walmsley of Blackburn. SWC II H 10.

WARDLE 5059035 Pte Ronald E., 11.7.43, aged 22. Born in Stoke-on-Trent, Staffordshire, son of Albert and Dorothy Maria Wardle of Stoke-on-Trent. SWC II H 11.

WATSON 2697410 Cpl James, 9.7.43, aged 23. Born in Stirlingshire, son of David and Euphemia Watson of Stenhousmuir, Stirlingshire. CASM P7.

WATT 3599143 Pte James, 10.7.43, aged 26. Born in Glasgow (ROH domiciled Glasgow), son of James and Hannah Watt of Cambuslang, Lanarkshire. SWC II G 1.

WEBSTER 3605434 Pte Terence Patrick, 10.7.43, aged 21. Born in Salford, Lancashire, son of John and Cecilia Webster of Stretford, Manchester. CASM P7.

WEIR 3708054 Pte Alexander, 10.7.43, aged 33. Born in Cumberland, son of Mrs J. Weir, husband of H. Weir of Egremont, Cumberland. CASM P7.

WEST 4981028 Pte Lionel Arthur, 9.7.43, aged 21. Born in Nottingham, son of Harry and Dorothy West of Woodthorpe, Nottingham. CASM P7.

WHITE 3596657 Pte Francois Samuel Fernand, 10.7.43, aged 27. Born in Pembrokeshire, son of Thomas and Madalaine White, husband of Irene White of Brixton, London. SWC II F 3.

WHITTON 3595863 Cpl Robert Walter, 10.7.43, aged 26. Born in Eire and domiciled in Northumberland, son of Robert and Margaret Whitton, husband of Clare Whitton. CASM P7.

WILLOUGBY 4622043 Cpl Joe, 14 Pl B Coy, 9.7.43, aged 28. Born in Yorkshire, son of Thomas and Sarah E. Willougby of Shipley, West Yorkshire. CASM P7.

WOOD 4546679 Pte William, 9.7.43, aged 20. Born in Dewsbury, West Yorkshire, son of Edwin and Martha Wood of Earlsheaton, Dewsbury. CASM P7.

WYATT 134114 Lt P. J. W., Queen's Regiment seconded to 1 Border, 10.7.43, aged 27. Son of John Lawrence and Dorothy Wyatt, husband of Lucy Theodora Wyatt. CASM P4.

NORTH AFRICA

El Alia Cemetery, Algiers

WHITE 3602723 Pte William James, 22.1.44, aged 25. Born in Exeter, Devon, son of Violet Louise White and stepson of John Henry Danning of Longecombe, Devon.

ARNHEM

OWC: Oosterbeek CWGC, Netherlands 260; GM: Groesbeek Memorial, Nijmegen. Other cemeteries as stated

ADAMS 4547065 Cpl William, 24.9.44, aged 21. Born in Buckinghamshire, son of Horace and Elizabeth Adams of Attercliffe, Sheffield. FB crossroads Van Borsselenweg/ Utrechtseweg, now OWC 21.B.18.

AGER 3599174 Pte Ernest, 22.9.44, aged 32. Born in Manchester, husband of Florence Ager of Chorlton-on-Medlock, Manchester.

Bugler John Pulford of the 1st Battalion sounds Last Post and Reveille at the first Memorial Service in the Oosterbeek Cemetery in September 1945. Pulford joined the 1st Battalion from The King's Own Yorkshire Light Infantry in 1941 and served in HQ Company. He was renowned for his bugling and blew Last Post and Reveille at General Hopkinson's funeral in Italy, at the 1st Airborne Division's Remembrance service at Grantham in December 1944 and at the first Commemoration service at Oosterbeek in 1945. He later became the Drum-Major of the 1st Battalion, then transferred in the same capacity to the 1st Battalion The Manchester Regiment, with whom he completed his service in 1958. *BRM/Ray Brown*

Body found together with that of Pte Lowery in February 1993 in the garden of a house on the north side of Van Lennepweg and re-interred in the Oosterbeek Cemetery 8 October 1993. GM P4, now OWC 25.C.4.

ALLEN 3598633 Sgt John, 22.9.44. Born in Whitehaven, Cumberland, wife and two children in Whitehaven. Called up with 5 Border in 1939 and later transferred to 1 Border. FB in front of the Tafelberg Hotel, now OWC 16.A.4.

ASHURST 4616055 Pte Tom, 24.9.44, aged 24. Born in Oldham, Lancashire, husband of May Ashurst of Waterhead, Oldham. FB sports ground behind Hartenstein, now OWC 26.B.6.

ASTON 3865747 Pte Frederick Joseph, 21.9.44, aged 26. Born in Cheshire, son of Samuel and Maggie Aston of Barnton, Cheshire. GM P4.

ATKINSON 3602709 Cpl Bernard S., 25.9.44, aged 28 (R M same day). Born and domiciled in Lancashire. Buried by the Germans in the dyke near 'Blauwe Kamer' at Rhenen and later re-interred in the General Cemetery at Rhenen 27.B.1.

AYRES 3596882 Pte William, ACC att'd 1 Border, 20.9.44, aged 36. Son of Charles and Edith Ayres. FB near Sonnenberg at side of Hoofdlaan, now OWC 5.C.14.

BARFOOT 3861738 L/Cpl James, 28.9.44, aged 33 (R W/M 21.9.44). Born in Oldham, Lancashire, son of James A. and Catherine Barfoot, husband of May of Oldham. DoW in hospital and buried in General Cemetery 'Heidehof' at Apeldoorn, now OWC 24.A.12.

BARNES 14641710 Pte Robert, 21.9.44, aged 20. Born in Cumberland, son of John and Margaret Barnes of Cleator Moor, Cumberland. FB access road to Driel Ferry, now OWC 30.C.8.

BARNES 3771478 Pte William Charles, 21.9.44, aged 26 (R M 26.9.44). Husband of L. Barnes of Bootle, Lancashire. GM P4.

BECK 3784044 Pte William, 24.9.44, aged 21. Born in St Helens, Lancashire, son of William and Lucy Ellen Beck of St Helens. GM P4.

BELL 3602774 Pte Albert, 22.9.44, aged 31 (R M 26.9.44). Born in Yorkshire, son of Albert and Alice Victoria Bell, husband of Annie Ruth Bell of Scarborough. FB in garden of house Hemelseberg, now OWC 18.A.3.

BORDERS 3602584 Pte Eric, 20.9.44, aged 27. Born in Stockport, Cheshire, son of William H. and Emily Borders, husband of Nellie Maud Borders of Stockport. FB garden of the Ter Horst family near Oosterbeek Church, now OWC 17.C.10.

BRAGG 3608284 Pte Henry 'Harry', 20.9.44, aged 21 (R W/M same day). Born in Cumberland, son of Jane Bragg of Egremont, Cumberland. GM P4.

BROWN 162499 Lt George Eric Tiplady, 21.9.44. Born in Yorkshire, only son of Mrs James Brown of Portinscale. Lived at Keswick for 23 years. At Stowe received his cap for rugby and cricket and played in the Junior Tennis Championship at Wimbledon. Played three-quarter for Cumberland. Received his BA from Cambridge in 1933 and was teaching in Yorkshire at the outbreak of the war. Served in the RAC for 2½

Oosterbeek, Airborne Cemetery

Oosterbeek, Airborne Cemetery

The Airborne Cemetery at Oosterbeek. *BRM*

years before joining 1 Border in January 1944. GM P4.

BRYSON 3602942 L/Cpl Thomas John W., 21.9.44, aged 28. Born in Roxburghshire, son of George and Isabel Bryson, husband of Gwendoline Bryson of North Kensington, London. FB at the corner Van Lennepweg and Utrechtseweg, now OWC 27.A.3.

BUCKLEY 14206592 Pte Frank, 21.9.44, aged 21 (R M 18.9.44). Born and domiciled in Cheshire. FB east of church near laundry Van Hofwegen, now OWC 26.B.15.

BURNS 176190 A/Capt William R., att'd HQ 1st Air-Landing Brigade as Intelligence Officer, 20.9.44, aged 31. Born in Whitehaven, Cumberland, son of Col and Mrs Sidney Burns of Cullercoats, Northumberland, husband of Elsie Burns of Kinsley, Yorkshire. FB 180 yards west of the Hartenstein Hotel, now OWC 1.A.16.

BURR 2878204 Sgt Hendry 'Hank', 18.9.44, aged 23 (R W/M same day). Born in

Aberdeenshire, son of Jane Warrender of St Fergus, Aberdeenshire. FB Renkum General Cemetery, now OWC 5.D.7.

CAIN 3783853 Pte Vincent Leslie, 20.9.44, aged 23. Born in Lancashire, son of Bartholomew and Rose Cain of Prescot, Lancashire. FB probably at the side of the Utrechtseweg by J. P. Heije Stichting, now OWC 28.C.5.

CARR 4397327 Cpl Jack, 25.9.44, aged 22 (R. M. 22.9.44). Born in Yorkshire, son of Walter and Maggie Elizabeth Carr of Keighley, West Yorkshire, husband of Catherine Peggy of Leyburn, Yorkshire. GM P4.

CAVEN 14563521 Pte James, 21.9.44, aged 19 (R M 26.9.44). Born in Dumfries, son of Charles A. and Thomasina Caven of Dumfries. FB 100 yards west of the Hartenstein Hotel, now OWC 26.B.14.

CERVI 3608007 L/Cpl Laurence, 18.9.44, aged 20 (R W/M same day). Born in Manchester,

son of Gladys Cervi of Manchester, husband of Margaret Cervi of Southrey, Lincolnshire. GM P4.

CHAPMAN 3602785 L/Cpl John, 20.9.44, aged 28. Born in West Hartlepool, son of John and Jane Mary Chapman, nephew of Mrs F. Graham of Billingham, Co Durham. FB garden of the Ter Horst family near Oosterbeek Church, now OWC 17.C.11.

CLAY 3390615 Pte George, 24.9.44, aged 22. Born and domiciled in Preston, Lancashire. FB possibly Ommershof, now OWC 23.C.1.

COATES 3602789 Cpl Thomas, 20.9.44, aged 28. Born in Sunderland, son of Thomas and Ada Coates, husband of Ivy Coates of Whitburn, Co Durham. FB possibly by road junction by Driel Ferry, now OWC 30.C.9.

COULSTON 228608 Lt Robert Hugh, 23.9.44, aged 24. Born in Cumberland, son of William James and Hannah Louisa. OWC 26.A.15.

COWIN 3602473 Cpl Lawrence 'Larry', KiA 25.9.44, aged 26 (R M. 26.9.44). Born in Cumberland, son of James Frederick and Agnes Cowin, husband of Margaret Annie Cowin of Newbiggin-on-Lune, Westmorland. FB area of Sonnenberg/ Hartenstein, now OWC 19.C.11.

Cpl Larry Cowin, Signaller attached to D Company. *BRM*

CRANSWICK 3602793 Pte Alfred H., 22.9.44, aged 28 (R W/M 20.9.44). Born and domiciled in Yorkshire. DoW in a hospital and buried in General Cemetery Soestbergen in Utrecht, Plot 12.D.1.11.

CRIMMEL 1142367 Pte John Henry, 20.9.44, aged 21 (R M 19.9.44). Born in East London, son of Henry E. and Maud A. J. Crimmel of Canvey Island, Essex. GM P4.

DALTON 7946561 Pte Charles William, 27.9.44, aged 22 (R M 25.9.44). Son of Mr and Mrs C. Dalton of York. DoW in hospital and buried in General Cemetery 'Heidehof' at Apeldoorn, now OWC 24.A.12.

DEIGHTON 3600684 Sgt Harold, 4.4.45, aged 26 (R M 26.9.44), died in hospital in PoW camp. PoW Stalag XIIA 91890. Born in Cumberland, son of George and Sarah Deighton of The Fleece Inn, Brough, Cumberland. Hannover War Cemetery, Germany (CWGC 748) 15.F.11.

DENTON 14583425 Pte Kenneth, 12.2.45, aged 20 (R M 26.9.44). Born in Bolton, Lancashire, son of James and Emilia Denton of Deane, Bolton. Taken prisoner and DoW in hospital at Apeldoorn. Buried in General Cemetery 'Heidehof' at Apeldoorn, now OWC 18.C.11.

DURBER 3607415 Pte Thomas, 21.9.44, aged 19. Born in Lancashire, son of Joseph and Mary Durber of Ashton-under-Lyne, Lancashire. FB near Utrechtseweg near junction with Hoofdlaan, now OWC 17.B.11.

EDEN 3603438 L/Cpl William, 22.9.44, aged 29 (R W/M same day). Born in Preston, Lancashire, son of the late Pte John Eden, 6th Battalion The King's Own Royal Regiment (Lancaster) who DoW at Gallipoli 24.8.15, and Mary Elizabeth Eden of Ribbleton, Preston. GM P4.

EDGAR 3603439 Cpl Thomas, DoW 24.9.44, aged 27. Born in Carlisle, Cumberland, son of John and Margaret Anne Edgar of Stanwix, Carlisle. GM P4.

EDGE 3600831 Pte Clifford, 19.9.44, aged 25 (R W/M 17.9.44). Born in Manchester, son of George William and Ethel Edge, husband of Elizabeth Edge of Miles Platting, Manchester. FB near Sonnenberg along the Hoofdlaan, now OWC 5.C.12.

ELLERY 3602808 Pte Robert, 21.9.44, aged 28 (R W/M same day). Born and domiciled in Sunderland. FB in front of the Tafelberg Hotel, now OWC 21.A.5.

ELLICOCK 4397165 Pte George Henry, 25.9.44, aged 21. Born in Wakefield, West Yorkshire, and domiciled in Bradford, West Yorkshire. GM P4.

ELVIN 14638663 Pte William Leonard, 25.9.44, aged 20. Born and domiciled in SE London. GM P4.

EVERINGTON 4615126 Pte George Charles Hugh, 22.9.44, aged 20 (R M 19.9.44). Born in Lincoln, son of George William and Freida Clare Everington, husband of Louisa Everington of Kippax, Yorkshire. FB 'Hoge Oorsprong' in field west of Van Borsselenweg, lower part, now OWC 18.B.14.

FIDDLER 3602545 Pte Telford, 23.9.44, aged 28. Born in Cumberland, son of the late Telford and Diane Fiddler of Broughton Moor, husband of Edith Mary Fiddler of Bolton Street, Workington, Cumberland. GM P4.

FITZPATRICK 14647194 Pte Francis 'Fitz', 25.9.44, aged 19 (R W/M same day). Born in Leeds and domiciled in Liverpool. FB likely to have been behind Pietersberg, now OWC 26.B.12.

FLETCHER 3597942 Cpl Walter D., 24.9.44 (R W/M 21.9.44). Born in Dumfriesshire and domiciled in Northumberland. DoW in hospital and buried in General Cemetery (Soestbergen) in Utrecht 12.D.1.12.

FOGGO 3602486 L/Cpl Eric Edward, 21.9.44, aged 27. Born in Liverpool, son of James and

Pte George C. H. Everington, 12 Platoon B Company. *BRM*

Lucy Foggo, husband of Kathleen Enid Foggo of Settle, West Yorkshire. FB possibly junction of road and field Oranjeweg/Bothaweg, now OWC 22.B.6.

FORD 3782886 Pte James Patrick, 29.9.44, aged 21 (R W/M 20.9.44). Born in Cheshire, son of James and Elizabeth Ford of Runcorn, Cheshire. FB in front of the Tafelberg Hotel, now OWC 16.B.20.

FOSTER 3601333 Pte Arthur, 21.9.44, aged 27 (R M 17.9.44). Born in Bolton, Lancashire, husband of Lily Foster of Stanwix, Carlisle, Cumberland. GM P4.

FOWLER 3602819 Pte Robert Ball, 22.9.44, aged 29 (R W/M same day). Born in Sunderland, Co Durham, son of Harry and Alice Fowler, husband of Florence E. Fowler of Monkwearmouth, Sunderland. GM P4.

FROUD 3596579 Cpl George, 21.9.44, aged 27 (R W/M same day). Husband of Vera Frances Froud of Headington, Oxford. GM P4.

GALLACHER 2697171 Pte Neil, 18.9.44, aged 27 (R M same day). Born in West Lothian, son of Neil and Helen Gallacher, Linlithgow, West Lothian. FB behind Chr Passberg School, now OWC 23.A.14.

GIBSON 3602826 Pte Joseph Henry, 23.9.44, aged 29. Born in Sunderland, son of Mr and Mrs J. Gibson, husband of Lilian May Gibson of Ryhope, Co Durham. FB in sports ground behind Hartenstein Hotel, now OWC 17.B.3.

GRAY 4397338 Pte William Frederick, 18.9.44, aged 21. Born in Hull, East Yorkshire, son of Mrs G. Fox of Hull, husband of Muriel Gray of Sowerby Bridge, West Yorkshire. OWC.15.A.10.

HALLIDAY 3602840 L/Cpl Raymond, 24.9.44, aged 28 (R W/M same day). Born in Co Durham, son of Henry and Nancy Halliday, husband of Lily Halliday of Stockton-on-Tees. GM P4.

HANSON 3596670 Sgt Robert, 21.9.44, aged 32. Born in Manchester, son of James Oswald and Ann Hanson, husband of Rachel Holiday Hanson of Stanwix, Carlisle. FB in front of house Hillock near Zilverberg, now OWC 16.A.11.

HARDY 14212903 Pte Stanley Ronald, 26.9.44, aged 22 (R W/M 20.9.44). Born and domiciled in SW London, son of Mr and Mrs J. W. Hardy of Edlington, West Yorkshire. GM P4.

HARTLEY 3604673 L/Sgt Edward, 20.9.44, aged 31 (R M 26.9.44). Born in Leeds, West Yorkshire, son of J. H. and Cissie Hartley, husband of Vera A. Hartley of Cookridge, Leeds. GM P4.

HIRD 1137162 Pte Edward E., 23.9.44, aged 21 (R M 26.9.44). Born in Staffordshire, son of Emmanuel and Annie Hird of Hanley, Staffordshire. GM P4.

HODGSON 129359 Capt William Kitching, DoW 26.9.44, aged 24. Born in Westmorland, son of John P. and Bertha Taylor Hodgson of Milnthorpe, Westmorland. FB Renkum General Cemetery, now OWC 1.C.2.

HOLDSWORTH 2696598 L/Cpl Herbert Arthur, 23.9.44, aged 22 (R M 17.9.44). Born and domiciled in Leeds, son of Edward and Zettee Caroline Holdsworth of Gildersome, West Yorkshire. FB near the Tafelberg Hotel, now OWC 16.A.14.

HOLME 3603471 Pte William Myles, 23.9.44, aged 29. Born in Westmorland, son of William James and Margaret Holme of Middleshaw, Westmorland. FB in small copse north of road, location unknown, now OWC 31.B.6.

HOLT 295834 Lt Philip Summer, 25.9.44, aged 19 (almost certainly killed on 21.9.44). Born in Stockport and domiciled in Manchester, son of Dorothy Holt of Wilmslow, Cheshire. FB in garden near the Van Borsselenweg, now OWC 22.C.18.

HOOD 3606832 L/Cpl Frank, died of dysentery in hospital 29.10.44, aged 21 (R M 25.9.44). PoW Stalag XIIA P/N 91945. Born in Cheshire, son of Mr Albert Edward Hood, Crewe, Cheshire. Rheinberg War Cemetery 10.D.21.

HORSLEY 164948 Lt John, att'd 21st Independent Company Parachute Regt, 27.9.44, aged 24. Born in Newcastle-upon-Tyne, son of Tom Mayson and Mildred Mary Horsley of Newcastle-upon-Tyne. OWC 18.C.6.

HOWE 14209659 L/Cpl George William, 24.9.44, aged 25 (R M 17.9.44). Born and domiciled in Cumberland, son of William and Mary J. Howe. FB 'Hoog Oorsprong' in field west of Van Borsselenweg, lower part, now OWC 18.B.18.

HULSE 3782658 Pte Philip A., 3.10.44, aged 21 (R M/PoW 18.9.44). Born and domiciled in Wallasey, Cheshire. DoW in hospital in Utrecht and buried in General Cemetery (Soestbergen) Utrecht 12.D.2.16.

HUNTER 3596717 L/Sgt Arthur, 18.9.44, aged 34. Born in Lancashire, son of Mr and Mrs Robert Hunter, husband of Vera Kathleen Hunter of Chorley, Lancashire. FB Renkum General Cemetery, now OWC 16.C.5.

HUNTER 3596799 Sgt John, 20.9.44, aged 30.

Born in Antrim, son of George and Elizabeth Hunter, husband of Lily Hunter of Prudhoe-on-Tyne, Northumberland. FB in wood at Westerbouwing, Valckeniersbossen, now OWC 28.A.3.

HURLEY 3450725 Pte Patrick, 22.9.44, aged 24 (R M same day). Born in Eire and domiciled in Manchester. FB in front of Tafelberg Hotel, now OWC 16.B.3.

ISHERWOOD 3600572 Pte Wallace, 23.9.44, aged 36 (R W/M same day). Born in Bolton, Lancashire, son of Mr and Mrs William Isherwood, husband of Lilian Isherwood of Bolton. FB in front of Tafelberg Hotel, now OWC 16.B.13.

JACKSON 3607911 Pte Robert, 23.10.44, aged 21. Born in Carlisle, son of J. T. and Elizabeth Jackson of Stanwix, Carlisle. DoW in hospital and buried in General Cemetery 'Heidehof', Apeldoorn, now OWC 24.A.16.

JARVIS 4398559 Pte Francis Edward, 24.9.44, aged 23 (R M 20.9.44). Born in Sunderland, son of Henry C. and Sarah Ann Jarvis of Sunderland, Co Durham. GM P4.

JOHNSON 3603507 Pte James 'Jimmy', 17.9.44, aged 29 (R W/M same day). Born in Lancashire, son of Mr and Mrs G. Johnson of Coppull, Lancashire, husband of Ina of Carlisle. GM P4.

JONES 14576638 Pte Thomas Donald, 22-25.9.44, aged 23 R M 20.9.44). Born in Birkenhead, Cheshire, son of Henry and Wilhelmina Jones, husband of Joyce A. Jones of Bidston, Cheshire. FB 'Hoog Oorsprong' in field west of Van Borsselenweg, lower part, now OWC 18.B.16.

LANGHORN 3601433 Cpl Thomas, 22.9.44, aged 29. Born in Blackburn, Lancashire, son of John Henry and Jane Langhorn, husband of Margaret Elizabeth Langhorn of Kendal, Westmorland. FB house 'Hoog Oorsprong' east of Van Borsselenweg, edge of Hemelseberg, now OWC 21.A.4.

LONG 4279402 L/Cpl George Edward Hearn, 24.9.44, aged 22 (R M same day). Born in Gateshead, son of Jasper and Beatrice Long, husband of Daphne Adeline Long of Andover, Hampshire. FB probably south of Tafelberg Hotel, now OWC 21.A.2.

LOWERY 4469819 Pte Douglas, 24.9.44, aged 21. Born in Gateshead, Co Durham, son of Thomas and Sarah Bell Lowery of Bensham, Gateshead. Body found in February 1993 in a garden on Van Lennepweg, Oosterbeek, with that of Pte Ager, re-interred in Oosterbeek Cemetery on 8 October 1993. GM P4, now OWC 25.C.1.

MANCHESTER 3606858 Pte Norman, 21/22.9.44, aged 20 (R M 19.9.44). Born in Lancashire, son of George and Ellen Manchester of Bury, Lancashire. FB along Veerweg, now OWC 21.C.17.

MARSLAND 3599161 L/Cpl William, 25.9.44, aged 30. Born in Manchester, son of Samuel and Catherine Marsland of Denton, Lancashire. FB Sonnenberg area at side of the Hoofdlaan, now OWC 16.C.8.

McDONALD 3602955 Pte Thomas, 24.9.44, aged 28 (R M 20.9.44). Born and domiciled in Co Durham. FB south of Westerbouwing, now OWC 27.A.5.

McGLADDERY 3595257 WO2 (CSM) Alfred, DoW 22.9.44, aged 36 (R M 20.9.44). Born in Maryport, Cumberland, son of the late Robert McGladdery, wife and two children living in Keddington, Suffolk. DoW in a hospital and buried in General Cemetery Soestebergen in Utrecht, Plot 12. D.1.9. Served with 1 Border before the war and received MiD for NW Frontier. Recalled at the outbreak of war and took part in the Sicily landings. Brother Robert killed at Dunkirk.

McMULLEN 3452886 Pte Denis, 26.9.44, aged 25 (R M same day). Born in Northumberland, son of James and Mary McMullen of Willington Quay, Northumberland. FB in garden of house Hemelsche Berg, now OWC 18.A.5.

MELLING 3597056 Pte William, 24/25.9.44, aged 29. Born and domiciled in Wigan, Lancashire. FB in grounds of Hartenstein Hotel, now OWC 16.B.4.

MELLING 3866035 L/Cpl Eric, 20.9.44, aged 21. Born in Wigan, Lancashire, son of Thomas and Helen Melling, husband of Annie Melling of Wigan. GM P4.

MIDGLEY 3604971 Pte Frank, 22.9.44, aged 22 (R W/M same day). Born and domiciled in Rochdale, Lancashire, son of Jesse and Ethel Jane Midgley. GM P4.

MONTGOMERY 160794 Major Thomas Everard, 21.11.44, aged 36. DoW in hospital at Lingen/Ems, Germany. Born in the Pacific Islands, son of Thomas Alexander and Gladys Montgomery, husband of Lavender Montgomery of Kilshannig, Co Cork, Eire. Buried by the Germans in the New Cemetery at Lingen/Ems, Row 13 Grave 11. Grave could not be located after the war. Special Memorial Type E with superscription 'Their Glory shall not be blotted out' erected in OWC at right from the entrance near the hedge.

Major Thomas E. Montgomery, OC A Company. *BRM*

NICHOLSON 3601635 Cpl Edward 'Ned', 23.9.44, aged 24. Born in Cumberland, son of Henry and Margaret Nicholson of Salterbeck, Workington, Cumberland. FB with Pte Clay possibly Ommershof, now OWC 23.C.2. Worked in the Workington Steelworks before the war, served in Sicily operations. Four brothers in the forces.

OWEN 3852653 L/Sgt Archibald, 24.9.44, aged 35. Born and domiciled in Liverpool. FB sports ground Hartenstein, now OWC 17.B.4.

PEARSON 4620133 Pte Jabez, 22.9.44, aged 28 (R W/M same day). Born in Newcastle-upon-Tyne, son of Robert and Mary Jane Pearson of New Washington, Co Durham. FB in front of the Tafelberg Hotel, now OWC 17.A.18.

PEAT 3603453 Cpl John, 20.9.44, aged 27. Born and domiciled in Lancashire. DoW in a hospital and buried in General Cemetery Soestbergen in Utrecht, Plot 12.D.1.10.

PECK 14674077 Pte Joseph, 24.9.44, aged 19 (R W/M same day). Born in Cheshire, son of Charles and Elizabeth Peck of Rudheath, Cheshire. FB in garden of the Ter Horst family near Oostebeek Church, now OWC 2.A.6.

PILLING 14671664 Pte Eric, 28.9.44, aged 18 (R W/M 26.9.44). Born and domiciled in Liverpool. DoW in hospital at Nijmegen and buried in temporary British cemetery at side of Sophiaweg, Nijmegen, now Jonkerbosch WC, Nijmegen 9.B.8.

PIPER 3600652 L/Cpl Thomas, 20.9.44, aged 25. Born in South Shields, son of Thomas and Agnes Piper, husband of Jessie Piper of South Shields, Co Durham. OWC 21.C.4.

POPE 3595025 WO1 (RSM) Albert 'Bish', DoW 22.9.44, aged 34. Born in Manchester, son of James and Harriet Pope, husband of Annie and father of Donald and Violet of Bolton, Lancashire. Enlisted in the Border Regiment in 1927. FB in front of Tafelberg Hotel, now OWC 22.B.13.

PRICE 3596981 Sgt Frederick William, 22.9.44, aged 35 (R W/M same day). Born in Shropshire and domiciled in Lancashire. FB 150 yards south of Tafelberg Hotel, now OWC 21.A.1.

RAYMOND 4345446 Pte Geoffrey, 17.9.44, aged 25. Born in Yorkshire, son of Mary Ellen Raymond of Silsden, West Yorkshire. FB near Sonnenberg along the Hoofdlaan, now OWC 16.C.8.

REVITT 2654814 Cpl Wilfred, 22.3.45, aged 34 (R W/M 24.9.44). PoW Stalag XIIA Transit Camp P/N 975355. Born in Sheffield, Yorkshire. NoK (M) Oughtibridge, Sheffield. Durnbach War Cemetery, Germany 3.D.19.

SEARS 3599001 L/Sgt Stanley William Charles, 18.9.44, aged 24. Born in Buckinghamshire, son of James William and Lydia Emily Sears, husband of Isabella Sears of Ibstone, Buckinghamshire. FB Renkum General Cemetery, now OWC 15.A.9.

SEED 3718807 Pte Fred, 21.9.44, aged 21 (R W/M same day). Born in Preston, son of James and Betsy Seed of Longridge, Lancashire. GM P4.

SKELTON 14662098 Pte Norman, 23.9.44, aged 21 (R W/M same day). Born in Cumberland, son of Mr and Mrs Robert Skelton of Brampton, Cumberland. FB behind Chr Paasberg School, now OWC 23.A.15.

SLOAN 3600657 Pte William, 24/25.9.44 (R M 20.9.44). Born and domiciled in Carlisle. FB 'Hoog Oorsprong' in field west of Van Borsselenweg, lower part, now OWC 18.B.17.

SMART 3602998 Pte Arthur Henry, 24.9.44, aged 28 (R M. 26.9.44). Born in Buckinghamshire, son of William Charles and Agnes Maud Smart, husband of Winifred Smart of Workington, Cumberland. FB Sonnenberg area at side of Hoofdlaan, now OWC 16.C.9.

SMITH 4540185 Pte Edward, 18.9.44, aged 25. Born and domiciled in Yorkshire, son of Albert Edward and Alice Smith. FB north of Hotel 'Klein Zwitserland' in middle of DZ by a glider, now OWC 29.B.8.

SMITH 14671694 Pte Frederick Aston, 25.9.44, aged 19. Born and domiciled in Liverpool. FB area of Hartenstein at side of the Utrechtseweg, now OWC 2.C.8.

SMITH 3597299 Pte Leo, 19.9.44, aged 35 (R M 25.9.44). Born in Manchester, son of William and Catherine Smith of Miles Platting, Manchester. DoW in St Joseph Mental Hospital, Apeldoorn. FB adjacent cemetery, now OWC 24.B.12.

SMITH 3608302 Pte Vernon, 22.9.44, aged 21. Son of George Albert and Harriet Emma Smith of Carlisle. FB along Utrechtseweg near Hartenstein, now OWC 16.A.19.

SMITHEN 3598950 Pte Joseph, 19.9.44, aged 27. Born in Salford, son of Harry and Mary Smithen, husband of Elsie Smithen of Pendleton, Salford, Lancashire. FB side of Utrechtseweg near crossroads Hoofdlaan/Hemelsche Berg, now OWC 17.B.12.

STANLEY 3606793 Pte Thomas Edward, 22.9.44, aged 21 (killed on the night of 19.9.44 according to Charles Coventry who was with him). Born in Cheshire, son of Thomas and Florence Stanley of Meols, Hoylake, Cheshire. GM P4.

STEPHENSON 3657621 Pte Frederick, 25.9.44, aged 28 (R M 20.9.44). Born and domiciled in Lancashire. Original grave, possibly on the Rhine embankment, found on 31.5.45. General Cemetery at Wageningen, Plot 2.793.

SYKES 3606231 Pte Lawrence, DoW 20.9.44, aged 21 (R W/M 24.9.44). Born in Leeds and domiciled in Preston, Lancashire. DoW in St Joseph Mental Hospital, Apeldoorn. FB adjacent cemetery, now OWC 24.B.13.

TATE 164866 Lt Joseph, DLI att'd 1 Border, 21/22.9.44, aged 26. Son of Joseph and Beatrice Mary Tate of Whickham, Co Durham. FB German military cemetery on Grebbeberg, east of Rhenen, now OWC 24.A.8.

THOMAS 153075 Lt Anthony Robert, OC 1st ALB HQ Defence Pl, KIA 20.9.44, aged 25. Born in Kent, son of Martin Lewis and Eleanor Thomas of Sydenham, London. FB probably west of the Hartenstein Hotel, now OWC 1.A.11.

THOMPSON 3602898 Pte Eric M., 25.9.44, aged 24 (R M same day). Born and domiciled in Yorkshire. GM P4.

THOMPSON 3602900 Pte William Nelson, 21/22.9.44, aged 24 (R W/M 22.9.44). Domiciled in Sunderland, son of William Henry and Elizabeth Thompson of Knowle Park, Bristol. FB possibly along Utrechtseweg near J. P. Heije Stichting, now OWC 28.C.4.

VASEY 3602906 Pte Harry, 23.9.44, aged 28 (R W/M same day). Born in Co Durham, son of Mrs A. Vasey of New Bowburn, Co Durham. GM P4.

WALKER 3603968 Pte Joseph, 18.9.44, aged 22. Born in Bury, Lancashire, son of James and Sarah Walker, husband of Irene Walker of Freetown, Bury. FB Renkum General Cemetery, now OWC 15.A.7.

WALL 3865803 Pte Harry, 21.9.44, aged 27 (R W/M same day). Born in Liverpool, son of Louisa Wall, husband of Dorothy L. Wall of Liverpool. GM P4.

WARREN 14641890 Pte William Scales, 22.9.44, aged 20. Born and domiciled in Wallasey, Cheshire. FB possibly in front of Tafelberg Hotel, now OWC 17.A.17.

WATSON 3602924 Sgt Thomas, 21.9.44, aged 28 (R M 20.9.44). Born in Northumberland, son of Joseph W. and Agnes Watson of Blyth, Northumberland. FB access road to Driel Ferry, now OWC 18.B.13.

WELLBELOVE CDN318 Lt John Arthur, Royal Canadian Infantry Corps att'd 1 Border, 25.9.44, aged 24 (date almost certainly 21.9.44). Son of John and Mary Eva Wellbelove of Eston, Saskatchewan, Canada. FB in the Valckeniersbossen, Westerbouwing, now OWC 30.C.2.

WELLS 3606343 Pte James, 20.9.44, aged 23. Born in Oldham, Lancashire, son of James and Mary Ann Wells of Glodwick, Oldham. FB by crossroads Van Borsselenweg/Utrechtseweg, opposite Koude Herberg Cafe, now OWC 17.A.14.

Private Jimmy Wells from the gun grew of 'Hellespont' Anti-Tank Platoon S Company attached C Company. *BRM*

WHITFIELD 3602916 Pte Francis George, 18.9.44, aged 30 (R W/M same day). Born in Yorkshire, son of George Edward and Ada Lavina Whitfield of Dormanstown, Redcar, North Yorkshire. FB Renkum General Cemetery, now OWC 15.A.12.

WIGHTMAN 3604115 Pte John, 25.9.44, aged 29. Born in Dumfriesshire and domiciled in Cumberland. OWC 22.A.10.

WILLIAMS 3523577 L/Cpl George Maurice, 20.9.44, aged 33 (R W/M same day). Born and domiciled in Oldham, Lancashire. GM P4.

WILSON 3606643 Pte George, 21/22.9.44, aged 22 (R W/M 21.9.44). Born in Lancashire, son of Joseph and Hettie Wilson of Haslingden, Lancashire. GM P4.

YAPP 3597285 Pte Francis 'Buster', 18.9.44, aged 26. Born in Surrey, husband of Joyce Yapp of Sale, Cheshire. FB near Sonnenberg, along the Hoofdlaan, now OWC 16.C.7.

An Unknown Soldier of The 1st Battalion. *BRM*

The Memorial tablet in Burford Priory Chapel, which was dedicated on 16 August 1946 in memory of all ranks of the Battalion who went to Arnhem. *BRM*

BELGIUM

LAYCOCK 13075435 Pte Norman, 25.10.44, aged 36. Born in Westmorland, son of Robert and Edith Laycock of Temple Sowerby, Westmorland. Buried in Ghent City Cemetery, Belgium, 18.B.19.

SMITH 3593710 WO2/CSM James MM, 25.10.44, aged 38. Born in Yorkshire, son of James and Ellen Smith, husband of Elizabeth Smith, Derrylin, Co Fermanagh, NI. Ghent City Cemetery, Belgium 18.B.4. Possibly killed with the above as a result of a V1 attack on an HQ near Ghent; 21 soldiers killed on the same day are buried in this cemetery. Awarded the MM for Sicily.

NORWAY

All in Oslo Western Civil Cemetery (NOR 1)

BROWN 3602780 Pte Frederick, 10.5.45, aged 25. Born in Middlesbrough, Yorkshire, son of James Henry and Dorothy Brown of Middlesbrough. I.A.19.

BROWN 3599063 Pte Thomas Dalrymple, 10.5.45, aged 26. Born in Dumfries, son of Thomas Carson and Janey Dalrymple Brown of Longtown, Cumberland. I.A.23.

GAVAGHAN 3443816 Cpl Charles, 10.5.45, aged 34. Born in Lancashire, son of John and Mary Elizabeth Gavaghan, husband of Annie Gavaghan of Todmorden, Yorkshire. I.A.17.

LAYCOCK 3602855 Pte Thomas, 10.5.45, aged 26. Born in Darlington, son of William and Margaret Laycock of Darlington, Co Durham. I.A.12.

LITTLE 3600359 Pte George Allan, 10.5.45, aged 25. Born in Carlisle, son of William and Rachel Little of Kirkbride, Cumberland. I.A.16.

McKEOWN 3604614 Pte Robert, 10.5.45, aged 30. Born in Cumberland, son of Robert and Jane McKeown, husband of Doris Ritson of Askham, Westmorland. I.A.25.

NEWBY 4465299 Pte Horace, 10.5.45. Born and domiciled in Blackburn, Lancashire. I.A.12.

PAGAN 3598670 Pte Joseph, 10.5.45, aged 25. Born in Carlisle, Cumberland, son of Thomas and Theresa A. Pagan of Carlisle. I.A.22.

Border Regiment graves in the Commonwealth War Graves Plot at Oslo Western Civil Cemetery, Vermoek, Oslo. *BRM*

PHIPPS 14642982 Pte George Thomas, 10.5.45, aged 25. Born in Cardiff, son of George and Rose Phipps of Radford, Warwickshire. I.A.24.

RICHARDSON 3598450 L/Cpl Thomas Errington, 10.5.45, aged 25. Born in Cumberland, son of Tom E. and Jane E. Richardson of Penrith, Cumberland. Had served with 4 Border from the outbreak of the war, BEF, Western Desert, India and Burma. Transferred to 1 Border on return to UK. I.A.8.

SAVILLE Lt Frederick Geoffrey, The Leicestershire Regt, att'd 1 Border, 10.5.45, aged 20. Son of Frederick and Evelyn Saville of Apsley, Nottingham. I.A.7.

SMETHURST 3593887 Pte Joseph, 10.5.45, aged 38. Born in Oldham, Lancashire, son of William and Mary Smethurst, husband of Jane Smethurst of Oldham. I.A.18.

TODD 3599329 L/Cpl Alexander Barr 'Sandy', 10.5.45, aged 25. Born in Northumberland, son of Robert and Mary Todd, husband of Mabel Todd of Dumfries. Served with 4 Border during the Second World War and transferred to 1st Battalion on return from Burma. I.A.20.

GERMANY

DEVLIN 2992686 Pte Francis J. 'Jock', died as the result of a PIAT accident whilst serving with 1 Border in Germany, 26.1.46, aged 20. Served in 14 Platoon B Company and had been taken PoW at Westerbouwing near Oosterbeek on 21.9.44 Stalag XIIA 075660. Re-joined the Battalion in 1945. Born in Glasgow, NoK (S) Mrs J. Rush, Balornock, Glasgow. Buried in Hannover War Cemetery, Germany (748), 14.C.19.

FORMER MEMBERS OF THE 1ST BATTALION killed with other units and others from the Regiment killed while serving with other Airborne Division units

ANDERSON 3606646 Pte Gilbert, 11th Bn Parachute Regt, 25.9.44, aged 21. Son of Thomas and Elizabeth Anderson of Blackpool, Lancashire. Known to have been buried at Onderlans, approximately opposite

St Elizabeth's Hospital, Arnhem, but grave not located. GM P8.

BOYLE 3596510 A/Cpl Francis, Royal Irish Fusiliers att'd No 3 Commando, 14.7.43. Catania War Cemetery, Sicily 1.E.1.

BULL 3602499 Pte Ernest, 6/7.6.44, aged 27. Son of William Joseph and Ada Bull of Stockport, Cheshire. Bayeux War Cemetery

CAIRNS 3602783 Cpl Leo, 1st Airborne Reconnaissance Squadron, 25/26.9.44, aged 29. Drowned during withdrawal from River Rhine, body recovered on 17.10.44 and buried in Rhenen General Cemetery, 27.C.13.

CHAMBERLAIN 3597618 Pte Charles A. Henry, 21.8.44, aged 28. AAC, 6 Border att'd 8th Bn Parachute Regt. Son of H. T. and Kathleen Chamberlain of Fallowfield, Manchester, husband of A. Chamberlain of Moss Side, Manchester. Ranville War Cemetery.

GIBB 3603036 Craftsman Alexander, REME 1st Airborne Div Workshop, 20.9.44, aged 24. FB 150 yards south of Tafelberg Hotel, now OWC 21.B.19.

HALL 3596685 Fusilier Joseph DCM, 1st Bn The Royal Irish Fusiliers, KIA Catania, Sicily, 6.8.43, aged 28. Son of Thomas and May Hall, husband of Nellie Mary Hall of Blackpool, Lancashire. Catania War Cemetery, Sicily, III F. 33.

HAMILTON 3051601 Pte John, AAC att'd 8th Bn Parachute Regt, 25.8.44, aged 31. Son of David and Agnes Sime Hamilton, husband of Catherine Nimmo of Edinburgh. Ranville War Cemetery.

McBRYDE Capt James Robert, att'd 6th Airborne Division, 18.6.44, aged 35. Son of William Orr and Jeanne Kerr McBryde, husband of Elizabeth Jean McBryde of Bowdon, Cheshire. Ranville War Cemetery.

NORBURY 3606701 Signaller Douglas J., 1st Airborne Division Signals, 19.9.44, aged 21. Son of James and Mary Norbury of Collyhurst, Manchester. GM P2.

OLIVER Lt Basil, 17.8.44, aged 23. Son of Thomas Sherwood and Dorothy Oliver, husband of Margaret Emily Oliver of Wallasey, Cheshire. Ranville War Cemetery.

POTTS 3602724 L/Cpl Richard, 1st Airborne Reconnaissance Squadron, 13.11.44, aged 29. DOW in hospital at Apeldoorn. Son of Richard and Mary Potts, husband of Kathleen Potts of Goosnargh, Lancashire. FB General Cemetery 'Heidehof', Apeldoorn, now OWC 14.B.13.

SHARROCK 3606728 Sgt James Johnson, C Squadron Glider Pilot Regiment AAC, 22.9.44, aged 21. Son of Thomas William and Elizabeth Ellen Sharrock of Westhoughton, Lancashire. GM P8.

STEVENS 3606335 Pte Thomas, 156th Bn Parachute Regt, 18.9.44, aged 21. Killed when C-47 Dakota 43-15180 of 314 Troop Carrier Group, 50 Troop Carrier Sqn USAF, crashed along the Bonegraafsweg at Ochten, commune of Echteld, Holland, 20 km SW of Oosterbeek; there were no survivors. FB near the crash site, now Jonkerbosch War Cemetery, Nijmegen, 8.B.6. As the individual remains could not be identified after the war, the headstone bears the inscription 'Buried near this spot'.

Appendix 2

The Battalion Roll, Arnhem

This roll is based on a Battalion Roll compiled on 2 October 1944 after the Battalion had returned to England, a Regimental Prisoner-of-War Register and the HMSO Register of British PoWs in Germany, March 1945. Information has been added from veterans and other verified sources, including Platoon and Company details, but the list should not be regarded as absolute and it does not include names from the Battalion Seaborne Tail and Home details, for which there are no lists available. Attempts have been made to locate original glider manifest lists (Form B Glider) for the Battalion, but these do not appear to have survived. Details include Platoon and Company, PoW No, Camp No in Roman numerals (eg XIIA) and location, home town and district.

Abbreviations

Arkdo	Arbeitskommando
CDN	Canadian CANLOAN officers
Coy	Company
Evac	Evacuated
Int	Intelligence
KiA	Killed in Action
M	Date reported missing
OC	Officer Commanding
Pl	Platoon
PoW	Prisoner-of-War
Rep	Repatriated
T/	Temporary rank
U/	Unpaid
W	Wounded, date reported wounded
W/M	Date reported wounded and missing
1/ALB	First Air-Landing Brigade

Locations of PoW Camps

Oflag VIIB	Eichstatt
Oflag IXA/H	Spangenburg bei Kassel
Oflag IXA/Z	Rotenburg Fulda
Oflag XIIB	Hadamar
Oflag 79	Braunschweig (formerly Oflag 8F)
Stalag IVA	Hohenstein
Stalag IVB	Muhlberg (Elbe)
Stalag IVC	Wistritz bei Teplitz
Stalag IVD	Torgau (Elbe)
Stalag IVF	Hartmansdorf Chemnitz
Stalag VB	Villingen Schwarzwald
Stalag VIC	Munster
Stalag VID	
Stalag VIIA	Moosburg (Isar)
Stalag VIIIB	Tenschen
Stalag VIIIC	Kunau Kz. Sprottau/Sagan
Stalag IXC	Muhlhausen
Stalag XIA	Attengrabow
Stalag XIB	Fallingbostel
Stalag XIIA	Limburg s. d. Lahn
Stalag XIIIC	Hammelburg am Main
Stalag XIIID	Nurnburg

OFFICERS

All were commissioned into The Border Regiment except where stated.

Battalion HQ

58141	T/Lt Colonel Tommy Haddon CO PoW Oflag XIIB 00594
63589	T/Major H. Stuart Cousens Royal Inniskilling Fusiliers 2i/c Evac
210784	T/Capt Colin M. Douglas Adjt Evac
187403	Lt Ronald C. Hope-Jones RA IO PoW Oflag 79 602
186152	Lt Douglas H. Skilton LO/AO Evac

HQ Company

130361	T/Major Dennis R. L. Morrissey OC Loyals W/PoW Stalag VIIA 140228
258048	Lt Joseph S. D. Hardy RSO Evac
264650	Lt Alan H. Cox Loyals OC Pioneer Platoon PoW Oflag 79 605
211739	Capt Graham-Jones RAMC RMO PoW Stalag IXC 52981

123723	Capt Rev John Rowell RAChD Evac
289184	Capt S.B. Birchmore RA attached as FOO PoW Oflag 79 01775

S Company

67798	T/Major Richard H. Stewart MC OC W/PoW Oflag IXA/H 2132
160854	T/Capt Thomas Wood Ingram Cleasby 2i/c and OC MMG Group W/PoW Oflag IX A/H 2122
105018	T/Capt Barry B. Ingram Royal Fusiliers OC Mortar Group PoW Oflag 7B 578
228610	Lt Mike R. Holman OC 23 Mortar Platoon Evac
204365	Lt George Blain Coulthard OC 24 Mortar Platoon PoW Oflag 79 621
124182	T/Capt Robert M. A. Reese OC A/T Group W/PoW Oflag 79 686
240675	Lt John Anthony Howe OC 25 A/T Platoon W/PoW Stalag VIIA 140229
96393	Lt Edward S. Newport DLI OC 26 A/T Platoon PoW Oflag 79 630
164866	Lt Joe Tate DLI OC 27 MMG Platoon KiA
143723	Lt John S. G. McCartney OC 28 MMG Platoon Evac

A Company

160794	T/Major Thomas Edward 'Tui' Montgomery OC DoW as PoW
182276	T/Capt Baldwin Wilson 2i/c W/PoW Oflag IX A/Z 2192
262135	Lt Pat Baillie King's Own OC 7 Platoon PoW Oflag IXA/H 2145
CDN285	Lt T. W. Aasen OC 8 Platoon W/PoW
228608	Lt Robert H. Coulston OC 9 Platoon KiA
292013	Lt Edmund F. Scrivener OC 10 Platoon PoW Oflag 79 601

B Company

159958	T/Major Tommy W. W. Armstrong OC W/PoW Oflag 79 91199
228611	Lt William Patrick Stott 2i/c W/PoW Oflag 79 619

295896   Lt Stanley Barnes OC 11 Platoon W/PoW Stalag VIIA 140225
268902   Lt Arthur Robert Royall OC 12 Platoon PoW Oflag 79 00632
CDN318   Lt John Arthur Wellbelove OC 13 Platoon KiA
3602924   Sgt Watson OC 14 Platoon KIA

C Company

200852   T/Major William 'Jock' Neill OC Evac
132473   T/Capt. W. Gordon Welch MC 2i/c W/PoW Oflag IX A/Z 2186
284010   Lt Alan D. Roberts OC 15 Platoon Evac
CDN139   Lt G. W. Comper OC 16 Platoon W/PoW
264942   Lt Robert Claude Crittenden OC 17 Platoon PoW Oflag IX A/Z 2176
CDN540   Lt P. G. Boville OC 18 Platoon CANLOAN W/PoW

D Company

66138   Major Charles Frederick Osborne Breese OC W/Evac
129359   Capt William K. Hodgson 2i/c DoW
138694   Lt Jack 'John' McKenzie Bainbridge King's Own OC 19 Platoon W/PoW Oflag IX A/H 2146
247201   Lt Alan Thomas Green OC 20 Platoon W/PoW Oflag IX A/Z 2177
295834   Lt Philip Sumner Holt OC 21 Platoon KiA
162499   Lt George Edward T. Brown OC 22 Platoon KiA

Attached 1st Air Landing Brigade HQ

176190   Lt William R. Burns Intelligence Officer KiA
153075   Lt Anthony Robert Thomas OC Brigade Defence Platoon KiA

Attached 1st Airborne Reconnaissance Squadron

112855   T/Capt Michael Watkins Grubb W/PoW Oflag IX A/H 2113
129356   T/Capt J. Geoffrey Costeloe

Seaborne Tail

          Major William E. Balmer OC 1st ALB Seaborne Tail
68097   Capt C. H. Baker
147625   Capt Harold S. Barnes QM
285338   Lt William A. H. Baldock

R Company/Home Details - UK

164643   Major W. Howard Wilkie
269419   Lt Ronald R. Jack Loyals MTO - unfit
189364   Capt J. C. Law
284513   Capt Arthur W. Springbett 2i/c B Coy - unfit
CDN538   Lt D. R. Boulter CANLOAN
295787   Lt S. N. Bragg
CDN138   Lt W. A. Colbert CANLOAN
295848   Lt S. B. Dwyer
CDN625   Lt G. F. Hatchette CANLOAN
CDN553   Lt B. J. Hayman CANLOAN
CDN431   Lt J. Ilsley CANLOAN

CDN647   Lt J. P. Rawling CANLOAN (in excess of War Establishment)
CDN626   Lt C. S. Heath CANLOAN (in excess of War Establishment)

ROLL - WOs, NCOs AND OTHER RANKS

ACTON 3606573 Pte Fred M 25.9.44 PoW XIIA 91792, Whitefield, Manchester
ACTON 3605400 Pte John M 26.9.44 PoW VIIIC, Northwich, Cheshire
ADAMS 4547065 Cpl William att'd Def Pl 1/ALB HQ KiA 24.9.44, Sheffield
ADDIS 4697979 Pte Jack M 26.9.44 PoW XIIA 92114, South Kirby, Pontefract
ADEY 3779204 Pte Horace
AGER 3599174 Pte Ernest C Coy KiA 22.9.44, Manchester
AINSWORTH 3606401 Pte Edwin 13 Pl B Coy M 23.9.44 PoW XIB 118133, Blackburn, Lancashire
ALLEN 3598633 Sgt John KiA 22.9.44, Whitehaven, Cumberland
ALLISON 3596711 L/Cpl Robert 20.9.44 W/M PoW VIIIC Apeldoorn, Meadowfield, Co Durham
ALLSOPP 4985513 Pte Clifford J. A/T Pl S Coy M 26.9.44 PoW XIB 118285, Ruddington, Nottingham
ANGELL 14237266 Pte Donald Francis M 26.9.44 PoW XIIA 91882, Calne, Wilts
ANTWISTLE 3602938 W/Cpl Norman Sig Pl HQ Coy
APPLEBY 14579657 Pte J. 11 Pl B Coy W/M 22.9.44 PoW IVB 075433, York
ARMER Pte W. J. (see DARLING)
ARNOLD 14679402 Pte L.
ASHBRIDGE 3602241 Pte Albert 13 Pl B Coy M 25.9.44 PoW IVB/IVF 91464, Workington, Cumberland
ASHCROFT 14563393 Pte H.
ASHTON 3771829 Pte Frederick Joseph W/M 20.9.44 PoW IVB/XIB 117682, Knotty Ash, Liverpool
ASHTON 3603315 Pte Gerard att'd Def Pl 1/ALB HQ PoW IVB 92162, Wigan, Lancashire. Brother of above
ASHURST 4616055 Pte Tom att'd Def Pl 1/ALB KiA 24.9.44, Oldham, Lancashire
ASTON 3865747 Pte Frederick Joseph 'Blondie' 11 Pl B Coy KiA 21.9.44, Barnton, Cheshire
ATHERTON 3660440 WS/Cpl Cyril M 25.9.44 PoW XIIA 91798, Litherland, Liverpool
ATHERTON 14583624 Pte George Frederick M 17.9.44 PoW XIIA 91476, Bradford, Manchester
ATKINSON 3602770 L/Cpl Albert William M 26.9.44 PoW XIIA 91879, Nafferton nr Driffield, E Yorkshire
ATKINSON 3602709 WS/Cpl Bernard S. 12 Pl B Coy KiA 25.9.44
ATKINSON 14258469 W/Cpl J. 24 Mortar Pl
ATKINSON 3602628 WS/Cpl William Haig 'Lofty' Sig Pl HQ Coy M 26.9.44 PoW VIIIC 92953, Whitchurch, Hants
ATTENBOROUGH 3605823 Pte George Sig Pl HQ Coy W
AUSTIN 4455267 Pte Norris PoW IVB/XIIA, Birtley, Co Durham

AYRES 3596882 Pte William ACC attached KiA 20.9.44
BAGNALL 3394032 A/Cpl A. 19 Pl D Coy
BAILEY 4349972 A/Cpl Robert 11 Pl B Coy W/M 20.9.44 PoW VIIIC, Easington, Co Durham.
BAKER 3603726 WS/Cpl Frederick John W/M 21.9.44 PoW XIB/VIIIC 118462, Ealing, London W5
BALL 3606989 Pte Noah W/M 23.9.44 PoW XIB-Rep 117505, Bradford, Manchester
BAMBER 3602725 Pte William 24 Mortar Pl M 26.9.44 PoW XIIA/IVB 91711, Preston, Lancashire
BANKS 3606859 Pte V. 'Ginger' 12 Pl B Coy or possibly 24 Mortar Pl
BARFOOT 3861378 L/Cpl James W/M 21.9.44 DoW 28.9.44, Oldham, Lancashire
BARKER 3604096 Pte Frederick W/M 22.9.44 PoW XIB 117671, Hexham, Northumberland
BARNES 14641710 Pte Robert M 19.9.44, KiA 21.9.44, Cleator Moor
BARNES 3771478 Pte William C. KiA 21.9.44, M 26.9.44
BARON 3600516 Pte Bernard HQ Coy
BARR 2888129 L/Cpl G. 'Taffy' A/T Pl S Coy M 26.9.44
BARRASS 3394020 Pte A.
BARRATT 3597114 WS/Cpl Ernest William M 19.9.44 PoW XIIA 91974, Hornchurch, Essex
BARTON 3606437 Pte E.
BATE 2888353 Sgt Thomas William A/T Pl S Coy, Warrington, Cheshire
BATES 4616913 WS/Cpl B. O. 23 Mortar Pl S Coy M 26.9.44 PoW XIIID Res Laz 15244, Totley Rise, Sheffield
BATESON 3776362 Pte Robert James M 21.9.44 PoW XIIA/IVB 075499, Walton, Preston, Lancashire
BATTEN 3598227 Pte L.
BEATY 3608089 Pte F. W 26.9.44
BECK 3596904 L/Cpl William W/M 25.9.44 PoW XIB 118314. Parents in Old Woodhouse, Whitehaven, wife in Failsworth, Manchester
BECK 3784044 Pte William 'Bill' 19 Pl D Coy M KiA 24.9.44. Nephew of the above, St Helens
BEDFORD 4345500 Pte S.
BELL 3602774 Pte Albert 24 Mortar Pl M 26.9.44 KiA 22.9.44, Scarborough
BENT 3596732 Pte William Steers PoW XIIA 075926, Leigh, Lancs
BETTS 3529476 Pte L.
BIRDSELL 4986009 Pte W. 8 Pl A Coy
BLACK 3770609 Cpl Richard Joseph 'Sammy' 16 Pl C Coy W 26.9.44, St Ives, Cornwall
BLACKWELL 14220922 Pte Eric George 15 Pl C Coy W 26.9.44, Carlisle
BLADES 3602778 Pte George Ernest 24 Mortar Pl M 26.9.44 PoW XIIA 91628, Fuston-on-the-Wold, Driffield, East Yorkshire
BLAKELE 4688888 Pte E.
BLYTHE 3603629 Pte Dennis Fernley Int Section HQ Coy PoW XIIA 075914, Wilmslow, Cheshire
BLYTON 3453168 Pte H. 10 Pl A Coy M 25.9.44 PoW XIIA 91790, Newton-le-Willows, Lancashire
BOARDMAN 3860413 Pte George 'Sammy'

14 Pl B Coy M 19.9.44 PoW XIB 118344, Bolton, Lancashire

BOOTH 3609643 Pte P. C Coy

BOOW 3602965 Pte J. 15 Pl C Coy

BORDERS 3602584 Pte Eric 14 Pl B Coy KiA 20.9.44, Stockport, Cheshire

BOSWORTH 3771147 Pte F. 'Bill' D Coy

BOWER 2886887 Pte James 'Jimmy' A/T Pl S Coy, Workington

BRADBURN 3657388 Pte E.

BRADDOCK 14217409 Pte S.

BRADFORD 5181493 Pte Edward Charles W/M 20.9.44 PoW XIB 117690, Prudhoe, Northumberland

BRAGG 3608284 Pte Henry 'Harry' 11 Pl B Coy KiA 20.9.44, Egremont, Cumberland

BRAITHWAITE 3604975 Pte R. 'Brad' 17 Pl C Coy

BRETT 2569961 WS/Cpl F. 11 Pl B Coy W/M 20.9.44 PoW Apeldoorn

BRETT 3596764 L/Cpl Thomas 10 Pl A Coy M 26.9.44 PoW XIIA 91625, Atherton, Manchester

BRIGGS 4346036 L/Cpl Kenneth William A/T Pl S Coy PoW XIIA 075674, Meanwood, Leeds, West Yorkshire

BROMILOW 14653229 Pte Willis Vincent W/M 22.9.44 PoW XIB 117623, Lostock, Bolton, Lancashire

BROOKE 4617138 Pte H. 14 Pl B Coy

BROOKS 14650833 Pte Jack W/M 20.9.44 PoW XIB 117535, Bolton, Lancashire

BROWN 14671516 Pte Edward Joseph M 20.9.44 PoW XIB 118276, Liverpool

BROWN 3602780 Pte Frederick, killed Norway, Middlesbrough, N Yorkshire

BROWN 4542186 WS/Cpl Joseph Potter 19 Pl D Coy M 20.9.44 PoW XIIA 075554, Burley, Bradford, West Yorkshire

BROWN 3605571 Pte L.

BRUFFELL 4546355 Pte Thomas 24 Mortar Pl S Coy

BRYSON 3602942 L/Cpl Thomas John W. C Coy KiA 21.9.44

BUCKLEY 3597954 Pte Charles M 22.9.44 PoW XIIA/IVA 91982, Failsworth, Manchester

BUCKLEY 14206592 Pte Frank M 18.9.44, KiA 21.9.44

BUDWORTH 826999 W/Cpl F. 8 Pl A Coy

BUNTING 3774432 A/Cpl George 9 Pl A Coy W/M 22.9.44 PoW XIIA 92109, Liverpool

BURDON 3191498 Pte Jack Forster 'Sam' 19 Pl D Coy M 20.9.44 PoW XIIA 075438, South Shields

BURR 2878204 WS/Sgt Hendry 'Hank' A/T Pl S Coy KiA W/M 18.9.44, St Fergus, Aberdeenshire

BURTON 3603554 WS/Sgt Herbert Munro Int Section HQ Coy M 26.9.44 PoW XIIA 91889, Chorlton-on-Medlock, Manchester

BUTTERWICK 3602782 W/Cpl F. 15 Pl C Coy

BYRNE 3782510 Pte Michael 18 Pl C Coy W/M 25.9.44 PoW XIB 118304, Bootle, Liverpool

CAIN 3783853 Pte Vincent Leslie C Coy KiA 20.9.44, Prescot, Lancashire

CAIN 3783397 Pte W. 'Cobber' A/T Pl S Coy

CALLAGHAN 3708684 Pte William M 21.9.44 PoW XIIA 075699, Pemberton, Wigan, Lancashire

CALVERT 3606482 Pte K.

CAMP 2619360 Pte Thomas Everard W/M 22.9.44 PoW XIB 118320, Derby

CAMPBELL 3598578 Pte Albert Sig Pl HQ Coy W/M 21.9.44 PoW XIB 118197, Kirby Stephen, Westmorland

CAMPBELL 3607715 Pte William MMG Pl S Coy W/M 26.9.44 PoW XIB 117637, Hebburn-on-Tyne, Newcastle

CAMPLIN 7392936 Pte F. RAMC

CARLILE 3772940 WS/Cpl Walter 19 Pl D Coy M 25.9.44 PoW XIIA 25001, Liverpool

CARR 4397327 WS/Cpl Jack M KiA 22.9.44, Leyburn, Yorkshire

CARR 3605943 ORSgt John Edward HQ Coy

CARTER 3599035 L/Sgt J.

CASWELL 14671529 Pte J. 11 Pl B Coy W 26.9.44

CAVEN 14563521 Pte James Sig Pl HQ Coy or B Coy KiA 21.9.44 M 26.9.44, Dumfries

CAWOOD 14202522 Pte Donald Samuel 24 Mortar Pl S Coy M 24.9.44 PoW IVB/XIIA 91629, York

CERVI 3608007 L/Cpl Laurence W/M KiA 18.9.44, Southrey, Lincolnshire

CHALET 4619738 Pte M. 23 Mortar Pl S Coy

CHAMBERS 14202524 Pte Kenneth, Beeston, Leeds

CHAPMAN 3602785 L/Cpl John 12 Pl B Coy KiA 20.9.44, Billingham, Co Durham

CHAPMAN 3602932 Pte T.

CHILTON 3191430 Pte 'Ned' or 'Nipper' Edward 19 Pl D Coy M 20.9.44 PoW XIIA 075497, Blaydon, Newcastle

CHISHOLM 3602786 Pte Alexander 8 Pl A Coy W/M 20.9.44 PoW XIB 118162, Millfield, Sunderland

CHRISTOPHER 3606086 Pte A. 24 Mortar Pl S Coy

CHURM 3718512 Pte E.

CLAGUE 3782692 A/Cpl E.

CLAGUE 3604114 A/Cpl Joseph 19 Pl D Coy W/M 18.9.44 PoW XIB 117759, Workington, Cumberland

CLARK 3191444 W/Cpl A. 12 Pl B Coy, Scotswood-on-Tyne, Northumberland

CLARK 3596467 Pte Donald Reginald Bernard M 20.9.44 PoW IXC 52883, London

CLARK 3594148 W/Cpl W., Leeds

CLARKE 3606510 Pte Charles James 10 Pl A Coy M 25.9.44 PoW XIB-Rep 118273, Oswaldtwistle, nr Accrington, Lancashire

CLARKE 24550695 Pte H.

CLARKE 3650449 W/Sgt Sidney Pl Sgt 7 Pl A Coy, Liverpool

CLARKSON 14206221 Pte George M 25.9.44 PoW IVA 91525, Lytham, Lancashire

CLAY 3390615 Pte George KiA 24.9.44, Preston, Lancashire

CLEGG 3451679 Pte Frank W/M 23.9.44 PoW XIB 118264, Oldham, Lancashire

CLEMENT 3602197 Pte P.

CLEMENTS 1077118 Pte Hector B Coy HQ M 19.9.44 PoW IVB/XIIA 075661, Barrow-in-Furness, Lancashire

CLOSE 3452698 Pte T.

CLOWES 3780000 Pte Albert M 26.9.44 PoW XIIA 26085, Bolton, Lancashire

COATES 3602789 Cpl Thomas 11 Pl B Coy KiA 20.9.44, Whitburn, Co Durham

COCKERILL 2992863 Pte Malcom Alistair M 17.9.44 PoW XIB 117776, Fulham, London SW6

COCKS 14642494 Pte Cecil M 26.9.44 POW XIIA 91707, Ulverston, Lancashire

COJEEN 14638737 Pte Robert 'Dad' 12 Pl B Coy, Isle of Man

COLLINGS 3606306 WS/Cpl Walter 10 Pl A Coy W/M 24.9.44, PoW VIIIC 93619, Fazakerley, Liverpool

COMMON 3191433 L/Cpl Albert MMG Pl S Coy M 25.9.44 XIIA/IVB 91457, Hexham, Northumberland

CONNETT 6198713 CSMI Frederick APTC

COOK 3594527 Pte W.

COOPER 1437623 Pte Dennis Patrick ACC att'd B Coy HQ PoW XIIA 075685, Coventry, Warwickshire

CORLESS 3606890 Pte John Bernard W/M 22.9.44 Oflag XIIB, Wigan, Lancashire

CORNMELL 3605244 L/Cpl John 12 Pl B Coy W/M 19.9.44 PoW XIIA 075430, Woodborough, Nottinghamshire

CORTON 14591265 Pte Bernard M 26.9.44 PoW XIIA/IVF 91520, Sleaford, Lincolnshire

COUPE 3599021 Pte Joe 23 Mortar Pl S Coy, Chapeltown, Leeds

COURTIE 3606306 Cpl Thomas PoW VIIA 140153, Liverpool

COVENTRY 3605422 Pte Charles William 16 Pl C Coy W/M 22.9.44 PoW XIB 117738, Port Sunlight, Cheshire

COWIN 3602473 WS/Cpl Lawrence Signal Pl att'd D Coy KiA 25.9.44, M 26.9.44, Newbiggin-on-Lune, Westmorland

COWPE 1787131 Pte V. 11 Pl B Coy

COX 3595390 W/Cpl William RAP

COYLE 3856497 Pte J. B. A/T Pl S Coy M 26.9.44 PoW XIIA 075693, Woodhall Spa, Lincolnshire

CRANSWICK 3602793 Pte Alfred H. 14 Pl B Coy W/M 20.9.44 KiA 22.9.44

CRAWFORD 3191949 Pte John 'Jack' 10 Pl A Coy M 25.9.44 PoW XIB 118016 Bishopbriggs, Lanarkshire

CRICKETT 3531268 Cpl Cyril 13 Pl B Coy W/M 21.9.44 PoW XIB-Rep 118348, Wigan, Lancashire

CRILLEY 3599221 Pte J. ACC

CRIMMEL 1142367 Pte John H. 11 Pl B Coy M 19.9.44, KiA 24.9.44, Canvey Island, Essex

CRINGLE 14525413 Pte John Sydney 23 Mortar Pl S Coy W/M 20.9.44 PoW XIB 117608, Castletown, Isle of Man

CRINION 3601758 Pte Joseph W/M 18.9.44 PoW VIIIC 93345, Morecambe, Lancashire

CRONSHAW 6471864 Pte A. M 26.9.44

CROSS 1146496 Pte Bernard Reginald 'Double Cross' 11 Pl B Coy M 17.9.44 PoW VB/VIIA 18654, Southall, Middlesex

CROSSLAND 4691419 L/Cpl Stanley W/M 22.9.44 PoW XIB 117619, Chapelthorpe, near Wakefield

CRUICKSHANK 2878988 Pte Ronald C Coy, Aberdeen

CULL 3608321 Pte P. M 25.9.44 PoW XIIA

CUMISKY 3596833 Pte William W/M 26.9.44

CUNLIFFE 14402790 Pte Robert M 23.9.44 PoW IVB/XIIA 077399, Lower Altham, Accrington, Lancashire

CUNNINGTON 4347247 Pte Joseph A/T Pl S Coy, Selby, West Yorkshire

CURTIS 3597790 Pte George Edward Medical Orderly 17 Pl C Coy W/M 20.9.44 PoW XIB 118189, London

DADDY 4547338 Pte Sidney 21 Pl D Coy M 25.9.44 PoW XIIA/IVB 24657, Hull, East Yorkshire

DALEY 3599017 Pte Joseph M 25.9.44 PoW XIIA 24651, Armadale, Midlothian

DALTON 7946561 Pte Charles William M 25.9.44, KiA 27.9.44, York

DARLING 3608290 Pte W. J. (served as ARMER, Pte W. J.)

DAVIDSON 3600318 W/Sgt J., Workington, Cumberland

DAVIDSON 6215510 UP/L/Cpl Richard Athony W/M 24.9.44 PoW XIIA 92034, Peckham, London SE15

DAVIES 14641926 Pte C. 12 Pl B Coy W/M 20.9.44

DAVIES 3782610 Pte Harry 12 Pl B Coy M 20.9.44 PoW XIB Arkdo 7001 117258, Manchester

DAVIES 1454411 Pte Robert William M 21.9.44 PoW XIIA 075695, Bagillt, Flintshire

DAVIS 1149539 Pte F.

DAVISON 3602799 Pte John Raymond 10 Pl B Coy, Sherburn, Yorkshire

DAVISON 3606047 Pte J. 24 Mortar Pl S Coy

DAVISON 4277712 U/L/Cpl Joseph Thomson 24 Mortar Pl W/M 22.9.44 PoW XIB 117479, Newcastle-upon-Tyne

DAWSON 3602979 Pte Richard Trevor Martin M 26.9.44 PoW VIIIC 93414, Appleby, Westmorland

DEER 3783622 Pte R.

DEIGHTON 3600684 WS/Sgt Harold MMG Pl S Coy M 26.9.44 PoW XIIA 91890 D 4.4.45, Brough, Westmorland

DEIGHTON 3597017 WS/Sgt Thomas Robinson Pl Sgt 24 Mortar Pl S Coy M 26.9.44 PoW VB 18676, Belfast, N Ireland

DEMPSEY 3783762 Pte Daniel M 19.9.44 PoW XIB 118123, West Derby, Liverpool

DEMPSEY 14403795 Pte Edward PoW XIB 118011, Dublin

DE MUYNCK 2885194 WS/Sgt Victor Pl Sgt 13 Pl B Coy W/M 25.9.44 PoW XIB/VIIIC 118021, Portobello, Edinburgh.

DENTON 3607127 Pte J.

DENTON 14583425 Pte Kenneth Signaller att'd A Coy M 26.9.44, DoW 12.2.45

DEVLIN 2992686 Pte Francis Joseph 'Jock' 14 Pl B Coy M 19.9.44 PoW XIIA 075660, Balornock, Glasgow

DEVONPORT 3529215 Cpl James A/T Pl S Coy, Carlisle

DICKINSON 14590913 Pte L.

DISLEY 3771562 L/Cpl Thomas J. M 26.9.44 PoW XIIA 075485, Liverpool

DITTE 4625954 L/Cpl Alfred John W/M 25.9.44 PoW XIB-Rep 118100, Bath, Somerset

DIXON 3607283 Pte F.

DIXON 3602801 Pte John Francis M 23.9.44 PoW IVB 24674, Sunderland, Co Durham

DIXON 4616865 L/Sgt J. 24 Mortar Pl S Coy W/M 25.9.44

DODD 3602971 Pte D.

DODD 3599568 Pte George M 26.9.44 PoW XIIA 91596, Brampton, Cumberland

DOGGART 3597969 WS/Cpl Adam 7 Pl A Coy W/M 21.9.44 PoW XIIA 91523, Workington, Cumberland

DORAN 3598669 Pte D.

DUCKWORTH 14584161 Pte Harry Signaller att'd C Coy, Blackpool, Lancashire

DUNNE 3771792 Pte J. B Coy HQ/Mortar Pl

DUNNE 7365473 L/Cpl J. 'Lofty' RAMC att'd B Coy HQ Medic

DURBER 3607415 Pte Thomas KiA 21.9.44, Ashton-under-Lyne, Lancashire

DURHAM 4279084 Pte John M 26.9.44 PoW IVB/IVA 91946, West Hartlepool, Co Durham

DURKIN 4614317 Pte James D Coy M 22.9.44 PoW XIIA/IVB 26024, Keighley, West Yorkshire

DURNIN 4347257 Pte Charles M 25.9.44 PoW XIIA 91969, Selby, West Yorkshire

DUROSE 3866081 Pte R.

EAGLETON 14671556 Pte John M 25.9.44 PoW XIIA/IVF 91521, Liverpool

EASTWOOD 3597698 L/Cpl J.

ECCLES 3445288 L/Cpl/Pte R. A/T Pl S Coy

EDEN 3603438 L/Cpl William 15 Pl C Coy W/M KiA 22.9.44, Ribbleton, Preston

EDGAR 3603439 Cpl Thomas 'Rocky' 8 Pl A Coy W/M KiA 22.9.44, Stanwix, Carlisle

EDGE 3600831 Pte Clifford 10 Pl A Coy W/M 17.9.44, KiA 19.9.44, Miles Platting, Manchester

EDGE 3607997 Pte Harold D. M 26.9.44 PoW XIIA 075523, Liverpool

EDWARDS 14632996 Pte F.

EDWARDS 3393498 Pte Montague M 21.9.44 PoW XIIA 075486, Birkenhead, Cheshire

EDWARDS 14761557 Pte S.

EGERTON 3607003 Pte K. 23 Mortar Pl S Coy

ELAND 3597588 Pte Albert William 'Ginger' W/M 24.9.44 PoW XIB 117565, Penrith, Cumberland

ELLERY 3602808 Pte Robert 23 Mortar Pl S Coy W/M KiA 21.9.44, Sunderland

ELLICOCK 4397165 Pte George Henry KiA 25.9.44, Bradford, West Yorkshire

ELLIOTT 3759659 Pte Arthur Lewis Shaw 'Joss' W/M 23.9.44 PoW XIB 118321, Ramsey, Isle of Man. At 42 the oldest man in the Battalion to serve at Arnhem. Originally with R Coy, went as replacement on 17.9.44.

ELLIOTT 14641936 Pte G.

ELLIOTT 3608489 Pte R. M 19.9.44 PoW XIIA

ELLIOTT 7371720 Pte W. RAMC

ELLIS 7367872 L/Cpl G. RAMC

ELLISON 4277251 Pte Anthony M 22.9.44 PoW XIIA 91930, Shotton, Co Durham

ELVIN 14638663 Pte William Leonard 'Parky' 19 Pl D Coy KiA 25.9.44, London

ENNION 3606251 L/Cpl Gordon A/T Pl S Coy M 26.9.44 PoW IVB/IVA 91949, Gatley, Cheshire

ENNIS 6412571 Pte Harold Colin 'Skip' 20 Pl D Coy M 22.9.44 PoW XIB 118613, Gillingham, Kent

ENTWISTLE 14373034 Pte B.

ENTWISTLE 14674222 Pte John Int Section HQ Coy M 22.9.44 PoW IVB 91780 Swinton, Lancs

ENTWISTLE 3596911 Pte S.

ENTWISTLE 3597692 Pte W.

EVANS 3864100 Pte Frank M 25.9.44 PoW XIIA 91881, Chester

EVANS 3602813 WS/Cpl Henry Willam W/M 25.9.44 PoW VIIA 140142, Sunderland, Co Durham

EVERINGTON 4615126 Pte George Charles Hugh 12 Pl B Coy M 19.9.44, KiA 22.9.44, Kippax, West Yorkshire

EVISON 4802610 WS/Cpl John Thomas M 26.9.44 PoW VIIIC 118053, Skegness,

Lincolnshire (M); Bicester, Oxfordshire (W)

FAHEY 3782770 Pte T. 12 Pl B Coy W/M 26.9.44

FELLOWS 14584168 Pte J. M 23.9.44 PoW XIIA

FALLON 3602815 W/Cpl R.

FARLEY 3190506 Pte P. 19 Pl D Coy M 20.9.44 PoW

FARRELL 3606147 Pte Daniel 'Danny' A/T Pl S Coy

FENWICK 3601885 Pte William 'Bill' Charles Medical Orderly 16 Platoon C Coy W/M 21.9.44 PoW XIB 118765, Burnley, Lancashire

FERGUSON 3596830 L/Sgt Thomas 'Pop' RAP, Workington, Cumberland

FIDDLER 3602545 Pte Telford 13 Pl B Coy KiA 23.9.44, Workington, Cumberland

FIELD 3381653 WS/Cpl William Gilbert M 25.9.44 PoW XIIA/VIIIB 91519, Crookham, Hampshire

FIELDING 3383531 W/CSM Leslie HQ Coy

FINCHAM 11421633 Pte Harry A/T Pl S Coy, Littleport

FISHER 3460941 Cpl Alan 21 Pl D Coy, Nelson, Lancashire

FISHER 4807422 WS/Sgt George M. A/T Pl S Coy M 26.9.44 PoW VIIIC 118658, Bermuda, West Indies

FISHWICK 3784140 Pte H.

FITZGERALD 3608276 Pte R. 14 Pl B Coy M 25.9.44 PoW XIIA 94474

FITZPATRICK 14647194 Pte Francis 15 Pl C Coy W/M KiA 25.9.44, Liverpool

FITZSIMMONS 3600823 Pte Thomas W/M 23.9.44 PoW IVB 91934, Collyhurst, Manchester

FLANNIGAN 3604940 Pte J. A. W/M 20.9.44 PoW VIIIC 92788, Berwick-on-Tweed, Northumberland

FLEMING 14632998 Pte John L. W/M 18.9.44 PoW XIB/079 118879, Bolton, Lancashire

FLETCHER 3597942 WS/Cpl Walter D. 12 Pl B Coy W/M 21.9.44 KiA 24.9.44

FLINN 14641105 Pte Edward 13 Pl B Coy M 20.9.44 PoW XIB 119415, Cleator Moor, Cumberland

FLINT 3603441 Pte H.

FLYNN 3602818 Pte Christopher Alexander M 17.9.44 PoW IXC 53397, Prudhoe, Northumberland

FLYNN 3595670 Pte James 'Paddy' Medical Orderly 18 Platoon C Coy M 19.9.44 PoW VIIA 140070, Raffles, Carlisle

FOGGO 3602486 L/Cpl Eric Edward B Coy HQ KiA 21.9.44, Settle, West Yorkshire

FORD 3782886 Pte James Patrick W/M 20.9.44, KiA 29.9.44, Runcorn, Cheshire

FOSBROOK 14643776 Pte J. C. 23 Mortar Pl S Coy M 26.9.44 PoW IVB 075653

FOSTER 3601333 Pte Arthur 11 Pl B Coy M 17.9.44, KiA 21.9.44, Stanwix, Carlisle

FOSTER 14584171 Pte Harry 11 Pl B Coy M 20.9.44 PoW IVB 075688, Birkenhead, Cheshire

FOTHERGILL 3602985 Pte T.

FOWLER 4546551 Pte Colin 'Danny' 20 Pl D Coy M 25.9.44 PoW XIIA 91931, Yeadon, Leeds

FOWLER 3602819 Pte Robert B. 24 Mortar Pl S Coy W/M KiA 22.9.44, Monkwearmouth, Sunderland

FOX 3860327 L/Cpl E. W 26.9.44

FOX 3603932 Pte Roland 8 Pl A Coy M
26.9.44 PoW XIIA 91706, Bolton,
Lancashire

FRENCH 4452476 WS/Cpl Frederick John
W/M 21.9.44 PoW XIB 118056, New
Durham

FRENCH 1824121 L/Sgt William Donaldson
A/T Pl S Coy W/M 21.9.44 PoW XIB
118752, Walkerdene, Newcastle-upon-Tyne

FREWIN 1150793 Pte Erice Sydney M 22.9.44
PoW XIIA 25560, Reading, Berkshire

FROUD 3596579 WS/Cpl George 'Tich' C
Coy W/M KiA 21.9.44, Headington,
Oxfordshire

GALLACHER 2697171 Pte Neil M. KiA
18.9.44, Linlithgow, West Lothian

GALLAGHER 14583434 Pte George M
20.9.44 PoW XIB 117322, St Helens,
Lancashire

GARDNER 14227732 Pte E. W/M 18.9.44
PoW VB 149757

GARDNER-ROBERTS 3603310 Sgt James
MM 17 Pl C Coy

GARVEY 3596852 Pte Thomas 19 Pl D Coy
M 22.9.44 PoW XIIA 91984, Salford,
Lancashire

GAVAGHAN 3443816 L/Cpl Charles Sig Pl
HQ Coy (killed Norway), Todmorden, West
Yorkshire

GETTINGS 3603443 Pte Joseph W/M 19.9.44
PoW XIB 117620, Darwen, Lancashire

GIBSON 3602826 Pte Joseph Henry KiA
23.9.44, Ryhope, Co Durham

GIBSON 3602827 Pte W. Brother of above

GILL 14674240 Pte Douglas Charles 19 Pl D
Coy M 25.9.44 PoW XIIA 25558, Gosport,
Hampshire

GILLIES 1799012 Pte William Stevenson M
25.9.44 PoW XIIA/IVB 92007, Kilmarnock

GLENN 14401972 Pte John 13 Pl B Coy M
19.9.44 PoW XIB 118102, Collyhurst,
Manchester

GODDARD 3771317 Pte A. W/M 19.9.44
PoW Hospital Ede, Holland

GOFF 3608161 Pte Harry att'd Def Pl 1/ALB
HQ PoW XIIA 92003, Lancaster

GORDON 3607023 Pte John 'Johnny'
Battalion Range Taker 23 Mortar Pl S Coy,
Manchester

GORMAN 3186358 Pte Alfred W/M 22.9.44
PoW XIB 117406, Dumfries

GOULDING 3599543 WS/Sgt Dennis D Coy
W/M 21.9.44 PoW VB/VIIA 18678, Temple
Sowerby, Cumberland

GRAHAM 14376148 Pte R. MMG Pl S Coy
M 25.9.44 PoW

GRANT 3607117 Pte Gerard 14 Pl B Coy M
17.9.44 PoW XIIA 91473, Waterloo,
Liverpool

GRAY 3603654 Pte Percy W/M 25.9.44 PoW
XIIA/IVB 92033, Sale, Cheshire.

GRAY 4397338 Pte William Frederick KiA
18.9.44, Sowerby Bridge, West Yorkshire

GRAYDON 3605381 Pre Ronald Signaller
att'd 19 Pl D Coy M 25.9.44 PoW XIIA/IVB
91874, Carlisle

GREASLEY 4277600 Pte Charles Ernest 13 Pl
B Coy M 19.9.44 PoW XIB 118067,
Grantham, Lincolnshire

GREEN 3598733 Pte Harry M 20.9.44 PoW
XIB 118182, Blackburn, Lancashire

GREEN 6210457 Pte R.

GREENALL 3606248 Pte John 14 Pl B Coy

W/M 20.9.44 PoW XIIA/IVB 075398,
Stranorum, Co Antrim

GRIMSHAW 3597341 WS/CSM Frederick A
Coy W/M 22.9.44 PoW-Rep XIB/VIIIC
117291, Miles Platting, Manchester

GRINDROD 1739180 Pte J M 25 9 44 PoW

GRINDROD 3607666 Pte Norman W/M
21.9.44 PoW XIB 117569, Chorley,
Lancashire

GROVER 3244797 W/Cpl A.

GRUNDY 14583673 Pte John A/T Pl S Coy
26.9.44 PoW XIIA Transit Camp 91928,
Atherton, Manchester

HAIGH 3599575 Pte Eric Douglas att'd Def Pl
1/ALB HQ M 25.9.44 PoW XIB 118108,
Andover, Hampshire

HALE 3600892 A/Cpl Ronald PoW XIIA
91789, Newtown, Carlisle

HALEY 3598957 Pte Richard GM Major
Armstrong's batman B Coy HQ W/M
19.9.44 PoW IXC 52918, Frizington,
Cumberland

HALL 14583675 Pte James Signaller att'd A
Coy W/M 26.9.44

HALLIDAY 3602840 L/Cpl Raymond W/M
KiA 24.9.44, Stockton-on-Tees, Co
Durham

HAMER 3607398 Pte John 24 Mortar Pl S
Coy

HAMLETT 4462122 Pte Ernest Signaller att'd
19 Pl D Coy M 26.9.44 PoW XIB 118075,
Whalley Range, Manchester

HAMPSON 14671580 Pte William Edward M
22.9.44 PoW XIB 118137, Seaforth,
Liverpool

HANNAH 3192167 Pte Andrew 'Andy' 10 Pl
A Coy W/M 24.9.44 PoW VIIA 140096,
Whithorn, Wigtownshire

HANNAH 3192337 Pte James Alexander
W/M 18.9.44 PoW XIB 117450, Stranraer.
Brother of above?

HANSON 3596670 Sgt Robert KiA 21.9.44,
Stanwix, Carlisle

HARDING 3770311 WS/Cpl T. MMG Pl S
Coy M 25.9.44

HARDWICK 4546599 Pte Jack 23 Mortar Pl S
Coy, Leeds

HARDY 14212903 Pte Stanley Ronald W/M
20.9.44, KiA 26.9.44, Edlington, West
Yorkshire

HARE 317746 W/Sgt N.

HARLEY 2981828 Pte T. possibly 15 Pl C Coy

HARRISON 14579662 Pte Eric George M
22.9.44 PoW XIIA 175991 Glasshoughton,
Castleford, West Yorkshire

HARRISON 3607402 Pte Henry M 26.9.44
PoW XIIA 075674, Moss Side, Manchester

HARRISON 3603444 L/Cpl Ivan M 25.9.44
PoW XIIA 91800, Darwen, Lancashire

HARRISON 3605423 L/Cpl K. W 25.9.44

HART 3606608 Pte John 23 Mortar Pl S Coy

HARTLEY 3604673 L/Sgt Edward MMG Pl S
Coy KiA 20.9.44, M 26.9.44, Leeds, West
Yorkshire

HARTSHORN 3603644 L/Sgt Andrew 10 Pl
A Coy W/M 20.9.44 PoW XIB 117811,
Bolton, Lancashire. Taken PoW 24.9.44

HARWOOD 3604043 WS/Cpl Frederick M
21.9.44 PoW XIIA/VIIIC 91994, Preston,
Lancashire

HASKINS 3598519 Pte George A/T Pl S Coy
M 26.9.44 PoW XIIA/XIB 118372, Blackley,
Manchester

HEARNE 14279315 Pte Eric Frank M 17.9.44
PoW-Rep XIB 117968 Penn, nr High
Wycombe, Buckinghamshire

HEATON 3782796 A/Cpl Jack 12 Pl B Coy,
Castleton, Rochdale, Lancashire

HERRING 3604134 Pte Norman S Coy M
29.9.44 PoW-Rep XIB 117743, Greaves,
Lancaster

HESLOP 14658513 Pte John George 8 Pl A
Coy M 26.9.44 PoW XIIA 92154,
Gateshead, Co Durham

HEWITSON 3595278 WS/Sgt John Pl Sgt 11
Pl B Coy W/M 18.9.44 PoW XIB/VIIIC
117918, Workington, Cumberland

HEWITT 3603323 Pte Thomas W/M 22.9.44
PoW XIB 117285, Scholes, Wigan,
Lancashire

HILL 7376940 Pte William RAMC att'd D
Coy PoW 23.9.44, Widnes, Lancashire

HILLARY 3605673 Pte William W/M 25.9.44
PoW XIB 118184, Aspatria, Cumberland

HILLS 3596885 L/Sgt Alfred William M
26.9.44 PoW XIB 117920, Belfast, N Ireland

HILTON 3600521 Pte Robert W/M 21.9.44,
PoW XIB 118260 Cleator Moor,
Cumberland.

HIRD 1137162 Pte Edward E. KiA 23.9.44, M
26.9.44, Manley, Staffordshire

HODGE 3866321 Pte Donald Hugh PoW
XIIID/XIIIC 15231, Heald Green, Cheshire

HODGES 14202223 Pte Frederick Albert 20
Pl D Coy W/M 22.9.44 PoW XIB 118141,
Hillfields, Coventry

HODGKISS 3782780 Pte P. 'Doodle'

HOGG 3601527 WS/Cpl Alec M 25.9.44
PoW XIIA 91985, Workington (P); Llanelli
(W)

HOGG 14642226 Pte N.

HOLDEN 14412163 Pte H. att'd Def Pl 1/ALB
HQ

HOLDSWORTH 2696598 L/Cpl Herbert
Arthur 14 Pl B Coy M 17.9.44, KiA 23.9.44,
Gildersome, Yorkshire

HOLME 3603471 Pte William Myles KiA
23.9.44, Middleshaw, Westmorland

HOMER 4469806 Pte V. William 'Bill' 24 Pl
Mortar S Coy

HOOD 3606832 L/Cpl Frank D Coy M
25.9.44 PoW XIIA 91976 D 29.10.44,
Crewe, Cheshire

HOOLE 3598735 Pte A. W 23.9.44

HOOPER 3599167 Pte Tom 8 Pl A Coy W/M
24.9.44 PoW IVB 92110, Wythenshaw,
Manchester

HORROCKS 3597315 W/Cpl Gerald Sig Pl
HQ Coy

HOWARD 3535545 Pte Harold W/M 20.9.44
PoW XIIA/XIIB 91945, Hulme, Manchester

HOWCROFT 3603473 WS/Cpl John M
21.9.44 PoW VIIIC 93205, Higher Ince,
Wigan, Lancashire

HOWE 14209659 L/Cpl George William 14 Pl
B Coy M 17.9.44, KiA 24.9.44

HOWE 1436252 Gnr W. V. RA att'd
batman/runner to Capt Birchmore RA FOO
PoW XIB/Oflag 79 117279, Hull, East
Yorkshire

HOYNE 3596668 L/Sgt William C Coy W/M
22.9.44 PoW VIIA 140120, Carlisle,
Cumberland

HUGHES 3783626 Pte Arthur 'Nellie' 23
Mortar Pl S Coy

HUGHES 3598821 Pte Benjamin W/M

17.9.44 PoW XIB 118525, Ancoats, Manchester

HUGHES 14642662 Pte Cyril W/M 24.9.44 PoW XIIA 075354, Stoke-on-Trent, Staffordshire

HUGHES 3596264 L/Cpl Edward M 26.9.44 PoW XIIA 975689, Belfast, N Ireland

HUGHES 4462782 W/Cpl V. Sig Pl HQ Coy

HULSE 3782658 Pte Philip A. 13 Pl B Coy M 18.9.44, D 3.10.44, Wallasey, Cheshire

HUNT 3606762 Pte A. W/M 20.9.44 PoW

HUNT 4626714 Pte William D Coy M 24.9.44 PoW XIIA 91979, Rotherham, West Yorkshire

HUNTER 3596717 L/Sgt Arthur B Coy HQ KiA 18.9.44, Chorley, Lancashire

HUNTER 6401490 WS/Cpl Ian Robert Martin 14 Pl B Coy W/M 20.9.44 PoW Hospital Stammlager VIC then XIB, Midhurst, West Sussex

HUNTER 3596799 Sgt John 10 Pl A Coy KiA 20.9.44, Prudhoe-on-Tyne, Nothumberland

HURLEY 3450725 Pte Patrick M KiA 22.9.44, Manchester

HUTCHINSON 3760569 Pte Edward George W/M 21.9.44 PoW XIB 117510, Liverpool

HUTCHINSON 14571018 L/Cpl John B Coy HQ M 18.9.44 PoW IVB 88790, Heysham, Lancashire

HUTCHINSON 3603576 Pte Joseph Edwin Signaller att'd 23 Mortar Pl S Coy, from Salford, later Bothel, Cumberland

INGHAM 3718775 Pte Hubert Leslie Int Section HQ Coy W/M 23.9.44 PoW XIIA 075357, Bamber Bridge, Preston, Lancashire

ISHERWOOD 3600572 Pte Wallace W/M KiA 23.9.44, Bolton, Lancashire

ISLES 14647208 Pte Francis James 13 Pl B Coy M 17.9.44 PoW VB/VIIA 18667, Thornton, Blackpool, Lancashire

IVISON 3602521 WS/Cpl Robert John 13 Pl B Coy M 20.9.44 PoW XIB/VIIIB 117658, Workington, Cumberland

JACKSON 3606483 Pte Frederick 14 Pl B Coy W/M 20.9.44 PoW XIIA/IVD 075440, Blackburn, Lancashire. One of the youngest to join the Battalion at 15 at Barton Stacey

JACKSON 3604090 Pte J. ACC

JACKSON 3607911 Pte Robert att'd Def Pl 1/ALB HQ DoW 23.10.44, Stanwix, Carlisle

JACOBS 6148183 Pte Thomas John 24 Mortar Pl S Coy M 26.9.44 PoW XIB 117522, London SE17

JAMES 3593825 W/Sgt G.

JARVIS 4398559 Pte Francis Edward 13 Pl B Coy M 20.9.44, KiA 24.9.44, Sunderland

JEFFRIES 3596949 CSM James att'd Def Pl 1/ALB HQ PoW XIIA 92164, Hindley, Wigan, Lancashire

JENKINS 3597283 Pte H.

JENKINS 14401388 Pte H.

JOHNSON 3603507 Pte James 15 Pl C Coy W/M KiA 17.9.44, Carlisle

JONES 3534132 Pte Alfred 21 Pl D Coy W/M 22.9.44 PoW XIB 118062

JONES 3973734 Pte Charles Ralph 10 Pl A Coy W/M 20.9.44 PoW XIB 118156, Longworth, nr Mansfield, Nottinghamshire

JONES 3595904 Pte John 10 Pl A Coy W/M 23.9.44 PoW XIB 118570, Egremont, Cumberland

JONES 3603955 Pte Richard 'Dick' A/T Pl S Coy W/M 20.9.44 PoW XIB 118146, Blackley, Manchester

JONES 3654511 Pte T. V. 12 Pl B Coy, Warrington, Lancashire

JONES 14576638 Pte Thomas Donald M 20.9.44, KiA 22-25.9.44, Bidston, Cheshire

JONES 3771510 Pte W.

JURY 3607532 Pte L. 'Taffy' 15 Pl C Coy

KEARN 3605243 Pte N. HQ Coy

KELLY 3595395 Pte John HQ Coy Despatch Rider M 26.9.44 PoW XIB 117724, Bolton, Lancashire

KELSEY 3763807 Pte James Harrison att'd Def Pl 1/ALB HQ, Liverpool

KENDAL 3535230 Pte J.J. 24 Mortar Pl S Coy M 26.9.44 PoW XIIA/IVB 91953, Cheetham, Manchester

KENNY 3537370 Pte M.

KENWORTHY 4467370 Pte Joseph W/M 20.9.44 PoW XIB 118066, Ashton-under-Lyne, Manchester

KERR 3602996 L/Sgt James Findlay Pl Sgt 7 Pl A Coy W/M 21.9.44 PoW XIB 118836, Whitehaven, Cumberland

KERR 3864762 Pte Robert W/M 21.9.44 PoW-Rep XIB 118318, Glasgow

KERWIN 3528087 Pte John 24 Mortar Pl S Coy Capt Ingram's batman/runner M 27.9.44 PoW XIIA/IVC 92161, Oldham, Lancashire

KILGOUR 2826259 Pte T.

KIMBER 2037096 L/Sjt John 'Jack' Matthewman 13 Pl B Coy W/M 20.9.44 PoW XIB 118888, North Shields, Northumberland

KIMNEL 11414036 Pte Clifford Ernest 10 Pl A Coy M 20.9.44 PoW XIIA/IVA 91522, Middleton Cheney, nr Bradbury, Oxon

KING 865794 Pte P. 16 Pl C Coy

KIRKBRIDE 3603328 WS/Cpl John W/M 23.9.44 PoW-Rep XIB 118837, Maryport, Cumberland (P); Whitchurch, Hampshire (W)

KNEALE 3604751 Pte Robert Lewis 24 Mortar Pl S Coy M 26.9.44 PoW XIIA 075679, Douglas, Isle of Man

KNEE 5347099 L/Cpl F. REME

KNIGHT 14209120 Pte Norman 'Jock' 23 Mortar Pl S Coy W 26.9.44

KNOTT 3603391 Pte Alfred

LACE 3603224 Pte Gordon PoW XIIA/IVB 92002, Workington, Cumberland

LAIDLOW 3454371 Pte J. 24 Mortar Pl S Coy, Bothel, Cumberland

LAITHWAITE 3596206 Pte F. 12 Pl B Coy W/M 20.9.44 PoW, Wigan, Lancashire

LANG 3606642 Pte Robert 18 Pl C Coy W/M 20.9.44 PoW XIB 117504, Anfield, Liverpool

LANGHORN 3601433 Cpl Thomas 'Tommy' 21 Pl D Coy KiA 22.9.44, Kendal, Westmorland

LARGE 14424577 Pte E. 'Larry' A/T Pl S Coy

LATCHFORD 3606788 Pte Ernest W/M 25.9.44 PoW XIB 118470, Bromley Cross, Bolton, Lancashire

LATHAM 3862736 Pte Alfred M 25.9.44 PoW XIIA 91801, Warrington, Lancashire

LAWSON 3601839 Pte H.

LAWSON 3603163 Pte James 18 Pl C Coy M 26.9.44 PoW XIIA 075973, Hendon, Sunderland

LAWTON 14617022 Pte James Henry M 21.9.44 PoW XIB-Rep 117539, Warrington, Lancashire

LAYCOCK 3602855 Pte Thomas, killed Norway, Darlington, Co Durham

LEAVER 4807737 WS/Cpl Frederick Henry M 26.9.44 PoW VIIIC 91981, Forest Gate, London E7

LEE 3602983 Pte N. W 26.9.44

LEE 14672528 Pte Robert 'Bob' 17 Pl C Coy W/M 20.9.44 PoW VIIA 140090, Abbeytown, Cumberland

LEVER 3776422 L/Cpl B. A/T Pl S Coy M 25.9.44 PoW XIIA 26083

LEWIS 3603448 Pte L.

LEWIS 14431937 Pte William 8 Pl A Coy M 26.9.44 PoW XIIA 92111, Hyde, Cheshire

LIPPETT 3594025 Sgt Leonard att'd Def Pl 1/ALB HQ PoW

LITTLE 4621936 Pte Wilfred 24 Mortar Pl S Coy M 26.9.44 PoW XIIA 91710, Norwood Green, Halifax, West Yorkshire

LIVESEY 3391440 Pte T. 24 Mortar Pl S Coy

LOCKE 14634816 Pte Arthur Charles 12 Pl B Coy W/M 25.9.44 PoW XIB 118509, Kilburn, London NW6

LOGAN 4467488 Pte Alan Mortar Pl S Coy

LOMAX 14217581 Pte W. 17 Pl C Coy

LONG 4279402 L/Cpl George Edward Hearn D Coy W/M KiA 24.9.44, Andover, Hampshire

LONGSON 3782025 Pte James MMG Pl S Coy M 25.9.44 PoW XIIA 075994, Whaley Bridge, nr Stockport

LONGTON 3603531 L/Cpl Timothy HQ Coy CO's driver

LOOKER 3778886 Pte John 'Jack' 10 Pl A Coy W/M 25.9.44 PoW XIB 118343, Birkenhead, Cheshire

LORD 3606663 W/Cpl Robert 23 Mortar Pl S Coy

LOWERY 4469819 Pte Douglas 17 Pl C Coy KiA 24.9.44, Bensham, Gateshead

LOWRY 3650291 Pte Patrick W/M 22.9.44 PoW XIB 118593, Eltham Park, London SE9

LOWTHER 3607787 Pte Edgar W/M 22.9.44 PoW XIB 118306, Barrow-in-Furness, Lancashire

McCABE 2991956 Pte John W/M 22.9.44 PoW XIB 117389, Johnstone, Renfrewshire

McCALLUM 3529863 Pte P.

McCLUE 2765123 WS/Cpl 14 Pl B Coy W 25.9.44

McCLUSKIE 3596965 WS/Sgt James MM Sig Pl HQ Coy M 26.9.44 PoW XIB 117454, Ecclefechan, Dumfries

McDONALD 3772203 Pte Robert H. 12 Pl B Coy M 25.9.44 PoW XIIA 91475, Litherland, Liverpool

McDONALD 3602955 Pte Thomas 13 Pl B Coy M 20.9.44, KiA 24.9.44

McDONALD 3606564 Pte Wilfred James M 25.9.44 PoW IVB/IVF 075851, Droylesden, Manchester

McDOWELL 3601450 W/Cpl James 23 Mortar Pl S Coy, Crofton, Cumberland

McFARLANE 3604945 L/Cpl George Sig Pl HQ Coy

McGARR 3604100 Pte F. 23 Mortar Pl S Coy

McGINNGLE 2926248 L/Cpl H. A/T Pl S Coy

McGLADDERY 3595257 A/CSM Alfred B Coy M 20.9.44, DoW 22.9.44, Keddington, Suffolk

McGUINESS 3597882 Pte Hugh D Coy M 25.9.44 PoW, Whitehaven, Cumberland

McHUGH 3599165 Pte James M 26.9.44 PoW IVA/IVB 91948, Stockport, Cheshire

McINNES 3771799 W/Cpl C. 23 Mortar Pl S Coy

McKENZIE 3606679 Pte D. 10 Pl A Coy

McKERR 3783311 Pte J.

McKINLAY 3056691 Pte J. 'Jock' MMG Pl S Coy Attd C Coy W/M 20.9.44 PoW VID

McMULLEN 3452886 Pte Denis 24 Mortar Pl S Coy M KiA 26.9.44, Willington Quay, Northumberland

McNAMARA 4462812 W/Cpl A.

McSHERRY 4266478 WS/Sgt Vincent Pl Sgt 15 Pl C Coy W/M 20.9.44 PoW XIB/A 117618, Woodhouse, Whitehaven, Cumberland. Killed in the William Pit coal mine disaster, Whitehaven, 1947

MAGUIRE 3604446 Pte James

MAGUIRE 14583475 Pte Joseph Sig Pl HQ Coy att'd D Coy M 25.9.44 PoW IVB 24938, Stoneycroft, Liverpool

MAGUIRE 3603450 Pte Stephen M 25.9.44 PoW XIIA 91933, Maryport, Cumberland

MALCOLM 3783576 Pte W.

MALONE 14230355 Pte C. 'Ginger' Int Section HQ Coy

MANCHESTER 3606858 Pte Norman 14 Pl B Coy M 19.9.44, KiA 21/22.9.44, Bury, Lancashire

MANLEY 3594205 L/Cpl M. HQ Coy

MANN 4276920 WS/Cpl Sydney George W/M 20.9.44 PoW VB/VIIA 18675, Dinnington, Newcastle-upon-Tyne

MARCHANT 14593477 Pte P.

MARRIOTT 4279974 Pte Charles Edward W/M 21.9.44 PoW XIB 117642, Northampton

MARSH 4465205 Pte Walter 24 Mortar Pl S Coy M 26.9.44 PoW XIIA/IVB 075665, Widnes, Lancashire

MARSHALL 4691562 L/Cpl Thomas William W/M 20.9.44 PoW XIB 117676, Batley, West Yorkshire

MARSLAND 3599161 L/Cpl William KiA 25.9.44, Denton, Lancashire

MARTIN 3600606 Pte Laurence 'Laurie' 19 Pl D Coy W 26.9.44, Whitehaven, Cumberland

MASON 3600775 Pte Edward 23 Pl S Coy M 26.9.44 PoW XIIA 91524, Moss Side, Manchester

MASTERTON 2981724 Pte Alexander 'Sandy' A/T Pl S Coy

MATTHEWS 3392036 Pte Frederick George 18 Pl C Coy W/M 21.9.44 PoW XIB 117499, Salford, Lancashire

MAWDSLEY 14672551 Pte Joseph James Sig Pl HQ Coy W/M 20.9.44 PoW XIB 118609, Aughton, nr Ormskirk, Lancashire

MAWDSLEY 14583478 Pte Ronald Signaller

MAWMAN 3453537 Pte Robert Peer W/M 18.9.44 PoW XIB 117774, Nelson, Lancashire

MEACHIN 3603633 Pte Charles 'Charlie' Sig Pl HQ Coy

MEADE 7366395 L/Cpl E. RAMC att'd C Coy

MEIN 3602433 Pte Leonard Int Section HQ Coy

MELLING 3866035 L/Cpl Eric B Coy KiA 20.9.44, Wigan, Lancashire

MELLING 3597056 Pte William KiA 24/25.9.44, Wigan, Lancashire

MERCER 14405579 Pte Thomas W/M 17.9.44 PoW XIB 118757, Boswells, Roxburghshire

MEREDITH 3860614 A/Cpl Patrick M 21.9.44 PoW XIIA 075556, Darwen, Lancashire

METCALFE 3602861 Pte Edwin W/M 24.9.44 PoW XIB 118844, N Frodingham, nr Driffield, East Yorkshire

METCALFE 3596078 W/Sgt Stanley Frear, Bowness-on-Windermere, Westmorland

MIDDLEMISS 3602863 Pte J. 23 Mortar Pl S Coy

MIDGLEY 3604971 Pte Frank W/M KiA 22.9.44, Rochdale, Lancashire

MIERS 3600748 Pte C.

MILES 5677735 L/Cpl C. REME

MILLER 2980246 L/Cpl George M 26.9.44 PoW XIIA/IVA 91878, Clydebank, Dumbartonshire

MILLINGTON 3856104 A/Cpl Arthur W/M 26.9.44 PoW XIIA/IVB 91880, Oldham, Lancashire

MILLINGTON 4984713 Pte J.

MOLLOY 3598825 A/Sgt John 'Johnny' A/T Pl S Coy M 26.9.44 PoW XIIA 91959, Moss Side, Manchester

MONTGOMERY 3718530 Pte J. 'Jock' 19 Pl D Coy

MOORCROFT 3777992 Pte Thomas 12 Pl B Coy W/M 23.9.44 PoW XIB 118507, Liverpool

MOORE 3602865 Pte F. W/M 25.9.44

MOORE 3854499 Pte Robert Henry MMG Pl S Coy W/M 21.9.44 PoW XIB 118544, Preston, Lancashire

MORFEE 6412595 Pte J. 10 Pl A Coy

MORRIS 4547329 Pte J.

MOSS 3603331 Pte Walter B Coy M 20.9.44 PoW XIIA 075500, Sandbach, Cheshire

MOUSLEY 3866119 Pte Frank PoW IVB 92095, Barnoldswick, Yorkshire

MUCKIAN 4277812 Pte N. 14 Pl B Coy W/M 20.9.44 PoW XIB 117474, Scotswood, Newcastle-upon-Tyne

MUIR 2922216 Pte Robert 8 Pl A Coy W/M 21.9.44 PoW XIB 117408, Handsworth, Birmingham

MULLINS 3850421 L/Cpl T.

MUMFORD 3606568 Pte H. 10 Pl A Coy

MURDOCH 14593067 Pte David

MURPHY 3772686 Pte Bernard Signal Pl HQ Coy, Liverpool

MURRAY 3606965 Pte Ronald Thomas PoW XIB 117549, Blackburn, Lancashire

MURRAY 3776281 A/Cpl Thomas 17.9.44 PoW XIIA 075673, Manchester

NADIN 3866328 Pte George E. att'd Div HQ PoW

NICHOL 3603479 Pte William Edward M 22.9.44 PoW XIIA 91983, Cleator Moor, Cumberland

NICHOLSON 3601635 Cpl Edward KiA 23.9.44, Workington, Cumberland

NIXON 3600613 Pte Charles Alfred M 26.9.44 PoW XIIA 91944, Scotswood, Newcastle-upon-Tyne

NOLAN 767839 L/Cpl Harold HQ Coy CO's batman W/M 26.9.44 PoW XIB 118802, Ainsworth, Bolton, Lancashire

NORMAN 3598872 Pte Roland Workington

NORTHGRAVES 3601365 WS/Sgt Thomas Pl Sgt 19 Pl D Coy M 25.9.44 PoW XIIA/VIIIC 91958, Appleby, Westmorland

OAKLEY 3602636 WS/Cpl Maurice Tabberer MMG Pl S Coy att'd A Coy M 25.9.44 PoW XIB 118708, South Gosforth, Newcastle-upon-Tyne

OAKLEY 2059230 L/Sgt Robert M 25.9.44

PoW XIIA 91907, Salford, Lancashire

OAKLEY 3608505 Pte William Christopher W/M 20.9.44 PoW XIIB/Oflag 79 118856, Ormskirk, Lancashire

O'CONNELL 3606705 Pte Thomas Henry W/M 24.9.44 PoW XIB 118689 Woolford, Bury, Lancashire

O'DOWD 3605513 Pte J. E. Batman to Major Bteese D Coy W/M 25.9.44, PoW St Deduine Hospital

OFFORD 14217970 Pte J.

OGLANBY 3600406 Pte John 24 Mortar Pl S Coy, Aspatria, Cumberland

O'GORMAN 3606318 Pte C.

O'HANLON 3783776 Pte Henry BEM W/M 20.9.44 PoW, Liverpool

OLDHAM 3391058 Pte Wilfred Edwards 12 Pl B Coy

OLIVER 3537403 Pte Leslie M 20.9.44 PoW XIIA 91793

O'NEILL 3783818 Pte J. possibly 15 Pl C Coy

O'NEILL 3772654 Pte Peter M 26.9.44 PoW IVB 91947, Liverpool

OTTO 3604135 A/Cpl W. MMG Pl S Coy

OVERY 14681067 Pte Frederick Leonard M 25.9.44 PoW XIIA 075946, Marlow, Buckinghamshire

OWEN 3852653 L/Sgt Archibald att'd Def Pl 1/ALB HQ KiA 24.9.44, Liverpool

PAGAN 3598670 Pte Joseph, killed Norway

PAGE 14673439 Pte J.

PARKER 14560262 Pte G. M 26.9.44 PoW XIIA

PARKER 3599034 Pte T.

PARRY 14658202 Pte R.

PATTERSON 3189340 WS/Cpl David Turnbull 13 Pl B Coy M 21.9.44 PoW XIIA 075670, Ilford, Essex

PAYNE 3597704 L/Cpl Douglas Arthur 'Jack' 17 Pl C Coy W/M 20.9.44 PoW XIB 118818, Teddington, Middlesex

PEACOCK 3598810 Pte E.

PEACOCK 4805802 Pte Frederick William M 25.9.44 PoW XIIA/IVF 25559, Burnham Market, King's Lynn, Norfolk

PEARSON 3602871 Pte George William M 26.9.44 PoW XIIA/IVB 975470, Boscombe, Bournemouth, Hampshire (W)

PEARSON 4620133 Pte Jabez W/M, KiA 22.9.44

PEAT 3603453 WS/Cpl John DoW 20.9.44, New Washington, Co Durham

PECK 14674077 Pte Joseph 9 Pl A Coy W/M KiA 24.9.44, Rudheath, Cheshire

PENNINGTON 3390631 Pte Alfred M 25.9.44 PoW XIB 118309, Bolton, Lancashire (W)

PETERS 3606148 Pte Edward John 'Johnnie' 14 Pl B Coy, Liverpool

PHILLIPS 14681071 Pte James W/M 22.9.44 PoW XIB 117609, Poole, Dorset

PHIPPS 14642982 Pte George Thomas, killed Norway

PHOENIX 3779040 Pte Trevor Francis W/M 26.9.44 PoW XIB 118250, Liverpool

PILLING 14671664 Pte Eric 10 Pl A Coy W/M 26.9.44, DoW 28.9.44, Liverpool

PINKNEY 3602873 WS/Cpl Hugh 14 Pl B Coy M 20.9.44 PoW XIIA/VIIIC 24889, Whitechurch, Hampshire (W)

PIPER 3600652 L/Cpl Thomas C Coy KiA 20.9.44, South Shields

PLIMLEY 3606327 Pte Thomas 18 Pl C Coy, Bury, Lancashire

POINTON 3718784 Pte G.

POOL 3862643 Pte F. 10 Pl A Coy W/M 21.9.44 PoW XIB 117643

POPE 3595025 RSM Albert HQ Coy DoW 22.9.44, Bolton, Lancashire

PORTER 3603481 Pte John W/M 26.9.44 PoW XIB-Rep 118219, Chorley, Lancashire

POWELL 3598899 Pte Geoffrey William M 26.9.44 PoW XIB 118278, Appleby, Westmorland

POWELL 14676439 Pte Leonard Robert, batman to Lt Green 20 Pl D Coy M 25.9.44 PoW XIIA 91988, Carmarthen

PRESTON 3600079 Pte Laurence Henry M 26.9.44 PoW XIIA 075484, Kendal, Westmorland

PRICE 3596981 WS/Sgt Frederick William 'Mickey' 23 Mortar Pl S Coy W/M KiA 22.9.44

PRICE 3600802 Pte R. 23 Mortar Pl S Coy W 25.9.44

PRIDMORE 3600733 L/Cpl Wilfred Isaac A/T Pl S Coy, Keswick, Cumberland

PRYKE 4691531 Pte Cyril, Ossett, Leeds

PULFORD 4690587 Pte John William HQ Coy, Burley, Leeds, West Yorkshire

PURSHOUSE 406274 A/Sgt S. P. 14 Pl B Coy W/M 20.9.44 PoW XIB/VIIIC 117639, Sheffield

PYE 3606658 Pte Edwin 18 Pl C Coy PoW XIB 118615, Blackburn, Lancashire

QUAIL 3601803 WS/Cpl John W. M 25.9.44 PoW XIIA 075943, Cockermouth, Cumberland

QUINN 4546937 Pte Albert Edward W/M 24.9.44 PoW IVD 075350, Leeds

QUINN 3602875 Pte James W/M 21.9.44 PoW XIB 117478, North Shields, Co Durham

QUINN 3607205 Pte P.

QUINTON 3454926 WS/Cpl Robert Beatty 24 Mortar Pl S Coy M 26.9.44 PoW XIIA 91623, Higher Broughton, Salford, Lancashire

RAFFERTY 3597639 U/L/Cpl Henry W/M 25.9.44 PoW XIB 118090, Middlesbrough, North Yorkshire

RAFFERTY 3597922 Pte N.

RAFFERTY 14642750 Pte William W/M 24.9.44 PoW IVB 077368, Stoke-on-Trent, Staffordshire

RAINFORD 3606807 Pte Joseph 18 Pl C Coy, Liverpool

RANGER 6412603 Pte John Kenneth Frederick 20 Pl D Coy, Forest Row, East Sussex

RANNARD 3606485 WS/Cpl John 10 Pl A Coy, Liverpool

RAYMOND 4345446 Pte Geoffrey 10 Pl A Coy KiA 17.9.44, Silsden, West Yorkshire

READY 3600975 A/Cpl Alfred Victor MMG Pl S Coy M 25.9.44 PoW XIIA 91562, Forest Gate, London E7

REED 4469834 Pte Ronald W/M 21.9.44 PoW XIB 118362, Shildon, Co Durham

RENTON 3192256 Pte John M 22.9.44 PoW XIIA 075503, Preston Duns, Berwickshire

REVITT 2654814 A/Cpl Wilfred D. 22.3.45 W/M 24.9.44 PoW XIIA/VIIIC 075355, Oughtibridge, Sheffield

REYNOLDS 14645531 Pte Cyril Wilfred M 25.9.44 PoW IVB 93366, Clifton, Bristol

RHODES 3606850 Pte Harry PoW IVB 93371, Oldham, Lancashire

RICHARDS 3605404 Pte J.12 Pl B Coy W PoW 25.9.44

RIDEALGH 3597839 W/Sgt G.

RIDING 3606398 Pte C. K. 12 Pl B Coy W/M 20.9.44 PoW XIB 118052, South Shore, Blackpool, Lancashire

RILEY 4546122 Pte Bernard M 26.9.44 PoW XIB 118191, Barnoldswick, Lancashire

RILEY 3866213 Pte Hugh 19 D Coy M 20.9.44 PoW XIIA 075496, Wigan, Lancashire

RILEY 3866330 Pte James M 25.9.44 PoW XIB 118157, Maulsfield, Cheshire

ROBERTS 14671681 Pte J. 12 Pl B Coy W/M 22.9.44 PoW VIC

ROBERTS 14657775 Pte W.

ROBINSON 3596663 Pte M. B Coy HQ

ROBSON 3603002 Pte E.

ROCKLIFFE 3391069 Pte Richard J. A/T Pl S Coy Ted Newport's driver W/M 20.9.44 VIIA-Rep RES LAZ 140282 (in hospital), Burnley, Lancashire

ROGERS 3771252 L/Sgt Lewis 24 Mortar Pl S Coy M 26.9.44 PoW XIIA 91518, Liverpool

RUTTER 14638717 Pte William Charles W/M 22.9.44 PoW XIIA 075672, Westminster, London SW1

SANDHAM 3602959 W/Cpl J. 17 Pl C Coy

SAVAGE 3606520 Pte N. 13 Pl B Coy

SAWYERS 3601500 Pte Robert MMG S Coy, batman to Capt Cleasby

SCALES 4616838 Cpl George Henry att'd Def Pl 1/ALB HQ PoW XIIA 92031, Mexborough, West Yorkshire

SCOTT 3603978 Pte Joseph James M 25.9.44 PoW XIB 118152, Chorlton-cum-Hardy, Manchester

SCULLY 3597845 Pte Leonard A/T Pl S Coy Ted Newport's batman, Swinton, Manchester

SEABURY 3597615 W/Cpl F.

SEALE 14645417 Pte Joseph Alexander 10 Pl A Coy W/M 20.9.44 PoW XIB 118574, Camberley, Surrey

SEARS 3599001 L/Sgt Stanley William Charles Pl Sgt 20 Pl D Coy KiA 18.9.44, Ibstone, Buckinghamshire

SEED 3718807 Pte Fred 23 Mortar Pl S Coy W/M KiA 21.9.44

SEYMOUR 14574818 L/Cpl Thomas Henry B Coy HQ M 21.9.44 PoW XIIA 075687, Yarm-on-Tees, Yorkshire

SHAW 3385677 Pte Albert 18 Pl C Coy, Cumberland

SHELDON 14201232 Pte Walter 'Sniper' 19 Pl D Coy M 25.9.44 PoW XIIA 91951, Newark, Nottinghamshire

SHELLARD 4984631 L/Cpl David Hattle M 26.9.44 PoW IVB 91705, Rushden, Northamptonshire

SHEPHERD 3600081 WS/Cpl Gordon Brown 20 Pl D Coy M 25.9.44 XIB 118055, Kendal, Westmorland

SHEPHERD 3604890 Pte Walter M 25.9.44 PoW XIIA 91785, Burnley, Lancashire

SIDEBOTTOM 3605953 Pte Samuel A Coy W/M 20.9.44 PoW XIB 117527, Southampton

SIMCOX 14257964 L/Cpl Sydney Alexander W/M 21.9.44 PoW XIB 117622, Scarborough

SIMPSON 4394930 WS/Cpl J. R. W/M 21.9.44 XIB/VIIIC 118326, Middlesbrough, North Yorkshire

SIMPSON 3594221 Pte J.

SKELTON 14662098 Pte Norman W/M KiA 23.9.44, Brampton, Cumberland

SKILKI 4467603 Pte J. ACC

SLOAN 3600657 Pte William M 20.9.44, KIA 24/25.9.44

SMALLMAN 14583529 Pte Albert Edward W/M 20.9.44 PoW XIB 118245, Tyldesley, Lancashire

SMART 3602998 Pte Arthur Henry 23 Mortar Pl S Coy KiA 24.9.44, M 26.9.44, Workington, Cumberland

SMART 3652125 Pte Wilfred James 10 Pl A Coy M 19.9.44 PoW IVB 077087, Runcorn, Cheshire

SMETHURST 3593887 Pte J. HQ Coy despatch rider, killed in Norway

SMITH 3606440 Pte Alexander William W/M 23.9.44 PoW XIIA/XIIID 15280, Eyemouth, Berwickshire

SMITH 14208566 Pte B. W/M 20.9.44 PoW XIB 118504, New Waltham, Grimsby

SMITH 4540185 Pte Edward KiA 18.9.44

SMITH 14671694 Pte Frederick Aston KiA 25.9.44, Liverpool

SMITH 3602988 W/Cpl G.

SMITH 3603487 Pte James M 26.9.44 PoW VB 18660, Botcherby, Carlisle

SMITH 3597299 Pte Leo KiA 19.9.44, M 25.9.44, Miles Platting, Manchester

SMITH 3605626 Pte Peter M 21.9.44 PoW VIIIC 93361, Gosforth, Newcastle-upon-Tyne

SMITH 3608302 Pte B. Vernon 24 Mortar Pl S Coy KiA 22.9.44, Carlisle

SMITH 3603365 UL/Cpl Vincent M 25.9.44 PoW XIIA 91456, Widnes, Lancashire

SMITHEN 3598950 Pte Joseph KiA 19.9.44, Salford, Lancashire

SMITHSON 14643562 Pte Silas Berty M 26.9.44 PoW IVB 93403, Ringstead, King's Lynn, Norfolk

SOUTHWOOD 3534520 A/Cpl J. H. 12 Pl B Coy M 25.9.44 PoW XIIA, Salford, Manchester

SPENCER 5883009 WS/Sgt Herbert Louis A/T Pl S Coy M 26.9.44 PoW XIIA/VIIIC 075524, Flore, Northamptonshire

SPINK 3601583 Pte Harold C Coy, Seacroft, Leeds

STANLEY 3606793 Pte Thomas Edward C Coy KiA 22.9.44, Hoylake, Cheshire

STEELE 14274547 L/Cpl J.

STEPHEN 1773177 WS/Cpl Daniel John Sutherland M 25.9.44 PoW XIIA 91975, Fraserburgh, Aberdeenshire

STEPHENSON 3657621 Pte Frederick 10 Pl A Coy M 20.9.44, KiA 25.9.44

STEVENS 3451004 L/Cpl E. 10 Pl A Coy

STEWART 2886642 Pte William M 26.9.44 PoW XIIA 92089, Aberdeen

STIMPSON 4656947 Pte J. W. M 25.9.44 PoW XIIA Transit Camp 91797, Sheffield, Yorkshire

STOCK 3861966 Pte E.

STONES 3601584 Pte C. MMG Pl S Coy, Seacroft, Leeds

STREETER 14319170 Pte Frederick Henry W/M 26.9.44 PoW XIIA/IVC 91725, Tunbridge Wells, Kent

STREETON 3606819 Pte F. 12 Pl B Coy

STRINGER 3594746 WS/CSM George Henry C Coy W/M 25.9.44 PoW XIB 118641, Wythenshawe, Manchester

STRIPP 6412612 Pte Ronald Sydney 20 Pl D Coy W/M 17.9.44 PoW XIIA 075518, Exwick, Devon

STUBBS 3597851 Pte David att'd 1/ALB HQ, Carlisle

SUTTON 14649939 Pte F. B Coy HQ

SWALLOW 14680661 Pte D.

SWAN 3057009 W/Cpl James Guard Section C Coy, Peebles

SWARBRICK 3718787 Pte Vincent 13 Pl B Coy W/M 19.9.44 PoW XIB 117702, Preston, Lancashire

SWIRE 14677968 Pte Leonard Robert M 20.9.44 PoW XIIA 075557, Whitstable, Kent

SYKES 3606231 Pte Lawrence 10 Pl A Coy DoW 20.9.44, W/M 24.9.44, Preston, Lancashire

SYRETT 3603597 Pte Robert C Coy

TANNER 3598667 W/Cpl J.

TATE 3602897 Pte George Cooper 20 Pl D Coy M 22.9.44 PoW XIIA 24253, Philadelphia, Co Durham

TAYLOR 1560536 Pte Henry M 17.9.44 PoW XIB 117656, Oldham, Lancashire

TAYLOR 3191411 Pte H.

TAYLOR 3597751 Pte J, Cleator Moor, Cumberland

TAYLOR 5333356 Pte J.

TEBAY 3601199 W/Cpl Eric 23 Mortar Pl S Coy

TELFORD 3604103 L/Cpl H.

TERRY 3602396 WS/Sgt Frederick Pl Sgt 13 Pl B Coy W/M 21.9.44 PoW XIB

THIRLWELL 3597977 Cpl Charles Raymond 'Chris' Int Section HQ Coy

THOMLINSON 3596347 Pte R.

THOMPSON 3602896 Pte Eric M. M KiA 25.9.44

THOMPSON 3602081 W/Sgt William Charles Pl Sgt 21 Pl D Coy, Barrow-in-Furness, Lancashire

THOMPSON 3602900 Pte William Nelson C Coy W/M 20.9.44, KiA 21/22.9.44, Bristol

THORN 3596600 Pte A.

THORNLEY 3598842 Pte Robert C Coy M 21.9.44 PoW IVB 075560, Raffles, Carlisle

THORNTHWAITE 14617377 Pte Richard M 26.9.44 PoW IVB 93405, Embleton, nr Cockermouth, Cumberland

THYER 3590119 WS/CSM Herbert D Coy W/M 25.9.44 PoW XIB 118313, Maryport, Cumberland

TICKLE 3603457 Pte William M 26.9.44 PoW IVA 91624, Hindley, nr Wigan, Lancashire

TIERNEY 3606330 Pte Ron 'Ginger' 23 Mortar Pl S Coy

TIMMONS 4985539 Pte William 8 Pl A Coy 26.9.44 PoW IVD 93403, Mansfield, Nottinghamshire

TITTERINGTON 3606464 Pte Thomas W/M 22.9.44 PoW XIB 118367, Preston, Lancashire

TOMLINSON 3602921 Pte R. 24 Mortar Pl S Coy

TONGE 3596735 UL/Cpl Fred C Coy W/M 23.9.44 PoW XIB 117321, Bolton, Lancashire

TRAVIS 3783718 Pte George E. M 20.9.44 PoW XIIA/IVC 92124, Knotty Ash, Liverpool

TROUGHEAR 14206269 Pte John Joseph M 20.9.44 PoW XIIA/IVB 075419, Workington, Cumberland

TUBB 14681079 Pte John 24 Mortar Pl S Coy W/M 22.9.44 PoW XIB 118528, Abingdon, Berkshire

TURNER 2765098 Pte John 'Jake' C Coy M 24.9.44 PoW XIB 118820, Coatbridge, Lanarkshire

TURNER 3600830 Pte John M 26.9.44 PoW XIB 118851, Clayton, Manchester

TURNER 3602904 Pte T.

TWEDDLE 3602822 Pte R. 24 Mortar Pl S Coy

TYRIE 4912825 L/Cpl Charles Ernest M 26.9.44 PoW XIB 118692, Garstang, nr Preston, Lancashire

UNSWORTH 14674370 Pte William M 22.9.44 PoW XIIA/IVB 91791, Farnworth, Bolton, Lancashire

URSELL 3594497 A/CSM Norman 'Monkey' A Coy

VASEY 3602906 Pte Harry C Coy W/M KiA 23.9.44, New Bowburn, Co Durham

VERRAL 7023138 Pte Cyril Albert Douglas M 26.9.44 PoW XIIA 075483, Bromley, Kent

VINE 3771185 Pte James M 25.9.44 PoW IVB 077039, Liverpool

WADDINGTON 14653122 Pte R.

WALKER 3596269 L/Sgt A.

WALKER 3603968 Pte Joseph 20 Pl D Coy KiA 18.9.44, Bury, Lancashire

WALKER 3600710 L/Sgt Vincent

WALKER 3606558 Pte W.

WALL 3600926 Pte A.

WALL 3865803 Pte Harry W/M, KiA 21.9.44, Liverpool

WALLACE 14209579 Pte Cyril W/M 22.9.44 PoW XIB 117940, Carlisle

WALLACE 14671726 Pte Samuel M 22.9.44 PoW XIIA 24363, Wavertree, Liverpool 15

WALLACE 3606540 Pte Thomas 26.9.44 PoW IVB/XIIA 91942, Ardwick, Manchester

WALLWORK 3606538 Pte Walter 11 Pl B Coy W/M 20.9.44 PoW XIIA 075414, Salford, Lancashire

WARBURTON 409967 L/Sgt Richard M 26.9.44 PoW XIIA 91973, Crook, Co Durham

WARD 3602909 W/Cpl W.

WARREN 14641890 Pte William Scales KiA 22.9.44, Wallasey, Cheshire

WARRENER 4279142 Pte Reginald Benjamin M 25.9.44 PoW IVB 91875, Rugby, Warwickshire

WATSON 3602912 WS/Cpl Stanley 19 Pl D Coy M 20.9.44 PoW XIIA/VIIIC 075558/93613, Garton, nr Scarborough, Yorkshire

WATSON 3602924 WS/Sgt Thomas Pl Sgt 14 Pl B Coy M 20.9.44 KiA 21.9.44 Blyth, Northumberland

WATSON 3533468 Pte Thomas M 26.9.44 PoW XIIA/IVF 075696, Hessle, East Yorkshire

WAUGH 3603460 Pte Joseph 21 Pl D Coy Lt Holt's batman W/M 26.9.44 Rep-PoW aged 29, Whitehaven, Cumberland

WAUGH 3602914 Pte R. W/M 25.9.44 PoW St Leduine Hospital

WEARDON 3603346 Pte John C Coy, Preston, Lancashire

WEBB 14424829 Pte Alexander Kenneth B. M 26.9.44 PoW XIIA 91622, Surbiton, Surrey

WEBSTER 3598296 L/Cpl Freddie 15 Pl C Coy

WEBSTER 3602915 Pte Leonard W/M 24.9.44 XIB 118634

WELCH 7368099 Pte J. RAMC B Coy

WELLS 3606343 Pte James A/T Pl S Coy KiA 20.9.44, Oldham, Lancashire

WELSH 14578423 Pte Thomas William QM Section HQ Coy

WEST 14654984 Pte T.

WESTERMAN 4546681 Pte Ernest 23 Mortar Pl S Coy, Holbeck, Leeds

WHAITES 3606572 Pte K. 10 Pl A Coy

WHEELER 4693666 L/Cpl William 19 Pl D Coy M 25.9.44 PoW XIIA 91950, Methley, nr Leeds

WHITE 4547299 Pte Bernard W/M 22.9.44 PoW XIB 117501, Doncaster, West Yorkshire

WHITE 14277883 Pte Roy Stanley PoW VIIIC/XIIA 91722, Southampton, Hampshire

WHITEHOUSE 3599019 Pte Joshua W/M 19.9.44 PoW XIB 117734, Lamplugh, Cumberland

WHITFIELD 3602916 Pte Francis George 'General' 11 Pl B Coy W/M KiA 18.9.44, Redcar, Yorkshire

WHITWORTH 3444052 WS/Cpl Samuel 24 Mortar Pl S Coy W/M 20.9.44 PoW-Rep VIIIC 117083/93731, Bury, Lancashire

WIGHTMAN 3604115 Pte John KiA 25.9.44

WILCOCK 3856386 Pte T.

WILCOCKS 1077110 Pte Victor M 22.9.44 PoW XIIA 25561, Miles Platting, Manchester

WILLIAMS 3523577 Pte George Maurice W/M, KiA 20.9.44, Oldham, Lancashire

WILLIAMS 3854155 Pte Samuel M 21.9.44 PoW XIIA 075559, Worsley, nr Manchester

WILLIAMSON 3596704 Pte Robert Hugh M 25.9.44 PoW XIIA 075948, Seaham, Co Durham

WILSON 3608673 L/Cpl Albert 'Ginger' 11 Pl B Coy M 21.9.44 PoW XIIA 92112, Heysham, Lancashire

WILSON 3598436 W/Sgt D. ACC

WILSON 3606643 Pte George W/M 21.9.44, KiA 21/22.9.44, Haslingden, Lancashire

WILSON 4467355 Pte J. W/M 26.9.44 PoW XIB-Rep 118716, Parbold, nr Wigan, Lancashire

WILSON 3604965 Pte Matthew W/M 21.9.44 PoW XIB-Rep 117648, Newcastle-upon-Tyne

WINDROSS 3593849 Pte W. 'Marmy'

WINSTANLEY 14652869 Pte Joseph 13 Pl B Coy M 20.9.44 PoW XIB/Oflag 79 117286, St Helens, Lancashire

WOMBWELL 3598515 Pte George William W/M 25.9.44 PoW XIB-Rep 118187, Newcastle-upon-Tyne

WOOD 3603488 Pte Ernest M 22.9.44 PoW IVB 93263, Wigan, Lancashire

WOOD 14671738 Pte J. M 22.9.44 PoW IVB 26084

WRAGG 3605695 Pte J.

WRIGHT 14641910 Pte E.

WRIGHT 14674405 Pte James Land M 22.9.44 PoW XIB 118283, Bolton, Lancashire

WRIGHTON 14595060 Pte Raymond Bernard M 25.9.44 PoW XIIA 075945, Smallheath, Birmingham

YAPP 3597285 Pte Francis KiA 18.9.44, Sale, Cheshire

YARMAN 3597286 Pte Andrew M 21.9.44 PoW XIIA/IVB 075659, Blackpool, Lancashire

YOUNG 14638447 Pte Frederick William M 26.9.44 PoW XIB 118777, Chesterfield, Derbyshire

YOUNG 4547346 Pte John James M 22.9.44 PoW IVB 91971, Sheep Ridge, Huddersfield, West Yorkshire

Appendix 3

Honours and Awards

For their campaign service during the Second World War members of the Battalion qualified for all or some of the following - 1939-45 Star, Africa Star, Italy Star, France and Germany Star, Defence Medal, War Medal.

Distinguished Service Order (DSO)

MORGAN A/Lieutenant-Colonel Farrer Robert,
LG 11.7.40 1st Battalion att'd Royal Sussex Regiment

'For conspicuous ability and leadership in command of his Battalion during the 27th & 28th of May, his Battalion, greatly reduced in numbers by casualties, held a long sector at Rouse-Croix. No reserve except the carrier platoon was available. By his personal example of bravery when under enemy pressure & by his able use of the carrier platoon he maintained his line intact against heavy attack both by AFVs and infantry.'

NEILL A/Major William,
LG 9.11.44

'At 17.30 hrs on the 23rd September 1944 at ARNHEM after a heavy artillery and mortar concentration the enemy carried out a strong counter-attack supported by S.P. guns on the battalion position and succeeded in making a considerable penetration. Major Neill who had been wounded in four places but had refused to leave his post immediately organised a counter-attack with a few men he could muster. Leading his small force with great determination and with complete disregard for his own safety he drove the enemy out of the battalion position and quickly rectified what might have been a disastrous situation. Not satisfied with this he organised and personally led a patrol after dark into the enemy lines destroying the enemy HQ and causing such confusion that it prevented

the enemy from making any further attempts to attack. Throughout the nine days of ARNHEM Major Neill's devotion to duty and utter contempt for danger was an inspiration to all who served under him.'

TARLETON T/Brigadier Gerald Walden Browne MC,
OC 17th Infantry Brigade 5th Division, LG 21.10.43

'The capture as per schedule of both Syracuse and Augusta is regarded as directly attributable to this officer's drive and coolness. Throughout the whole of 10th of July he was constantly up with troops mortar and sniper fire. On the 12th of July when strong German resistance was first encountered in Priolo he immediately went forward to the front of the village which was then being heavily shelled. Having made a personal recce he got his brigade moving on the Augusta track by his own energy and drive in spite of considerable enemy resistance. During the move to Augusta he continually went forward under mortar and machine-gun fire. After arrival at Augusta late at night he was faced with an extremely difficult situation at dawn finding his brigade in a cup with enemy on two sides on the hills. Under heavy mortar and machine-gun fire he personally redisposed his brigade, driving the enemy in the surrounding lip of hills. His coolness and confidence have throughout all the operations in Sicily have been most inspiring to all ranks in his Brigade.'

Member of the Most Excellent Order of The British Empire (MBE)

BARNES Captain (QM) Harold S.,
LG 1.1.46 New Year Honours

SMITH Lieutenant T/Captain (QM) James William,
Border Regiment att'd HQ 50th Division, LG 18.2.43

'During operations 27 May to 2 July, Captain Smith as Camp Commandant 50 Div rendered

conspicuous service. In these five weeks of withdrawal of Rear H.Q., it was largely due to his efforts that, notwithstanding the frequent change of location necessitated by the battle, Rear H.Q. was always organised, the men fed and looked after. In addition to his manifold routine duties, he organised a reception station for stragglers and escaped Prisoners of War and looked after many units besides his own. Early in June, in order to meet the deficiency of RASC drivers, he organised a relief of drivers to take over the work of driving maintenance lorries up the GAZALA Pass. Day and night he never relaxed, and his constant cheerfulness and care of their welfare contributed greatly to the morale of the troops under his command. He has been Camp Commandant of this Div HQ for 2 years during which his work was first class.'

Military Cross (MC)

BUDGEN Lieutenant William George,
LG 23.12.43

'On the night of the glider borne operations against Sicily Lt. Budgen's glider landed about six miles from his correct landing place. He at once set off to join his Brigade & on route cut telephone wires. Later he fell in with a party from Brigade HQ & showed great dash & determination in leading his men in an attack on an enemy outpost. On the morning of the 10th Lt. Budgen acted as leading scout of a recce patrol which located an enemy coastal defence battery, in the subsequent attack Lt Budgen again distinguished himself. He showed great personal gallantry facing enemy machine-gun & rifle fire. By the end of the attack there were six enemy killed, five wounded and 40 prisoners. Throughout the whole period he remained cool calm & collected & by his bearing he inspired confidence in all those around him.'

GIBBON Major John,
Border Regiment att'd 46 Royal Marine Commando, LG 12.7.45

'On the night of 23rd March 1945 during the assault on the Rhine near Wesel, Capt. Gibbon commanded the leading troops of his command, in the first wave of the assault. Immediately before touching down, one of his LTV was hit and burst into flames thus reducing his strength by a quarter. Capt. Gibbon however led his troops inland at such a pace and with such determination that the enemy on the river bank were unable to check his advances. His objective was a farmhouse 500 yds inland and he pressed his advance so relentlessly behind the barrage put down by our guns that his Sergeant Major and another soldier fell by his side, casualties to our own shell fire. Without hesitation and with complete disregard for his own personal safety he led his men on to the objective where he killed three officers and took sixty prisoners. The capture of this vital position was entirely due to the dash and determination displayed by this officer.'

HARDY Lieutenant Joseph Stephenson, LG 9.11.44

'On the 18th at ARNHEM Lt. Hardy as signal officer was ordered to lay a signal cable from Battalion HQ to B Company which was an isolated detachment two miles from the remainder of the Battalion. Shortly after arrival in the Company area the enemy attacked in considerable strength and the Company was surrounded. Lt. Hardy immediately assumed duties as 2i/c and under the intense mortar and artillery fire he toured the Company area encouraging the men to greater efforts, when orders eventually reached the Company to break out and rejoin the Battalion. Lt. Hardy personally led the first troops through, still under fire he again went back and led some more men back to the Battalion position. Lt. Hardy's vigour and utter contempt for danger were an inspiration and source of encouragement to all around him.'

OLIPHANT Captain William Kingston Blair, 1 Border att'd 5 Border, LG 22.10.40

'At Tournai between May 16th & May 22nd Major Blair Oliphant's Company had a difficult and dangerous position on the banks of the Escaut Canal. For three days and nights his positions were subjected to incessant bombardment by air, mortar and enemy artillery fire. No inch of ground was at any time yielded by his Company. Through all the operations Major Blair Oliphant has shown the greatest devotion to duty & utter contempt for danger & his conduct has been an inspiration to all those serving under his command.'

WELCH Lieutenant William Gordon, LG 21.10.43 (recommended by Brig P. H. W. Hicks DSO MC)

'Lt. Welch who was commanding my Brigade Defence Platoon landed with his glider load in approximately the right area. He should normally have joined up with the remainder of the Brigade HQ, but no gliders were forthcoming. He immediately organised his force of 44 men & proceeded to Syracuse. On this journey he met & fought several small parties of Italians capturing nine. He arrived at the bridge at Syracuse & found it in possession of a platoon of the South Staffordshire Regiment. He at once helped to clarify the situation & organised

the two platoons in a defensive position. The bridge was heavily attacked with mortar and machine-gun fire from 11.00 hrs. to 17.00 hrs. when owing to casualties he was forced to surrender. As the enemy approached the bridge at about 16.00 hrs. Lt. Welch was wounded in the hip in a rough and tumble with three Italians. He feigned death & remained at his post with seven survivors until the bridge was retaken.'

George Medal (GM)

HALEY 3598957 Private Richard, LG 16.11.43

'During the airborne invasion of Sicily, the glider in which Haley was an occupant, came down in the sea. Between 8 pm on July 9th and 5.30 am on July 10th, the occupants of the glider were picked up by Landing Craft. On no fewer than nine occasions Pte Haley swam from the glider to the Landing Craft. The glider was swept by heavy seas and some of the crew, suffering from exposure, were unable to cling to the glider. Pte. Haley secured them to the fuselage. At least four members of the glider crew owe their lives to the gallantry and entire disregard for his own safety shown by Pte Haley.'

Distinguished Conduct Medal (DCM)

CLARK 3650449 Sergeant Sidney, LG 9.11.44

'At ARNHEM on the 28th September Sgt Clark was in command of a platoon detailed to clear the enemy from some woods who were becoming a threat to our main position. On entering the wood the platoon was pinned down by enemy fire from inside the wood. Sgt Clark however, regardless of his own personal safety carried on by himself, throwing grenades amongst the enemy. At the far end of the wood there was a tank, in a hull-down position engaging the main position from the flank. Sgt Clark immediately collected some grenades rushed to the tank, opened the top of the turret and dropped the grenades inside setting the tank on fire. During this whole period he was under very heavy enemy fire. His gallantry and leadership and devotion to duty were beyond all praise.'

HALL 3596685 L/Corporal Joseph, LG 12.2.42

(No citation details. Hall was captured whilst serving with the 1st Battalion in France in May 1940. After seven months in a PoW camp at Strasbourg, he escaped with a Capt Richard Broad, who had been taken PoW at St Valery and who was awarded the MC for escaping.)

USHER 3590496 Platoon Sergeant Major, later Lieutenant, Sidney Lewis, LG 11.9.40

'For exemplary courage and devotion to duty. On two consecutive occasions this Platoon Sergeant Major was in charge of an isolated rear-guard position when the posts on his right and left were destroyed by the enemy. Under heavy artillery and mortar fire, he, by his example, of cool determination inspired his platoon

to maintain the position until ordered to withdraw according to plan.'

Military Medal (MM)

GARDNER-ROBERTS 3603310 L/Sergeant Jackson LG 23.12.43, p5573

'At about 16.00hrs on 10th July 1943, Lance-Sergeant Gardner-Roberts, although severely wounded in the left shoulder and having wounds in the head, seeing that a handcart containing ammunition and a mine had caught fire in the vicinity of his post, moved out from cover under heavy fire and attempted to push the handcart over a bank out of range of the post. As he was unable to push the handcart he lifted the mine clear of the handcart before the remaining ammunition exploded. By his cool action under fire and disregarding his personal safety, Lance-Sergeant Gardner-Roberts probably saved serious casualties amongst the men of his post.'

McCLUSKIE 3596965 Private John, LG 10.3.42 p1109

'For devotion to duty under fire. On 21st. May, 1940, on the river ESCAUT this man as a regimental signaller, was a member of a line party sent out under shell fire to repair damaged cables. While the work was in progress a heavy concentration of H.E. and shrapnel came down on several other members of the party. This man regardless of personal safety, led the way back to go to their assistance. The following day he was again sent out as a linesman and despite bombing and machine gunning he remained at work for eleven hours until the line was repaired. His coolness and devotion to duty was a splendid example to others.'

O'NEILL 3783818 Private J. J., LG 9.11.44 p5130

'At Arnhem on 25 Sep 1944 C Company was ordered to evacuate its position at 23.00 hrs. At 22.00 hrs the enemy mounted a very strong counter attack against this company position which was successfully repulsed. A few minutes before the evacuation was due to commence a wounded man was seen lying near the enemy position. Pte. O'Neill immediately went out in an attempt to rescue him. Very heavy fire came down and Pte. O'Neill was pinned to the ground. Still determined, however, to rescue this wounded man, Pte. O'Neill again went forward and this time succeeded in reaching him. With complete disregard for his personal safety he carried the wounded man back to his Company lines under very heavy mortar and MG fire. Pte. O'Neill's contempt for danger at a time when the situation was extremely grave was an inspiration to all those around him. His fearlessness and devotion to duty were of a very high order.'

SMITH 3593710 CQMS James, LG 21.10.43 p4663

'Sicily 9/10 July 1943
CQMS Smith's glider landed away from the main body of the Bn. The glider load moved off

under the command of the Coy. Comd. On the move up an Italian position was encountered. This was attacked and captured. During the action the Coy Comd was very severely wounded and Smith received injuries in the hand and the head. He had his wounds dressed but insisted on accompanying the party to Bn. H.Q. Throughout the remainder of the day he displayed great courage and devotion to duty organising the defence of his Coy under fire. He did not proceed to hospital until the embarkation of his unit took place from Syracuse. His presence and unfailing cheerfulness in the face of adversity contributed largely to the spirit of optimism which remained with his unit throughout the battle.'

SWAN 3057009 Corporal James, LG 9.11.44 p5130

'At Arnhem on the 21 Sep 1944 the enemy carried out a strong frontal attack on C Company. While this very depleted company was engaging the enemy to its front, an enemy platoon with MG support attacked from the left. Cpl. Swan was in charge of the Company Support Group of six men. Without waiting orders he immediately engaged the enemy who were extremely determined, and pressed home their attack - Cpl. Swan however, so handled his small force that he halted the enemy. Not content, however, he attacked with bayonet and grenades and killed the greater proportion of the enemy platoon, the remainder fled. Cpl. Swan's gallant action undoubtedly saved a very critical situation. His leadership and devotion to duty were of a high order.

WARING 3597789 Corporal John, LG 21.10.43 p4663 (recommended for the DCM, granted an Immediate MM)

'Sicily 9/10 July 1943
Cpl Waring is Bn Signal Cpl. His glider crash landed on the beach during the night 9/10 Jul 43. There was no medical orderly in the glider and Cpl Waring dealt with the injured. While moving to join his Bn. a second glider was found which had also crashed. The glider was under light automatic fire from an Italian post nearby. Both glider pilots were injured and unable to move. Cpl. Waring approached the glider and managed to drag both glider pilots to a place of safety. He then dug a small slit trench for each of them with his entrenching tool. At this time grass and gorse caught fire close to the wounded pilots. Cpl. Waring at once attacked the fire and prevented it reaching the wounded men. All this was done under fire from the Italian position 100 yds. away. Having made the injured pilots as comfortable as possible, Cpl. Waring organised a small party of men and with one 2" Mortar which he had never fired before, assaulted and captured the Italian pill-box. He then proceeded on his way and during the march to rejoin his Bn encountered two more small Italian posts both of which he liquidated. At arrival at his BN H.Q. he continued to succour the wounded in the neighbourhood and to search for others who had been reported to be lying by crashed gliders. He was working incessantly from the time of landing until mid-day Jul 10 when he was picked up in an exhausted condition. It was

due to the self-sacrifice and devotion to duty of Cpl Waring that two glider pilots were brought to a position of safety and also to his powers of leadership and the initiative shown by him that three enemy posts were captured and the occupants killed.'

British Empire Medal (BEM)

O'HANLON 3783776 Private Henry, LG 24.2.44

'During the airborne operation on Sicily, on 9th July, 1943, the glider in which this man was flying came down in the sea at night some five miles off the coast of Sicily. Seeing two non-swimmers washed off the glider he went to their rescue in a very heavy swell and managed, although almost exhausted, to bring one man back to the glider, which had drifted about two hundred yards away, thus saving the man's life. Thereafter he kept up the spirits of the exhausted men on the glider until rescue craft arrived some seven hours later. He showed great courage and a complete disregard for his personal safety.'

C-in-C's Certificate

CONNETT 6198713 WO2 Fred, APTC att'd 1st Battalion (recommended for MM)

'At Arnhem on 23 September, during a critical phase of the battle communications were in grave danger of breaking down owing to the lack of wireless batteries. The route to the divisional dump itself was under constant artillery and mortar fire, and one party had already been killed in an attempt to get through the woods to the dump for fresh batteries. CSMI Connett realising the hazards, immediately volunteered to go personally for a re-supply of batteries. In spite of intense mortar and shell fire, and the danger of snipers in the woods, CSMI Connett made his way to the divisional dump and returned to Bn. HQ with them in time to keep communications open. No sooner had he completed this task than he again volunteered to carry ammunition to A Coy who were being very hard pressed, and were running short of supplies. Having carried out this task he then proceeded to organise and lead carrying parties for ammunition forward from the divisional dump.
This WO's utter disregard of danger, his outstanding devotion to duty, and his cheerful disposition under the most arduous conditions were an inspiration to all who came in contact with him.'

HUGHES 4462782 Corporal Vincent (recommended for MM)

'At ARNHEM on the 23 Sept. 1944 the enemy carried out a strong attack on C Company. Cpl. Hughes was signal NCO at Company HQ. His 18 set was rendered useless by enemy mortar fire. Cpl. Hughes immediately, on his own initiative, and in spite of heavy mortar and MG fire went out into the enemy positions and retrieved a new 18 set from a container which had been dropped into the enemy lines 38 hours previously. In a short time Cpl Hughes

had communications working again. Later in the same day his batteries ran down, and he again faced heavy fire to go out for fresh batteries. By his prompt action, and daring, communications were maintained at a time when the battle had reached a critical stage. His fearlessness and devotion to duty were of a very high order and contributed in no mean way to the success of the battle.'

KNOTT 3603391 Private Alfred (recommended for MM)

'At ARNHEM (HOLLAND) on the 21 September 1944, word was received at Bn. HQ that B Coy was surrounded by the enemy, and getting dangerously short of ammunition. Pte. Knott hearing this immediately volunteered to try and break through to them with a carrier. He was warned that the whole route to B Coy was under mortar and shell fire, and probably held by the enemy in places. Undaunted, he set off and managed to break through, delivered his ammunition and brought 8 prisoners back with him. His vehicle was hit and destroyed on the return journey, yet within an hour he again volunteered to make the same journey with extra ammunition and food. When on 22 Sept. the Bn. ammunition dump was set on fire he for two hours amidst exploding ammunition vehicles, dragged clear as many trailers, handcarts and boxes of ammunition as were still not burning, the whole area was being mortared all the time. Pte. Knott's cheerfulness, courage and devotion to duty was an example of the British soldier at his best.'

STEELE 14274547 L/Corporal James (recommended for MM)

'At ARNHEM on 23 Sep. 1944 A Coy area was in immediate danger of being overrun by SP guns and flame-thrower tanks. An urgent call for No. 82 grenades (Gammon Bombs) was made by the Coy, but there were none in the dump. L/Cpl. Steele had seen a container dropped by parachute in the woods some 500 yards from Bn. HQ. Although the woods were being subjected to heavy mortar and shell fire, and several men had been killed by snipers whilst trying to get supplies from the containers, L/Cpl. Steele volunteered to get into the woods and bring back some of the grenades. He completed his task, assembled the grenades and carried them to A Coy under heavy fire from the tanks. His gallant action enabled A Coy to beat off the tank attack and restore the situation. Throughout the action his devotion to duty was of the highest order.'

WRAGG 3605695 Private John (recommended for MM)

'At ARNHEM (HOLLAND) on the 25 Sept. 99, Pte. Wragg was a member of my section. At about 22.30hrs. on that date, as a sentry, he pointed out the fact that some enemy infantry had infiltrated to a nearby wood, some 70 yards distant. I went to explain the situation to my section and made plans to attack as we all know the enemy must be cleared to enable that the enemy retire. Pte. Wragg however, noticed in my absence that the enemy were putting a heavy MG in position, and realised that the few minutes it would take to lay on an attack might be fateful. Without any thought for his own safety he rushed the enemy post with grenades before the gun opened up and thereby saved the situation. He also gained information about the enemy which was passed to my Company Commander.'

Mention-in-Despatches (MiD)

BLAIR-OLIPHANT Lieutenant-Colonel

BOOTH 3603643 Private J.

BUTLER 3595096 L/Sergeant Cyril
(recommended for MM 6.40)

'For exemplary courage in the saving of life. On the ESCAUT CANAL on 20th May, 1940, a section post was destroyed by mortar fire. This N.C.O. exposed to heavy direct machine-gun fire from the enemy made his way to the post three times carrying back two wounded and one killed, and helping the two other wounded members of the section to get back.'

COWBURN Captain John Cyril Livingstone
(recommended for MC 6.40)

'For persistent devotion to duty. On 28th May, 1940, this officer set off to reconnoitre the route to bring up rations to the Battalion in the front lines. He was captured and disarmed by the enemy, escaped and immediately set out again with the ration party in an attempt to force his way through the enemy lines to deliver rations to his Battalion.'

FAIRWEATHER 3595171 L/Corporal Alfred Patterson
(recommended for MM 19.6.40)

'For conspicuous courage near FROYENNES on 20th. May, 1940. For five hours he made repeated journeys as a stretcher bearer evacuating wounded from a post which was being mortared, across an anti tank ditch, and over open ground. The whole was continually under machine gun fire and in full view of the enemy.'

GAVAGHAN 3443816 L/Corporal Charles
(recommended for MM)

'At ARNHEM (HOLLAND) on the 22 September 1944 the wireless communication from C Coy to Bn. HQ had completely broken down. C Coy at that time were being attacked by a greatly superior enemy force. L/Cpl. Gavaghan, who by that time was the only signaller available at Bn. HQ, volunteered to attempt to break through to C Coy with a telephone line and equipment to repair the wireless set. The route to C Coy was under extremely heavy Mortar and artillery fire, and enemy snipers had infiltrated into the woods and were sniping at the slightest movement. L/Cpl. Gavaghan, without any regard for his personal safety, took the line, managed to get to the forward positions at the time of the attack, and sent back information that enabled Bn. HQ to lay on artillery support. The fact that communication was re-opened, saved the Company from being overrun and it was the courage and devotion to duty of L/Cpl.

Gavaghan only that opened communications. His action was an outstanding example, and an inspiration to all that were in the same area as he was working.'

GRINLEY Lieutenant P. N.

HASWELL Major R. H.

INGRAM T/Captain Harry Barnett
(recommended for MC)

'On 23 Sep 1944 at ARNHEM Capt. Ingram was Commander of the three inch Mortar Group. A very heavy enemy attack began to develop at 10.00hrs. with very heavy mortar, shell and MG fire. The Mortar positions were well registered by the enemy, but Capt. Ingram continued to move about under heavy fire encouraging his men, and, when his Communications broke down, he personally directed the fire of his mortars, until one by one his mortars were knocked out. About this time the enemy attacked A Company with tanks, and Capt. Ingram was sent to take over command of A Company which had now lost all its officers and was in a very critical situation with two enemy tanks in the middle of the Company area. Still under heavy fire Capt. Ingram immediately proceeded to the Company area, quickly appreciated the situation and rectified it, causing one enemy tank to be destroyed and the other driven off, and the company front to be stabilised. Capt. Ingram both as Mortar group commander and as company commander was a continual source of inspiration to his men, showing at all times gallantry and devotion to duty of a high order. PTO'

MACKAY Major C. S., twice

MILLER Major Arthur Summers (twice)

'For gallantry and devotion to duty at Lille. On 28th May 1940, this young officer showed a complete disregard for personal danger when, under shell fire and machine-gun fire, he carried out a lone reconnaissance to a distance of 4 kilometres, located the enemy and brought back most useful information.'

MORGAN A/Lieutenant-Colonel F. R. H.

ROWELL Captain Rev John 123732 RAChD att'd

'At ARNHEM during the operation of the 1st Airborne Division Capt. Rev. Rowell CF worked in the RAP assisting the Medical Officer. Throughout the whole of this period Capt. Rowell was a continuous source of comfort to the wounded, and his tirelessness and fearlessness in working at the RAP, which was frequently under accurate and heavy shell fire was an inspiration to all who saw him. His continual energy in nursing the wounded resulted in the saving of the lives of many who might otherwise have died of their wounds.'

SKILTON Lieutenant Douglas Harry
(recommended for MC)

'On the 23 September at ARNHEM, Lieut. Skilton was acting Intelligence Officer, and administrative officer. Bn. HQ was accurately

registered by the enemy, and any movement around it brought down a hail of fire. At the same time the entire Battalion area was being subjected to continuous mortar and shell fire. Ignoring all dangers, Lieut Skilton was constantly moving around the Battalion positions collecting information, keeping abreast of the ever-changing situation and answering the urgent requests of companies for more ammunition and supplies by organising and conducting carrying parties. Although men were falling on all sides he continued to carry out his most hazardous tasks with great daring and utter contempt of danger. It was largely through his untiring efforts that the supplies reached the forward companies, enabling them to continue the battle.'

STOCKWELL Captain Robert
(recommended 19.6.40)

'For cool courage and devotion to duty. On the beach at DUNKIRK on 29th. & 30th. May, 1940 when the sands were heavily shelled by the enemy, this young officer in charge of three companies of the Battalion, by his sangfroid and personal example restrained his men from the general rush to embark, maintained complete control and discipline, thereby obviating unnecessary casualties, and finally embarked his men as an organised body on one ship, in spite of severe enemy bombing from the air.'

WOODS 3595644 L/Corporal Albert Frank
(recommended for MM 19.6.40)

'For persistent devotion to duty and conspicuous courage on 20th. & 21st. May, near FROYENNES. With total disregard of personal danger he repeatedly exposed himself to Rifle and Machine gun fire to tend the wounded and without hesitation cleared casualties on his Company's front from positions which were under heavy mortar and shell fire.'

FOREIGN AWARDS

Dutch Bronze Lion/Star

HOLMAN Lieutenant Michael Robert,
LG 18.3.47/20.3.47 (recommended for MC)

'On 23 September 1944 at ARNHEM the enemy carried out a very strong counter attack on the Battalion positions, and defensive fire from our three inch mortars was urgently required. The enemy counter-battery fire had accurately registered our mortar positions, and many of the mortars and their teams had been destroyed; furthermore the least activity on the part of our mortars brought down heavy fire on their positions. Knowing full well the dangers about him, Lieut. Holman immediately organised further mortar teams and brought them into action with great accuracy, causing confusion in the enemy attacks. Although his men were being killed and wounded around him, Lieut. Holman continued to move from one mortar team to another directing their fire and giving them encouragement until, when all his ammunition was exhausted, and all his mortars had been knocked out, he was forced to collect his few remaining men together as an infantry section, which he proceeded to lead with the same vigour and disregard of danger as he displayed with his mortars.'

Dutch Bronze Cross

GAVAGHAN 3443816 L/Corporal Charles, 20.3.47
(See entry for MiD above)

US Distinguished Service Cross

BREESE Major Charles Frederick Osborne, LG 14.11.47

'On September 22 an unpleasant situation had developed on the south of the Brigade sector in the Arnhem position. All officers had become casualties and the enemy by persistent attacks had effected a penetration. Major Breese with a scratch force of one platoon Border Regiment, 40 Parachutists and 35 Poles was sent down with orders to stabilize the situation and be prepared to counter-attack the enemy. As soon as the area was reached heavy mortar and artillery fire was laid on by the enemy and the Poles were reduced to 16 men, other units also suffering heavily. The situation was critical, but Major Breese immediately asserted his authority, and by his own personal bearing scothed the remainder of his force and within an hour was able to report "All in order". The area occupied by his force was subjected, until the evacuation, to some of the most intense fire, but the troops held, and offensive patrols were sent out with good results. Major Breese was wounded on September 23, but refused to be evacuated until south of the river. It was entirely due to this officer's strong personality, fine example and fearless behaviour that his force was able to hold on to a position that was of paramount importance to the Divisional perimeter.'

US Silver Star

ROBERTS Captain A. D.,
LG 16.1.47/20.3.47

WEBSTER Corporal Frederick, 14.11.47

US Bronze Star

DUNNE 7265478 L/Corporal John Gerald
(recommended for MM)

'At ARNHEM on September 18 1944, L/Cpl. Dunne was medical orderly to B Company which was on an isolated detachment. The Company was subjected to very heavy mortar and MG fire and there were numerous casualties. L/Cpl. Dunne, entirely oblivious of all danger went out in the face of this fierce fire to attend to the wounded and to bring them back to the company aid post. In order to reach the

crew of an anti-tank gun who had been badly wounded, L.Cpl. Dunne had to climb a six-foot wall still under intense fire. Wherever the battle was fiercest, L.Cpl. Dunne was to be found, tending the wounded with no thought for himself. His courage and devotion to duty in the face of grave danger were of the highest order.'

FIELDING 3383531 CSM Leslie S.,
LG 14.11.47

TARLETON Brigadier G. W. B.,
LG 23.7.48

Norway - King Haakon VII Liberty Cross

BREESE Lieutenant-Colonel C. F. O.,
LG 16.3.48/19.3.48

Norway - King Haakon VII Liberty Medal

DOUGLAS T/Captain Colin Martin, 19.3.48

KEARNS WO1 (RSM) Patrick,
LG 16.3.48/19.3.48

RECOMMENDATIONS

BENNETT 3595204 L/Sergeant Joseph
(recommended for Medal of the Order of the British Empire 6.10.40 for NYHL 1941)

'From September, 1939 until October, 1940 this N.C.O. has been in charge of the stretcher bearers of this unit, and has carried out his duties in a highly meritorious manner in circumstances both dangerous and trying in France, and on the sea crossing back from Dunkirk. He has shown himself untiring both in the dangerous work and tending the wounded in the field, and in training stretcher bearers for this work.'

BLACK Captain Godfrey Greenwell RAMC, att'd
(recommended for MBE 6.10.40 for NYHL 1941)

'This officer by his devotion to duty and untiring work throughout the campaign in France, has guarded the health of his unit in a most remarkable manner. Throughout this time, whatever the danger, and however long the stretch of his working hours, he has tended the wounded and sick without fail.'

BRADSHAW 3592640 QMS (ORS) Thomas
(recommended for MBE 6.10.40 for NYHL 1941)

'This W.O. has performed service of a high degree of merit during the period September,

1939 to October, 1940. In particular, after all the Orderly Room documents had been lost at Dunkirk, by his untiring devotion to duty, by his long hours of work and unruffled temper has very greatly facilitated the reorganisation of his unit in extremely trying conditions.'

CLARK 3596467 Bandsman Donald Reginald Bernard
(recommended for MM 19.6.40)

'For conspicuous devotion to duty and courage on 22nd. May, 1940, near TOURNAI when he advanced alone under machine gun and rifle fire to a section post, which was in full view of the enemy and was being heavily shelled, to tend the wounded. Later he returned, led forward a party of stretcher bearers and brought back his casualties under heavy fire.'

GORBELL 3593885 Corporal Harry
(recommended for the Medal of The Order of The British Empire 6.10.40 for NYHL 1941)

'This N.C.O. throughout the whole of the period from September, 1939 to October, 1940 - more particularly during the reorganisation after Dunkirk - he has by long hours of work and exceptional ability greatly contributed to the maintenance, equipment, and rationing of the Battalion.'

MILLER Lieutenant Arthur Sumner
(recommended for MBE 6.10.40 for NYHL 1941)

'As Battalion Liaison Officer at Brigade Headquarters in France in May, 1940 this officer showed remarkable zeal, courage and devotion to duty in keeping the Battalion in touch with Brigade Headquarters in most dangerous and trying conditions. Throughout the period from September, 1939 to October, 1940, the work of this young officer as Company Commander and Acting/Adjutant has been exceptionally faithful and meritorious.'

STOCKWELL Captain Robert
(recommended for MBE 6.10.40 for NYHL 1941)

'This officer from September, 1939, until October, 1940, has carried out with remarkable zeal and devotion to duty his work as Signal Officer in trying and dangerous conditions. At Dunkirk, by his example and initiative, he enabled three companies of his Unit to be embarked as organised Units on a destroyer without loss of lives. Throughout the Campaign in France he was untiring in his efforts to keep the Signal communications working, often in dangerous and trying conditions.'

Appendix 4

Gliders and Loads, Glider and Personnel Casualties for Operation LADBROKE/HUSKY

Gliders and their loads for Operation 'Ladbroke'

This Appendix is based on the original loading manifests in 1st Battalion operational orders, the official report on the 1st Air-Landing Brigade's part in the operation, and personal reminiscences of veterans. The names of the Glider Pilots are also taken from the above-named report and research collated by Major H. N. Andrews DFM and Bar. Where Glider Pilots lost their lives, the Memorial or Cemetery reference is included in brackets after their names. Some of the pilots and loads may have been altered prior to take-off; certainly RSM Gardner, listed in Waco No 127, actually flew to Sicily, landed and was killed on 10 July.

Abbreviations
AFU   Army Film Unit
MT   Motor Transport
CM   Cassino Memorial, Italy
SWC   Syracuse War Cemetery, Sicily
BB   'Blitz Buggy' or Jeep

Airfield C - all Wacos towed by C-47s

55   SEA Major J. Place and Major-Gen Hopkinson - 15 Pl C Coy: Officer and 15 ORs

56   SEA S/Sgt Reg Dance and Sgt Ernest Barker (10.7.43 CM) - 19 Pl D Coy: Officer and 15 ORs

57   SEA Lt Buchan and F/O Rau - Bn HQ I:

CO, Batman, Adjt, RSO with 18 Set, Man Defence Section, 2 Signallers with 18 Sets, 2 Signallers with 68 Sets, MO, Intelligence Sgt, 1 man Intelligence Section, handcart

58   SEA Lt Michael Bourke Connel (10.7.43 CM) and Sgt Herbert D. J. Hill (10.7.43 CM) - Bn HQ II: 2i/c, Batman, IO, Signal Sgt with 18 Set, 1 man Defence Section, 2 Signallers with 18 Sets, 2 Signallers with 68 sets, RAMC Sgt, 2 men Intelligence Section, handcart

59   SEA S/Sgt Barclay and Sgt Shirley - 15 Pl C Coy: Sgt and 8 men, 2 men R Coy, Policeman Bn HQ, handcart

60   SEA S/Sgt John Arthur Boorman (10.7.43 CM) and F/O Diewaltowski - 19 Pl D Coy: Sgt and 8 men, 2 men R Coy, Provost Sgt Bn HQ, handcart

61   SEA Lt Iremonger and Sgt Cole - A Coy: OC Coy, Batman, CSM, Clerk, Nursing Orderly, Bugler, 2 Signallers with 18 Sets, Bren Cpl, 3 Pioneers, 2 Bren Nos, 2 2-inch Mortar men

63   LAND SSM Wally Masson and Sgt Denis L. Casson - C Coy: OC Coy, Batman, CSM, Clerk, Nursing Orderly, Bugler, 2 Signallers with 18 sets, 2 Bren Nos, 2 2-inch Mortar men, 3 Pioneers, Bren Cpl

64   SEA Lt Godman and Lt Hayes USAF - D Coy: OC Coy, Batman, CSM, Clerk, Nursing Orderly, Bugler, 2 Signallers with 18 sets, 2 Bren Nos, 2 2-inch Mortar men, 3 Pioneers, Bren Cpl

65   SEA/LAND Sgt D. E. Baker and Sgt Robert Risdale Burton (9.7.43 CM), and Sgt E. D. Baker - 7 Pl A Coy: Officer and 15 ORs

67   LAND Sgt Jack Battersby and Sgt Richard N. Clarke - C Coy: 2 2-inch Mortar men, 2 3-inch Mortar men, 2 MT, 2 Signallers Bn HQ, trolley, 2 handcarts

68   SEA Sgt Ellis and Sgt Bates - 20 Pl D Coy: Officer and 15 ORs

69   LAND Sgt Lawrence Nicholas Ryan (9.7.43 CM) and Sgt C. J. Smith - 7 Pl

A Coy: Sgt, 8 men, 2 men R Coy, 1 man Intelligence Section, handcart

71   SEA S/Sgt George Arthur Leonard Reeves (9.7.43 CM) and F/O Daves - 16 Pl C Coy: Officer and 15 ORs

72   SEA S/Sgt Hay and Sgt George Albert Victor Hill (10.7.43 SWC 5.A.10) - 20 Pl D Coy: Sgt and 8 men, 2 men R Coy, Loading Officer, handcart

73   SEA Sgt Geoffrey Scriven and Sgt Donald Edwin Witham (9.7.43 CM) - 8 Pl A Coy: Officer and 15 ORs

74   SEA Sgt Leadbetter and F/O Dees - B Coy: OC, Batman, CSM, Clerk, Nursing Orderly, Bugler, 2 Signallers with 18 sets, Bren Cpl, 3 Pioneers, 2 Bren Nos, 2 2-inch Mortar men

75   SEA Sgt Peter Mansfield and Sgt Robert Alistair McLeod - 16 Pl C Coy: Sgt and 8 men, 2 men R Coy, Nursing Orderly Bn HQ, handcart

76   LAND Sgt Stewart and Sgt Joyce - 21 Pl D Coy: Lt Sainty and 15 ORs

77   SEA S/Sgt Peter Lawrence Gray Hampshire (10.7.43 CM) and Sgt John Elliott Randall (10.7.43 CM) - 8 Pl A Coy: Sgt J. Davidson, 8 men, 2 men R Coy, Orderly Room Clerk, handcart

78   SEA Sgt McLean and Sgt H. Brown - B Coy HQ: Sgt Support Group, 2 Bren Nos, 3 3-inch Mortar men, 1 MT, 2 handcarts

79   LAND Sgt Len Raggett and Sgt Harvey Rossdale - C Coy: Sgt Support Group, 2 Bren Nos, Nursing Orderly, 3 3-inch Mortar men, MT

80   LEFT ON AIRFIELD/LAND Sgt Owen Morgan and Sgt Russell - 21 Pl D Coy: Sgt, 8 men, 2 men R Coy, AFU man, handcart

Airfield D - all Wacos towed by C-47s
Nos 101A, 102A, 103A and 104A added to Load Table. EX-BIGOT instructions to 1 Border Appendix F 7.7.43.

81   LAND Lt Ian Alexander McArthur and

Lt Tom Breach - 17 Pl C Coy: Lt Crittenden and 15 ORs

82 SEA Sgt Stan Peacock and Sgt George Cushing - D Coy: 2i/c Coy, Batman, Signaller with 18 Set, Nursing Orderly, 3 3-inch Mortar men, Storeman, 2 handcarts

83 RETURNED TO MALTA WITHOUT RELEASING S/Sgt Stan Coates and Sgt Vic Perry - A Coy: 2i/c, Batman, Signaller with 18 Set, Nursing Orderly, 3 3-inch Mortar men, Storeman, 2 handcarts

84 SEA S/Sgt Bridges and Sgt David Goode Jones (9.7.43 CM) - 11 Pl B Coy: Lt Louden and 15 ORs

85 RETURNED S/Sgt Stewart and Sgt Guinan - 17 Pl C Coy: Sgt and 8 men, 2 men R Coy, man Divisional Provost, handcart

86 LAND Capt T. D. M. McMillan and Lt Bernard Halsall - D Coy: Sgt Support Group, 2 Bren Nos, Nursing Orderly, 3 3-inch Mortar men, 1 MT, 2 handcarts

87 SEA S/Sgt Alec George Shepherd (9.7.43 CM) and F/O McCullem - A Coy: Sgt Support Group, 2 Bren Nos, Nursing Orderly, 3 3-inch Mortar men, 1 MT, 2 handcarts

88 LAND Sgt Ken A. Evans and Sgt Richard E. Martin - 11 Pl B Coy: Sgt and 8 men, 2 men R Coy, Signaller Bn HQ, handcart

89 SEA Sgt Henry James Aylott (9.7.43 CM) and F/O Wilson - C Coy: 2i/c, Batman, Signaller with 18 Set, Nursing Orderly, 3 3-inch Mortar men, Storeman, 2 handcarts

90 SEA Sgt Jack Frampton and Sgt Paddy Cooke - D Coy: 2 2-inch Mortar men, 2 3-inch Mortar men, 2 MT, Nursing Orderly Bn HQ, Policeman Bn HQ, 2 handcarts

91 SEA Sgt Anderson or possibly Sgt Jack Caslaw and Sgt Frederick Highfield Street (14.7.43 CM) - A Coy: 2 2-inch Mortar men, 2 3-inch Mortar men, 2 MT, Padre Rowell Bn HQ, Pioneer Sgt Bn HQ, 2 handcarts

92 SEA Sgt Hill and F/O Gunter - 12 Pl B Coy: Lt A. R. Royall and 15 ORs

93 LAND Sgt Douglas Edward Kent (10.7.43 SWC II.F.11) and Sgt Purcell - C Coy: Signaller, Nursing Orderly, NCO and 3 men R Coy, MO's Batman, Nursing Orderly Bn HQ, 2 handcarts

94 SEA Sgt Robert Brown Hall (9.7.43 CM) and Flying Officer Hollinshead - D Coy: Signaller, Nursing Orderly, NCO and 3 men R Coy, Signaller and Medical Orderly Bn HQ, 3 handcarts

95 LAND Sgt Mick Pryor and Sgt Eric Rowbotham - A Coy: Signaller, NCO and 3 men R Coy, Nursing Orderly, RSO's Batman, one man AFU or CSM H Coy, 2 handcarts

96 SEA Lt Stevens and F/O White - 12 Pl B Coy: Sgt V. De Muynck and 8 men, 2 men R Coy, Policeman Bn HQ, handcart

97 SEA Sgt William John Percy (9.7.43 CM) and Sgt Reddish - 18 Pl C Coy: Officer and 15 ORs

98 SEA Sgt William Joseph Sleigh and Sgt Donald Tasker - 22 Pl D Coy: Officer and 15 ORs

99 SEA Sgt Victor Taylor and F/O Samek USAF - 9 Pl A Coy: Officer and 15 ORs

100 SEA Sgt Worley and F/O Capite - 13 Pl B Coy: Lt McCartney and 15 ORs

101 SEA S/Sgt Henden and Sgt L. Turner - 18 Pl C Coy: Sgt and 8 men, 2 men R Coy, Medical Orderly Bn HQ, handcart

101A SEA Sgt Jeavons and Sgt Westerby - H Coy: Officer and 12 ORs

102 SEA Sgt Cole and Sgt Dennis Norman Willis (9.7.43 CM) - 22 Pl D Coy: Sgt and 8 men 22 Pl D Coy, 2 men R Coy, Nursing Orderly 181 Field Ambulance, 2 handcarts

102A DID NOT TAKE OFF/NO TUG AVAILABLE H Coy: Officer and 12 men

103 SEA Sgt Tommy Gillies and F/O Browning USAF - 9 Pl A Coy: Sgt and 8 men, 2 men R Coy, man Divisional Provost, handcart

103A DID NOT TAKE OFF/NO TUG AVAILABLE H Coy: Officer and 12 ORs

104 SEA Sgt Turner and Sgt Flanders - 13 Pl B Coy: Sgt and 8 men, 2 men R Coy, Nursing Orderly 181 Field Ambulance, handcart

104A DID NOT TAKE OFF/NO TUG AVAILABLE H Coy: 13 ORs

Airfield F - all Wacos towed by Albemarles

106 LAND S/Sgt Kay Cawood and S/Sgt Bert Holt - Bn HQ III: Pioneer Officer, Batman, OC S Coy, man Defence Section, 2 men Recce Pl, Nursing Orderly, Sgt Smith (QM), handcart Recce Pl, handcart Pioneer Pl

107 LAND S/Sgt James Cyril Carr (10.7.43 SWC II.F.7) and S/Sgt Matthews - 10 Pl A Coy: Officer and 15 ORs

108 LAND S/Sgt Douglas and Sgt Donald - B Coy: Coy 2i/c, Batman, Signaller with 18 Set, Nursing Orderly, 3 3-inch Mortar men, Storeman, handcart

109 LAND S/Sgt Wood and Sgt Isaacs - H Coy: Lt E. S. Newport OC Pl, 2 men 6-pounder gun

110 LAND Lt Boucher-Giles and Sgt Miller - H Coy: Sgt Hodge, 2 men, 6-pounder gun

111 SEA S/Sgt Arthur Prescott and Sgt Scott - 10 Pl A Coy: Sgt and 8 men, 2 men R Coy, Medical Orderly Bn HQ, handcart

112 SEA Sgt Bayley and Sgt Linscott - B Coy: 2 2-inch Mortar men, 2 3-inch Mortar men, 2 men MT, Medical Orderly and Signaller Bn HQ, 2 handcarts

113 RETURNED S/Sgt MacDonald and Sgt Welsh - H Coy: 4 men, BB, 20 6-pounder rounds

114 SEA Sgt Struthers and Sgt Southey - H Coy: 4 men, BB, 20 6-pounder rounds

115 LAND S/Sgt Ferguson and Sgt Rye - Recce Pl: OC Pl, Batman, Officer, 8 men, Signaller Bn HQ with 18 set, handcart

116 LAND Sgt Sharpe and Sgt V. C. Webb - B Coy: Signaller, Nursing Orderly, NCO and 3 men R Coy, 2 Signallers Bn HQ, Signal Trolley, 2 handcarts

117 SEA S/Sgt Whale and S/Sgt John Russell Wheatley (19.7.43 CM) - H Coy: Batman, 2 men 6-pounder

118 SEA S/Sgt Roddy MacKenzie and Sgt Ralph Webb - H Coy: 2 men 6-pounder

119 SEA S/Sgt Waldron and Sgt Harris - Recce Pl: 2i/c Pl Lt Costeloe, Batman, Lt Coulston, 8 men, Signaller Bn HQ, 2 handcarts

120 RETURNED Sgt Reed and Sgt W. Gill - 14 Pl B Coy: Lt W. P. Stott and 15 ORs

121 RETURNED S/Sgt MacKenzie and S/Sgt Edwards - H Coy: 4 men, BB, 20 6-pounder rounds

122 LAND (N AFRICA) Sgt Gordon Patterson and an American WO Locart - H Coy: 4 men, BB, 20 6-pounder rounds

123 LAND S/Sgt Chapman and Sgt Kelly - Recce Pl: Sgt, Orderly, Officer, 8 men, Nursing Orderly, handcart

124 SEA S/Sgt Hedley James Iron (9.7.43 CM) and Sgt Geoffrey Edward Nelson (9.7.43 CM) - 14 Pl B Coy: Sgt Gorbells and 8 men, 2 men R Coy, Signaller Bn HQ, handcart

125 RETURNED Sgt John T. Braybrook and Sgt Atkins - Mortar Pl: Officer, Batman, 10 Mortar men, 9 men R coy, 5 trolleys, 2 3-inch Mortars and 132 bombs. (Tug aircraft Albemarle had oil leak in engine - returned to strip and not allowed to take off again. Men divided between 125 and 125A.)

125A LAND Lt W. J. Carn MC and Sgt David William John Richards (12.7.43 SWC III.G.10) - Mortar Platoon

126 LAND S/Sgt Chandler and S/Sgt Torrance - Mortar Pl: Sgt, Orderly, 10 Mortar men, Anti-tank man, 8 men R Coy, 5 trolleys, 2 3-inch Mortars, 132 bombs. (Men divided between 126 and 126A.)

126A RETURNED S/Sgt Nutton and Sgt Davitt - Mortar Platoon

127 PULLED OFF AFTER TAKE-OFF Sgt Pavitt and Sgt Boucher - Bn HQ IV: RSM, NCO R Coy, 6 men R Coy, handcart

Gliders taking off from Airfields C and F carrying non-Battalion personnel

62 C SEA Sgt Dixie Lee and F/O Johnson USAF - Section 181 Field Ambulance

66 C SEA S/Sgt T. G. Laidlaw and Sgt Simons - Section 181 Field Ambulance

70 C SEA Sgt Dilnutt and F/O Birdewick - Section 181 Field Ambulance

105 F LAND Capt Boyd and Sgt Bannister - RE Sub-Section: Officer and 11 ORs, handcart

Y F SEA Sgt Jim Pearson and Sgt George Curry - RE Sub-Section: Sgt and 11 men, handcart

Glider and personnel casualties for Operation 'Husky'

Gliders

Took off	72
Landed in sea	44
Landed in Sicily	20
Landed in Africa	7
Landed in Malta	1

Personnel

	Officers	ORs	
Took off	43	753	
Landed in sea	28	478	= 64%
Landed in Sicily	11	191	= 25%
Landed in Africa	3	77	= 10%
Landed in Malta	1	7	= 1%

Analysis - Sea personnel

Landed in sea	28	478	
Drowned		2	
Missing believed drowned	1	71	} = 23%
Missing at sea	1	39	
Killed enemy action at sea		2	
Wounded enemy action at sea		2	} = 1%
Picked up	14	275	= 57%
Swam ashore	12	86	= 19%
Swam ashore wounded in action	2	4	
Swam ashore killed in action		1	

Analysis - Land personnel

Landed in Sicily	11	191	
Wounded in crashes	4	34	} = 19%
Killed in crashes		1	
Wounded in action	1	18	} = 12%
Killed in action		6	

Casualties

Killed in crash, action, or drowned and buried		12	
Wounded	7	58	
Missing believed drowned, or missing	2	110	
Total casualties	9	180	= 24%

BNAF   *Signed by Colin Douglas Capt*
3 Aug 43. NAK.   *Adjt 1st Bn The Border Regiment*

Distribution: CO, 2IC, Adjt, IO, All Coys, War Diary (2)

Appendix 5

Officers' Roll for North Africa and Sicily

Lt Col George V. Britten MBE, Commanding Officer
Major Tommy Haddon, 2i/c
Captain N. A. H. Stafford, Adjutant
Lt Ronald C. Hope-Jones, IO
Lt Douglas H. Skilton, OC Pioneer Platoon

Capt Geoffrey Costeloe, Recce Platoon
Lt William G. Budgen, Recce Platoon
Lt J. C. Law, Recce

Lt Joe S. D. Hardy, RSO
Capt C. R. W. Scruby, MTO
Lt J. Horsley, A/MTO
Lt H. S. Barnes, QM
Capt Godfrey G. Black, MO
Rev John Rowell, Padre

Lt Barry B. Ingram, LO
2/Lt Ronald R. Jack, ALO

Lt Gordon Welch, OC Brigade Defence Platoon

Capt W. Howard Wilkie, OC R Coy
Capt T. W. Ingram Cleasby
Capt Dennis R. L. Morrissey, rear party for ops
Capt Bob Stockwell, OC Training Compamy

Major T. P. H. Du Boulay, OC S Company
Capt Richard H. Stewart MC, 2i/c
Lt Robert M. A. Reese, A/T
Lt Edward S. Newport, A/T
Lt Colin M. Douglas
Lt George B. Coulthard, Mortar

Major John D. Gibbon, OC A Company
Capt William K. Hodgson, 2i/c
Lt John M. Bainbridge
2/Lt J. Anthony Howe
Lt Robert H. Coulston
Lt Baldwin Wilson

Capt T. W. Armstrong, OC B Coy
Capt W. Neill, 2i/c
Lt Grant Louden
2/Lt Arthur R. Royall
Lt John S. G. McCartney
Lt W. Pat Stott

Major Freddie W. Fineron, OC C Company
Capt T. E. Montgomery, 2i/c
Lt Arthur W. Springbett
2/Lt Alan T. Green
2/Lt Robert C. Crittenden
Lt Mike R. Holman

Major H. Stuart Cousens, OC D Company
Capt Ernie W. R. Gaff, 2i/c
Lt Joe Tate
Lt Philip J. Wyatt
2/Lt W. C. Sainty

Lt J. H. Rees
Lt J. Mears
2/Lt J. MacFadyen
2/Lt Pat Baillie
2/Lt Alan H. Cox

Appendix 6

Proposed Establishment of an Air Landing Battalion, August 1943, and Composition of the Seaborne Tail

Airborne Infantry Battalion - Proposed War Establishment, August 1943

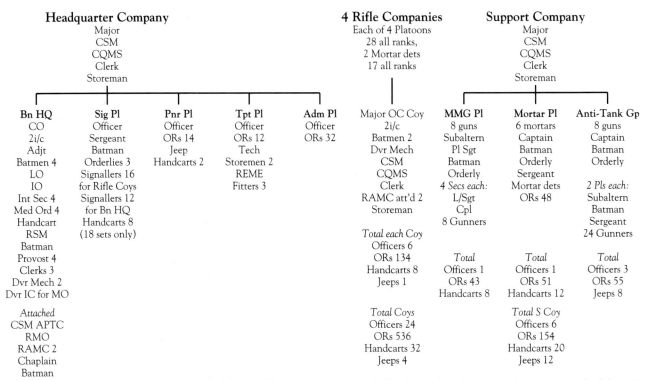

Headquarter Company
Major
CSM
CQMS
Clerk
Storeman

4 Rifle Companies
Each of 4 Platoons
28 all ranks,
2 Mortar dets
17 all ranks

Support Company
Major
CSM
CQMS
Clerk
Storeman

Bn HQ
CO
2i/c
Adjt
Batmen 4
LO
IO
Int Sec 4
Med Ord 4
Handcart
RSM
Batman
Provost 4
Clerks 3
Dvr Mech 2
Dvr IC for MO

Attached
CSM APTC
RMO
RAMC 2
Chaplain
Batman

Total Bn HQ
Officers 7
ORs 29
Jeeps 3

Total HQ Coy
Officers 12
ORs 132
Jeeps 15
Handcarts 11

Grand total Bn
Officers 42
ORs 818
Handcarts 63
Jeeps 34

Sig Pl
Officer
Sergeant
Batman
Orderlies 3
Signallers 16
for Rifle Coys
Signallers 12
for Bn HQ
Handcarts 8
(18 sets only)

Pnr Pl
Officer
ORs 14
Jeep
Handcarts 2

Tpt Pl
Officer
ORs 12
Tech
Storemen 2
REME
Fitters 3

Adm Pl
Officer
ORs 32

Major OC Coy
2i/c
Batmen 2
Dvr Mech
CSM
CQMS
Clerk
RAMC att'd 2
Storeman

Total each Coy
Officers 6
ORs 134
Handcarts 8
Jeeps 1

Total Coys
Officers 24
ORs 536
Handcarts 32
Jeeps 4

MMG Pl
8 guns
Subaltern
Pl Sgt
Batman
Orderly
4 Secs each:
L/Sgt
Cpl
8 Gunners

Total
Officers 1
ORs 43
Handcarts 8

Mortar Pl
6 mortars
Captain
Batman
Orderly
Sergeant
Mortar dets
ORs 48

Total
Officers 1
ORs 51
Handcarts 12

Total S Coy
Officers 6
ORs 154
Handcarts 20
Jeeps 12

Anti-Tank Gp
8 guns
Captain
Batman
Orderly

2 Pls each:
Subaltern
Batman
Sergeant
24 Gunners

Total
Officers 3
ORs 55
Jeeps 8

Note This does not include the first line reinforcements held in R Company, which brings the Battalion strength to well over 900 all ranks. The Battalion basically operated to this establishment in North Africa and Sicily, except that there was one MMG Platoon and one Platoon of 20mm Hispano cannon and one Mortar Platoon with eight 3-inch Mortars. When the Battalion returned to the UK in late 1943, Support Company was increased. The Hispano Platoon was disbanded and another MMG Platoon was formed with a Captain in overall command of the Group, and a Subaltern commanding each Platoon. The Mortar Platoon was increased to two (one using handcarts, the second jeeps), each with six 3-inch Mortars with a similar command structure, personnel being found from R and the Rifle Companies.

Appendix C Issued in conjunction with 1 Border Administrative Instruction No 3 of 28 May 1944

Composition of the Seaborne Tail

1. Personnel

	Officers	OR	Remarks
(a) **Admin Platoon**			
QM and Batman	1	1	
Clerks		2	
Equipment repairer		1	
Storeman		1	
Sanitary man		2	
Postman		1	
Water Duty man		1	
Armourer		1	
Shoemaker		1	
ACC Cooks		7	(one NCO)
Total Admin Platoon	1	18	
(b) **Transport Platoon**			
MTO and Batman	1	1	
MT Sergeant		1	
Storeman		1	
Sergeant Tech Stores		1	
Fitters REME		2	
Drivers (incl Veh Mechanics)		15	
Total Tpt Pl	1	21	
(c) CQMS and Storeman (per Coy)		12	
(d) Any personnel of airborne portion which does not take off			
Total personnel	2	51 excl airborne surplus	

2. Transport

Nature of vehicle	Allotted to	To carry	Remarks
(a) 1 x 3 Tonner	Each Rifle Coy and HQ Coy	1 groundsheet per man 2 blankets per man 1 haversack per man 1 pair boots per man hydro burners 5 cooking containers 5 dixies	see para 3 for composition
		5 water containers minimum officers mess haircutting tools shoemaker's tools Coy office box, spare handcarts	tin plate only
(b) 2 x 3 Tonners	S Coy	As for Rifle Coys as in (a) above with in addition fitters tools for 6-pdrs spare parts for weapons	
(c) 1 x 3 Tonner; 3 x 15 cwts	QM	minimum res clothing set armourers tools set shoemakers tools Any MOs equipment MT spares and fitters tools Personnel Reserve wireless batteries spare signals equipment spare Pioneers tools NAAFI packs	if necessary
(d) 1 x 15 cwt	MTO	MT spares, fitters tools etc	
(e) 2 water carts	QM		provided from outside source
(f) 1 car 4 seater	CO		
(g) 7 BB and 7 trailers		To carry normal load	to include op veh. not carried by air

3. Packing of Groundsheets, Blankets and Haversacks

(a) Groundsheet to contain:
   2 blankets
   1 pair boots
   1 haversack containing: 2 pairs socks
                            1 suit denims
                            1 shirt
                            1 towel
                            soap
                            1 set underclothes
                            1 pair PT shoes

(b) All (a) above to be securely tied up inside the groundsheet and man's name and number to be stencilled on outside. In the event of large packs being available, these will be used.

Appendix 7

Battalion Operational Orders for Operation MARKET

SECRET

1 Border OO No. 1 Operation "MARKET"   Copy No ....
                                                        14 Sep 1944

Ref Maps:
1/25,000   GSGS 4427 Sheets GINKEL 386, EDE 387, REMEN 5NE and
           ARNHEM 6 NW
1/100,000 GSG 2541 sheets 2 & 5
           "   4416 sheet P1

INFM:

1   **Enemy:** summary issued separately

    Own Tps:

2   General: Operation "MARKET" is a development of Op "COMET".
    It envisages the use of three Airborne divs carrying out the same task
    as one airbrone div in "COMET". I Airborne Div is responsible for
    area ARNHEM.
    82 American Airborne Div for area NIGMEGEN
    and 101 American Airborne Div for area GRAVE, and adjacent brs.

3   **Air Plan:** 1 Airborne Div lands in three lifts:-
    1st Lift: H plus 45 mins 1 Para Bde   DZ 'X'
                   H hr 1 Air Ldg Bde (less certain sub units)   LZ 'S'
                   H hr 9 Fd Coy RE   LZ 'Z'
                   H hr plus 19 mins 181 Fd Amb   LZ 'S'
                   H hr plus 19 onwards certain Div Tps   LZ 'Z'

    2nd Lift: X hr 4 Para Bde   DZ 'Y'
                   X plus 17 mins onwards remainder 1 Air Ldg Bde   LZ 'S'
                   X plus 32 mins onwards remainder Div Tps   LZ 'X'
    3rd lift: Z hr 1 Polish Para Bde   DZ 'K'
                   Z plus 20 mins onwards 1 Polish Para Bde   DZ 'L'
                   (DZs and LZs which affect Bn shewn on attd trace)

4   **Timings:** D Day is first day of op.
                  H hr is time of landing of 1st lift
                  D plus 1 early morning 2nd lift lands X hr
                  D plus 1 evening 3rd lift lands Z hr

5   **Tasks:**
    (a) **1 Para Bde:**
        (i) Seize and hold ARNHEM and secure brs over the NEDER RIJN
        (ii) Occupy that portion of the town shown on trace attd.

    (b) **1 Air Ldg Bde:**
        (i) Cover the unloading of 1st and 2nd lifts.
        (ii) After unloading of 2nd lift seize and occupy the sector of the
        town allotted.
        (iii) Protect LZ for landing of 3rd lift gliders.

    (c) **4 Para Bde and 1 Polish Para Bde:** occupy sector of town
        allotted.

    (d) Outpost line and standing patrols will be pushed fwd as far as
        possible as for normal telescopic defence.

6   **Recce Sqn** Lands LZ 'Z' (1st lift) and seizes main br at ARNHEM.

7   **Arty:** 1 Lt Bty in sp 1 Air Ldg Bde with initial gun area 6779.

8   **RE:** One tp 9 Fd Coy RE under comd 1 Air Ldg Bde.

9   **GP:** one Bn under comd 1 Air Ldg Bde.

10 **Bombline:**
    (i) From H hr until 2nd lift plus 6 hrs:
        785855 - 768852 - 750846 - 737845 - 730844 - 715845 - 708851
        - 695852 - 767853 - 659853 - 639853 - 628853 - 613855

    (ii) As from 2nd Lift plus 6 hrs (ie not before 1100 hrs D plus 1):
        629852 - 629842 - 630821 - 628807 - 623788 - 616772 - 614759

    Prebriefed tgts will be engaged from D - 1 to H hr. Those will
        incl barracks at EDE and WOLFHEZEN and all known flak.

11 **1 Air Ldg Bde Plan:**
    (a) **General:** Tasks are (i) Protect ldg of 2nd and 3rd Lifts
                                (ii) occupy ARNHEM within bdys shown on
                                attd trace.

These tasks will form two phases.

PHASE I

(b) **Tasks**

    (i) **7 KOSB:**

        (a) Est strong coy gp at PLANKEN WAMBUIS 6683.

        (b) Protect DZ 'Y' until 4 Para Bde are clear.

    (ii) **1 Border:**

        (a) Est strong coy gp at RENKUM 6276.

        (b) Protect DZ 'X' and LZ 'Z' until Div tps are clear.

    (iii) **2 S Staffords:**

        (a) Seize and occupy WOLFHEZEN 6680.

        (b) Protect LZ 'S'.

    (iv) **Glider Pilot Bn:**

        (a) Remain with units as far as unit RVs.

        (b) RV under own arrangements thereafter and occupy EAST end of WOLFHEZEN.

PHASE II

(c) **Tasks**

    (i) **7 KOSB:**

        (a) move as soon as 4 Para Bde are clear of DZ Y into bde res in area H on rd 7279.

        (b) protect LZ L until 1 Polish Para Bde gliders are clear with one coy gp.

        (c) est post at rd and rly br 715780.

        (d) dominate area bounded by pts   H on rd 7279

                                        X rds 726797

                                        X rds 733785

    (ii) **1 Border:**

        (a) move on orders Bde HQ to occupy area KOUDE HERBERG 6873.

        (b) est post in HEVEADORP area.

        (c) route along main RENKUM - ARNHEM rd.

        (d) dominate area bounded on NORTH by main rd, on EAST by rly and on SOUTH by river with special reference to ferries.

    (iii) **2 S Staffords:**

        (a) move as soon as joined by own 2nd lift to occupy area to include H on rd at 7080 and rd junc 713798

        (b) est post at rd junc 717806 to contact 4 Para Bde.

        (c) route along rd n of rly through JOHANNA HOEVE 6980.

    (iv) **Glider Pilots:**

        (a) move on orders Bde HQ along rd NORTH of rly to occupy wood 697787 with posts from HALTE X rds 699792 to main rd at 696784.

        (b) dominate the area bounded on the NORTH by the rly, on the EAST by the rly and on the SOUTH by the main rd.

(d) **RE:**

    (a) one Pl 9 Fd Coy under comd 1 Airldg Bde - primary task rd blocks on main EDE - ARNHEM rd in area 2 S Staffords during Phase II.

    (b) the tasks of the remainder incl

        (i) seizing and holding rly br at 7076.

        (ii) removal of all boats to NORTH bank of NEDER RIJN.

INTENTION:

12 1 Border will

    (a) Protect DZ 'X' and LZ 'Z' until Div tps are clear.

    (b) thereafter occupy the area KOUDE HERBERG.

METHOD:

13 **Landing Plan:**

    (a) Bn RV - SE corner of wood 649811 - see attached trace. Coys will NOT have independent assembly areas. Glider loads will move independently direct to the Bn RV where they will be directed to Coy areas on arrival. Coys will then be despatched independently to their allotted areas (see trace attd for Phase I).

PHASE I:

14 **Rifle Coy Areas:** see attd trace. In addition B Coy will be responsible for seizing and holding ferry at RENKUM 623764.

15 **S Coy:** Sub units will be placed under comd of rifle coys as follows:- (Sub units join coys at Bn RV)

    (a) **MMG Gp:** one sec per rifle coy.

    (b) **A tk Gp:** two dets per rifle coy

    (c) **Mortar Gp:**

        (i) Two secs to B Coy

        (ii) Two secs to A Coy

        (iii) One sec to each D & C Coys.

PHASE II (when ordered).

16 **Rifle Coy areas:** see attd trace.
In addition B Coy will be responsible for seizing and holding ferry at 687767.

17 **S Coy:**

    (a) **MMG Gp:**

        (i) One sec in sp C Coy for use in outpost posn.

        (ii) One pl in sp A Coy in area pt 63.5 6878

        (iii) One sec in sp D Coy in area pt 63.2

    (b) **A tk Gp:** Two dets in sp each rifle coy

    (c) **Mortar Gp:**

        (i) One sec under comd B Coy

        (ii) One sec under comd C Coy

        (iii) Remainder under comd Gp Comd in area of wood NORTH of rd in 687784. Probable DF tasks later.

18 **Patrols:** Area of responsibility as shown on trace attd. A Coy will be prepared to provide any special patrols which may be required.

19 **Recce:** If the situation permits 2IC and one offr per coy with protection party of one sec found by C Coy will recce Bn posn for Phase II before move takes place.

20 **Pnr Pl:** Be prepared to assist B, C & D Coys in the construction of rd blocks and removal of any enemy mines.

ADM:

21 **Resup:**

    SDP   (i) LZ 'L' at X plus 10 hrs.

             (ii) SOUTH of HOOGERF 7180 from Z plus 30 onwards.

22 **Med:**

    (a) Cas on all LZs and DZs will be evacuated to 181 Fd Amb in WOLFHEZEN until Phase II.

    (b) At Phase II MDS will be est in 1 Airldg Bde sector of the town in a hospital to be recced.

    (c) RAP will be near Bn HQ in both phases.

23 **Amn:** Tpt pl jeeps and trailers will be called to Bde HQ in Phase II.

24 **POW:** may have to be held by coys in Phase I.

25 **Civilians:**

    (a) As for Op "COMET"

    (b) Dep Comd 1 Airldg Bde has been appointed Town Comdt and will control all I (b) matters.

26 **Tpt:** Every effort will be made to acquire all available tpt to replace handcarts and make Bn mobile.

INTERCOMN:

27 **WT:** open on landing

28 **Line:** will be laid in Phase II

29 **Pigeon messages:** will be added to "HQ Br Airborne Tps (rear)"

30 **Recognition:**
(a) as for Op "COMET".
(b) 21 Indep Para Coy will display yellow smoke and triangles if engaged on the LZ.
(c) Triangles will be shewn to all br a/c operating overhead.

31 **Passwords:** as for Op "COMET".

32 **HQs:**
(a) **Div:**　(i) Lands on LZ Z.
(ii) RV track junc 657797.
(iii) Moves by main rd WAGENINGEN - ARNHEM.
(iv) Opens at ARTILLERIE PARK 7378 on arrival.

(b) **Bde:**　(i) RV WOLFHEZEN.
(ii) Moves along 2 S Staffords route.
(iii) est in KOEPEL 7179 on arrival.

(c) **Bn:**　Phase I - JONKERSHOEVE 6479.

Phase II - in D Coy's area

Signed T. Haddon Lt Col
Comd 1st Bn The Border Regiment.

DISTRIBUTION:

No. 1	A Coy		No. 16	Ldg Offr
2	B Coy		17	MO
3	C Coy		18	FOO
4	D Coy		19	QM
5	HQ Coy		20	RSM
6	S Coy		22	Capt Scott RAMC
7	Comd MMG Gp		23	HQ 1 A L Bde
8	Comd A tk Gp		24	7 KOSB
9	Comd Mtr Gp		25	2 S Staffords
10	RSO		26	War Diary
11	Comd Pnr Pl		27	File
12	CO		28-30	Spare
13	2IC			
14	Adjt			
15	IO			

Appendix 8

Badges and Insignia

Cap Badges

Officers wore the OSD bronze badge in the Service Dress and Field Service side-cap. Some officers may have worn the silver or silver-plated cap badge, usually worn in the Dress Blues cap, with the maroon beret. The white-metal cap badge was also worn in the maroon beret.

NCOs and ORs wore the white-metal cap badge in the Service Dress cap, the Field Service side-cap and in the maroon beret from mid-1942. The grey plastic cap badge was issued to recruits at No 18 ITC during training c1943-46, but was universally disliked and exchanged as quickly as possible for the white-metal example.

Collar Badges

Officers wore the OSD bronzed badges (left and right facing) on the lapels of Service Dress, the design identical to the OSD cap badge.

NCOs and ORs wore the white-metal collar badges (left and right facing), which continued to be worn by NCOs and ORs on Service Dress until the re-kitting of the Battalion with Battle Dress in early 1940.

Shoulder Titles

1. The pre-war curved brass title BORDER continued to be worn until early 1940 on the ORs' Service Dress and Battle Dress tunics.

2. Rectangular cloth title BORDER in black cotton on a khaki/green woollen ground worn on Battle Dress, 1940-41. Normally worn as a slip-on title on the epaulette, but was later sewn on at the shoulder, due to the wearing of the Company colour on the epaulette in late 1941/early 1942.

3. Title BORDER woven in yellow cotton on green cloth ground, this stitched in green thread on a purple cloth backing, worn 1942-1951.

4. White BORDER on red ground, 1944-59. Worn by recruits to the Regiment, but exchanged on joining the 1st Battalion, when the green, yellow and purple titles were taken into wear. Produced in both screen-printed cotton and woven.

5. CANLOAN officers serving with the Battalion in 1944-45 wore, in addition to the normal insignia of the Battalion, the title CANADA in white on a khaki background between the shoulder title and the Divisional patch on both sleeves of the Battle Dress.

Divisional and Brigade Badges

1. Brigade badge of the 31st Independent Infantry Brigade worn on Battle Dress when the Battalion was in South Wales in 1941. The badge comprised a heraldic bull in red rising from a crown on a dark blue background.

2. Airborne Division badge of Bellerophon and Pegasus in pale blue on a maroon background was designed by Major Edward Seago in May 1942. The patch was worn with Pegasus facing forward on each shoulder of the Battle Dress blouse below the Battalion shoulder title. Below the Airborne patch on each sleeve was the title AIRBORNE. Both badges were produced in screen-printed cotton or woven. The Museum's collection includes an un-issued pair with the maroon painted on to thin backed cotton and the Pegasus stencilled over in pale blue paint.

3. 5th Infantry Division, a white Y on a mid-brown background, screen-printed cotton. Worn by the Battalion from October 1945 after leaving the Airborne Division.

Qualification badges

1. Glider badge: Horsa glider woven in blue cotton on a khaki oval, granted as a glider qualification badge after three flights and worn in most cases by members of the Battalion on the lower right sleeve of the Battle Dress blouse.

2. Parachute qualification badge: awarded to all ranks who had passed through parachute training school, but who were not regular parachute troops or instructors. White parachute on khaki square, screen-printed or woven on cotton. Commonly referred to as the 'light-bulb'. Members of 1 Border who qualified for the badge wore it on the lower right sleeve above the Glider badge.

Company Colours

Company colour distinctions were introduced after the Battalion joined the 1st Air-Landing Brigade, almost certainly by Lt Col Roger Bower. The practise was continued after the war by the 1st Battalion until 1959, and from 1959 by the 1st Battalion The King's Own Royal Border Regiment until Battle Dress was withdrawn from use c1964. The tabs were slip-on silk or cotton bands worn on each epaulette of the Battle Dress as follows:

HQ Company - yellow
A Company - green
B Company - white, then purple (to avoid being confused with officer cadet shoulder strip designations)
C Company - red
D Company - pale blue
S Company - dark blue
T, later R Company - black

The GLIDER Badge

In May 1946 Brigadier R. H. Bower, who had commanded the 1st Battalion and both the 1st and 6th Air-Landing Brigades, proposed the granting of a badge in recognition of the service of the units involved. Bower contacted the commanding officers of the four battalions concerned; in the case of 1 Border, the CO, Lt-Col C. F. O. Breese, contacted the then Colonel of the Regiment, Brigadier G. Hyde Harrison DSO, who gave his full backing to the idea. Bower then wrote the following letter:

'SUBJECT: Airborne Emblems

The Under Secretary of State,
The War Office

1. As 6 Airlanding Brigade is now reverting to a normal establishment and ceasing to have an airborne role, there will no longer be any Airlanding Infantry units in the Army.

Certified True Copy.

VICtoria 6622/253.

68/GEN/8236 (Ord 17E).

Sir,

Award of distinction - Units of 1st. Airborne Division.

1.　　I am directed to inform you that H.M. The King has been graciously pleased to approve the award of a distinction to the following Units to mark the part played by them in the 1st. Airlanding Brigade, 1st. Airborne Division, at the invasion of Sicily on the night of 9th/10th. July 1943, this being the first occasion on which British Gliderborne troops took part in a major tactical operation:-

　　9th. Airborne Squadron, Royal Engineers.
　　1st. Battalion, The Border Regiment.
　　2nd. Battalion, The South Staffordshire Regiment.
　　1st. Glider Pilot Regiment.

2.　　The distinction will be in the following forms:-

(A)　9th. Airborne Squadron　）　The Unit to be awarded a commemorative
　　　Royal Engineers.　　　　）　parchment.

(B)　1st. Battalion　　　　　）　　All Ranks to wear an embroidered
　　　The Border Regiment.　）　glider badge on each sleeve of the
　　　　　　　　　　　　　　　）　No 1. dress jacket and battle dress
　　　2nd. Battalion　　　　　）　blouse (only).
　　　The South Staffordshire　）
　　　Regiment.　　　　　　　　）
　　　　　　　　　　　　　　　）
　　　1st. Glider Pilot Regiment. ）

The above distinctions will be provided at public expence.

(Note; the reason for the difference between the two forms of distinctions is that in the Corps of Royal Engineers it is an established practice for all units to be dressed alike.)

3.　　With Battle Dress, the glider badge will be incorporated in the regimental arm title, in pairs, so that the glider is facing forward.

4.　　The production of prototype badges for wear with No 1. dress and Battle dress is already in hand and a further communication in this connection will be forwarded in due course.

　　　　　　　　　　　　　I am,
　　　　　　　　　　　　　　Sir,
　　　　　　　　　　　　　Your obedient Servant,
　　　　　　　　　　　　　Signed. XXXXXXXXXXXXXXXX

　　　　　　　　　　　　　for Director of Ordnance Services.

Major General P.J. Shears, CB.,
Colonel, The Border Regt,
36, Bramerton Street, London S.W. 3.

THE WAR OFFICE,
LONDON, S.W. 1.

5th August 1949.

Having now commanded both 1 and 6 Airlanding Brigades and having presided over the disbandment of the former and the re-conversion of the latter I would like to put forward a strong case for some permanent recognition of the operational airborne activities of the following Battalions:
　　1 Border Regiment
　　2 South Staffordshire Regiment
　　2 Oxfordshire and Buckinghamshire Light Infantry
　　1 Royal Ulster Rifles

1 Argyll and Sutherland Highlanders are not included as they have never in fact been airborne. 12 Devonshire Regiment and 7 Kings Own Scottish Borderers are not included as both Battalions have already been disbanded.

2. The above four Regular Battalions constituted the 31 Independent Infantry Brigade in October 1941 and, being given a glider role, became 1 Airlanding Brigade. They carried out all the experimental glider training, developed the technique of an airlanding operation, and each battalion took part in two airborne operations of the first magnitude and acquitted themselves in the succeeding battles with no small degree of credit.

3. All these battalions have left Airborne Forces with very great regret. They have acquired a tremendous airborne esprit de corps in addition to that of their own Regiments. It would be a thousand pities to allow this to fade when it is probable that it can be secured for all time. I therefore suggest that to keep this invaluable tradition and spirit alive, and to perpetuate the memory of their airborne achievements, all ranks of each of these battalions should wear a small silver Pegasus badge on the upper sleeve of the right arm in all forms of dress. This should be a unit award and not an individual one: only those on the strength of these four battalions should wear the badge and nobody else.

4. I understand that suggestions of this kind have been made already though not officially. Having obtained the approval of the Commanding Officers of the four battalions concerned I am now anxious to put forward this proposal officially and as strongly as I can for I am confident that morale and esprit de corps would be greatly enhanced by its sanction. I request that this proposal, having first been discussed with the Colonels of the Regiments concerned, should be submitted to His Majesty the King for his consideration and approval.'

On 31 May 1946 Major-General H. Murray CB DSO, the Director of Personal Services at The War Office, wrote to Brigadier Hyde-Harrison asking for his opinion on such a special emblem. Murray referred to two possible emblems, the first being a small silver Pegasus badge, and the second the 'Glider Badge' as worn by the air-landing units. Harrison replied on 4 June that the Regiment favoured the silver Pegasus badge.

　　The matter was subsequently discussed later that year by the Honours and Distinctions Committee of the War Office. Meanwhile, after 1 Border had resumed a normal infantry role in 5th Division, all airborne distinctions were lost and the matter appeared to have been forgotten. However, in August 1949, much to the delight of the Regiment, His Majesty King George VI granted 1 Border the right to wear a glider badge, which was taken into wear in April 1951.

Detail of Glider Badges

1. Shoulder title comprising yellow BORDER and Horsa glider on maroon ground, 1951-59. Produced both screen-printed and woven. Worn in pairs on the Battle Dress blouse with glider facing forward. Officially taken into wear on 7 April 1951. Worn only by 1st Battalion personnel with the Battalion, serving at the Depot or attached to the 4th (TA) Battalion Border Regiment.

2. Horsa glider in gold bullion wire on dark blue background worn immediately below the shoulder on the right arm of No 1 Dress approved in 1952. Worn by the 1st Battalion from 1952 and by the 1st Battalion The King's Own Royal Border Regiment from 1959.

3. Shoulder title with wording KING'S OWN BORDER and Horsa glider in yellow woven in cotton on green cloth ground stitched on black/blue backing. Worn in pairs on the Battle Dress blouse with glider facing forward by the 1st Battalion The King's Own Royal Border Regiment 1959-1964.

4. Horsa glider in gold bullion wire on khaki ground worn by Officers and WOs of the 1st Battalion The Border Regiment from about 1952 to 1959 on Service Dress and by Officers and WOs of the 1st Battalion The King's Own Royal Border Regiment from 1959 to date on Service Dress and the woollen pullover.

5. Horsa glider in gold bullion on scarlet background worn by Officers, WOs and Sergeants of the King's Own Royal Border Regiment on the Mess Jacket and by Bandsmen and Drummers on the scarlet full-dress Tunic.

6. Horsa glider in yellow cotton worn on No 2 Dress and the woollen pullover by NCOs and ORs of the King's Own Royal Border Regiment.

Appendix 9

Sky Battlefleet to Arnhem - Colin Fowler's Poems

This anthology of poetry was composed by the late Colin Fowler, who served with 20 Platoon D Company 1 Border.

Sky Battlefleet to Arnhem

Tribute to the 1st Battalion The Border Regiment 1st Air-Landing Brigade

With glowing cheeks and shining eyes,
Superbly fit, as fit could be,
The Border lads set out to fight
July the ninth, in forty-three;
Then glider borne on Arnhem day
Their part, in that great epic quest,
They fought, they lost, but gave their best.
Alas, so many fought so well, that stories
Unbelieved, they tell, of comrades, who
Were laid to rest, That Time, That Place,
That glorious past.

Now Red Beret and polished Badge,
Are all the lads who lived do have;
The cheeks and eyes no longer gleam,
For many years have passed between
That battle fought and the present scene.
We stand up tall on memory days,
As thoughts go back to all who played,
With pride we think of all those friends,
A Memory Chain, which has no ends;
The Border lads will stand and drink,
With heads held high, some shoulders bent,
Their thoughts of loyal sentiment,
The Toast, My Friends, `The Regiment'.

One Way Ticket

Those lazy coils of tow ropes laid
Along the runways all displayed,
To herald an amazing feat,
The take-off, of an Airborne fleet;
Dakotas, Stirlings, in position
Airborne troops of the First Division,
All waiting for the last command
To lift this army from the land.

The word at last, the engines roared,
The tow-ropes leapt with one accord
Between the planes and Horsa gliders,
Linking tugs and glider riders.
Lifting the first the gliders rose,
The tow-ropes whipped from tail to nose.

September Forty Four it was, at noon as I recall,
A sunny day, a pleasant day, a day to suit us all,
And as we climbed into the sky,
A sight so marvellous met the eye,
Three hundred Horsa gliders flew,
Above the slipstream, straight and true.

Then out unto the Netherlands,
This giant fleet prepared to land,
The canopies of parachutes
Just filled the air like summer fruits.
As idle domes they floated down,
To land so softly on the ground;
Then suddenly our hearts stood still,
The tow-ropes gone, and what a thrill
To watch the ground come up to meet
The gliders of this airborne fleet.

We hit the ground and skidded on,
The landings safe, the first job done,
Machine-guns chattered, rifles cracked,
But through all this the troops unpacked,
Then moved off at a hasty pace,
Eight miles to go, to each that place,
Called ARNHEM.

Feeling the Pinch

So quickly dawned the second day,
Our second lift came in to play.
It seemed that all the Hell let loose,
The screaming tracers, quite profuse,
A gun, a jeep, shot through the air,
A plane's on fire, Oh God look there,
Another one is coming down,
The cries of wounded all around,
This battle we had come to fight
Went on and lasted through the night.

The days that followed made it plain,
That officers and men again would suffer
What with wounds and rain;

Yes, that awful rain came on us,
Every day throughout the week,
Making harder our resistance,
Testing patience, tempting sleep,
Our dying friends and injured mates
Were transferred to hospital gates,
Some kept in cellars, some on stairs,
Some went alone, some went in pairs.

The numbers of our wounded grew,
To such proportions that we knew
If helping troops didn't reach us quick,
With food and clothing for the sick,
Our chances of a victory here
Were very slight and that was clear;
But hold out lads, and do this chore
And put your faith in Thirty Corps.
Guards with armour moving slowly,
To this cauldron, that we know.

Listen now a tank is coming,
Is it friend? Or is it foe?
Can your hear it? Can you see it?
Piat and mortars have a go,
Then we see the cross it's wearing
Painted black, and starkly staring,
With its cannon blazing shell
Blasting us with armour piercing,
Making this a living Hell.

Oh, God our help throughout the ages
Give us strength to battle on
Soldiers here are tired and weary
Starved and wounded, nearly done.
Our chief commander's lost, he's stranded;
We know not what we have to do,
The courage of the men here with us
Can do it with some help from you.

Sosabowski's Men

The independent Polish Airborne,
With Sosabowski in command
Came over in their planes and gliders
Our third lift was here at hand.
The German guns were pointed at them
Spitting steel and lead to boot,
Breaking up the close formations
Ripping wide their parachutes;

Still these gallant Polish soldiers,
Dropped from the sky in disarray
But quickly closed on their commander
Leader of this great brigade.

Bloodshot eyes in pallid faces,
Watched this carnage from below,
Helpless as we watched in horror,
How we hate this German foe;
Now the Polish drop had landed,
Can relief be our reward,
For holding out against the Panzers,
Fighting off the German horde.
Or is this just a flight of fancy?
Can they come to our defence?
Can they come to our advantage?
Christ Almighty, not a chance.

Surely must the tide be turning
Guards with armour must appear,
News of gun fire in the distance
Gave us views of what we feared,
All those tanks and troops awaited,
Had their moments of defeat,
Cut off by the German forces, and
Weary with the lack of sleep;
Slowly, oh so very slowly,
Moving up to join the fray,
Radio the troops in Arnhem,
Cannot meet them here today.

Determined now to hold positions
Troops in Arnhem battle on,
Climatised to these conditions
Holding firm to what we've won.
Never will the Germans beat us
This is what they've never done.
Come on chaps and clean their weapons
Fire them with the keenest eye
Make the shots you have left in them
Hit their marks before we die.
God is with us in this contest
Settle down and keep your nerve
Keep contact with the men around you
Cheer them up, they've seen the worst.

Dug In

On the heights of Westerbouwing,
Positioned firmly in the woods,
Fighting off the infiltrators
Doing now the best we could;
We have no food, we have no water,
Ammunition is running low,
Our first aid post is filling slowly,
With the soldiers that we know.
Mortar bombs and spandau firing
Start and end the waiting days,
Cutting down surviving members
In the trenches they had made.

Now we have patrols of Germans
Calling round at early dawn,
We must let them all come closer
Before we drop them one by one.
Dressed in capes from head to shoulder,
Bucket helmets on their heads,
What a mess to see them falling,
As defenders shoot them dead.
Then we search them for tobacco,
Cigarettes and matches that we crave,
For our supplies you see have missed us;
The Germans got them by mistake.

One time we found a lonely basket,
Hung on a tree inside a wood.
Volunteers from those around us
Fetched this in, it did us good,
Till we opened up the treasure
That our courageous friends had brought.
Food and smokes, and drugs and bandage
These were going through our thoughts
Can you imagine our amazement
When the contents came to light?
Red Berets and clean pyjamas,
What a let down, what a sight.

Now many men round Arnhem town
Were fighting very well,
Some stories of those episodes
Are left for me to tell.
My friend was in the 'Tafelberg'
A clean and smart hotel;
We used it as a hospital
Conditions there were hell,
Some patients on the tables lay
Already under care,
Were watching all the rafters burn,
And sparks fly through the air.

Some wounded men were hit again
As shells and bullets flew
Across the rooms made up as wards,
They hit the doctors too.
So hectic was the mess in there,
A two hour truce was called
To move the soldiers from that place
And into safer halls.

A tiny church at Oosterbeek
Watched o'er an epic fight,
Its pitted walls and half its roof
Laid open to the night.
A motley group of Airborne men
Collected round its square,
Dick Lonsdale was the man in charge,
He made them all aware
Of what the situation was
And why he'd got them there.

We met the Germans once before,
And found them second rate,
Now we meet them once again
With too much on their plate.
So quickly clean your weapons,
Let nothing pass this way,
We are waiting for that Thirty Corps
Who have had a slight delay.

Supply Drop Tribute

Above our heads, but flying low
Supplies in planes cruised round,
The contents of those heroes' ships
Were thrown out to the ground.
Though wreathed in flames and coils of smoke,
The aircraft without knowing
Had missed our frantic signals
From the heights of Westerbouwing.
They carried on regardless
Of the trouble they had found,
Their mission was to drop supplies,
Then slowly circle round.

We saw one plane come overhead,
Both engines were on fire,
The men inside we saw quite plain
Dispatching our desires.
Those lovely baskets sailing past
With baited breath we waited,
But in our hearts we knew the worst,
They supplied the men we hated.
But how were they to know the truth
Of how we held the ground?
Their mission was to drop supplies
Then slowly circle round.

Now anyone who watched that day
And saw those pilots make their way
Along the shell and shrapnel path,
Ignoring all the German wrath,
Saw aircraft crews of high renown,
Whose task was get those baskets down,
And this they did, a job well done,
For some it took a second run.
Determined men whose hearts were strong,
Dispatching all they'd brought along,
They did not know the drop was wrong,
Their mission was to drop supplies,
Then slowly circle round.

Call for Our Surrender

The swish of bullets through the trees,
The sound of branches falling,
Accustomed as we were to these
Some results were quite appalling.
For soldiers, just like anyone,
Would look to see what's there;
Some men stood up to look around
But most stayed as they were,
The latter were the lucky ones
The others, well you know,
A few of them were slightly hurt,
A few were maimed for life,
But quite a few whose names we knew
Would never greet their wives.

Accompanied by boos and jeers
Loud speaker music reached our ears.
Dear Tommies, called a female voice,
Think of your girls and wives and boys;
Surrender now and don't delay
Please don't get hurt, or killed today.
These Germans never miss a trick,
But here we are and here we'll stick
Until our guns and tanks arrive;
We hope they find us, still alive,
But doubt is creeping through our minds,
Our thoughts are fastened on the Rhine
And of that bridge we came to get,
That bridge we haven't seen it yet.

Only hunger now beset us,
Water we contrived to get
By stretching out our groundsheets
Over bushes that were wet.
Surrounded now was our position
Sixty yards of no-mans-land
Separated both the armies,
Desperation made our stand.
We were told to hold this cross-roads
Leading down to Heveadorp.
So we'll hold it, just believe it
Surrender was not in our thoughts.

Mixed News

At Westerbouwing stands a cottage
Painted white and looking trim,
This was where we kept our wounded
Orderlies just packed them in.
Those who died were laid outside it
Altogether in one line,
Covered up with sheets and blankets;
These men we knew had served their time.
Some others, only slightly wounded,
Lived in trenches they had made,
We were very close beside them
With the Germans in the glade.

The Second Army's on the move
The word was passed along;
A barrage of our heavy guns
Were soon to sing a song
And under cover of this fire,
Some troops would come across
To help restore the balance
That our famous Div had lost.
We felt more heartened by the news
That contact had been made
With Horrocks and his Thirty Corps
Of armoured tank brigades.

About this time we got the news
John Frost had lost the bridge,
So now our task was more defined,
We have to hold this ridge.
The ferry down at Heveadorp
Remains our only chance
Of getting help, or getting out,
Depending how we stand.
Now here we are and here we stay,
So wet and cold and weary,
Both officers and men alike
Red-eyed, grey-cheeked, but cheery.

Taking Stock

An eerie day the Twenty-Fifth,
Our guns from across the Rhine
Were falling short among our friends
And adding to our plight.
We could not see the ring of tanks
Beyond the woods of course,
But someone was directing fire
And cutting it quite close.
A rumour now was spreading round
Somehow we got the name
`John Bull' they said, remember that,
We thought it was a game.

That night it rained and black as pitch
It covered all the sounds
Of Airborne troops, all moving back
Out of the battle grounds.
We never got the word to go,
Or when to leave our posts,
We carried on without regard
And tried to find a smoke;
Later on that evening though
The few that still remained
Just crossed the road into the house
To shelter from the rain.

We checked our kit and found that we
Had used up all our rations.
We'd fired all our Three O Threes
In that nine days of passion.
But now the truth was sinking in
To all our tired brains,
Our trenches just across the road
Had filled up with the rains.
So flinging bolts from rifles,
As far as we could throw,
We realised our war was done
And that we'd have to go.

The seven men who walked about
Were cold and very weak,
We joined the wounded laid about
And gladly went to sleep.
Spasmodic fired ripped through the house
From Germans who we'd seen
Had occupied the trenches,
Where these Airborne troops had been.

Last Day

Today is Tuesday, Twenty-Six, September '44,
Last night we slept and then we woke
And then we slept some more.
Demoralised and quite ashamed
With what we had to do,
Someone must tell the Germans
That our fighting days are through.
We could not bear to see them gloat,
To find us in this state,
They'd met their match and this we knew,
We thought we'd pulled our weight.

So curled up in the warmest spot,
We tried to find a way
To save our pride and try to hide
Our feelings of that day.
Although we did our best to seek
A method of escape,
We could not leave the wounded,
Who were weakened by their fate.
So making up a flag of truce
From sheets and pillow slips,
White strips of cloth around our arms,
The sheet stuck on a stick.

The stick we waved from side to side
And made up our decision
To call out to the German troops
And surrender our position.
A pal of ours, a youngish lad
Came with me on this task,
We walked across the road to where
The German HQ was;
The officer who was in charge
Stepped forward from his hut.
He first shook hands, then
Stood erect and gave a smart salute.

Acknowledgements

The book would not have been produced without the help of many former members of the Battalion and their families, to whom the authors are grateful for their tremendous interest, support, kindness and hospitality in allowing access to photographs, papers, memorabilia and their personal recollections, some good, some not so happy, in order that we can tell a story. Many provided detailed information for Alan Green in 1988-89 and have done so again in 1993-4. They have patiently answered letters and questionnaires and made great efforts to recall events and names of 50 years ago. Others, sadly no longer alive, have left a historical legacy of their service with the Battalion in the form of letters, articles, original documents, notes and taped interviews, which are lodged in the Regimental Museum archives.

The authors wish to thank the following wartime members of the 1st Battalion and their families for all their help:

James Absalom, Norman Antwistle, the late George Attenborough, the late Pat Baillie, Colonel John Bainbridge TD, Capt Bill Baldock, Bill Bate, Eric Blackwell, George Boardman, the late Brigadier Charles Breese CBE, Ken Briggs, George Bunting, Bill Campbell, Rev T. W. I. Cleasby, Walter Collings, Captain Geoffrey Costeloe, Charles Coventry, Cyril Crickett, Syd Cringle, the late Bob Crittenden, Ron Cruickshank, Mike Curran, Alfred Davey, John Davison, Owen Delvoir, Mrs C. H. Denby (widow of the late Capt Alan Cox), Jimmy Devonport, the late Capt Colin Douglas, Harry Duckworth, Harold Ennis, John Entwistle, Mrs R. Etteridge (widow of the late Freddie Webster), Leslie Fielding, Tom Ferguson (son of the late Sgt Tom 'Pop' Ferguson), the late Harry Fincham, Alan Fisher, George Fisher, Bill George, Major John Gibbon OBE MC, John Gordon, the late Dennis Goulding, Dr J. Graham-Jones, Gerry Grant, Ron Graydon, Canon Alan Green, the late Major Michael Grubb, the late Brigadier Tommy Haddon CBE, Mrs C. Haddon, Dick Haley GM, Jim Hall, Jack Hardwick, Captain Joe Hardy MC, Andrew Hartshorn, Jack Heaton, Norman Herring, William Hill, Fred Hodges, Bill Homer, Ronald Hope-Jones CMG,

Capt Ron Jack, Bill Hoyne, Ian Hunter, Joe Hutchinson, Jock Hyndman, Les Ingham, the late Capt Barry Ingram, Ron Jack, Fred Jackson, Jim Kelsey Norman Knight, Jack Looker, Jim Longson, Jimmy McDowell, Sandy Masterton, the late Joseph Maguire, Stanley Metcalfe, Tom Metcalfe (nephew of the late Pte Tom Metcalfe), Bernard Murphy MBE, Mr V. G. Murray (son of the late Sgt V. De Muynck), Colonel Ted Newport TD, Tom Northgraves, Maurice Oakley, Wilf Oldham, Doug Payne, Johnnie Peters, Thomas Plimley, Len Powell, Wilf Pridmore, Henry Rafferty, John Ranger, the late John Rannard and Mrs A. Rannard, the late Colonel Bob Reese OBE, Tom Reeves, Capt Alan Roberts, Prebendary Arthur Royall, Cedric Sanders, Eric Scrivener, Leonard Scully, Samuel Sidebottom, C. T. Smith, Major Arthur Springbett, Major Tony Stafford, Capt Pat Stott, David Stubbs, Jim Swan MM, Ian Thirlwell (son of the late Sgt Chris Thirlwell), Bob Thornley, Alex Turner, Reg Vowles, Joseph Weardon, Tom Welsh, Ernie Westerman, Joe Whelan, Albert 'Ginger' Wilson, and Capt Baldwin Wilson.

Many others have freely given their time, knowledge of Airborne operations and access to their research. For their help, patience, hospitality and knowledge of the Arnhem-Oosterbeek area and the events of 1944 Dr Adrian Groeneweg (Director), Berry de Reuss (Curator) and the Staff of the Airborne Museum Hartenstein at Oosterbeek deserve a special thanks. Adrian and his wife Marianne kindly hosted Messrs Eastwood and Gray for five days in October 1993, and Adrian gave us four valuable days of his time to walk the areas where 1 Border served during the Battle and gave the authors a far better understanding of the events of September 1944, for which we are extremely grateful. The kindness shown to us and others on visits to Holland is beyond praise. Peter Taylor of Barnsley has provided numerous photographs and documents from his library for us to use. Harry Foote the archivist at the Museum of Army Flying, Middle Wallop, has provided a number of photographs, copies of documents and research, which have proved invaluable. This includes a considerable

amount of work by David Hall on the details of glider loads and tugs for 'Market'.

The two chapters on the Sicily landings would have been somewhat thinner but for research material made available by Major H. N. 'Andy' Andrews DFM and Bar, formerly of the Glider Pilot Regiment. A veteran of Sicily, Normandy, Arnhem and the Rhine Crossing, he was introduced to the authors by Harold Ennis, formerly of 20 Platoon D Company 1 Border, in whose Platoon Andy flew to Arnhem. Over many years he and others have collated reports by those Glider Pilots involved in the Sicily landings from sources other than those used by the authors. His research confirmed much of our information, as well as providing new material for which we are most grateful.

Many others have helped in various ways and include Davie Orr, Paul Rea and David Truesdale of the Airborne Battle Study Group, Cliff Blood, Ray Brown, Colonel Clive Elderton OBE, Tony Goddard, Fred Gray, Secretary of the 9th Airborne Squadron RE Association, Joe Hodgson, Max Hutton, John Mallinson, Rowland McFarlane, ex-RAMC 1st Airborne Division, Alan Pawson, David Raw and Bob Walker; Jim Templeton for all his work copying, developing and printing photographs; Craig Smith and Paul Greenwood at Norwyn Photographic at Preston for their attention to detail in copying original photographs and making a number of silk purses out of sow's ears; and Paul Thompson and Wendy Moore of Lancaster City Museum for kindly producing the various maps.

There has been tremendous support from many others within the Regiment; Brigadier James Howard CBE, the Regimental Secretary, and Captain Ian Banks, the Assistant Regimental Secretary at RHQ King's Own Royal Border Regiment in Carlisle Castle, Major Bill Alexander, the Chairman, and the members of the Regimental Museum Committee, Lt Colonel Dennis Flynn, the Commanding Officer of the 1st Battalion King's Own Royal Border Regiment, and WO2 Mark Graham, also of the 1st Battalion, who took many of the photographs on Sicily in 1993. The authors would also like to thank John Peaty and the staff of the MoD Historical Branch for their help with records; John Delaney and other members of Staff of the Department of Photographs at The Imperial War Museum; the staff of the Commonwealth War Graves Commission; Alan Brown and Mrs Diane Andrews at The Airborne Forces Museum at Aldershot; HMSO for permission to reproduce the maps from the Cabinet Papers for Operation 'Market'; and Colonel John Young,

Royal Signals, the Defence Attaché in The Hague.

A special thanks is due to Patricia Hutchinson and Geoff Ellis BEM, the Museum's two custodians, who have dealt with the public and answered numerous enquiries and the telephone while the Curator has been busy with 'the Book'.

For permission to reproduce photographs thanks are due to the Airborne Forces Museum at Aldershot, the Bundesarchiv Koblenz, the Trustees of The Imperial War Museum, the

Municipal Archives of Renkum and Mr J. van der Zeyden of the Municipal Archives in Arnhem, the Smithsonian Institution in Washington DC and the Taylor Library, Barnsley. The photographs have been acknowledged accordingly. The credit 'BRM' indicates that the print and/or negative is held in the Regimental Museum's photographic collections. Where a copy of a photograph is available, or the source is The Imperial War Museum, the relevant negative number has been quoted.

Bibliography

Published Sources

Books and articles

Atkin, Ronald *Pillar of Fire - Dunkirk 1940* (Sidgwick & Jackson, London 1990)

Baynes, John *Urquhart of Arnhem - The Life of Major-General R. E. Urquhart CB DSO* (Brasseys, London 1993)

Border Magazine, 1947-1959

Breese, Major C. F. O. 'The Airborne Operations in Holland September 1944', *Border Magazine*, September 1948 and March 1949

'Operation Husky, The Planning', *Border Magazine*, March 1950

'1 Border in Norway', *The Lion and The Dragon*, Spring 1977

Chatterton, George *Wings of Pegasus* (Battery Press, Nashville 1982)

Commonwealth War Graves Commission Cemetery and Memorial Registers

Cowper, J. M. *The King's Own - The Story of A Royal Regiment Vol 3 1914-50* (Gale & Polden, Aldershot and London 1957)

Davies, Brian L. *British Army Uniforms and Insignia of WW2* (Arms and Armour Press, London 1983)

D'Este, Carlo *Bitter Victory - The Battle for Sicily 1943* (Collins, London 1988)

Devlin, Gerald M. *Silent Wings - The Story of The Glider Pilots of WW2* (W. H. Allen, London 1985)

Fairley, John *Remember Arnhem* (Peaton Press, Bearsden 1990)

Frost, Major-General John CB DSO MC *A Drop Too Many* (Buchan & Enright, London 1982)

Gibbon, Major John OBE MC 'Operation "Husky"', Part II, *Border Magazine*, September 1954

Green, Alan, *1st Battalion The Border Regiment, Arnhem 17-26 September 1944* (Border Regimental Museum, Carlisle 1991)

Hallam, John, *The History of The Lancashire Fusiliers 1939-45* (Alan Sutton, Stroud 1993)

Harman, Nicholas *Dunkirk - The Necessary Myth* (Hodder & Stoughton, London 1980)

Hey, J. A. *Roll of Honour Battle of Arnhem 17-26 September 1944* (Society of Friends of the Airborne Museum, Oosterbeek 1986)

Hibbert, Christopher, *The Battle of Arnhem* (B. T. Batsford Ltd, London 1962)

Kent, Ron, *First In Parachute Pathfinder Company* (Batsford, London 1979)

Kershaw, Robert J. *It Never Snows in September - The German View of the Battle of Arnhem* (The Crowood Press, Marlborough 1990)

The Lion and The Dragon, The Regimental Magazine of The King's Own Royal Border Regiment, 1960-1993

Longson, J. and Taylor, C. *Arnhem Odyssey* (Pen and Sword Books, 1991)

Lord, Walter *The Miracle of Dunkirk* (Viking Press, New York 1982)

Middlebrook, Martin *Arnhem 1944 - The Airborne Battle* (Viking/Penguin Books, London 1994)

Otway, Lt-Col J. B. H. DSO *The Second World War 1939-45 Army, Airborne Forces* (Imperial War Museum, London 1990)

Powell, Geoffrey *The Devil's Birthday* (Buchan & Enright, London 1984; Leo Cooper, London 1992)

Prisoners of War, British Army 1939-1945, originally published by HMSO in 1945 and reprinted by J. B. Hayward & Son, Polstead, Suffolk, with The Imperial War Museum, 1990

Purves, Tom *The 9th - The History of the 9th (Parachute) Squadron RE* (1988)

Seth, Ronald *Lion With Blue Wings - The Story of The Glider Pilot Regiment 1942-45* (Victor Gollancz Ltd, London 1956)

Shears, P. J. *The Story of The Border Regiment 1939-1945* (Nisbet & Co Ltd, London 1948)

'The Story of The Border Regiment 1939-45', *Border Magazine*, September 1949

Shepperd, G. A. *The Italian Campaign 1943-45* (Morrison & Gibb Ltd, London 1968)

Smith, Claude *The History of The Glider Pilot Regiment* (Leo Cooper, London 1992)

Stafford, N. A. H. 'Operation "Husky"', *Border Magazine*, March 1954

Sutherland, Douglas C. H. *Tried and Valiant - The Story of The Border Regiment 1702-1959* (Leo Cooper, London 1972)

Urquhart, Major-General R. E. CB DSO *Arnhem* (Cassell & Co, London 1958)

Wood, Alan *The Glider Soldiers* (Spellmount, Tunbridge Wells 1992)

History of the World's Glider Forces (Patrick Stephens Ltd, Wellingborough 1990)

Unpublished sources

Numerous written reminiscences in the Regimental Museum Archives

War Diary, 1st Battalion The Border Regiment, Sept 1939-Oct 1945

War Diary, Seaborne Tail, 1st Airborne Division

Report on 1st Air-Landing Brigade's Operations in Sicily, July 1943

Report on Operation 'Market Garden'

Report on Operation 'Doomsday'

Cabinet Papers - Report on 'Market Garden'

Cabinet Papers - Report on Operation 'Husky'

Index